VALU, AVX and GPU Acceleration Techniques for Parallel FDTD Methods

The ACES Series on Computational Electromagnetics and Engineering (CEME)

Andrew F. Peterson, PhD – Series Editor

The volumes in this series encompass the development and application of numerical techniques to electrical systems, including the modeling of electromagnetic phenomena over all frequency ranges and closely-related techniques for acoustic and optical analysis. The scope includes the use of computation for engineering design and optimization, as well as the application of commercial modeling tools to practical problems. The series will include titles for undergraduate and graduate education, research monographs for reference, and practitioner guides and handbooks.

Titles in the Series

Elsherbeni and Demir – The Finite-Difference Time-Domain Method for Electromagnetics: With MATLAB® Simulations, Second Edition (2014)

Elsherbeni, Nayeri, and Reddy – Antenna Analysis and Design Using FEKO Electromagnetic Simulation Software (2014)

Yu, Yang, and Li – VALU, AVX and GPU Acceleration Techniques for Parallel FDTD Methods (2014)

Warnick – Numerical Methods for Engineering: An Introduction Using Computational Electromagnetics and MATLAB® (2011)

VALU, AVX and GPU Acceleration Techniques for Parallel FDTD Methods

ACES Series

Wenhua Yu
2COMU and Harbin Engineering University

Xiaoling Yang
2COMU

Wenxing Li
Harbin Engineering University

Edison, NJ
scitechpub.com

Published by SciTech Publishing, an imprint of the IET.
www.scitechpub.com
www.theiet.org

10 9 8 7 6 5 4 3 2 1

ISBN 978-1-61353-174-7 (hardback)
ISBN 978-1-61353-178-5 (PDF)

Typeset in India by MPS Limited
Printed in the USA by Sheridan Books, Inc.

Contents

Series Editor Foreword

The ACES series on Computational Electromagnetics and Engineering strives to offer titles on the development and application of numerical techniques, the use of computation for engineering design and optimization, and the application of commercial modeling tools to practical problems. The discipline of computational electromagnetics has always pushed the limits of the available computer power, and will continue to do so. Recent developments in multiprocessor computer hardware offer substantial gains in performance, if those features can be fully utilized by software developers. Unfortunately, compilers that automatically exploit hardware advances usually lag the development of the hardware.

The present book is a valuable addition that should help readers meet the challenges provided by modern hardware, and improve the performance of their codes. This text provides a significant level of detail about issues such as the optimization of cache memory, control of the vector arithmetic logic unit, and use of the graphical processing unit to improve computational performance. These techniques are described in the context of the popular finite-difference time domain (FDTD) method of electromagnetic analysis. The authors have also included source code to facilitate the implementation of their ideas. While the authors use the FDTD approach for illustration, readers who are primarily interested in other methods should also benefit. The book also offers an introduction to cloud computing, with a discussion of a wide range of issues related to that type of service.

Andrew F. Peterson
July 18, 2013

Preface

Multi-core CPU computers, multi-CPU workstations, and GPU are popular platforms for scientific research and engineering applications today. Achieving the best performance on existing hardware platforms is, however, a major challenge. In addition, distributed computing has become a primary trend due to its high performance at low cost for hardware and network devices. This book introduces the vector arithmetic logic unit (VALU), advanced vector extensions (AVX) and graphics processor unit (GPU) acceleration techniques to (1) speed up the electromagnetic simulations significantly and (2) use these acceleration techniques to solve practical problems in the parallel finite difference time domain (FDTD) method. Both VALU and AVX acceleration techniques do not require any extra hardware devices.

Three major computational electromagnetic methods – FDTD method, method of moments (MoM), and the finite element method (FEM) – are popularly used in solving various electromagnetic problems concerned with antennas and arrays, microwave devices and communication components, new electromagnetic materials, and electromagnetic radiation and scattering problems. Among these methods, the FDTD method has become most popular due to its simplicity, flexibility, and ability to handle the complex environment of electromagnetic problems. In this book, we apply VALU and AVX capabilities inside the standard CPUs and GPU to accelerate the parallel FDTD method. VALU is operated by the streaming SIMD extensions (SSE) instruction set originally designed by Intel and AMD for the multimedia area. AVX, released in 2011, is the extension of VALU, and its vector length is extended from 128 bits to 256 bits. GPU is a popular topic today in computational techniques, so we discuss its application in the parallel FDTD method in this book. Compute unified device architecture (CUDA) allows the programming of GPUs for parallel computation without any graphics knowledge. We introduce how to implement CUDA in the parallel FDTD method.

Cloud computing is one of the popular computing services that does not require end-user knowledge of both physical location and configuration of the computing resource. Cloud computing includes two key aspects, namely, virtual resources and web browser tools. This book introduces the basic idea of cloud computing related to the electromagnetic simulation techniques.

A high-performance code is a key to achieve the best simulation performance on a given hardware platform. This book demonstrates a parallel 3-D FDTD code enhanced by the VALU acceleration techniques. The superior performance has been validated in Chapter 6 for various engineering problems on both Intel and AMD processors.

This book includes seven chapters and one appendix. The first chapter briefly introduces the parallel FDTD method. Chapter 2 presents the VALU and AVX acceleration techniques using the SSE and AVX instruction sets in the parallel FDTD method followed by three simple examples to demonstrate the acceleration performance. Chapter 3 shows how to implement the SSE instructions to accelerate the CPML boundary condition. Chapter 4 introduces the three-level parallel processing techniques, including OpenMP, MPI, and their combination with the SSE instruction set. Chapter 5 presents the basic concept, implementation, and engineering applications of GPU acceleration techniques. Chapter 6 presents some engineering problems in various applications such as antenna arrays, radiation and scattering problems, microwave components, and finite and curved frequency selective surface (FSS) structures. Finally, Chapter 7 introduces the cloud computing technique and its applications in the electromagnetic field area. The appendix includes a 3-D parallel FDTD code with the CPML boundary condition enhanced by the VALU acceleration technique.

This book is appropriate for advanced senior and graduate students in electrical engineering and for professors in areas related to electromagnetic computing techniques, computer science, and hardware acceleration techniques. This book is also good for any students, engineers, or scientists who seek to accelerate numerical simulation and data processing techniques.

The authors would like to thank Prof. Atef Elsherbeni and Prof. Veysel Demir for their contributions to Chapter 5.

The authors would like to thank the following colleagues and friends for their help during the manuscript preparation: Mr. Yongjun Liu, Mr. Akira Motu, Dr. Yong Zhang, Prof. Wenwu Cao, Prof. Erping Li, Dr. Jian Wang, Dr. Yan Zhang, and Dr. Xiande Wang.

CHAPTER 1

Introduction to the Parallel FDTD Method

The finite-difference time domain (FDTD) method is a numerical technique based on the finite difference concept. It is employed to solve Maxwell's equations for the electric and magnetic field distributions in both the time and spatial domains. The FDTD method utilizes the central difference approximation to discretize two of Maxwell's curl equations, namely, Faraday's and Ampere's laws, in both the time and spatial domains, and then solve the resulting equations numerically to derive the electric and magnetic field distributions at each time step and spatial point using the explicit leap-frog scheme. The FDTD solution, thus derived, is second-order accurate, although the difference formulation is first order, and is stable if the time step size is chosen to satisfy the special criterion [1].

1.1 FDTD Updated Equations

In Yee's scheme [2] the computational domain is discretized by using the rectangular grids. The electric fields are located along the edges of electric elements, while the magnetic fields are sampled at the center of electric element surfaces and are normal to these surfaces. This is consistent with the duality property of electric and magnetic fields in Maxwell's equations. A typical Yee's electric element is shown in Fig. 1.1.

The FDTD method utilizes the rectangular pulse as the base function in both the time and spatial domains, indicating that the electric field is uniformly distributed along the edge of the electric element, while the distribution of the magnetic fields is uniform on the surface of the electric unit. In addition, in the time domain the electric fields are sampled at times $n\Delta t$ and are assumed to be uniform in the time period of $(n-1/2\Delta t)$ to $(n+1/2\Delta t)$. Similarly, the magnetic fields that are sampled at $(n+1/2\Delta t)$ have a shift of a half-time step with respect to the sampling of the electric fields, and they are assumed to be uniform in the period of $n\Delta t$ to $(n+1)\Delta t$. Two of Maxwell's curl equations are expressed as follows:

$$\nabla \times \vec{E} = -\mu \frac{\partial \vec{H}}{\partial t} - \sigma_M \vec{H} \quad \text{(Faraday's law)} \tag{1.1a}$$

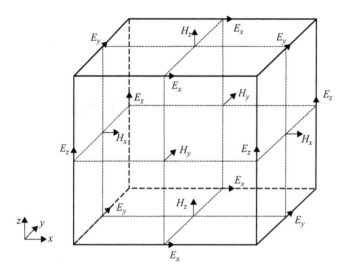

Figure 1.1 Positions of the electric and magnetic fields in Yee's electric element.

$$\nabla \times \vec{H} = \varepsilon \frac{\partial \vec{E}}{\partial t} + \sigma \vec{E} \qquad \text{(Ampere's law)} \tag{1.1b}$$

In the Cartesian coordinate system, we can rewrite (1.1a) and (1.1b) as the following six coupled partial differential equations:

$$\frac{\partial H_x}{\partial t} = \frac{1}{\mu_x} \left(\frac{\partial E_y}{\partial z} - \frac{\partial E_z}{\partial y} - \sigma_{Mx} H_x \right) \tag{1.2a}$$

$$\frac{\partial H_y}{\partial t} = \frac{1}{\mu_y} \left(\frac{\partial E_z}{\partial x} - \frac{\partial E_x}{\partial z} - \sigma_{My} H_y \right) \tag{1.2b}$$

$$\frac{\partial H_z}{\partial t} = \frac{1}{\mu_z} \left(\frac{\partial E_x}{\partial y} - \frac{\partial E_y}{\partial x} - \sigma_{Mz} H_z \right) \tag{1.2c}$$

$$\frac{\partial E_x}{\partial t} = \frac{1}{\varepsilon_x} \left(\frac{\partial H_z}{\partial y} - \frac{\partial H_y}{\partial z} - \sigma_x E_x \right) \tag{1.2d}$$

$$\frac{\partial E_y}{\partial t} = \frac{1}{\varepsilon_y} \left(\frac{\partial H_x}{\partial z} - \frac{\partial H_z}{\partial x} - \sigma_y E_y \right) \tag{1.2e}$$

$$\frac{\partial E_z}{\partial t} = \frac{1}{\varepsilon_z} \left(\frac{\partial H_y}{\partial x} - \frac{\partial H_x}{\partial y} - \sigma_z E_z \right) \tag{1.2f}$$

where ε and σ, μ, and σ_M are the electric and magnetic parameters of the material. The anisotropic material can be described by using different values of dielectric parameters along the respective directions. Equations (1.2a)–(1.2f) form the foundation of the FDTD algorithm for modeling propagation of electromagnetic waves and interaction of the electromagnetic waves with arbitrary 3-D objects embedded in arbitrary media. Using the conventional notations, the discretized fields in the time and spatial domains can be written in the following format:

$$E_x^n(i+1/2,j,k) = E_x\left((i+1/2)\Delta x, j\Delta y, k\Delta z, n\Delta t\right) \tag{1.3a}$$

$$E_y^n(i,j+1/2,k) = E_y\left(i\Delta x, (j+1/2)\Delta y, k\Delta z, n\Delta t\right) \tag{1.3b}$$

$$E_z^n(i,j,k+1/2) = E_z\left(i\Delta x, j\Delta y, (k+1/2)\Delta z, n\Delta t\right) \tag{1.3c}$$

$$H_x^{n+1/2}(i,j+1/2,k+1/2) = H_x\left(i\Delta x, (j+1/2)\Delta y, (k+1/2)\Delta z, (n+1/2)\Delta t\right) \tag{1.3d}$$

$$H_y^{n+1/2}(i+1/2,j,k+1/2) = H_y\left((i+1/2)\Delta x, j\Delta y, (k+1/2)\Delta z, (n+1/2)\Delta t\right) \tag{1.3e}$$

$$H_z^{n+1/2}(i+1/2,j+1/2,k) = H_z\left((i+1/2)\Delta x, (j+1/2)\Delta y, k\Delta z, (n+1/2)\Delta t\right) \tag{1.3f}$$

It is useful to note that the electric and magnetic fields in the discretized version are staggered in both time and space. For instance, the electric and magnetic fields are sampled at the time steps $n\Delta t$ and $(n+1/2)\Delta t$, respectively, and are also displaced from each other in space, as shown in Fig. 1.1. Therefore, we need to interpolate the sampled electric and magnetic fields in order to measure the electric and magnetic fields in the continuous spatial and time domains. Ignoring this field-sampling offset in the Fourier transforms may result in a significant error at high frequencies.

Using the notations in (1.3a)–(1.3f), we can represent Maxwell's equations (1.2a)–(1.2f) in the following explicit formats [2–4]:

$$H_x^{n+1/2}(i,j+1/2,k+1/2) = \frac{\mu_x - 0.5\Delta t\sigma_{Mx}}{\mu_x + 0.5\Delta t\sigma_{Mx}} H_x^{n-1/2}(i,j+1/2,k+1/2)$$

$$+ \frac{\Delta t}{\mu_x + 0.5\Delta t\sigma_{Mx}} \left[\begin{array}{c} \dfrac{E_y^n(i,j+1/2,k+1) - E_y^n(i,j+1/2,k)}{\Delta z} \\[2mm] - \dfrac{E_z^n(i,j+1,k+1/2) - E_z^n(i,j,k+1/2)}{\Delta y} \end{array} \right] \tag{1.4a}$$

$$H_y^{n+1/2}(i+1/2,j,k+1/2) = \frac{\mu_y - 0.5\Delta t \sigma_{My}}{\mu_y + 0.5\Delta t \sigma_{My}} H_y^{n-1/2}(i+1/2,j,k+1/2)$$

$$+ \frac{\Delta t}{\mu_y + 0.5\Delta t \sigma_{My}} \left[\begin{array}{c} \dfrac{E_z^n(i+1,j,k+1/2) - E_z^n(i,j,k+1/2)}{\Delta x} \\[2mm] -\dfrac{E_x^n(i+1/2,j,k+1) - E_x^n(i+1/2,j,k)}{\Delta z} \end{array} \right] \qquad (1.4b)$$

$$H_z^{n+1/2}(i+1/2,j+1/2,k) = \frac{\mu_z - 0.5\Delta t \sigma_{Mz}}{\mu_z + 0.5\Delta t \sigma_{Mz}} H_z^{n-1/2}(i+1/2,j+1/2,k)$$

$$+ \frac{\Delta t}{\mu_z + 0.5\Delta t \sigma_{Mz}} \left[\begin{array}{c} \dfrac{E_x^n(i+1/2,j+1,k) - E_x^n(i+1/2,j,k)}{\Delta y} \\[2mm] -\dfrac{E_y^n(i+1,j+1/2,k) - E_y^n(i,j+1/2,k)}{\Delta x} \end{array} \right] \qquad (1.4c)$$

$$E_x^{n+1}(i+1/2,j,k) = \frac{\varepsilon_x - 0.5\Delta t \sigma_x}{\varepsilon_x + 0.5\Delta t \sigma_x} E_x^n(i+1/2,j,k)$$

$$+ \frac{\Delta t}{\varepsilon_x + 0.5\Delta t \sigma_x} \left[\begin{array}{c} \dfrac{H_z^{n+1/2}(i+1/2,j+1/2,k) - H_z^{n+1/2}(i+1/2,j-1/2,k)}{\Delta y} \\[2mm] -\dfrac{H_y^{n+1/2}(i+1/2,j,k+1/2) - H_y^{n+1/2}(i+1/2,j,k-1/2)}{\Delta z} \end{array} \right] \qquad (1.4d)$$

$$E_y^{n+1}(i,j+1/2,k) = \frac{\varepsilon_y - 0.5\Delta t \sigma_y}{\varepsilon_y + 0.5\Delta t \sigma_y} E_y^n(i,j+1/2,k)$$

$$+ \frac{\Delta t}{\varepsilon_y + 0.5\Delta t \sigma_y} \left[\begin{array}{c} \dfrac{H_x^{n+1/2}(i,j+1/2,k+1/2) - H_x^{n+1/2}(i,j+1/2,k-1/2)}{\Delta z} \\[2mm] -\dfrac{H_z^{n+1/2}(i+1/2,j+1/2,k) - H_z^{n+1/2}(i-1/2,j+1/2,k)}{\Delta x} \end{array} \right] \qquad (1.4e)$$

$$E_z^{n+1}(i,j,k+1/2) = \frac{\varepsilon_z - 0.5\Delta t \sigma_z}{\varepsilon_z + 0.5\Delta t \sigma_z} E_z^n(i,j,k+1/2)$$

$$+ \frac{\Delta t}{\varepsilon_z + 0.5\Delta t \sigma_z} \left[\begin{array}{c} \dfrac{H_y^{n+1/2}(i+1/2,j,k+1/2) - H_y^{n+1/2}(i-1/2,j,k+1/2)}{\Delta x} \\[2mm] -\dfrac{H_x^{n+1/2}(i,j+1/2,k+1/2) - H_x^{n+1/2}(i,j-1/2,k+1/2)}{\Delta y} \end{array} \right] \qquad (1.4f)$$

We point out that, for simplicity, the explicit indices are omitted for the material para-meters, which share the same indices with the corresponding field components. Equations

(1.4a) through (1.4f) are valid at the spatial points and do not contain any explicit boundary information, and we need to augment them with an appropriate boundary condition in order to truncate the computational domain. In the FDTD simulation, some of the commonly used boundary conditions include those associated with the perfect electric conductor (PEC), the perfect magnetic conductor (PMC), the absorbing boundary condition (ABC), and the periodic boundary condition (PBC). In addition to the above boundary conditions, we also need to handle the interfaces between different media in an inhomogeneous environment. In accordance with the assumption of the locations of the electric and magnetic fields, the magnetic field is located along the line segment joining the two centers of adjacent cells. Consequently, the effective magnetic parameter corresponding to this magnetic field is the weighted average of the parameters of the magnetic material that fills in the two adjacent cells. Unlike the magnetic field, the loop used to compute the electric field is likely to be distributed among four adjacent cells. Therefore, the effective electric parameter corresponding to this electric field is equal to the weighted average of electric parameters of the material that fills in these four cells. In addition, the curved PEC and dielectric surfaces require the use of the conformal FDTD technique [5, 6] for accurate modeling.

In recent years, research on FDTD methods has focused on the following five topics:

1) Improving the conventional FDTD algorithm and instead employing the conformal version in order to reduce the error introduced by the staircasing approximation [5, 6].
2) Using a subgridding scheme in the FDTD techniques to increase the local resolution [7–9].
3) Employing the alternative direction implicit (ADI) FDTD algorithm [10, 11] to increase the time step size.
4) Utilizing the computer clusters combining with the message passing interface (MPI) library [4, 12, 13] to speed up the FDTD simulation and solve electrically large and complex electromagnetic problems.
5) Using hardware [14–16] options to accelerate the FDTD simulation.

In addition, the alternative FDTD algorithms such as the multi-resolution time domain (MRTD) method [17] and the pseudo-spectrum time domain (PSTD) technique [18] have been proposed with a view to lowering the spatial sampling. Yet another strategy, which has been found to be more robust as compared to the MRTD and PSTD, is to parallelize the conformal code [4, 19, 13] and enhance it with the subgridding, ADI algorithm, and VALU/AVX/GPU hardware acceleration techniques.

We express the electric and magnetic fields in the updated equations (1.4a)–(1.4f) according to their positions in space. However, we index both the electric and magnetic fields from zero rather than using the leap-frog time-stepping scheme in order to reduce the memory usage. Namely, if there are n_x, n_y, and n_z cells in the x-, y-, and z-directions, respectively, the electric field arrays E_x, E_y, and E_z, and the magnetic field arrays H_x, H_y, and H_z are located in the following way:

$$E_x[n_x][n_y + 1][n_z + 1] \tag{1.5a}$$

$$E_y[n_x + 1][n_y][n_z + 1] \tag{1.5b}$$

$$E_z[n_x + 1][n_y + 1][n_z] \qquad (1.5c)$$

$$H_x[n_x + 1][n_y][n_z] \qquad (1.5d)$$

$$H_y[n_x][n_y + 1][n_z] \qquad (1.5e)$$

$$H_z[nx][ny][nz + 1] \qquad (1.5f)$$

Since the data inside memory is continuous in the z-direction, to match the VALU/AVX format, we usually allocate several more cells in the z-direction. Generally speaking, the electric fields can start from the index 0 that is allocated on the boundary of the computational domain, as shown in Fig. 1.2.

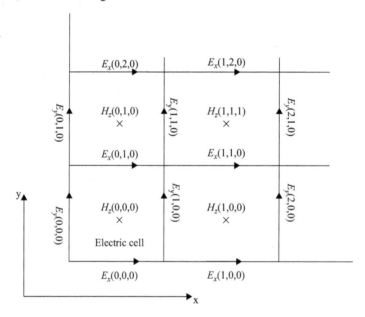

Figure 1.2   Relative locations of the electric and magnetic fields in the FDTD method.

Using the definition in Fig. 1.2, the first index of both the electric and magnetic fields starts from zero. The update of electric fields on the domain boundary requires the magnetic fields outside the domain. However, these magnetic fields outside the domain are not available and require special treatment in both the regular FDTD method and the VALU/AVX acceleration code. We can write the updated equations in the following format:

Electric field update:

$$E_x^{n+1}(i,j,k) = E_x^n(i,j,k) + \frac{\Delta t}{\varepsilon}\left[\frac{H_z^{n+1/2}(i,j,k) - H_z^{n+1/2}(i,j-1,k)}{\Delta y} \right.$$

$$\left. - \frac{H_y^{n+1/2}(i,j,k) - H_y^{n+1/2}(i,j,k-1)}{\Delta z} \right] \qquad (1.6a)$$

$$E_y^{n+1}(i,j,k) = E_y^n(i,j,k) + \frac{\Delta t}{\varepsilon} \left[\frac{H_x^{n+1/2}(i,j,k) - H_x^{n+1/2}(i,j,k-1)}{\Delta z} \right.$$

$$\left. - \frac{H_z^{n+1/2}(i,j,k) - H_z^{n+1/2}(i-1,j,k)}{\Delta x} \right] \qquad (1.6b)$$

$$E_z^{n+1}(i,j,k) = E_z^n(i,j,k) + \frac{\Delta t}{\varepsilon} \left[\frac{H_y^{n+1/2}(i,j,k) - H_y^{n+1/2}(i-1,j,k)}{\Delta x} \right.$$

$$\left. - \frac{H_x^{n+1/2}(i,j,k) - H_x^{n+1/2}(i,j-1,k)}{\Delta y} \right] \qquad (1.6c)$$

Magnetic field update:

$$H_x^{n+1/2}(i,j,k) = H_x^{n-1/2}(i,j,k) + \frac{\Delta t}{\mu} \left[\frac{E_y^n(i,j,k+1) - E_y^n(i,j,k)}{\Delta z} \right.$$

$$\left. - \frac{E_z^n(i,j+1,k) - E_z^n(i,j,k)}{\Delta y} \right] \qquad (1.7a)$$

$$H_y^{n+1/2}(i,j,k) = H_y^{n-1/2}(i,j,k) + \frac{\Delta t}{\mu} \left[\frac{E_z^n(i+1,j,k) - E_z^n(i,j,k)}{\Delta x} \right.$$

$$\left. - \frac{E_x^n(i,j,k+1) - E_x^n(i,j,k)}{\Delta z} \right] \qquad (1.7b)$$

$$H_z^{n+1/2}(i,j,k) = H_z^{n-1/2}(i,j,k) + \frac{\Delta t}{\mu} \left[\frac{E_x^n(i,j+1,k) - E_x^n(i,j,k)}{\Delta y} \right.$$

$$\left. - \frac{E_y^n(i+1,j,k) - E_y^n(i,j,k)}{\Delta x} \right] \qquad (1.7c)$$

In Fig. 1.2, the electric cell is located most outside and the absorbing boundary is applied to the electric fields.

1.2 Stability Analysis

One of the challenging issues that we must address in the marching-on-time technique like the FDTD method is the stability in the time domain solution. The stability characteristic of the FDTD algorithm depends upon the nature of the physical model, difference scheme employed, and the quality of the mesh structure. To understand the nature of the stability characteristic, we express the dispersion relationship as follows [4]:

$$\omega = \frac{2}{\Delta t}\sin^{-1}\left(c\Delta t\sqrt{\frac{1}{\Delta x^2}\sin^2\left(\frac{k_x\Delta x}{2}\right) + \frac{1}{\Delta y^2}\sin^2\left(\frac{k_y\Delta y}{2}\right) + \frac{1}{\Delta z^2}\sin^2\left(\frac{k_z\Delta z}{2}\right)}\right) \quad (1.8)$$

If ω is an imaginary number, the electromagnetic wave, $\psi(t,\vec{r}) = \psi_0 e^{j(\omega t - \vec{k}\cdot\vec{r})}$, either will attenuate rapidly to zero or will grow exponentially and become divergent, depending on whether the imaginary part of ω is positive or negative. In order to ensure that ω is a real number instead, the expression inside the larger round bracket in (1.8) must satisfy the condition:

$$c\Delta t\sqrt{\frac{1}{\Delta x^2}\sin^2\left(\frac{k_x\Delta x}{2}\right) + \frac{1}{\Delta y^2}\sin^2\left(\frac{k_y\Delta y}{2}\right) + \frac{1}{\Delta z^2}\sin^2\left(\frac{k_z\Delta z}{2}\right)} \leq 1 \quad (1.9)$$

Since the maximum possible value of the sine-square term inside the square root is 1, the time step size must satisfy:

$$\Delta t \leq \frac{1}{c\sqrt{\dfrac{1}{\Delta x^2} + \dfrac{1}{\Delta y^2} + \dfrac{1}{\Delta z^2}}} \quad (1.10)$$

in order for the solution to be stable. The criterion above is called the stability condition for the FDTD method, and it is referred to as the Courant condition (or the Courant, Friedrichs, and Lewy criterion) [20]. Equation (1.10) indicates that the time step size is determined by the cell sizes in the x-, y-, and z-directions and the speed of electromagnetic wave in the medium.

1.3 Boundary Conditions

It is well known that boundary condition plays a very important role in the FDTD simulations when it is used to truncate the computational domain for open space problems. Though the original FDTD algorithm was proposed as early as 1966, it was not really applied to solve practical problems until the early 1980s when Mur's absorbing boundary [21] was proposed. Though Mur's absorbing boundary condition is relatively simple and has been used successfully to solve many engineering problems, it has room for improvement in terms of accuracy of the solution it generates. To improve its accuracy, Mei and Fang [22] have introduced the so-called super-absorption technique, while Chew [23] has proposed to employ Liao's boundary condition [24] – both of which exhibit better characteristics than Mur's, especially for obliquely incident waves. However, many of these absorbing boundary conditions were found to suffer from either an instability problem or an inaccurate solution, and the request for robust and effective boundary conditions continued until the perfectly matched layers (PMLs) were introduced by Berenger [25], and several other versions [26–28] have been proposed since then. In contrast to the other boundary conditions such as those of Mur and Liao, PML can absorb the incoming waves at all frequencies as well as for all incident angles. PEC is a natural boundary for electromagnetic waves since it totally reflects the waves falling upon it. When the PEC condition is applied to truncate the FDTD computational domain, it simply forces the tangential electric fields on the domain boundary to be zero. In common with PEC, PMC is also a natural type of boundary condition for electromagnetic waves and it also totally reflects the waves illuminating upon it. However, unlike PEC, the PMC boundary is not physical but is merely an artifice. Both the PEC and PMC boundaries are often used to take advantage of the symmetry of the object geometry with a view toward reducing the size of the computational domain. In this section, we focus on the convolution PML (CPML) [29], one of the most popular PML formats. Although the PML boundary is named to be an absorbing boundary condition, in fact it is an anisotropic material – albeit mathematical – which is inserted in the periphery of the computational domain in order to absorb the outgoing waves.

Before introducing the PML boundary conditions, we first investigate their role in the FDTD simulations. In the FDTD method, Maxwell's equations that govern the relationship between the electric and magnetic fields in the time and spatial domains are discretized into a set of difference equations that do not explicitly contain any boundary information. It is necessary, therefore, to combine the difference equations with the appropriate boundary conditions in order to carry out the mesh truncation as a preamble to solving these equations. Generally speaking, there are two types of boundary conditions required in the FDTD simulations: (1) the interface condition between different media and (2) the outer boundary condition for the domain mesh truncation. In this chapter we only discuss the latter, namely, the boundary that is used to truncate the computational domain.

CPML is based on the stretched coordinate PML [21, 22], and the six coupled Maxwell's equations in CPML can be written in the following form:

$$j\omega\varepsilon\tilde{E}_x + \sigma_x\tilde{E}_x = \frac{1}{S_y}\frac{\partial\tilde{H}_z}{\partial y} - \frac{1}{S_z}\frac{\partial\tilde{H}_y}{\partial z} \tag{1.11a}$$

$$j\omega\varepsilon\tilde{E}_y + \sigma_y\tilde{E}_y = \frac{1}{S_z}\frac{\partial\tilde{H}_x}{\partial z} - \frac{1}{S_x}\frac{\partial\tilde{H}_z}{\partial x} \tag{1.11b}$$

$$j\omega\varepsilon\tilde{E}_z + \sigma_z\tilde{E}_z = \frac{1}{S_x}\frac{\partial\tilde{H}_y}{\partial x} - \frac{1}{S_y}\frac{\partial\tilde{H}_x}{\partial y} \tag{1.11c}$$

$$j\omega\mu_x\tilde{H}_x + \sigma_{Mx}\tilde{H}_x = \frac{1}{S_z}\frac{\partial\tilde{E}_y}{\partial z} - \frac{1}{S_y}\frac{\partial\tilde{E}_z}{\partial y} \tag{1.11d}$$

$$j\omega\mu_y\tilde{H}_y + \sigma_{My}\tilde{H}_y = \frac{1}{S_x}\frac{\partial\tilde{E}_z}{\partial x} - \frac{1}{S_z}\frac{\partial\tilde{E}_x}{\partial z} \tag{1.11e}$$

$$j\omega\mu_z\tilde{H}_z + \sigma_{Mz}\tilde{H}_z = \frac{1}{S_y}\frac{\partial\tilde{E}_x}{\partial y} - \frac{1}{S_x}\frac{\partial\tilde{E}_y}{\partial x} \tag{1.11f}$$

To derive the updated equations for CPML from (1.11a), we first take its Laplace transform to obtain the following equation in the time domain:

$$\varepsilon_x\frac{\partial E_x}{\partial t} + \sigma_x E_x = \overline{S}_y(t) * \frac{\partial H_z}{\partial y} - \overline{S}_z(t) * \frac{\partial H_y}{\partial z} \tag{1.12}$$

where S_y and S_z are the Laplace transforms of $1/S_y$ and $1/S_z$, respectively. The asterisk "*" indicates the convolution of two time domain terms.

CPML is derived by converting (1.12) to a form that is suitable for explicit updating. Furthermore, to overcome the shortcomings of the split field and unsplit PML insofar as the effectiveness at the low frequencies and the absorption of the surface waves are concerned, we modify S_x, S_y, and S_z as follows:

$$S_x = K_x + \frac{\sigma_{x,\mathrm{PML}}}{\alpha_x + j\omega\varepsilon_0} \tag{1.13a}$$

$$S_y = K_y + \frac{\sigma_{y,\mathrm{PML}}}{\alpha_y + j\omega\varepsilon_0} \tag{1.13b}$$

$$S_z = K_z + \frac{\sigma_{z,\mathrm{PML}}}{\alpha_z + j\omega\varepsilon_0} \tag{1.13c}$$

where $\alpha_{x,y,z}$ and $\sigma_{x,y,z,\mathrm{PML}}$ are real numbers, and K is greater than 1. $\overline{S}_x$, $\overline{S}_y$, and $\overline{S}_z$ can be obtained from the Laplace transforms:

$$\overline{S}_x = \frac{\delta(t)}{K_x} - \frac{\sigma_x}{\varepsilon_0 K_x}\exp\left[-\left(\sigma_{x,\mathrm{PML}}\big/_{\varepsilon_0 K_x} + \alpha_{x,\mathrm{PML}}\big/_{\varepsilon_0}\right)tu(t)\right] = \frac{\delta(t)}{K_x} + \xi_x(t) \tag{1.14a}$$

$$\overline{S}_y = \frac{\delta(t)}{K_y} - \frac{\sigma_y}{\varepsilon_0 K_y}\exp\left[-\left(\sigma_{y,\mathrm{PML}}\big/_{\varepsilon_0 K_y} + \alpha_{y,\mathrm{PML}}\big/_{\varepsilon_0}\right)tu(t)\right] = \frac{\delta(t)}{K_y} + \xi_y(t) \tag{1.14b}$$

$$\overline{S}_z = \frac{\delta(t)}{K_z} - \frac{\sigma_z}{\varepsilon_0 K_z}\exp\left[-\left(\sigma_{z,\mathrm{PML}}\big/_{\varepsilon_0 K_z} + \alpha_{z,\mathrm{PML}}\big/_{\varepsilon_0}\right)tu(t)\right] = \frac{\delta(t)}{K_z} + \xi_z(t) \tag{1.14c}$$

where $\delta(t)$ and $u(t)$ are an impulse function and a step function, respectively. Substituting (1.14a) and (1.14c) into (1.12), we have:

$$\varepsilon_x\varepsilon_0\frac{\partial E_x}{\partial t} + \sigma_x E_x = \frac{1}{K_y}\frac{\partial H_z}{\partial y} - \frac{1}{K_z}\frac{\partial H_y}{\partial z} + \xi_y(t) * \frac{\partial H_z}{\partial y} - \xi_z(t) * \frac{\partial H_y}{\partial z} \tag{1.15}$$

It is not numerically efficient to compute the convolution directly appearing in (1.15), and to address this issue we introduce a quantity $Z_{0y}(m)$ in order to calculate it efficiently, as follows:

$$Z_{0y}(m) = \int_{m\Delta t}^{(m+1)\Delta t} \xi_y(\tau)\mathrm{d}\tau$$

$$= -\frac{\sigma_y}{\varepsilon_0 K_y^2} \int_{m\Delta t}^{(m+1)\Delta t} \exp\left[-\left(\frac{\sigma_{y,\mathrm{PML}}}{\varepsilon_0 K_y} + \frac{\alpha_{y,\mathrm{PML}}}{\varepsilon_0}\right)\tau\right]\mathrm{d}\tau \qquad (1.16)$$

$$= a_y \exp\left[-\left(\frac{\sigma_{y,\mathrm{PML}}}{K_y} + \alpha_{y,\mathrm{PML}}\right)\left(\frac{m\Delta t}{\varepsilon_0}\right)\right]$$

where:

$$a_y = \frac{\sigma_{y,\mathrm{PML}}}{\sigma_{y,\mathrm{PML}}K_y + K_y^2 \alpha_y}\left(\exp\left[-\left(\frac{\sigma_{y,\mathrm{PML}}}{K_y} + \alpha_y\right)\left(\frac{m\Delta t}{\varepsilon_0}\right)\right] - 1\right) \qquad (1.17)$$

A similar expression can be derived for $Z_{0z}(m)$. Using (1.16) and (1.17), (1.15) can be written as:

$$\varepsilon_x \varepsilon_0 \frac{E_x^{n+1}(i+1/2,j,k) - E_x^n(i+1/2,j,k)}{\Delta t} + \sigma_x \frac{E_x^{n+1}(i+1/2,j,k) + E_x^n(i+1/2,j,k)}{2}$$

$$= \frac{H_z^{n+1/2}(i+1/2,j+1/2,k) - H_z^{n+1/2}(i+1/2,j-1/2,k)}{K_y \Delta y}$$

$$- \frac{H_y^{n+1/2}(i+1/2,j,k+1/2) - H_y^{n+1/2}(i+1/2,j,k-1/2)}{K_z \Delta z}$$

$$+ \sum_{m=0}^{N-1} Z_{0y}(m) \frac{H_z^{n-m+1/2}(i+1/2,j+1/2,k) - H_z^{n-m+1/2}(i+1/2,j-1/2,k)}{K_y \Delta y}$$

$$- \sum_{m=0}^{N-1} Z_{0z}(m) \frac{H_y^{n-m+1/2}(i+1/2,j,k+1/2) - H_y^{n-m+1/2}(i+1/2,j,k-1/2)}{K_z \Delta z}$$

$$(1.18)$$

Finally, the updated formula of (1.18) takes the following form:

$$\varepsilon_x \varepsilon_0 \frac{E_x^{n+1}(i+1/2,j,k) - E_x^n(i+1/2,j,k)}{\Delta t} + \sigma_x \frac{E_x^{n+1}(i+1/2,j,k) + E_x^n(i+1/2,j,k)}{2}$$

$$= \frac{H_z^{n+1/2}(i+1/2,j+1/2,k) - H_z^{n+1/2}(i+1/2,j-1/2,k)}{K_y \Delta y}$$

$$- \frac{H_y^{n+1/2}(i+1/2,j,k+1/2) - H_y^{n+1/2}(i+1/2,j,k-1/2)}{K_z \Delta z}$$

$$+ \psi_{exy}^{n+1/2}(i+1/2,j,k) - \psi_{exz}^{n+1/2}(i+1/2,j,k)$$

$$(1.19)$$

where:

$$\psi_{exy}^{n+1/2}(i+1/2,j,k) = b_y\psi_{exy}^{n-1/2}(i+1/2,j,k)$$
$$+a_y\frac{H_z^{n+1/2}(i+1/2,j+1/2,k) - H_z^{n+1/2}(i+1/2,j-1/2,k)}{\Delta y}$$

$$(1.20)$$

$$\psi_{exz}^{n+1/2}(i+1/2,j,k) = b_z\psi_{exz}^{n-1/2}(i+1/2,j,k)$$
$$+a_z\frac{H_y^{n+1/2}(i+1/2,j,k+1/2) - H_y^{n+1/2}(i+1/2,j,k-1/2)}{\Delta z}$$

$$(1.21)$$

$$b_x = \exp\left[-\left(\sigma_{x,\mathrm{PML}}/K_x + \alpha_x\right)\left(\Delta t/\varepsilon_0\right)\right] \qquad (1.22a)$$

$$b_y = \exp\left[-\left(\sigma_{y,\mathrm{PML}}/K_y + \alpha_y\right)\left(\Delta t/\varepsilon_0\right)\right] \qquad (1.22b)$$

$$b_z = \exp\left[-\left(\sigma_{z,\mathrm{PML}}/K_z + \alpha_z\right)\left(\Delta t/\varepsilon_0\right)\right] \qquad (1.22c)$$

Equation (1.19) is the desired updated equation that we have been seeking in order to retain the advantages of the unsplit PML and overcome its drawback at the same time. In common with the conventional FDTD method, the electric field updating inside the PML region only requires the magnetic fields around it and the value of ψ at the previous time step. The same statement is true for the magnetic field update as well. CPML does not require additional information exchange in the parallel FDTD simulation over and above that in the conventional FDTD method.

Supposing the variable x is the distance measured from the outer boundary of the PML region, the conductivity distribution in the PML region is given by:

$$\sigma(x) = \sigma_{\max}\left(\frac{d-x}{d}\right)^m \qquad (1.23)$$

where the index m is taken to be either 2 or 4. In addition, in (1.23), d is the thickness of PML region and $\sigma_{\max}$ is the maximum value of the conductivity, which can be expressed as:

$$\sigma_{\max} = \frac{m+1}{200\pi\sqrt{\varepsilon_r}\Delta x} \qquad (1.24)$$

Supposing that y is a distance measured from the outer boundary of the PML region, then the distribution of K_y is given by:

$$K_y(y) = 1 + (K_{\max} - 1)\frac{|d-y|^m}{d^m} \qquad (1.25)$$

The implementation of CPML in the FDTD code is relatively simpler than most of the other types of PMLs. Also, CPML does not depend on the properties of the materials being simulated. In addition, it has a good performance at low frequencies.

1.4 Parallel FDTD Method

In this section, we briefly introduce the parallel FDTD method [4], which is widely used in electromagnetic simulations. The basic idea here is to help readers understand the simulation procedure when a parallel code runs on a parallel platform. One compute unit can be a compute core, a compute CPU including multiple physical cores, or a compute node that contains multiple CPUs. The different partition schemes of the compute units will significantly affect the parallel performance that determines the amount of the information exchange among the compute units.

In the parallel processing technique, the original problem is divided into small pieces that the FDTD code assigns to each compute unit. Each compute unit in the cluster only needs to simulate one specified sub-domain, as shown in Fig. 1.3. Each sub-domain is not independent and requires the information from its neighbors to calculate the fields on the interface of sub-domains. The information exchanging procedure is demonstrated in Fig. 1.4.

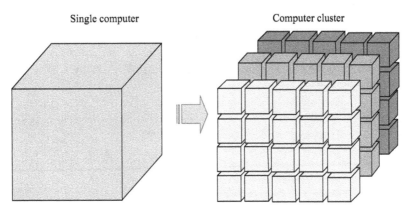

Single computer   Computer cluster

Figure 1.3   Basic idea of parallel processing FDTD simulation on a computer cluster. The original problem is split into small pieces and each compute unit in the cluster only needs to simulate one piece.

A complete FDTD simulation is carried out in three steps: project pre-processing, project simulation, and data post-processing. In the first step, the parallel FDTD code generates the material distribution based on the geometry information and the specified mesh distribution. In this procedure, each compute unit in a cluster does not have to wait for others since it does not need to borrow any information from its neighbors. For the complex geometry problems, the job load in each sub-domain may be significantly different, and the processing time required in each sub-domain may vary on different compute units. In order to speed up the pre-processing procedure, we do not have to let the number

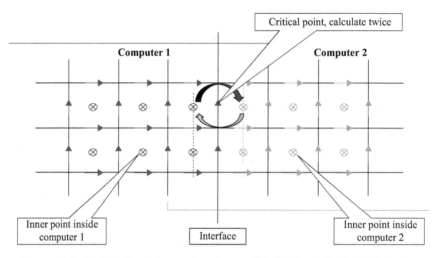

Figure 1.4   Field information exchanging on the interface of the sub-domains.

of sub-domains be equal to the number of compute units. Also, the compute units carrying on the simple sub-domains can work on more sub-domains without the need to wait for the other compute units, as illustrated in Fig. 1.5. In contrast to the project pre-processing, the parallel FDTD update processing in each sub-domain must be synchronized at each time step. Therefore, we will not allow the compute unit to switch from one sub-domain to another during the simulation. The data post-processing will not require the data exchange among the compute units.

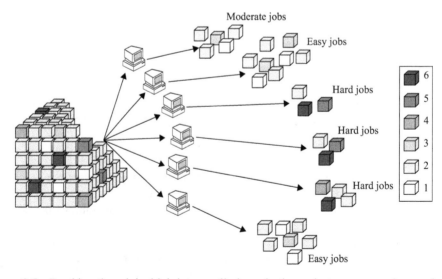

Figure 1.5   Breaking the original job into small pieces in the project pre-processing, each compute unit in the cluster will handle one piece at one time. The number of small pieces may be much larger than the number of compute units in the cluster.

Since the field update in the FDTD method only requires the information around it, it is one of the highly parallelized methods. Let us start from one component of Maxwell's equations [1, 2]:

$$\frac{\partial E_z}{\partial t} = \frac{1}{\varepsilon_z}\left(\frac{\partial H_y}{\partial x} - \frac{\partial H_x}{\partial y} - \sigma_z E_z\right) \tag{1.26}$$

Using the central difference scheme, we can get the following discretization formulation for (1.26):

$$E_z^{n+1}(i,j,k+1/2) = \frac{\varepsilon_z - 0.5\sigma_z\Delta t}{\varepsilon_z + 0.5\sigma_z\Delta t}E_z^n(i,j,k+1/2)$$

$$+\frac{1}{\varepsilon_z+0.5\sigma_z\Delta t}\left[\begin{array}{c}\dfrac{H_y^{n+1/2}(i+1/2,j,k+1/2) - H_y^{n+1/2}(i-1/2,j,k+1/2)}{0.5[\Delta x(i)+\Delta x(i-1)]} \\[3mm] -\dfrac{H_x^{n+1/2}(i,j+1/2,k+1/2) - H_x^{n+1/2}(i,j-1/2,k+1/2)}{0.5[\Delta y(j)+\Delta y(j-1)]}\end{array}\right] \tag{1.27}$$

For a serial code, the field solution in the entire FDTD domain can be solved by forcing the fields to satisfy the proper condition on the domain boundary. However, for the parallel code, the fields on the boundary of each sub-domain are unknown, but they are calculated by borrowing some information from the adjacent sub-domains. Therefore, we need the high-performance network to transform the information from one compute unit to another one at each time step. In contrast to other electromagnetic simulation techniques, the parallel FDTD method only requires passing the fields on the interface between the adjacent compute units.

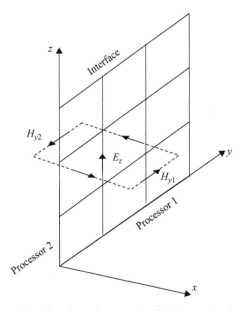

Figure 1.6   Distribution of the electric and magnetic fields near the interface between two adjacent processors.

For example, considering (1.27) in Fig. 1.6, the electric field E_z is located on the interface between the processors 1 and 2. Update of this electric field needs two magnetic fields: H_{y1}, i.e., $H_y^{n+1/2}(i+1/2,j,k+1/2)$, and H_{y2}, i.e., $H_y^{n+1/2}(i-1/2,j,k+1/2)$, which are located in the processors 1 and 2, respectively.

Rewriting (1.27) for the processors 1 and 2, the electric fields on the interface can be expressed as:

$$E_z^{n+1,\text{processor }1}(i,j,k+1/2) = \frac{\varepsilon_z - 0.5\sigma_z\Delta t}{\varepsilon_z + 0.5\sigma_z\Delta t} E_z^n(i,j,k+1/2)$$

$$+ \frac{1}{\varepsilon_z + 0.5\sigma_z\Delta t} \left[\begin{array}{c} \dfrac{H_y^{n+1/2}(i+1/2,j,k+1/2) - H_{y1}}{0.5[\Delta x(i) + \Delta x(i-1)]} \\[2mm] -\dfrac{H_x^{n+1/2}(i,j+1/2,k+1/2) - H_x^{n+1/2}(i,j-1/2,k+1/2)}{0.5[\Delta y(j) + \Delta y(j-1)]} \end{array} \right]$$

$$(1.28)$$

$$E_z^{n+1,\text{processor }2}(i,j,k+1/2) = \frac{\varepsilon_z - 0.5\sigma_z\Delta t}{\varepsilon_z + 0.5\sigma_z\Delta t} E_z^n(i,j,k+1/2)$$

$$+ \frac{1}{\varepsilon_z + 0.5\sigma_z\Delta t} \left[\begin{array}{c} \dfrac{H_{y2} - H_y^{n+1/2}(i-1/2,j,k+1/2)}{0.5[\Delta x(i) + \Delta x(i-1)]} \\[2mm] -\dfrac{H_x^{n+1/2}(i,j+1/2,k+1/2) - H_x^{n+1/2}(i,j-1/2,k+1/2)}{0.5[\Delta y(j) + \Delta y(j-1)]} \end{array} \right]$$

$$(1.29)$$

The magnetic fields H_{y1} and H_{y2} are exchanged through the high-performance network at each time step. The data exchange happens only on the interface between two adjacent sub-domains, and not on the edges and corners of the sub-domains.

References

[1] A. Taflove and S. Hagness, *Computational Electromagnetics: The Finite-Difference Time-Domain Method*, 3rd ed., Artech House, Norwood, MA, 2005.

[2] K. Yee, "Numerical Solution of Initial Boundary Value Problems Involving Maxwell's Equations in Isotropic Media," *IEEE Transactions on Antennas and Propagation*, Vol. 14, No. 5, 1966, pp. 302–307.

[3] W. Yu and R. Mittra, *Conformal Finite-Difference Time-Domain Maxwell's Equations Solver: Software and User's Guide*, Artech House, Norwood, MA, 2003.

[4] W. Yu, X. Yang, Y. Liu, et al., *Parallel Finite Difference Time Domain Method*, Artech House, Norwood, MA, 2006.

[5] W. Yu, and R. Mittra, "A Conformal FDTD Software Package for Modeling of Antennas and Microstrip Circuit Components," *IEEE Antennas and Propagation Magazine*. Vol. 42, No. 5, 2000, pp. 28–39.

[6] W. Yu and R. Mittra, "A Conformal Finite Difference Time Domain Technique for Modeling Curved Dielectric Surfaces," *IEEE Microwave and Guided Wave Letters*, Vol. 11, No. 1, 2001, pp. 25–27.

[7] B. Wang, Y. Wang, W. Yu, et al., "A Hybrid 2-D ADI-FDTD Subgridding Scheme for Modeling On-Chip Interconnects," *IEEE Transactions on Advanced Packaging*, Vol. 24, No. 11, 2001, pp. 528–533.

[8] W. Yu and R. Mittra, "A New Subgridding Method for Finite Difference Time Domain (FDTD) Algorithm," *Microwave and Optical Technology Letters*, Vol. 21, No. 5, 1999, pp. 330–333.

[9] M. Marrone, R. Mittra, and W. Yu, "A Novel Approach to Deriving a Stable Hybrid FDTD Algorithm Using the Cell Method," *Proceedings of the IEEE AP-S URSI*, Columbus, OH, 2003, pp. 1–4.

[10] T. Namiki, "A New FDTD Algorithm Based on Alternating-Direction Implicit Method," *IEEE Transactions on Microwave Theory and Techniques*, Vol. 47, No. 10, 1999, pp. 2003–2007.

[11] F. Zheng, Z. Chen, and J. Zhang, "Toward the Development of a Three-Dimensional Unconditionally Stable Finite-Difference Time-Domain Method," *IEEE Transactions on Microwave Theory and Techniques*, Vol. 48, No. 9, 2000, pp. 1550–1558.

[12] C. Guiffaut and K. Mahdjoubi, "A Parallel FDTD Algorithm Using the MPI Library," *IEEE Antennas and Propagation Magazine*, Vol. 43, No. 2, 2001, pp. 94–103.

[13] W. Yu, Y. Liu, Z. Su, et al., "A Robust Parallel Conformal Finite Difference Time Domain Processing Package Using MPI Library," *IEEE Antennas and Propagation Magazine*, Vol. 47, No. 3, 2005, pp. 39–59.

[14] W. Yu, X. Yang, T. Su, et al., *Advanced FDTD Method: Parallelization, Acceleration and Engineering Applications*, Artech House, Norwood, MA, 2011.

[15] W. Yu, X. Yang, Y. Liu, et al., "New Development of Parallel Conformal FDTD Method in Computational Electromagnetics Engineering," *IEEE Antennas and Propagation Magazine*, Vol. 53, No. 3, 2011, pp. 15–41.

[16] A. Elsherbeni and V. Demir, *The Finite Difference Time Domain Method for Electromagnetics: With MATLAB Simulations*, SciTech Publisher Inc., Raleigh, NC, 2009.

[17] Y. Chao, Q. Cao, and R. Mittra, *Multiresolution Time Domain Scheme for Electromagnetic Engineering*, John Wiley & Sons, New York, NY, 2005.

[18] Q. Liu, "The PSTD Algorithm: A Time-Domain Method Requiring Only Two Cells Per Wavelength," *Microwave and Optical Technology Letters*, Vol. 15, 1997, pp. 158–165.

[19] W. Yu, X. Yang, Y. Liu, et al., "New Direction in Computational Electromagnetics Solving Large Problems Using the Parallel FDTD on the BlueGene/L Supercomputer Yielding Teraflop-Level Performance," *IEEE Antennas and Propagation Magazine,* Vol. 50, No. 23, 2008, pp. 20–42.

[20] R. Courant, K. Friedrichs, and H. Lewy, "Uber die partiellen Differenzengleichungen der math_ematischen Physik," *Mathematische Annalen*, Vol. 100, 1928, pp. 32–74.

[21] G. Mur, "Absorbing Boundary Conditions for the Finite-Difference Approximation of the Time-Domain Electromagnetic Field Equations," *IEEE Transactions on Electromagnetic Compatibility*, Vol. 23, No. 3, 1981, pp. 377–382.

[22] K. Mei, and J. Fang, "Superabsorption – a Method to Improve Absorbing Boundary Conditions," *IEEE Transactions on Antennas and Propagation*, Vol. 40, No. 9, 1992, pp. 1001–1010.

[23] M. Moghaddam, E. Yannakakis, W. Chew, and C. Randall, "Modeling of the subsurface interface radar," *J. Electromag. Waves Appl.* Vol. 5, No. 1, 1991, pp. 17–39.

[24] Z. Liao, H. Wong, Y. Baipo, et al. "A Transmitting Boundary for Transient Wave Analyzes," *Scientia Sinica* (Series A), Vol. 27, No. 10, 1984, pp. 1062–1076.

[25] J. Berenger, "A Perfectly Matched Layer for the Absorption of Electromagnetic Waves," *Journal of Computational Physics*, Vol. 114, 1994, pp. 185–200.

[26] S. Gedney, "An Anisotropic Perfectly Matched Layer-Absorbing Medium for the Truncation of FDTD Lattices," *IEEE Transactions on Antennas and Propagation*, Vol. 44, No. 12, 1996, pp. 1630–1639.

[27] W. Chew and W. Wood, "A 3-D Perfectly Matched Medium from Modified Maxwell's Equations with Stretched Coordinates," *Microwave and Optical Technology Letters*, Vol. 7, 1994, pp. 599–604.

[28] W. Chew, J. Jin, and E. Michielssen, "Complex Coordinate Stretching as a Generalized Absorbing Boundary Condition," *Microwave and Optical Technology Letters*, Vol. 15, No. 6, 1997, pp. 363–369.

[29] J. Roden and S. Gedney, "Convolution PML (CPML): An Efficient FDTD Implementation of the CFS-PML for Arbitrary Medium," *Microwave and Optical Technology Letters*, Vol. 27, No. 5, 2000, pp. 334–339.

CHAPTER 2

VALU/AVX Acceleration Techniques

Popular central processing units (CPUs) for high-performance workstations and servers are made by either AMD (www.amd.com) [1] or Intel (www.intel.com) [2]. Both are useful for general purposes. It is difficult to compare the performance of AMD and Intel CPUs because there are no absolute rules to judge CPU performance in a given system. Regardless of using AMD or Intel CPUs, we consider the following important parameters that significantly affect simulation performance:

- Clock frequency: An important factor for simulation performance, which usually is directly proportional to simulation performance.
- Number of cores: Determines the number of vector arithmetic logic units (VALUs).
- Manufacturing process: Indicates the different generation manufacturing techniques, for example, 32-nm CPUs are better than 45-nm CPUs for the same technical specifications.
- L1 cache: Determines the CPU performance. Each core has its own L1 cache.
- L2 cache: Shared by all the cores in an Intel CPU and independent for each core in AMD CPU. Determines the CPU performance.
- L3 cache: Shared by all the cores and is not important as L1 and L2 caches.
- HyperTransport (AMD)/Quick Path Interconnect (Intel): Significantly affects the performance of multi-CPU workstations. The multi-CPU workstation uses this technique to extend the memory bandwidth. For parallel FDTD code, this allows a CPU to allocate its data in its own local memory.
- Memory: Significantly affects the simulation performance. In most cases, the memory bandwidth is the major simulation performance bottleneck.
- Maximum CPU configuration: Determines how many CPUs we can install on a single motherboard.
- Thermal design power (TDP): Indicates the power consumption by a CPU.

When an FDTD code starts running, it first allocates memory for the declared variables and arrays, and then starts executing each statement in a compiler optimized order. The most often used data will be placed in the L1 and L2 caches in Intel CPUs. The most recently used data will be placed in the L1 and L2 caches in AMD CPUs. When the arithmetic logic unit (ALU) needs the data, as shown in Fig. 2.1, it will get the data from the L1 cache. If the required data is not in the L1 cache, the system will deliver the data from the L2 cache or memory to the L1 cache. This is an automatic procedure and we do not need to get involved in the data transfer procedure. What we can do is to make the data continuous inside memory wherever it is possible to improve the cache hit ratio. The cache line containing multiple bytes is a basic unit of cache operation, and therefore the cache hit ratio is determined by the data continuity inside memory. Usually, L1 cache is much faster than L2 cache, and L2 cache is much faster than regular memory. The amount of the L1 cache is much smaller than the L2 cache, and the L2 cache is much smaller than the regular memory. The caches usually occupy the most space on a CPU chip, and the regular memory is outside the CPU and connected to the CPU through a data bus.

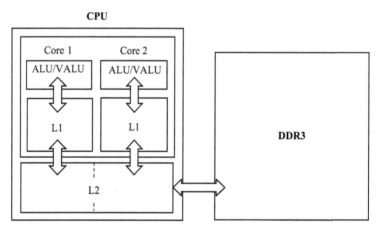

Figure 2.1   A simplified flowchart for the data processing inside an Intel CPU. Each core inside an AMD CPU has its own L2 cache. All the cores inside an Intel CPU share the L2 cache.

Each core has its own L1 cache, which ensures fast L1 cache performance. In practical applications, CPU manufacturers use the L2 cache in different strategies to increase L2 cache performance, as shown in Fig. 2.2. L2 cache in an AMD CPU belongs to each core.

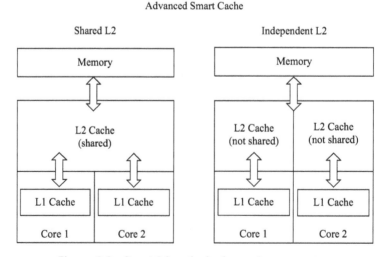

Figure 2.2   Smart L2 cache in the modern processor.

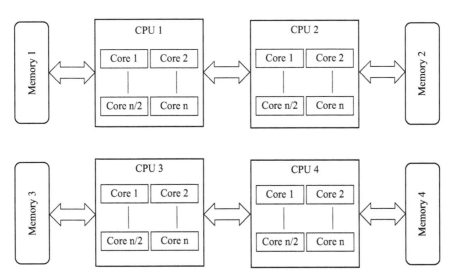

Figure 2.3   NUMA architecture in the multi-CPU workstation.

Intel uses shared L2 cache. In both AMD and Intel CPUs, the L3 cache is not as important as the L1 and L2 caches.

Most of the time, the system bottleneck is the memory bandwidth. Today, the most popular memory is DDR3 that has a speed selected to match the CPU. The non-uniform memory allocation (NUMA) architecture is used in both AMD (hyper transport technology) [3] and Intel (quick path technology) [4] processors to increase memory bandwidth, as shown in Fig. 2.3. Inside the NUMA architecture, each CPU can have access to its own memory independently.

From the Intel Pentium III of the 1990s, Intel added VALU to its processors for multi-media applications. However, it is rarely used in engineering applications. Since VALU [5] can produce four result-based 128-bit registers with a single instruction, it can speed up simulation four or eight times compared to an ALU. Next, we describe how to use VALU to accelerate FDTD simulation.

2.1 Introduction to SSE Instructions

Previously, microprocessors employed an architecture called single instruction single data (SISD) [6] where a processor applied an instruction to a single data element. Today, modern processors are single instruction multiple data (SIMD) CPU and simultaneously handle multiple data using a single instruction. SIMD extensions called streaming SIMD extensions (SSE) allow one instruction to operate on multiple data elements. VALU is the hardware component inside CPU that is controlled by the SSE instruction set. The SSE instruction set is a kind of assembly language that can be invoked through the high language application program interface (API). This reduces the burden on programmers.

Intel has a long history of implementing SIMD extensions that include both new instructions and the microarchitecture resources that can accelerate these instructions.

The trend started with a floating point unit (FPU) first integrated in the 80486 family in 1999, and followed by extended temperature Pentium processor with the multimedia extensions (MMX) technology, and then several evolutions of SSE. SSE first came to the Intel Pentium III processor through eight 128-bit registers known as XMM0 through XMM7 with floating point math support. Subsequently SSE2 added double-precision math, and SSE3 added digital signal processor (DSP)-oriented instructions. Today, the state of the art are SSE4.1, which was implemented in microarchitecture processors when Intel migrated to the 45-nm design code named Penryn, and SSE4.2, which was implemented in the newest microarchitecture code named Nehalem.

Intel offers a library of software functions called Intel integrated performance primitives (IPP). Combined with a compiler, IPP allows users to write an application code once that will run on any Intel architecture processor and leverage the most advanced SSE instructions and the underlying hardware accelerators that are available on the target platform.

AMD added SSE to its Athlon microprocessors in 1999. SSE adds a separate register space to the microprocessor. Because of this, SSE can only be used on operating systems that support it. Fortunately, the most recent operating systems support the SSE instruction set. All versions of Windows since Windows 98 support SSE, as do Linux kernels since version 2.2.

SSE gives users access to 70 new instructions that operate on these 128-bit registers, MMX registers, and sometimes even regular 32-bit registers.

Multimedia extensions control and status register (MXCSR) is a 32-bit register that contains masks and flags for control and status information regarding the SSE instructions. As of SSE3, only 16 bits from 0 to15 have been defined.

Pnemonic	Bit Location	Description
FZ	bit 15	Flush to zero
R+	bit 14	Round positive
R−	bit 13	Round negative
RZ	bits 13 and 14	Round to zero
RN	bits 13 and 14 are 0	Round to nearest
PM	bit 12	Precision mask
UM	bit 11	Underflow mask
OM	bit 10	Overflow mask
ZM	bit 9	Divide by zero mask
DM	bit 8	Denormal mask
IM	bit 7	Invalid operation mask
DAZ	bit 6	Denormals are zero
PE	bit 5	Precision flag
UE	bit 4	Underflow flag
OE	bit 3	Overflow flag
ZE	bit 2	Divide by zero flag
DE	bit 1	Denormal flag
IE	bit 0	Invalid operation flag

FZ mode causes all under flowing operations to simply go to zero. This saves some processing time, but loses precision.

R+, R−, RN, and RZ rounding modes determine how the lowest bit is generated. Normally, RN is used.

PM, UM, OM, ZM, DM, and IM are masks that tell the processor to ignore the exceptions. They can keep the program from having to deal with problems, but might cause invalid results.

DAZ tells CPU to force all denormals to zero. A denormal is a number that is so small that ALU cannot renormalize it due to limited exponent ranges. They are just like normal numbers, but they take considerably longer time to process.

PE, UE, OE, ZE, DE, and IE are the exception flags that are set if they happen. Programs can check these to see if something interesting happened. Once these bits are set, they stay set forever until the program clears them. This means that the indicated exception could have happened several operations ago, but the program did not clear it.

DAZ was not available in the first version of SSE. Since setting a reserved bit in MXCSR causes a general protection fault, we need to be able to check the availability of this feature without causing problems. To do this, we need to set up a 512-byte area of memory to save the SSE state using the *fxsave* instruction, and then we need to inspect bytes 28 through 31 for the MXCSR_MASK value.

The category and instructions of the SSE set are listed below:

Arithmetic

addps	Adds four single-precision (32-bit) floating-point values to four other single-precision floating-point values.
adds	Adds the lowest single-precision values; the top three values remain unchanged.
subps	Subtracts four single-precision floating-point values from four other single-precision floating-point values.
subss	Subtracts the lowest single-precision values, the top three values remain unchanged.
mulps	Multiplies four single-precision floating-point values with four other single-precision values.
mulss	Multiplies the lowest single-precision values; the top three values remain unchanged.
divps	Divides four single-precision floating-point values by four other single-precision floating-point values.
divss	Divides the lowest single-precision values; the top three values remain unchanged.
rcpps	Reciprocates ($1/x$) four single-precision floating-point values.
rcpss	Reciprocates the lowest single-precision values; the top three values remain unchanged.
sqrtps	Square root of four single-precision values.
sqrtss	Square root of lowest value; the top three values remain unchanged.
rsqrtps	Reciprocal square root of four single-precision floating-point values.
rsqrtss	Reciprocal square root of lowest single-precision value; the top three values remain unchanged.

maxps	Returns maximum of two values in each of four single-precision values.
maxss	Returns maximum of two values in the lowest single-precision value; the top three values remain unchanged.
minps	Returns minimum of two values in each of four single-precision values.
minss	Returns minimum of two values in the lowest single-precision value; the top three values remain unchanged.
pavgb	Returns average of two values in each of 8 bytes.
pavgw	Returns average of two values in each of four words.
psadbw	Returns sum of absolute differences of eight 8-bit values. Result in bottom 16 bits.
pextrw	Extracts one of four words.
pinsrw	Inserts one of four words.
pmaxsw	Returns maximum of two values in each of four signed word values.
pmaxub	Returns maximum of two values in each of eight unsigned byte values.
pminsw	Returns minimum of two values in each of four signed word values.
pminub	Returns minimum of two values in each of eight unsigned byte values.
pmovmskb	Builds mask byte from top bit of 8-byte values.
pmulhuw	Multiplies four unsigned word values and stores the high 16-bit result.
pshufw	Shuffles four word values. Takes two 128-bit values (source and destination) and an 8-bit immediate value, and then fills in each destination 32-bit value from a source 32-bit value specified by the immediate. The immediate byte is broken into four 2-bit values.

Logic

andnps	Logically ANDs four single-precision values with the logical inverse (NOT) of four other single-precision values.
andps	Logically ANDs four single-precision values with four other single-precision values.
orps	Logically ORs four single-precision values with four other single-precision values.
xorps	Logically XORs four single-precision values with four other single-precision values.

Compare

cmpxxps	Compares four single-precision values.
cmpxxss	Compares lowest two single-precision values.
comiss	Compares lowest two single-precision values and stores result in EFLAGS.
ucomiss	Compares lowest two single-precision values and stores result in EFLAGS. (QNaNs don't throw exceptions with ucomiss, unlike comiss).

Compare Codes

eq	Equal to.
lt	Less than.
le	Less than or equal to.
ne	Not equal.
nlt	Not less than.
nle	Not less than or equal to.

ord   Ordered.
unord   Unordered.

Conversion
cvtpi2ps   Converts two 32-bit integers to 32-bit floating-point values. The top two values remain unchanged.
cvtps2pi   Converts two 32-bit floating-point values to 32-bit integers.
cvtsi2ss   Converts one 32-bit integer to 32-bit floating-point value. The top three values remain unchanged.
cvtss2si   Converts one 32-bit floating-point value to 32-bit integer.
cvttps2pi Converts two 32-bit floating-point values to 32-bit integers using truncation.
cvttss2si Converts one 32-bit floating-point value to 32-bit integer using truncation.

State
fxrstor   Restores floating-point and SSE state.
fxsave   Stores floating-point and SSE state.
ldmxcsr   Loads the MXCSR register.
stmxcsr   Stores the MXCSR register.

Load/Store
movaps   Moves a 128-bit value.
movhlps   Moves high half to a low half.
movlhps   Moves low half to upper halves.
movhps   Moves 64-bit value into top half of an XMM register.
movlps   Moves 64-bit value into bottom half of an XMM register.
movmskps   Moves top bits of single-precision values into bottom four bits of a 32-bit register.
movss   Moves the bottom single-precision value; the top three values remain unchanged in another XMM register; otherwise they are set to zero.
movups   Moves a 128-bit value. Address can be unaligned.
maskmovq   Moves a 64-bit value according to a mask.
movntps   Moves a 128-bit value directly to memory, skipping the cache. (NT stands for "non-temporal.")
movntq   Moves a 64-bit value directly to memory, skipping the cache.

Shuffling
shufps   Shuffles four single-precision values.
unpckhps   Unpacks single-precision values from high halves.
unpcklps   Unpacks single-precision values from low halves.

Cache Control
prefetchT0   Fetches a cache-line of data into all levels of cache.
prefetchT1   Fetches a cache-line of data into all but the highest levels of cache.
prefetchT2   Fetches a cache-line of data into all but the two highest levels of cache.
prefetchNTA Fetches data into only the highest level of cache, not the lower levels.

sfence   Guarantees that every store instruction that precedes the store fence instruc-
                tion in program order is globally visible before any store instruction that
                follows the fence.

The *prefetches* instructions may be used to access an invalid memory location (i.e., off
the end of an array) – however, the address must be generated without error.

2.2 SSE in C and C++

The SSE instructions [7] operate on either all or the least significant pairs of packed data
operands in parallel. The *packed instructions* (with PS suffix), as shown in Fig. 2.4, operate
on a pair of operands, while the *scalar instructions* (with SS suffix), as shown in Fig. 2.5,

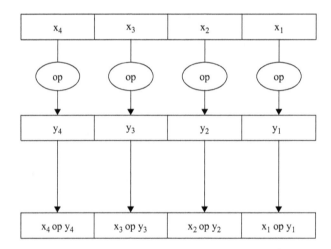

Figure 2.4   SSE packed instruction works on four pairs of data at the same time.

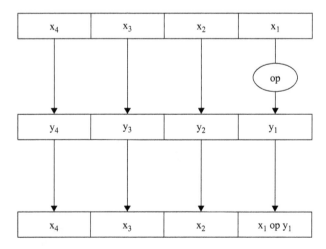

Figure 2.5   SSE scalar instruction only works on a single pair of data.

always operate on the least significant pair of two operands. For scalar operations, the three upper components from the first operand are passed to the destination.

The C version of an SSE register is the user-friendly and self-explanatory type __m128. All the instructions start with _mm_ (i.e., multimedia). The suffix indicates the data type. We describe four floats below, which use the suffix _ps (packed single-precision floats). For example, _mm_load_ps loads four floats into a __m128, and _mm_add_ps adds four corresponding floats together. Major useful operations are listed in Table 2.1.

Table 2.1 Major operations in the SSE instruction set.

__m128 _mm_load_ps(float *src)	Load 4 floats from a 16-byte aligned address (Warning: Segfaults if the address is not a multiple of 16!)
__m128 _mm_loadu_ps(float *src)	Load 4 floats from an unaligned address (4 × slower!)
__m128 _mm_load1_ps(float *src)	Load 1 individual float into all 4 fields of an __m128
__m128 _mm_setr_ps(float a,float b,float c, float d)	Load 4 separate floats from parameters into an __m128
void _mm_store_ps(float *dest,__m128 src)	Store 4 floats to an aligned address
void _mm_storeu_ps(float *dest,__m128 src)	Store 4 floats to unaligned address
__m128 _mm_add_ps(__m128 a,__m128 b)	Add corresponding floats (also "sub")

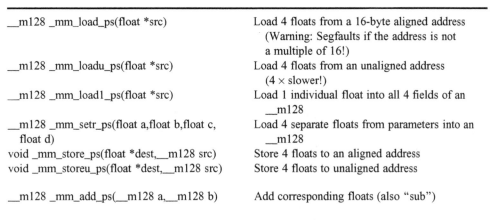

dest[31-0] ← dest[31-0] + src[31-0];
dest[63-32] ← dest[63-32] + src[63-32];
dest[95-64] ← dest[95-64] + src[95-64];
dest[127-96] ← dest[127-96] + src[127-96];

dest[31-0] ← dest[31-0] − src[31-0];
dest[63-32] ← dest[63-32] − src[63-32];
dest[95-64] ← dest[95-64] − src[95-64];
dest[127-96] ← dest[127-96]−src[127-96];

__m128 _mm_mul_ps(__m128 a,__m128 b)   Multiply corresponding floats (also "div", but it is slow)

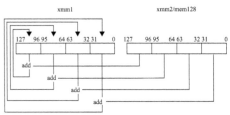
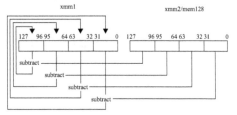
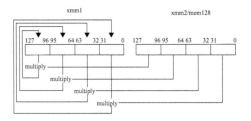
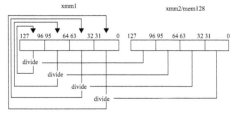

dest[31-0] ← dest[31-0] * src[31-0];
dest[63-32] ← dest[63-32] * src[63-32];
dest[95-64] ← dest[95-64] * src[95-64];
dest[127-96] ← dest[127-96] * src[127-96];

dest[31-0] ← dest[31-0] / (src[31-0]);
dest[63-32] ← dest[63-32] / (src[63-32]);
dest[95-64] ← dest[95-64] / (src[95-64]);
dest[127-96]← dest[127-96]/(src[127-96]);

__m128 _mm_min_ps(__m128 a,__m128 b)

Take corresponding minimum (also "max")

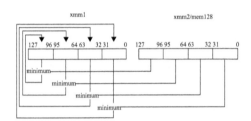

dest[63-0] ← if ((dest[31-0] = 0.0) and
  (src[31-0] = 0.0)) then src[31-0]
else if (dest[31-0] = snan) then src[31-0];
else if src[31-0] = snan) then src[31-0];
else if (dest[31-0] > src[31-0])
then dest[31-0]
else src[31-0];
repeat operation for 2nd and 3rd doublewords
dest[127-64] ← if ((dest127-96] = 0.0) and
  (src[127-96] = 0.0))
then src[127-96]
else if (dest[127-96] = snan) then src[127-96];
else if src[127-96] = snan) then src[127-96];
else if (dest[127-96] < src[127-96])
then dest[127-96]
else src[127-96];

dest[31-0] ← if ((dest[31-0] = 0.0) and
  (src[31-0] = 0.0)) then src[31-0]
else if (dest[31-0] = snan) then src[31-0];
else if src[31-0] = snan) then src[31-0];
else if (dest[31-0] > src[31-0])
then dest[31-0]
else src[31-0];
repeat operation for 2nd and 3rd doublewords
dest[127-64] ← if ((dest[127-96] = 0.0) and
  (src[127-96] = 0.0))
then src[127-96]
else if (dest[127-96] = snan) then src[127-96];
else if src[127-96] = snan) then src[127-96];
else if (dest[127-96] > src[127-96])
then dest[127-96]
else src[127-96];

__m128 _mm_sqrt_ps(__m128 a)

Take square roots of 4 floats

dest[31-0] ← sqrt(src[31-0]);
dest[63-32] ← sqrt(src[63-32]);

dest[95-64] ← sqrt(src[95-64]);
dest[127-96] ← sqrt(src[127-96]);

__m128 _mm_rcp_ps(__m128 a)

Compute rough (12-bit accuracy) reciprocal of all 4 floats (as fast as an add!)

dest[31-0] ← approximate(1.0/(src[31-0]));
dest[63-32] ← approximate(1.0/(src[63-32]));
dest[95-64] ← approximate(1.0/(src[95-64]));
dest[127-96] ← approximate(1.0/(src[127-96]));

__m128 _mm_rsqrt_ps(__m128 a)

Rough (12-bit) reciprocal-square-root of all 4 floats (fast)

dest[31-0] ← approximate(1.0/sqrt(src[31-0]));
dest[63-32]←approximate(1.0/sqrt(src[63-32]));
dest[95-64]←approximate(1.0/sqrt(src[95-64]));
dest[127-96]←approximate(1.0/sqrt(src[127-96]));

__m128 _mm_shuffle_ps(__m128 lo,__m128 hi, _mm_shuffle(hi3,hi2,lo1,lo0))

Interleave inputs into low 2 floats and high 2 floats of output. Basically
out[0]=lo[lo0];   out[1]=lo[lo1];
out[2]=hi[hi2];   out[3]=hi[hi3];
For example, _mm_shuffle_ps(a,a,_mm_shuffle (i, i,i,i)) copies the float a[i] into all 4 output floats

2.3 SSE Programming Examples

VALU is a hardware vector unit that allows users to place four floating numbers or two double-precision numbers in a vector register. Today, the second generation Intel i7 and the latest AMD processors have extended the length of the vector unit to 256 bits (eight floating numbers or four double-precision numbers). Both AMD and Intel plan to extend the length of the vector unit to 1,024 bits. One vector unit may include many registers, for example, eight 128-bit registers in the Intel Pentium III processor. The SSE instructions use the SSE functions to operate on four numbers in the register. VALU is an SIMD-style arithmetic logic unit in which a single instruction performs the same operation on all the data elements in each vector.

2.3.1 SSE

SSE adds a series of packed and scalar single-precision floating-point operations, and some conversions between single precision and integer. SSE uses the XMM register file, which is distinct from the MMX register file and does not alias the ×87 floating-point stack.

All operations under SSE are done under the control of MXCSR, a special purpose control register that contains IEEE-754 flags and mask bits. SSE is enabled using the GCC compiler flag -msse. SSE is enabled by default on gcc-4.0. If SSE is enabled, the C preprocessor symbol __SSE__ is defined.

2.3.2 SSE2

SSE2 adds a series of packed and scalar double-precision floating-point operations. Like SSE, SSE2 uses the XMM register file. All floating point operations under SSE2 are also done under the control of MXCSR to set rounding modes, flags, and exception masks. In addition, SSE2 replicates most of the integer operations in MMX, besides being modified appropriately to fit the 128-bit XMM register size. SSE2 also adds a large number of data type conversion instructions.

SSE2 is enabled using the GCC compiler flag -msse2. It is also enabled by default on gcc-4.0. If SSE2 is enabled, the C preprocessor symbol __SSE2__ is defined.

2.3.3 SSE3

SSE3 adds some instructions mostly geared to making the complex floating-point arithmetic unit work better in some data layouts. However, since it is possible to get the same or better performance by repacking data as uniform vectors rather than non-uniform vectors ahead of time, it is not expected that most developers will need to rely on this feature. Finally, it adds a small set of additional permutes and some horizontal floating-point adds and subtracts that may be of use to some developers. SSE3 is enabled using the GCC compiler flag -msse3.

2.3.4 SSE4

SSE4 is an another major enhancement, adding a dot product instruction, additional integer instructions, a *popcnt* instruction, and more.

2.3.5 Programming examples

Each core in the multi-core processor has its own cache, ALU and VALU, as shown in Fig. 2.6. Unlike the ALU, the VALU allows users to operate on four numbers at the same time. We use a VALU that includes a 128-bit vector unit through the SIMD instruction set to accelerate parallel FDTD code.

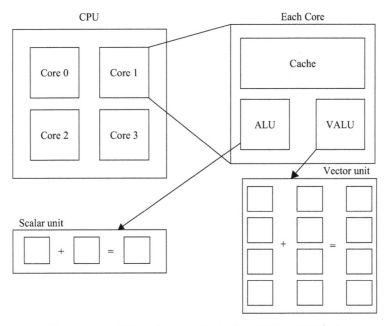

Figure 2.6 CPU architecture including ALU and VALU.

SIMD computations were introduced to the Intel architecture with the MMX technology. The MMX technology allows the SIMD computations to be performed on a packed byte. The Pentium III processor extended the SIMD computation model with the introduction of SSE. SSE allows SIMD computations to be performed on operands that contain four packed single-precision floating-point data elements. The operands can be in memory or in a set of eight 128-bit XMM registers. Fig. 2.7 shows typical SIMD computation procedure.

The following simple example is employed to demonstrate the advantage of using SSE. Consider an operation like the vector addition, which is often used in the FDTD update.

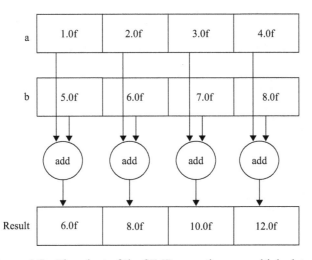

Figure 2.7 Flowchart of the SIMD operation on multiple data.

Adding two single-precision four-component vectors together using ×86 code requires four floating-point addition instructions [8].

```
vec_res.x = v1.x  + v2.x;
vec_res.y = v1.y  + v2.y;
vec_res.z = v1.z  + v2.z;
vec_res.w = v1.w  + v2.w;
```

This would correspond to four ×86 floating-point ADD (FADD) instructions in the object code. On the other hand, as the following pseudo-code shows, a single 128-bit packed-add instruction can replace the four scalar addition instructions.

```
movaps xmm0, [v1]; xmm0 = v1.w | v1.z | v1.y | v1.x;
addps xmm0,  [v2]; xmm0 = v1.w+v2.w | v1.z+v2.z | v1.y+v2.y | v1.x+v2.x;
movaps [vec_res], xmm0;
```

The various intrinsic functions are available in one of the four headers, one each for MMX, SSE, SSE2, and SSE3, when the corresponding *instruction set architecture* (ISA) appeared:

```
MMX    mmintrin.h
SSE    xmmintrin.h
SSE2   emmintrin.h
SSE3   pmmintrin.h
```

Here is a demo code segment that calculates the summation of two vectors without the SSE acceleration:

```
#include <iostream>
using namespace std;
int main(int argc, char **argv)
{
        //Declare the vectors a and b.
        float a[4], b[4];

        //Assign the vectors with the given values.
        a[0] = 1.0f;
        a[1] = 2.0f;
        a[2] = 3.0f;
        a[3] = 4.0f;
        b[0] = 5.0f;
        b[1] = 6.0f;
        b[2] = 7.0f;
        b[3] = 8.0f;

        //Execute the multiplication operation four times.
        a[0] = a[0] * b[0];
        a[1] = a[1] * b[1];
        a[2] = a[2] * b[2];
```

```
        a[3] = a[3] * b[3];

        //Output the results
        cout << a[0] << endl;
        cout << a[1] << endl;
        cout << a[2] << endl;
        cout << a[3] << endl;

        return 0;
}
```

The code segment with SSE acceleration is expressed as follows:

```
#include <iostream>
using namespace std;

//Header file for the SSE intrinsics.
#include <xmmintrin.h>

int main(int argc, char **argv)
{
        //The operand is aligned on the 16-byte boundary.
        #ifdef LINUX
        //FLOAT_ALN16 on LINUX
        typedef float FLOAT_ALN16 __attribute__((aligned(16)));
        #else
        //FLOAT_ALN16 on Windows
        typedef __declspec(align(16)) float FLOAT_ALN16;
        #endif

        //Declare the vectors a and b
        FLOAT_ALN16 a[4], b[4];

        //Assign the vectors with the given values
        a[0] = 1.0f;
        a[1] = 2.0f;
        a[2] = 3.0f;
        a[3] = 4.0f;
        b[0] = 5.0f;
        b[1] = 6.0f;
        b[2] = 7.0f;
        b[3] = 8.0f;

        //Convert the data type to the SSE format
        __m128 *va = (__m128 *)a;
        __m128 *vb = (__m128 *)b;

        va[0] = _mm_mul_ps(va[0], vb[0]);

        //Output the results
        cout << a[0] << endl;
        cout << a[1] << endl;
```

```
    cout << a[2] << endl;
    cout << a[3] << endl;

    return 0;
}
```

2.4 Compile and Execute SSE Code

In order to compile SSE code, we add the SSE header file #include <xmmintrin.h> to the code if the compiler and CPU supports the SSE instructions. Both C/C++ and FORTRAN compilers in the operating system Windows (Windows 98 or newer version) or Linux (its kernels are newer than version 2.2) support SSE instructions, and so do Intel Pentium IV or AMD Athlon 64 and newer CPUs. Compiling is exactly same as for C/C++ and FORTRAN code. The SSE executive file can be run on Intel or AMD CPUs in the Windows or Linux environment.

When the SSE header file #include <xmmintrin.h> is included in the code, the SSE intrinsic functions are available. The compilation and execution procedure is exactly same as that for regular C/C++ and FORTRAN code. A detailed explanation of the compilation and execution of SSE code is beyond the scope of this book.

There are three popular compilers. Microsoft Visual Studio is a very popular compiler for Windows because it has a good and user-friendly integrated development environment (IDE). The Microsoft compiler optimizes reasonably well, but not as well as the Intel and Gnu compilers.

The Intel Studio/Composer compiler optimizes very well. Intel also provides some of the best optimized function libraries for mathematical and other purposes. Unfortunately, the Intel compilers and some of the function libraries favor Intel CPUs, and often produce code that runs slower on CPUs of other brands.

Gnu C++ compiler produces the best optimizations in most cases. The g++ compiler is currently available for all ×86 and ×86-64 platforms.

2.5 VALU Implementation in the FDTD Method

A 3-D array in FDTD code [9] is allocated by using the *_aligned_malloc* function in the SSE instructions. For example, if we need a 3-D array *array_name*[*x_size, y_size, z_size*], we can first define one 1-D array *array_name_tmp*[*N*] whose size is *N*=*x_size**y_size*z_size, and then map the 1-D memory address to a 3-D array *array_name*. The pseudo-code segment is demonstrated as follows:

```
//allocate 1-D memory
array_name_tmp=(float*)_aligned_malloc(sizeof(float)*x_size*y_size*
    z_size,16);
array_name=(float ***)_aligned_malloc (sizeof(float**)*x_size,16 );
for( i = 0; i < x_size; i++){

    array_name[i]=(float **)_aligned_malloc(sizeof(float*)*y_size,16 );
    for( j = 0; j < y_size; j++){
```

```
        map_address = i * y_size * z_size + j * z_size;
        array_name[i][j] = &array_name_tmp[map_address];
    }
}
```

In the C programming language, the data in memory is continuous in the *y-z* plane. Suppose that *x_size, y_size*, and *z_size* are equal to n_x, n_y, and n_z, respectively, with the data structure in the *y-z* plane shown in Fig. 2.8. The memory addresses of the data elements (0, 0, 0), (0, 0, 1), ..., (0, 0, n_z) are continuous. Likewise, the addresses of (0, 1, 0), (0, 1, 1), ..., (0, 1, n_z) are continuous too. The address of (0, 0, n_x) is followed by the element (0, 1, 0). When we calculate the electric and magnetic fields in the *y-z* plane, we only need to know the address of the first element and the entire array.

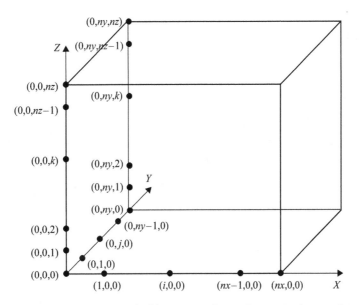

Figure 2.8   Data structure inside memory is continuous in the *y-z* plane.

Actually, the number of unknowns for the different field components in the different directions is different; for example, the computational domain is discretized into n_x cells in the *x*-direction, n_y cells in the *y*-direction, and n_z cells in the *z*-direction, respectively. The number of the electric and magnetic field unknowns in each direction inside the computational domain has the following patterns:

- E_x: Number of unknowns is n_x, $n_y + 1$, and $n_z + 1$ in the *x*-, *y*-, and *z*-directions, respectively.
- E_y: Number of unknowns is $n_x + 1$, n_y, and $n_z + 1$ in the *x*-, *y*-, and *z*-directions, respectively.
- E_z: Number of unknowns is $n_x + 1$, $n_y + 1$, and n_z in the *x*-, *y*-, and *z*-directions, respectively.
- H_x: Number of unknowns is $n_x + 1$, n_y, and n_z in the *x*-, *y*-, and *z*-directions, respectively.

- H_y: Number of unknowns is n_x, $n_y + 1$, and n_z in the x-, y-, and z-directions, respectively.
- H_z: Number of unknowns is n_x, n_y, and $n_z + 1$ in the x-, y-, and z-directions, respectively.

It is important to know that each component shifted in the x- or y-direction is aligned in the z-direction. That is, we can assign two adjacent array segments to two vectors without defining new vectors and moving the data from one vector to another. For example, we can assign $E_z(i, j, k)$ to the *vEz* vector, and $E_z(i, j + 1, k)$ to the *vEz1* vector as follows:

```
vEz  = (__m128 *)(Ez[i][j]);
vEz1 = (__m128 *)(Ez[i][j+1]);
```

and then calculate their difference:

```
xmm1 = _mm_sub_ps(vEz1[kk], vEz[kk]);
```

which is more efficient than the following:

```
vEz  = (__m128 *)(Ez[i][j]);
xmm1 = _mm_loadu_ps(&Ez[i][j+1]);
xmm1 = _mm_sub_ps(xmm1, vEz[kk]);
```

If a shift of two array segments occurs in the z-direction, for example, $E_y(i, j, k + 1)$ and $E_y(i, j, k)$, we have to define an intermediate vector to store either $E_y(i, j, k + 1)$ or $E_y(i, j, k)$ since we cannot align $E_y(i, j, k + 1)$ and $E_y(i, j, k)$ at the same time.

```
vEy  = (__m128 *)(Ey[i][j]);
xmm0 = _mm_loadu_ps(&Ey[i][j][k+1]);
xmm0 = _mm_sub_ps(xmm0, vEy[kk]);
```

It is worthwhile to notice that the start index of the six field components is (0, 0, 0).

2.5.1 Magnetic fields

We demonstrate the VALU implementation in the parallel FDTD code next and explain the programming techniques for both regular and SSE FDTD code development. A complete parallel FDTD code enhanced by VALU is presented in the appendix. Suppose that the computational domain is filled with an isotropic and homogenous medium and that the magnetic field H_x update can be expressed as follows:

$$H_x^{n+1/2}\left(i, j+\frac{1}{2}, k+\frac{1}{2}\right) = H_x^{n-1/2}\left(i, j+\frac{1}{2}, k+\frac{1}{2}\right)$$
$$+\frac{\Delta t}{\mu}\left[\frac{E_y^n\left(i, j+\frac{1}{2}, k+1\right) - E_y^n\left(i, j+\frac{1}{2}, k\right)}{\Delta z} - \frac{E_z^n\left(i, j+1, k+\frac{1}{2}\right) - E_z^n\left(i, j, k+\frac{1}{2}\right)}{\Delta y}\right] \quad (2.1)$$

In a regular FDTD update, the magnetic field $H_x^{n+1/2}(i, j + 1/2, k + 1/2)$ is calculated by using its value $H_x^{n-1/2}(i, j + 1/2, k + 1/2)$ at the previous time step, and its four electric field neighbors $E_y^n(i, j + 1/2, k + 1)$, $E_y^n(i, j + 1/2, k)$, $E_z^n(i, j + 1, k + 1/2)$, and $E_z^n(i, j, k + 1/2)$ at the previous half time step, as shown in Fig. 2.9.

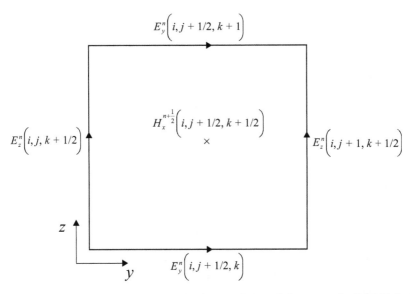

Figure 2.9   Distribution of the electric fields E_y and E_z and the magnetic field H_x in (2.1).

In code development, both the electric field E and the magnetic field H have independent indices, as shown in Fig. 2.10. That is, they are not in a "leap-frog" format to reduce the memory usage and to maintain data continuity in memory. Therefore, the updates for the electric field E and the magnetic field H have different expressions.

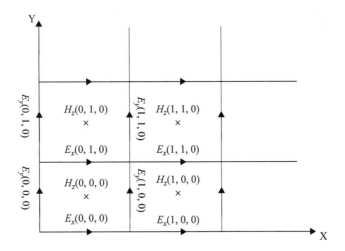

Figure 2.10   Electric and magnetic field indices in the FDTD code.

Due to the continuous data along the z-direction, the magnetic field H_x update loop in the regular FDTD update should be written as:

```
//Hx update
Coefficient_Ey = Dt/(Mu0*Dz);
Coefficient_Ez = Dt/(Mu0*Dy);
for( i = 0; i <= nx; i++){
    for( j = 0; j < ny; j++){
        for( k = 0; k < nz;k++){

            Hx[i][j][k] = Hx[i][j][k] + Coefficient_Ey * (Ey[i][j][k+1] -
                          Ey[i][j][k])] - Coefficient_Ez *
                          (Ez[i][j+1][k]- Ez[i][j][k]);
        }
    }
}
```

One update procedure in the code above generates one magnetic field at a time. The i loop is the outside loop and the k loop is the inside loop. This generates better code performance by keeping the data structure together inside memory. Follow the steps below to use the SSE instructions to accelerate the H_x update.

1) Declare all the variables and arrays as the SSE data type.
2) Load the coefficient of electric field E_y into the SSE vectors. Convert the single floating number (the coefficient of E_y difference) to one floating vector. The four element values inside the vector are equal to the single floating number.
3) Load the coefficient of electric field E_z into the SSE registers. Convert a single floating number (the coefficient of E_z difference) to one floating vector.
4) Convert H_x, E_y, and E_z to SSE 128-bit pointers. The simulation will take four numbers in each vector in each operation.
5) Since the electric field E_y is not aligned in the z-direction, define an intermediate vector to store either $E_y(i, j, k + 1)$ or $E_y(i, j, k)$ in order to carry out the subtraction of $E_y(i, j, k)$ from $E_y(i, j, k + 1)$ in the z-direction, as shown in Fig. 2.11.
6) Carry out the multiplication operation of the difference of the electric field E_y by its coefficient in the vector format.

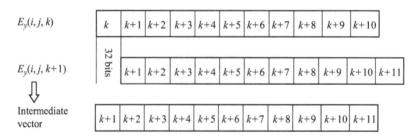

Figure 2.11 $E_y(i, j, k)$ and $E_y(i, j, k + 1)$ cannot be aligned to each other. An intermediate vector is used to align the two electric fields in the z-direction.

7) Calculate the difference of the electric field E_z in the y-direction. Since E_z at j and $j + 1$ are aligned on 16-byte boundaries, we can carry out the subtraction of the two E_z in the y-direction directly by assigning $E_z(i, j + 1, k)$ and $E_z(i, j, k)$ to two different vectors, as shown in Fig. 2.12.

8) Multiply the difference of two electric fields E_z in the y-direction by its coefficient in vector format.

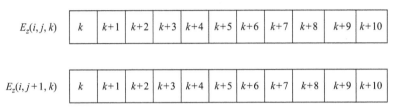

Figure 2.12 $E_z(i, j, k)$ and $E_z(i, j + 1, k)$ can be aligned to each other without requiring an intermediate vector.

9) Calculate the contributions from E_y and E_z to the magnetic field H_x.

10) Calculate the contribution of the previous magnetic field H_x and produce four H_x at one time.

11) Move four indices forward in the z-direction.

The SSE code segment for the update of the magnetic field H_x is given below:

```
void Hx_Update_SSE(){
//Hx is continuous along the z-direction and the update should start
//from the z-direction to improve cache hit ratio.
//Hx[*][*][0], Ey[*][*][0] and Ez[*][*][0] are aligned on the 16-byte
//boundary.

int i, j, k, kk;
__m128 *vHx, *vEy, *vEz, *vEz1, vehcoefz, vehcoefy, xmm0, xmm1;

vecoefz = _mm_load1_ps(&ecoefz); //Coefficient of Ey
vecoefy = _mm_load1_ps(&ecoefy); //Coefficient of Ez

for (i = 1; i <= nx; i ++){
    for (j = 1; j < ny; j ++){

        vHx = (__m128 *)(Hx[i][j]);   //convert the floating array
        vEy = (__m128 *)(Ey[i][j]);   //to the group of 4 numbers.

        vEz = (__m128 *)(Ez[i][j]);
        vEz1 = (__m128 *)(Ez[i][j+1]);

        k = kk = 0;
        do {
                xmm0 = _mm_loadu_ps(&Ey[i][j][k+1]);
                xmm0 = _mm_sub_ps(xmm0, vEy[kk]);
```

```
xmm0 = _mm_mul_ps(xmm0, vefoefz);


xmm1 = _mm_sub_ps(vEz1[kk], vEz[kk]);
xmm1 = _mm_mul_ps(xmm1, vecoefy);

xmm0 = _mm_sub_ps(xmm0, xmm1);
vHx[kk] = _mm_add_ps(vHx[kk], xmm0);

k += 4;
kk ++;

} while (k <= nz);
}
}
}
```

We next explain the important lines in the code segment above:

1) vecoefz = _mm_load1_ps(&ecoefz): Load the single-precision floating-point value of coefficient *ecoefz* into the vector *vecoefz*, and copy it into the vector *vecoefz* as four 32-bit numbers. The SSE instruction uses SIMD to operate on the four numbers, which requires that the four numbers in vector 1 and another four numbers in vector 2 should have the same operation. When we use a floating number to multiply a vector, we need to convert the floating number to a floating vector.

2) vecoefy = _mm_load1_ps(&ecoefy): Load the single-precision floating-point value of coefficient *ecoefy* into the vector *vecoefy* and copy it into the vector *vecoefy* as four 32-bit numbers.

   Similar to the order found in regular FDTD code, the outside loop index is *i* followed by the index *j*, and the inner loop index is *k*. The data structure is determined by the memory allocation method.

3) vHx = (__m128 *)(Hx[i][j]): Convert the array H_x into the vector format required by SSE instructions. The SSE instruction then operates on the vectors.

4) vEy = (__m128 *)(Ey[i][j]): Convert the array E_y into the vector format required by SSE instructions. To calculate the magnetic field H_x, we need two electric field components E_y that are at different positions in the spatial domain. Since $E_y(i, j, k)$ and $E_y(i, j, k + 1)$ have a 32-bit shift in memory, as shown in Fig. 2.13, we cannot align them at

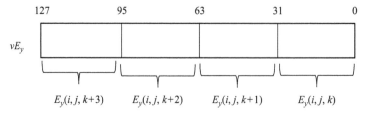

Figure 2.13   Relative locations of the electric field $E_y(i, j, k)$ inside the vector *vEy*.

the same time. To do so, we need to load one of them into a temporary vector *xmm0*, and then carry out the operation of two vectors $E_y(i, j, k)$ and *xmm0*.

5) vEz=(__m128 *)(Ez[i][j]): Convert the array E_z into the vector format required by SSE instructions. Since the field $E_z(i, j, k)$ inside memory is not continuous along the *y*-direction, we need to assign the electric fields $E_z(i, j, k)$ and $E_z(i, j + 1, k)$ to two vectors. Hence, the two electric fields $E_z(i, j, k)$ and $E_z(i, j + 1, k)$ can be subtracted directly, as shown in Fig. 2.14.

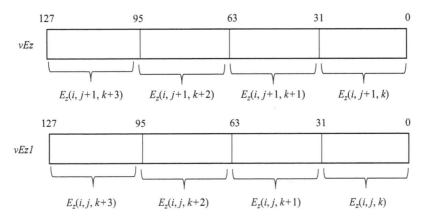

Figure 2.14   Relative locations of the electric fields $E_z(i, j, k)$ and $E_z(i, j, k + 1)$ in the vectors *vEz* and *vEz1*.

6) vEz1=(__m128 *)(Ez[i][j+1]): Convert the array E_z into the vector format required by SSE instructions, which is aligned with the *vEz* vector.

7) xmm0=_mm_loadu_ps(&Ey[i][j][k+1]): Load the array $E_y(i, j, k + 1)$ into an intermediate vector *xmm0*.

8) xmm0=_mm_sub_ps(xmm0, vEy[kk]): Subtract the vector *xmm0* from *vEy*, and store the four results in the vector *xmm0*. Since the electric field $E_y(i, j, k + 1)$ cannot be aligned with $E_y(i, j, k)$ at the same time, we need to place $E_y(i, j, k + 1)$ into an intermediate vector. Then, we can calculate the difference of the two electric fields $E_y(i, j, k + 1)$ and $E_y(i, j, k)$, as shown in Fig. 2.15.

9) xmm0=_mm_mul_ps(xmm0, vefoefz): Use the constant vector *vefoefz* to multiply the difference of the two electric fields $E_y(i, j, k + 1)$ and $E_y(i, j, k)$ and store the results in the *xmm0* vector. This removes the difference of the two electric fields $E_y(i, j, k + 1)$ and $E_y(i, j, k)$ in the *xmm0* vector.

   The two electric fields $E_z(i, j + 1, k)$ and $E_z(i, j, k)$ are in two vectors *vEz* and *vEz1*, respectively. Because they have been aligned with each other, we can carry out the operation on them directly.

10) xmm1=_mm_sub_ps(vEz1[kk], vEz[kk]): Calculate the difference of the two electric fields $E_z(i, j + 1, k)$ and $E_z(i, j, k)$ and store the results in the *xmm1* vector.

11) xmm1=_mm_mul_ps(xmm1, vecoefy): Multiply the difference of the two electric fields $E_z(i, j + 1, k)$ and $E_z(i, j, k)$ by the constant coefficient *vecoefy* vector, and store the results in the *xmm1* vector.

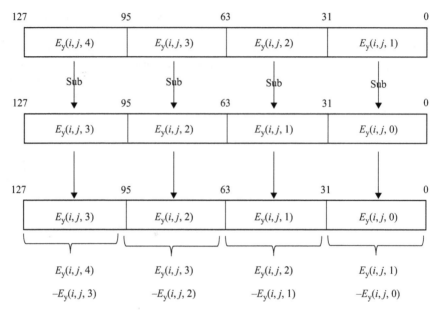

Figure 2.15   Relative locations of the electric fields $E_y(i, j, k)$ and $E_y(i, j, k+1)$ in the vectors *xmm0* and *vEy*.

12) xmm0=_mm_sub_ps(xmm0, xmm1): Calculate the contribution of electric fields E_y and E_z to the magnetic field H_x.

$$\frac{\Delta t}{\mu}\left[\frac{E_y^n\left(i,j+\frac{1}{2},k+1\right) - E_y^n\left(i,j+\frac{1}{2},k\right)}{\Delta z} - \frac{E_z^n\left(i,j+1,k+\frac{1}{2}\right) - E_z^n\left(i,j,k+\frac{1}{2}\right)}{\Delta y}\right]$$

13) vHx[kk]=_mm_add_ps(vHx[kk], xmm0): Add the magnetic field H_x contribution from the magnetic field H_x determined in the previous time step.

$$H_x^{n-1/2}\left(i,j+\frac{1}{2},k+\frac{1}{2}\right)$$
$$+\frac{\Delta t}{\mu}\left[\frac{E_y^n\left(i,j+\frac{1}{2},k+1\right) - E_y^n\left(i,j+\frac{1}{2},k\right)}{\Delta z} - \frac{E_z^n\left(i,j+1,k+\frac{1}{2}\right) - E_z^n\left(i,j,k+\frac{1}{2}\right)}{\Delta y}\right]$$

14) $k += 4$ and kk ++: Move four grids forward along the z-direction.

The update procedure of magnetic field component H_y is similar to that of H_x. For the update of component H_z, the electric fields E_x and E_y are aligned in the z-direction. Therefore, we do not need the intermediate vector to provide alignment for the load operation.

2.5.2 Electric fields

Different from the update formulation of the magnetic fields, the electric field E_x update can be expressed as follows:

$$E_x^{n+1}\left(i+\frac{1}{2},j,k\right) = E_x^n\left(i+\frac{1}{2},j,k\right) + \frac{\Delta t}{\varepsilon}\left[\frac{H_z^{n+1/2}\left(i+\frac{1}{2},j+\frac{1}{2},k\right) - H_z^{n+1/2}\left(i+\frac{1}{2},j-\frac{1}{2},k\right)}{\Delta y}\right.$$

$$\left. - \frac{H_y^{n+1/2}\left(i+\frac{1}{2},j,k+\frac{1}{2}\right) - H_y^{n+1/2}\left(i+\frac{1}{2},j,k-\frac{1}{2}\right)}{\Delta z}\right] \tag{2.2}$$

In the regular FDTD update, the electric field $E_x^{n+1}(i+1/2,j,k)$ is calculated by using $E_x^n(i+1/2,j,k)$ from the previous time step, and four magnetic field neighbors $H_y^{n+1/2}(i+1/2,j,k+1/2)$, $H_y^{n+1/2}(i+1/2,j,k-1/2)$, $H_z^{n+1/2}(i+1/2,j+1/2,k)$, and $H_z^{n+1/2}(i+1/2,j-1/2,k)$ from the previous one-half time step, as shown in Fig. 2.16.

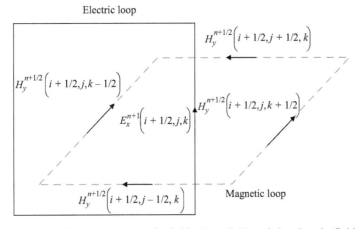

Figure 2.16   Distribution of the magnetic fields H_y and H_z and the electric field E_x in (2.2).

Differing from the magnetic field indexing style, the index of the electric field E_x in the y-direction is the same as that of magnetic field H_z on the right-hand side. Similarly, the index of electric field E_x in the z-direction is the same as that of magnetic field H_y into the paper. Because we have continuous data along the z-direction, the electric field E_x update in the regular FDTD method should be as follows:

```
//Ex update
Coefficient_Hz = Dt/(Dy*Epsilon0);
Coefficient_Hy = Dt/(Dz*Epsilon0);
for( i = 0; i < nx; i++){
    for( j = 0; j <= ny; j++){
        for( k = 0; k <= nz; k++){
```

```
    Ex[i][j][k] = Ex[i][j][k] + Coefficient_Hz * (Hz[i][j][k]-
        Hz[i][j-1][k]) - Coefficient_Hy * (Hy[i][j][k]-
        Hy[i][j][k-1]);

    }

  }

}
```

One update procedure in the code above generates one electric field E_x each time because the index k moves forward one grid for each operation. For the same reason, we place the index i in the outmost level of the *for* loop statement to achieve better code performance. Since the data is continuous in the z-direction, the index k is always in the inner loop. Follow the steps below to use the SSE instructions to accelerate the update.

1) Declare variables and arrays to be of the SSE data type, which is required by the SSE instructions.
2) In the SSE instructions, a constant must be converted to a constant vector to operate with a constant or a vector; therefore, for a floating constant, load the coefficient of the magnetic field H_z into the *vhcoefy* vector and make each element value inside the vector equal to the constant.
3) Similarly, load other constants into vectors and make each element value inside the vectors equal to the constant accordingly.
4) Convert E_x, H_y, and H_z to SSE 128-bit pointers so that SSE instructions can operate on four numbers in a single instruction.
5) Since the magnetic fields $H_y(i, j, k + 1)$ and $H_y(i, j, k)$ cannot be aligned at the same time due to their continuous properties, load one of them into an intermediate vector so that they can be operated on by SSE instructions.
6) Subtract the magnetic field $H_y(i, j, k)$ from $H_y(i, j, k + 1)$, and store the results in a temporary vector.
7) Multiply the difference of magnetic field H_y in the z-direction by its coefficient in vector format and store the results in a temporary vector.
8) Similarly, calculate the term associated with the magnetic field H_z in the E_x update. However, since the magnetic fields $H_z(i, j + 1, k)$ and $H_z(i, j, k)$ are aligned with each other, load them into two separate vectors.
9) Subtract the magnetic fields $H_z(i, j, k)$ from $H_z(i, j + 1, k)$ and store the result in a temporary vector.
10) Multiply the difference of the two magnetic fields $H_z(i, j, k)$ and $H_z(i, j + 1, k)$ in the y-direction by their coefficient.
11) Calculate the contribution of magnetic fields H_y and H_z to the electric field E_x.
12) Calculate the contribution of electric field E_x from the previous step and assign the results to the electric field E_x.
13) Move four indices forward in the z-direction.

The SSE code segment for the update of the magnetic field E_x is given below:

```
void Ex_Update_SSE()
{
//Ex is continuous along the z-direction and the update should start
//from the z-direction to improve cache hit ratio. Ex[*][*][0],
//Hz[*][*][0] and Hy[*][*][0] are aligned on the 16-byte boundary.
```

```
int i, j, k, kk;
__m128 *vEx, *vHz, *vHz1, *vHy, vhcoefy, vhcoefz, xmm0, xmm1;

vhcoefy = _mm_load1_ps(&hcoefy);
vhcoefz = _mm_load1_ps(&hcoefz);

for (i = 0; i < nx; i++) {
    for (j = 0; j<= ny; j++){

        vEx = (__m128 *)(Ex[i][j]);
        vHy = (__m128 *)(Hy[i][j]);
        vHz = (__m128 *)(Hz[i][j]);
        vHz1 = (__m128 *)(Hz[i][j-1]);

        k = kk = 0;
        xmm0 = _mm_shuffle_ps(vHy[0], vHy[0], _MM_SHUFFLE(2,1,0,0));

        do {
                xmm0 = _mm_sub_ps(vHy[kk], xmm0);
                xmm0 = _mm_mul_ps(xmm0, vhcoefz);

                xmm1 = _mm_sub_ps(vHz[kk], vHz1[kk]);
                xmm1 = _mm_mul_ps(xmm1, vhcoefy);

                xmm0 = _mm_sub_ps(xmm1, xmm0);
                vEx[kk] = _mm_add_ps(vEx[kk], xmm0);

                k += 4;
                kk ++;

                xmm0 = _mm_loadu_ps(&Hy[i][j][k-1]);
    } while (k <= nz);
    }
  }
}
```

Below, we explain the important line in the code segment above:

1) vhcoefy=_mm_load1_ps(&hcoefy): Load the floating number *hcoefy* into the vector *vhcoefy* and copy into the vector *vhcoefy* as four 32-bit numbers. The SSE instruction uses SIMD to accelerate evaluation with the four numbers in vector 1 and four numbers in vector 2 subject to the same operation. When we use a floating number to multiply a vector, we need to change the floating number to vector format.

2) vhcoefz=_mm_load1_ps(&hcoefz): Load the floating coefficient *hcoefz* into the vector *vhcoefz*, and copy it into the vector *vhcoefz* as four 32-bit numbers.

3) vEx=(__m128 *)(Ex[i][j]): Convert the array E_x into the vector format required by SSE instructions so that we can pick up four numbers each time.

4) vHy=(__m128 *)(Hy[i][j]): Convert the array H_y into the vector format required by SSE instructions. To calculate the electric field component E_x, the magnetic field component H_y is required at different locations. For the floating numbers H_y, $H_y(i, j, k)$, and $H_y(i, j, k-1)$, there is a 32-bit shift in memory, and therefore these cannot be aligned at the same time, as shown in Fig. 2.17. In order to perform the operation, load one of them into a vector *xmm0*, and then carry out the operation of $H_y(i, j, k)$ and *xmm0*.

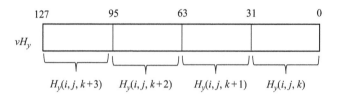

Figure 2.17 Magnetic field $H_y(i, j, k)$ inside the vHy vector.

5) vHz=(__m128 *)(Hz[i][j]): Convert the array H_z into the vector format required by SSE instructions. Since the magnetic field $H_z(i, j, k)$ inside the memory is not continuous along the y-direction, place the magnetic fields $H_z(i, j, k)$ and $H_z(i, j - 1, k)$ in different vectors. Hence, two magnetic fields $H_z(i, j, k)$ and $H_z(i, j - 1, k)$ can be subtracted directly.

6) vHz1=(__m128 *)(Hz[i][j-1]): Convert the array H_z into the vector format required by SSE instructions, as shown in Fig. 2.18.

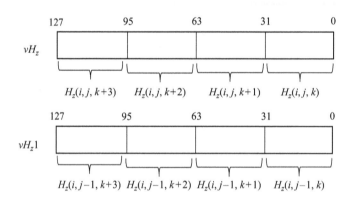

Figure 2.18 Magnetic fields $H_z(i, j, k)$ and $H_z(i, j - 1, k)$ inside the vHz and $vHz1$ vectors.

7) xmm0=_mm_shuffle_ps(vHy[0], vHy[0], _MM_SHUFFLE(2, 1, 0, 0)): The first index in the array $H_y(i, j, k - 1)$ is -1 for $k = 0$. This makes the value of magnetic field $H_y(i, j, -1)$ invalid. Fortunately, this value is of no use in the E_x update. Here, the _mm_shuffle_ps function is used to assign the value of $H_y(i, j, 0)$ to $H_y(i, j, -1)$.

8) xmm0=_mm_sub_ps(vHy[kk], xmm0): Subtract $H_y(i, j, k)$ from $H_y(i, j, k - 1)$ in vector format.

9) xmm0=_mm_mul_ps(xmm0, vhcoefz): Use the constant vector *vhcoefz* to multiply the difference of the two magnetic fields $H_y(i, j, k)$ and $H_y(i, j, k - 1)$.

   The two magnetic fields $H_y(i, j, k)$ and $H_y(i, j, k - 1)$ are in two vectors vHy and $vHy1$, respectively. Because they have been aligned with each other, we can carry out the operations on them directly, as shown in Fig. 2.19.

10) xmm1=_mm_sub_ps(vHz1[kk], vHz[kk]): Subtract the two magnetic fields $H_z(i, j, k)$ and $H_z(i, j - 1, k)$ and store the result in the *xmm1* vector.

11) xmm1=_mm_mul_ps(xmm1, vhcoefy): Multiply the difference of the two magnetic fields $H_z(i, j, k)$ and $H_z(i, j - 1, k)$ by the constant coefficient *vecoefy* vector.

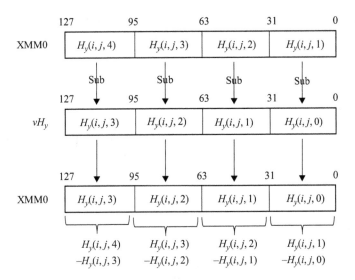

Figure 2.19   Using a vector operation on *xmm0* and *vHy* to get four results in a single operation.

12) xmm0=_mm_sub_ps(xmm0, xmm1): Calculate the contribution of magnetic fields H_y and H_z to the electric field E_x:

$$\frac{\Delta t}{\varepsilon} \left[\frac{H_z^{n+1/2}\left(i+\frac{1}{2},j+\frac{1}{2},k\right) - H_z^{n+1/2}\left(i+\frac{1}{2},j-\frac{1}{2},k\right)}{\Delta y} \right.$$

$$\left. - \frac{H_y^{n+1/2}\left(i+\frac{1}{2},j,k+\frac{1}{2}\right) - H_y^{n+1/2}\left(i+\frac{1}{2},j,k-\frac{1}{2}\right)}{\Delta z} \right]$$

13) vEx[kk] = _mm_add_ps(vEx[kk], xmm0): Add the electric field contribution from the value in the previous time step and assign the result to the electric field E_x:

$$E_x^n\left(i+\frac{1}{2},j,k\right)$$

$$+ \frac{\Delta t}{\varepsilon} \left[\frac{H_z^{n+1/2}\left(i+\frac{1}{2},j+\frac{1}{2},k\right) - H_z^{n+1/2}\left(i+\frac{1}{2},j-\frac{1}{2},k\right)}{\Delta y} \right.$$

$$\left. - \frac{H_y^{n+1/2}\left(i+\frac{1}{2},j,k+\frac{1}{2}\right) - H_y^{n+1/2}\left(i+\frac{1}{2},j,k-\frac{1}{2}\right)}{\Delta z} \right]$$

14) $k + = 4$ and kk ++: Move four grids forward along the z-direction.

The update procedure of the electric field component E_y is similar to E_x. For the update of component E_z, the magnetic fields H_x and H_y are aligned with the electric field E_z in the z-direction. Therefore, we do not need the intermediate vector to realize alignment for the load operation.

2.6 AVX Instruction Set

Advanced vector extension (AVX) [10–13] is an extension to the $\times 86$ instruction set architecture for microprocessors proposed by Intel in March 2008 and first supported by Intel with the Sandy Bridge processor shipping in Q1 2011 and later on by AMD with the Bull-dozer processor shipping in Q3 2011. AVX provides new features, new instructions, and a new coding scheme. Some of the new instructions in AVX that are distinct from SSE are listed in the Table 2.2.

Table 2.2 Typical AVX instructions.

Instruction	Description
VBROADCASTSS, VBROAD-CASTSD, VBROADCASTF128	Copy a 32-bit, 64-bit, or 128-bit memory operand to all elements of an XMM or YMM vector register
VINSERTF128	Replaces either the lower half or the upper half of a 256-bit YMM register with the value of a 128-bit source operand. The other half of the destination is unchanged
VEXTRACTF128	Extracts either the lower half or the upper half of a 256-bit YMM register and copies the value to a 128-bit destination operand
VMASKMOVPS, VMASKMOVPD	Conditionally reads any number of elements from an SIMD vector memory operand into a destination register, leaving the remaining vector elements unread and setting the corresponding elements in the destination register to zero. Alternatively, conditionally writes any number of elements from an SIMD vector register operand to a vector memory operand, leaving the remaining elements of the memory operand unchanged
VPERMILPS, VPERMILPD	Shuffle 32-bit or 64-bit vector elements, with a register or memory operand as selector
VPERM2F128	Shuffle the four 128-bit vector elements of two 256-bit source operands into a 256-bit destination operand, with an immediate constant as selector
VZEROALL	Set all YMM registers to zero and tag them as unused. Used when switching between 128-bit use and 256-bit use
VZEROUPPER	Set the upper half of all YMM registers to zero. Used when switching between 128-bit use and 256-bit use

The width of the SIMD register file, XMM0–XMM15, is increased from 128 bits to 256 bits and is renamed YMM0–YMM15. In processors with AVX support, the legacy SSE instructions, which previously operated on 128-bit XMM registers, now operate on the lower 128 bits of the YMM registers, as shown in Fig. 2.20.

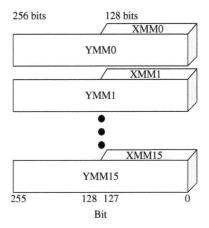

Figure 2.20   XMM registers overlay the YMM registers.

AVX introduces a three-operand SIMD instruction format, where the destination register is distinct from the two source operands. For example, the SSE instruction using the conventional two-operand form $a = a + b$ can now use a non-destructive three-operand form, $c = a + b$. This preserves both source operands, as shown in Fig. 2.21. AVX's three-operand format is limited to instructions with SIMD operands (YMM) and does not include instructions using the general-purpose registers.

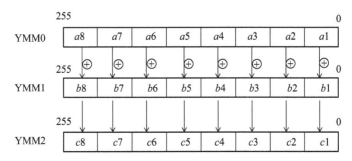

Figure 2.21   Results can be stored in the third vector in AVX operations.

AVX is a new 256-bit instruction set extension to the Intel SSE and is designed for applications that are floating-point intensive. It was released in early 2011 as part of the Intel microarchitecture processor family code named Sandy Bridge and is present on platforms ranging from notebooks to servers. Intel AVX improves performance due to wider vectors, new extensible syntax, and rich functionality.

Figure 2.22 illustrates the data types used in the SSE and AVX instructions. Typically, for AVX, any multiple of 32-bit or 64-bit floating-point types whose total length adds up to 128 or 256 bits is allowed as well as multiples of any integer type whose total length adds up to 128 bits or 256 bits.

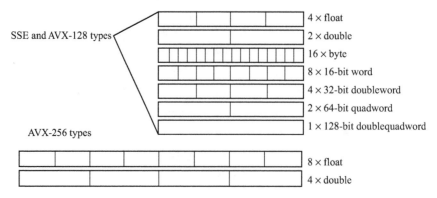

Figure 2.22   AVX and SSE data types.

Next, we use the AVX instructions to write the update code segment for the E_z component.

```
void Ez_Update_AVX(){
//Ez is continuous along the z-direction and the update should start
//from the z-direction to improve cache hit ratio.
//Ez[*][*][0], Hx[*][*][0] and Hy[*][*][0] are aligned on the 16-byte
//boundary.

int i, j, k, kk;
__m256 *vEz,*vHx,*vHx1,*vHy,*vHy1,vhcoefx,vhcoefy,ymm0,ymm1;

    vhcoefx = _mm256_broadcast_ss(&hcoefx);
    vhcoefy = _mm256_broadcast_ss(&hcoefy);

    for (i = 0; i <= nx; i++){
        for (j = 0; j <= ny; j++){

            vEz = (__m256 *)(Ey[i][j]);
            vHx = (__m256 *)(Hx[i][j]);
            vHx1 = (__m256 *)(Hx[i][j-1]);
            vHy = (__m256 *)(Hy[i][j]);
            vHy1 = (__m256 *)(Hy[i-1][j]);

            k = kk = 0;
            do {
                ymm0 = _mm256_sub_ps(vHy[kk], vHy1[kk]);
                ymm0 = _mm256_mul_ps(ymm0, vhcoefx);

                ymm1 = _mm256_sub_ps(vHx[kk], vHx1[kk]);
                ymm1 = _mm256_mul_ps(ymm1, vhcoefy);

                ymm0 = _mm256_sub_ps(ymm0, ymm1);
                vEz[kk] = _mm256_add_ps(vEz[kk], ymm0);

                k += 8;
                kk ++;

            } while (k < nz);
        }
    }
}
```

It is evident from the AVX code segment above that AVX is about eight times faster than a single floating-point unit.

2.7 VALU Performance Investigation

In this section, we first use an ideal case to investigate the performance of the parallel FDTD code enhanced by VALU on the same hardware platform using different operating systems. Then we explore the performance of AMD and Intel processors enhanced by the VALU acceleration. The parallel FDTD code used for these comparisons runs on a 2-CPU workstation for Windows and Linux operating systems, respectively. The test problem is a hollow box that is discretized into a uniform mesh of $300 \times 300 \times 300$ to $800 \times 800 \times 800$. The performance on Windows and Linux operating systems is shown in Fig. 2.23. We see that the performance of parallel FDTD code with the SSE acceleration on a Linux platform is two times faster than that with the SSE acceleration on a Windows platform.

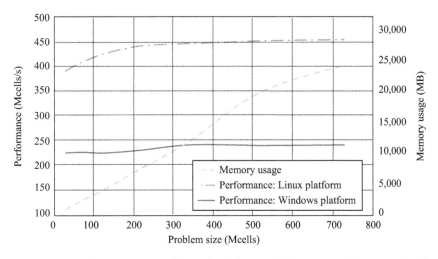

Figure 2.23   Performance comparison of Windows and Linux on a 2-CPU workstation.

An Intel Xeon X5550 contains four physical and four logical cores. If each physical core includes 8 VALUs, an Intel Xeon X5550 CPU has total 32 VALUs. However, an AMD Opteron 6168 CPU includes 12 physical cores; therefore, it has total 96 VALUs. We have four workstations with eight Intel Xeon X5550 CPUs, which are connected by using the Infiniband network system. The AMD workstation includes four AMD Opteron 6168 CPUs. The test problem is a hollow box discretized into a uniform mesh of $300 \times 300 \times 300$ to $1,000 \times 1,000 \times 1,000$. The performance on an eight Intel Xeon X5550 cluster and an AMD workstation is shown in Fig. 2.24. We see that the performance of eight Intel Xeon X5550 cluster has similar performance to that of the four AMD Opteron 6168 CPU workstation for the same problem. However, the price for eight Intel CPUs is much more than that for four AMD CPUs with comparable performance.

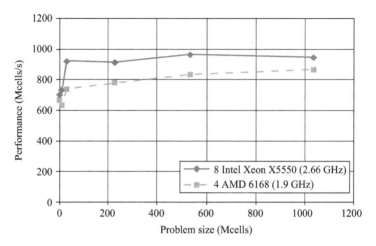

Figure 2.24   Performance comparison of an eight Intel Xeon X5550 cluster and a four AMD CPU workstation.

Next, we use three simple examples to demonstrate the performance of VALU acceleration in the FDTD simulations. The hardware platform is a laptop whose configuration is:

CPU: Intel Core i7 2.3 GHz
Memory: 8 GB
Operating system: 64-bit Windows 7

In the simulations, the computational domain is divided into one single sub-domain, and OpenMP (open multi-processing) is employed to use all the cores inside the computer. The ideal performance of VALU acceleration should be four times faster than the case without the VALU acceleration. However, it will be less than four due to the following three reasons:

1) Memory bandwidth is the major bottleneck limiting simulation performance. The CPU performance determines only a portion of the overall performance.
2) The Intel compiler has partially used VALU to improve simulation performance even if VALU has not been explicitly used in the FDTD code. In all the examples in this book, the reference is a fully optimized parallel FDTD code. Therefore, the improvement due to VALU is the real benefit from the VALU acceleration.
3) The data in memory might not be continuous in practical problems such as the equivalent currents on the Huygens' surface [9], and hence, its performance is degraded accordingly.

2.7.1 Hollow box benchmark

The first example is a hollow box, as shown in Fig. 2.25, which includes only a simple voltage excitation source and a voltage output. The domain size is 300 mm × 300 mm × 300 mm that is discretized into 300 × 300 × 300 uniform cells. The domain is truncated by a PEC boundary. We run the problem twice, with and without the VALU acceleration option, and check the VALU performance for this simple problem. For the multi-core processor, we use OpenMP to speed up the simulation for both cases with and without the VALU acceleration option.

A differential Gaussian pulse is selected as the excitation signature, which does not generate a DC component in the frequency domain. We run the problem for 1,000 time steps and summarize the performance of the VALU acceleration in Table 2.3. The time domain signature measured at an observation point is shown in Fig. 2.26. VALU accelerates the simulation almost two times with the same memory usage.

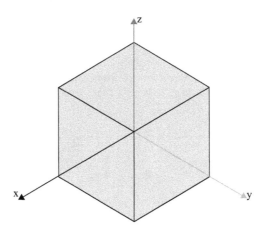

Figure 2.25   Test benchmark for the VALU acceleration.

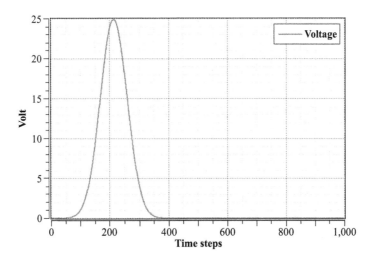

Figure 2.26   Measured time domain voltage signature at the observation point.

Table 2.3   Simulation summary for the hollow box benchmark.

	Simulation Time	Memory Usage	Problem Size	Number of Time Steps
With VALU	175 s	744 MB	27 Mcells	1,000
Without VALU	328 s	744 MB	27 Mcells	1,000

2.7.2 Dipole antenna

The second example is a dipole antenna, as shown in Fig. 2.27(a), whose length and cross section are 100 mm and 1 mm × 1 mm, respectively. A voltage source with a pure resistor at the feed gap is used to excite the dipole, as shown in Fig. 2.27(b). The internal impedance helps reduce the absorption of the resonant power inside the feed gap and speeds up the simulation convergence. The computational domain is larger than the space occupied by the dipole antenna structure to achieve a good simulation result. The equivalent current on the Huygens' surface is calculated through the interpolation of electric and magnetic fields near the Huygens' surface. If the Huygens' surface is designed to be too close to the antenna, this interpolation introduces error into the equivalent currents. The radiation pattern is not

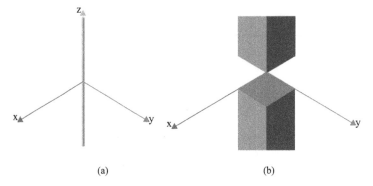

(a)   (b)

Figure 2.27   Dipole antenna with a length of 100 mm is excited by a voltage source: (a) dipole configuration, (b) zoomed feed area.

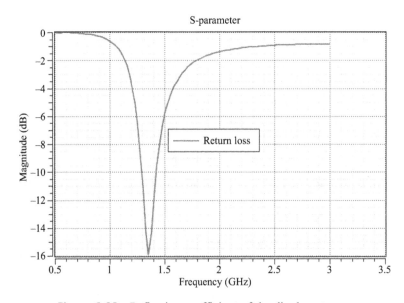

Figure 2.28   Reflection coefficient of the dipole antenna.

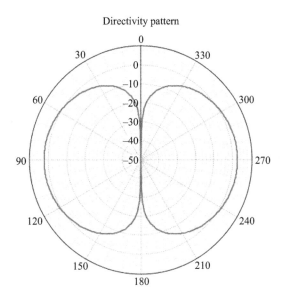

Figure 2.29   Directivity pattern of the dipole antenna at 1.37 GHz.

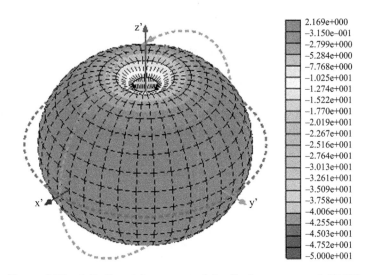

Figure 2.30   3-D directivity pattern of the dipole antenna at 1.37 GHz.

sensitive to the variation of equivalent currents. However, the calculations of the antenna directivity and gain require the value of the radiated power, but the radiated power is usually calculated from the equivalent currents on the Huygens' surface instead of directly from the far fields in order to improve the simulation performance. The number of non-uniform meshes in the x-, y- and z-directions are 22, 22, and 88, respectively. A six-layer CPML is used to truncate the computational domain in the six directions.

A differential Gaussian pulse is selected as the excitation signature. We run the problem for 4,650 time steps corresponding to −30 dB convergent criterion. The output parameters include the reflection coefficient and far-field patterns at selected frequencies, as shown in Figs. 2.28–2.30. Simulation performance with and without the VALU acceleration option is summarized in Table 2.4.

Table 2.4   Simulation summary for the dipole antenna.

	Simulation Time	Memory Usage	Problem Size	Number of Time Steps
With VALU	3 s	5.96 MB	0.04 Mcells	4,650
Without VALU	13 s	5.96 MB	0.04 Mcells	4,650

2.7.3 Patch antenna

The last example, as shown in Fig. 2.31, is a patch antenna whose horizontal dimensions are much larger than its vertical dimensions. The dimensions of substrate in the x-, y-, and z-directions are 25 mm, 50 mm, and 0.794 mm, respectively. For the finite size of substrate and ground plane, the white space between the antenna and domain boundary is selected to ensure an accurate simulation result. The surface mesh for the surface current distributions is shown in Fig. 2.32(a) and (b). The surface mesh is employed to calculate the surface current distribution on the conductor surface.

A voltage source between the feed stripline and the ground plane is used to excite the patch antenna, and a 50-Ω internal resistance is placed inside the feed gap. The patch structure is a perfect electric conductor without thickness. The output parameters include the current distributions on the patch, reflection coefficients, and far-field patterns at the specified frequencies.

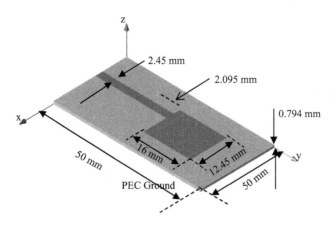

Figure 2.31   Configuration of the patch antenna.

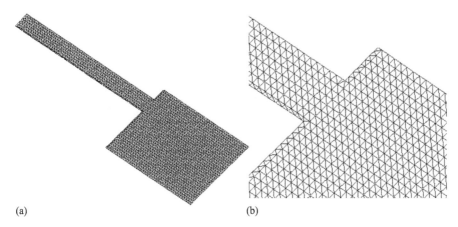

(a)   (b)

Figure 2.32   Surface mesh distribution of the patch structure: (a) mesh distribution on the entire
patch, (b) mesh distribution on the partial patch.

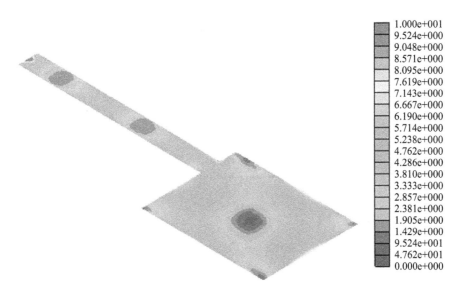

	1.000e+001
	9.524e+000
	9.048e+000
	8.571e+000
	8.095e+000
	7.619e+000
	7.143e+000
	6.667e+000
	6.190e+000
	5.714e+000
	5.238e+000
	4.762e+000
	4.286e+000
	3.810e+000
	3.333e+000
	2.857e+000
	2.381e+000
	1.905e+000
	1.429e+000
	9.524e+001
	4.762e+001
	0.000e+000

Figure 2.33   Surface current distribution at 10 GHz on the patch surface.

A differential Gaussian pulse is selected as the excitation source. We run the problem for
7,080 time steps corresponding to a −30 dB convergence criterion. The surface current
distribution at 10 GHz is plotted in Fig. 2.33. The reflection coefficient and directivity
patterns are plotted in Figs. 2.34–2.36. The simulation performance with and without the
VALU acceleration is summarized in Table 2.5.

It is obvious from the three simple examples that the VALU acceleration technique can
significantly improve the FDTD simulation without requiring any extra hardware devices.

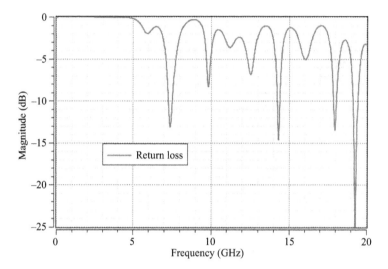

Figure 2.34 Reflection coefficient of the patch antenna array.

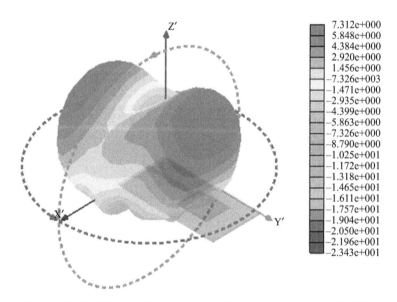

Figure 2.35 3-D directivity pattern of the patch antenna at 10 GHz.

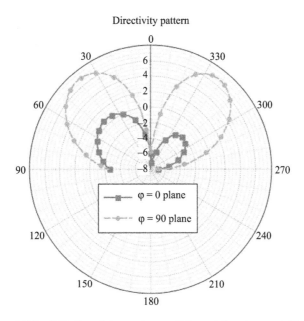

Figure 2.36   2-D directivity patterns of the patch antenna at 10 GHz.

Table 2.5   Simulation summary for the patch antenna.

	Simulation Time	Memory Usage	Problem Size	Number of Time Steps
With VALU	49 s	18.5 MB	0.225 Mcells	7,080
Without VALU	91 s	18.5 MB	0.225 Mcells	7,080

References

[1] http://www.amd.com

[2] http://www.intel.com

[3] http://www.intel.com/content/www/us/en/io/quickpath-technology/quickpath-technology-general.
html

[4] http://sites.amd.com/us/documents/48101a_opteron%20_6000_qrg_rd2.pdf

[5] http://en.wikipedia.org/wiki/Streaming_SIMD_Extensions

[6] http://softpixel.com/~cwright/programming/simd/sse.php

[7] http://neilkemp.us/src/sse_tutorial/sse_tutorial.html

[8] https://developer.apple.com/hardwaredrivers/ve/sse.html

[9] W. Yu and R. Mittra, *Conformal Finite-Difference Time-Domain Maxwell's Equations Solver: Software and User's Guide*, Artech House, Norwood, MA, 2004.

[10] http://en.wikipedia.org/wiki/Advanced_Vector_Extensions

[11] http://software.intel.com/en-us/avx

[12] http://devgurus.amd.com/thread/159669

[13] http://lomont.org/Math/Papers/2011/Intro%20to%20Intel%20AVX-Final.pdf

CHAPTER 3

PML Acceleration Techniques

Perfectly matched layers (PMLs) [1–5] play an important role in the FDTD method for simulation of the open space problems. PML is a special anisotropic absorbing material located outside the computational domain, as shown in Fig. 3.1.

3.1 Field Update Equations in CPML Layers

We describe how to use VALU to accelerate the CPML simulation in the parallel FDTD method. In the CPML equations, there are two extra terms inside the CPML layers compared to the regular FDTD updated equations. One of the updated equations inside the CPML region can be expressed as [6–8]:

$$
\begin{aligned}
H_x^{n+1/2}\left(i,j+\frac{1}{2},k+\frac{1}{2}\right) &= H_x^{n-1/2}\left(i,j+\frac{1}{2},k+\frac{1}{2}\right) \\
&+\frac{\Delta t}{\mu}\left[\frac{E_y^n\left(i,j+\frac{1}{2},k+1\right)-E_y^n\left(i,j+\frac{1}{2},k\right)}{K_z\Delta z}-\frac{E_z^n\left(i,j+1,k+\frac{1}{2}\right)-E_z^n\left(i,j,k+\frac{1}{2}\right)}{K_y\Delta y}\right. \\
&\left.+\Psi_{hxy}^n\left(i,j+\frac{1}{2},k+\frac{1}{2}\right)-\Psi_{hxz}^n\left(i,j+\frac{1}{2},k+\frac{1}{2}\right)\right]
\end{aligned}
$$

(3.1)

where Ψ_{hxy}^n and Ψ_{hxz}^n terms can be expressed as follows:

$$
\begin{aligned}
\Psi_{hxy}^n\left(i,j+\frac{1}{2},k+\frac{1}{2}\right) &= b_y\Psi_{hxy}^{n-1}\left(i,j+\frac{1}{2},k+\frac{1}{2}\right) \\
&+a_y\left[\frac{E_z^n\left(i,j+1,k+\frac{1}{2}\right)-E_z^n\left(i,j,k+\frac{1}{2}\right)}{K_y\Delta y}\right]
\end{aligned}
$$

(3.2a)

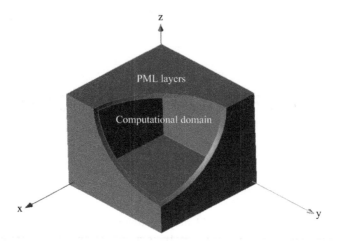

Figure 3.1 Relative location of the PML region and the computational domain in the FDTD method.

$$\Psi_{hxz}^n\left(i,j+\frac{1}{2},k+\frac{1}{2}\right) = b_z\Psi_{hxz}^{n-1}\left(i,j+\frac{1}{2},k+\frac{1}{2}\right)$$

$$+ a_z\left[\frac{E_y^n\left(i,j+\frac{1}{2},k+1\right) - E_y^n\left(i,j+\frac{1}{2},k\right)}{K_z\Delta z}\right] \tag{3.2b}$$

The coefficients a and b are related to the y- and z-directions, respectively. The coefficients in the equations above are defined as:

$$b_y = e^{-\left(\frac{\sigma_{y,\mathrm{PML}}}{\varepsilon_0 K_y} + \frac{\alpha_y}{\varepsilon_0}\right)} \tag{3.3a}$$

$$a_y = \frac{\sigma_{y,\mathrm{PML}}}{\sigma_{y,\mathrm{PML}}K_y + K_y^2\alpha_y}\left[\exp\left(-\left(\frac{\sigma_{y,\mathrm{PML}}}{\varepsilon_0 K_y} + \frac{\alpha_y}{\varepsilon_0}\right)\Delta t\right) - 1\right] \tag{3.3b}$$

$$\sigma_y = \sigma_{\max}\frac{|d-y|^4}{d^4} \tag{3.3c}$$

$$\sigma_{\max} = \frac{5}{200\sqrt{\pi}\Delta_{x,y,z}} \tag{3.3d}$$

$$K_y = 1 + K_{\max}\left(1 + \frac{|d - y|^4}{d^4}\right) \tag{3.3e}$$

$$b_z = e^{-\left(\frac{\sigma_{z,\mathrm{PML}}}{\varepsilon_0 K_z} + \frac{a_z}{\varepsilon_0}\right)} \tag{3.3f}$$

$$a_z = \frac{\sigma_{z,\mathrm{PML}}}{\sigma_{z,\mathrm{PML}} K_z + K_z^2 a_z}\left[\exp\left(-\left(\frac{\sigma_{z,\mathrm{PML}}}{\varepsilon_0 K_z} + \frac{a_z}{\varepsilon_0}\right)\Delta t\right) - 1\right] \tag{3.3g}$$

$$K_z = 1 + K_{\max}\left(1 + \frac{|d - z|^4}{d^4}\right) \tag{3.3h}$$

$$K_{\max} \geq 1 \tag{3.3i}$$

where $\sigma_{x,y,z,\mathrm{PML}}$ and $a_{x,y,z}$ are real numbers, d is the thickness of CPML region, and the variables y and z are measured from the outer boundary of the PML region. The $K_{\max}$ value is 1 by default and should increase (larger than 1) when the late time instability occurs, caused by the CPML layers. $\sigma_{\max}$ is a real number related to the cell size and conductivity distribution inside the CPML region. The expression (3.3d) is selected based on authors' experience.

We can observe from (3.1) that the electric field update inside the PML region has the formulation similar to the update inside the computational domain. However, there is one difference, namely, the K factor is an extra term in the denominator of the electric fields. The K factor corresponds to the dielectric constant distribution inside the PML region, which varies from one at the interface between the computational domain and the PML region to the maximum value at the outer boundary of the CPML region. If we introduce the K factor in the update inside the computational domain and set it to 1, then we can carry on the regular update formula in the entire domain, including the computational domain and the CPML region. We only need to add two Ψ terms to the magnetic field inside the CPML region, as shown in Fig. 3.2.

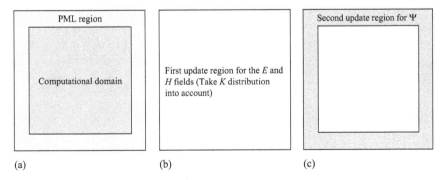

Figure 3.2   Update procedure in the FDTD domain and the CPML regions: (a) PML and regular regions, (b) update inside entire domain, (c) update in the PML region only.

The magnetic field update is split into two steps [2]. In the first step, the contribution from the electric fields is calculated in the entire computational domain.

$$H_x^{n+1/2}\left(i,j+\frac{1}{2},k+\frac{1}{2}\right) = H_x^{n-1/2}\left(i,j+\frac{1}{2},k+\frac{1}{2}\right)$$

$$+\frac{\Delta t}{\mu}\left[\frac{E_y^n\left(i,j+\frac{1}{2},k+1\right)-E_y^n\left(i,j+\frac{1}{2},k\right)}{K_z\Delta z}-\frac{E_z^n\left(i,j+1,k+\frac{1}{2}\right)-E_z^n\left(i,j,k+\frac{1}{2}\right)}{K_y\Delta y}\right]$$

In the second step, the contribution from two Ψ terms is calculated inside the CPML region.

$$H_x^{n+1/2}\left(i,j+\frac{1}{2},k+\frac{1}{2}\right) = H_x^{n+1/2}\left(i,j+\frac{1}{2},k+\frac{1}{2}\right)$$

$$+\frac{\Delta t}{\mu}\left[\Psi_{hxy}^n\left(i,j+\frac{1}{2},k+\frac{1}{2}\right)-\Psi_{hxz}^n\left(i,j+\frac{1}{2},k+\frac{1}{2}\right)\right]$$

The H_y component inside the CPML layers can be written in the following format:

$$H_y^{n+1/2}\left(i+\frac{1}{2},j,k+\frac{1}{2}\right) = H_y^{n-1/2}\left(i+\frac{1}{2},j,k+\frac{1}{2}\right)$$

$$+\frac{\Delta t}{\mu}\left[\begin{array}{c}\dfrac{E_z^n\left(i+1,j,k+\frac{1}{2}\right)-E_z^n\left(i,j,k+\frac{1}{2}\right)}{K_x\Delta x}-\dfrac{E_x^n\left(i+\frac{1}{2},j,k+1\right)-E_x^n\left(i+\frac{1}{2},j,k\right)}{K_z\Delta z}\\[4mm]+\Psi_{hyx}^n\left(i+\frac{1}{2},j,k+\frac{1}{2}\right)-\Psi_{hyz}^n\left(i+\frac{1}{2},j,k+\frac{1}{2}\right)\end{array}\right]$$

$$(3.4)$$

where Ψ_{hyx}^n and Ψ_{hyz}^n terms can be expressed as follows:

$$\Psi_{hyx}^n\left(i+\frac{1}{2},j,k+\frac{1}{2}\right) = b_x\Psi_{hyx}^{n-1}\left(i+\frac{1}{2},j,k+\frac{1}{2}\right)$$

$$+a_x\left[\frac{E_z^n\left(i+1,j,k+\frac{1}{2}\right)-E_z^n\left(i,j,k+\frac{1}{2}\right)}{K_x\Delta x}\right] \qquad (3.5a)$$

$$\Psi_{hyz}^n\left(i,j+\frac{1}{2},k+\frac{1}{2}\right) = b_z\Psi_{hyz}^{n-1}\left(i,j+\frac{1}{2},k+\frac{1}{2}\right)$$

$$+a_z\left[\frac{E_x^n\left(i+\frac{1}{2},j,k+1\right)-E_x^n\left(i+\frac{1}{2},j,k\right)}{K_z\Delta z}\right] \qquad (3.5b)$$

The coefficients a_z and b_z for the magnetic fields H_x and H_y have the same location and value along the z-direction. The coefficients a_x and b_x for the magnetic fields H_y and H_z along the x-direction can be expressed as:

$$b_x = e^{-\left(\frac{\sigma_{x,\text{PML}}}{\varepsilon_0 K_x} + \frac{\alpha_x}{\varepsilon_0}\right)} \tag{3.6a}$$

$$a_x = \frac{\sigma_{x,\text{PML}}}{\sigma_{x,\text{PML}} K_x + K_x^2 \alpha_x} \left[e^{-\left(\frac{\sigma_{x,\text{PML}}}{\varepsilon_0 K_x} + \frac{\alpha_x}{\varepsilon_0}\right)\Delta t} - 1 \right] \tag{3.6b}$$

$$\sigma_x = \sigma_{\max} \frac{|d - x|^4}{d^4} \tag{3.6c}$$

$$K_x = 1 + K_{\max}\left(1 + \frac{|d - x|^4}{d^4}\right) \tag{3.6d}$$

The H_z component inside the PML layers can be written in the following format:

$$H_z^{n+1/2}\left(i + \frac{1}{2}, j + \frac{1}{2}, k\right) = H_y^{n-1/2}\left(i + \frac{1}{2}, j + \frac{1}{2}, k\right)$$

$$+ \frac{\Delta t}{\mu}\left[\begin{array}{c} \dfrac{E_x^n\left(i + \frac{1}{2}j + 1, k\right) - E_x^n\left(i + \frac{1}{2}, j, k\right)}{K_y \Delta y} - \dfrac{E_y^n\left(i + 1, j + \frac{1}{2}, k\right) - E_y^n\left(i, j + \frac{1}{2}, k\right)}{K_x \Delta x} \\[4mm] + \Psi_{hzy}^n\left(i + \frac{1}{2}, j + \frac{1}{2}, k\right) - \Psi_{hzx}^n\left(i + \frac{1}{2}, j + \frac{1}{2}, k\right) \end{array} \right]$$

$$\tag{3.7}$$

where Ψ_{hzx}^n and Ψ_{hzy}^n terms can be expressed as follows:

$$\Psi_{hzy}^n\left(i + \frac{1}{2}, j + \frac{1}{2}, k\right) = b_y \Psi_{hzy}^{n-1}\left(i + \frac{1}{2}, j + \frac{1}{2}, k\right)$$

$$+ a_y \left[\frac{E_z^n\left(i + \frac{1}{2}, j + 1, k\right) - E_z^n\left(i + \frac{1}{2}, j, k\right)}{K_y \Delta y} \right] \tag{3.8a}$$

$$\Psi_{hzx}^n\left(i + \frac{1}{2}, j + \frac{1}{2}, k\right) = b_x \Psi_{hzx}^{n-1}\left(i + \frac{1}{2}, j + \frac{1}{2}, k\right)$$

$$+ a_x \left[\frac{E_y^n\left(i + 1, j + \frac{1}{2}, k\right) - E_y^n\left(i, j + \frac{1}{2}, k\right)}{K_x \Delta x} \right] \tag{3.8b}$$

The coefficients a_y and b_y for the magnetic fields H_x and H_z have the same location and value along the y-direction. The coefficients a_x and b_x for the magnetic fields H_y and H_z have the same location and value along the x-direction. The E_x component inside the CPML region can be written in the following format:

$$
E_x^{n+1}\left(i+\frac{1}{2},j,k\right) = E_x^n\left(i+\frac{1}{2},j,k\right)
$$

$$
+\frac{\Delta t}{\varepsilon}\left[
\begin{array}{c}
\dfrac{H_z^{n+1/2}\left(i+\frac{1}{2},j+\frac{1}{2},k+1\right) - H_z^{n+1/2}\left(i+\frac{1}{2},j+\frac{1}{2},k\right)}{K_y\Delta y} \\[3ex]
-\dfrac{H_y^{n+1/2}\left(i+\frac{1}{2},j+1,k+\frac{1}{2}\right) - H_y^{n+1/2}\left(i+\frac{1}{2},j,k+\frac{1}{2}\right)}{K_z\Delta z} \\[3ex]
+\Psi_{exy}^{n+1/2}\left(i+\frac{1}{2},j,k\right) - \Psi_{exz}^{n+1/2}\left(i+\frac{1}{2},j,k\right)
\end{array}
\right]
$$

$$(3.9)$$

where $\Psi_{exy}^{n+1/2}$ and $\Psi_{exz}^{n+1/2}$ terms can be expressed as follows:

$$
\Psi_{exy}^{n+1/2}\left(i+\frac{1}{2},j,k\right) = b_y\Psi_{exy}^{n-1/2}\left(i+\frac{1}{2},j,k\right)
$$

$$
+a_y\left[\dfrac{H_z^{n+1/2}\left(i+\frac{1}{2},j+\frac{1}{2},k\right) - H_z^{n+1/2}\left(i+\frac{1}{2},j-\frac{1}{2},k\right)}{K_y\Delta y}\right]
$$

$$(3.10a)$$

$$
\Psi_{exz}^{n+1/2}\left(i+\frac{1}{2},j,k\right) = b_z\Psi_{exz}^{n-1/2}\left(i+\frac{1}{2},j,k\right)
$$

$$
+a_z\left[\dfrac{H_y^{n+1/2}\left(i+\frac{1}{2},j,k+\frac{1}{2}\right) - H_y^{n+1/2}\left(i+\frac{1}{2},j,k-\frac{1}{2}\right)}{K_z\Delta z}\right]
$$

$$(3.10b)$$

The coefficients a_y and b_y for the electric field E_x and the magnetic field H_y have the same location and value along the y-direction. The coefficients a_z and b_z for the electric field E_x and the magnetic field H_z have the same location and value along the z-direction. The E_y component inside the PML region can be written in the following format:

$$E_y^{n+1}\left(i,j+\frac{1}{2},k\right) = E_y^n\left(i,j+\frac{1}{2},k\right)$$

$$+\frac{\Delta t}{\varepsilon}\begin{bmatrix} \dfrac{H_x^{n+1/2}\left(i,j+\frac{1}{2},k+\frac{1}{2}\right) - H_x^{n+1/2}\left(i,j+\frac{1}{2},k-\frac{1}{2}\right)}{K_z\Delta z} \\[2ex] -\dfrac{H_z^{n+1/2}\left(i+\frac{1}{2},j+\frac{1}{2},k\right) - H_z^{n+1/2}\left(i-\frac{1}{2},j+\frac{1}{2},k\right)}{K_x\Delta x} \\[2ex] +\Psi_{eyz}^{n+1/2}\left(i,j+\frac{1}{2},k\right) - \Psi_{eyx}^{n+1/2}\left(i,j+\frac{1}{2},k\right) \end{bmatrix} \quad (3.11)$$

where $\Psi_{eyz}^{n+1/2}$ and $\Psi_{eyx}^{n+1/2}$ terms can be expressed as follows:

$$\Psi_{eyz}^{n+1/2}\left(i,j+\frac{1}{2},k\right) = b_z\Psi_{eyz}^{n-1/2}\left(i,j+\frac{1}{2},k\right)$$

$$+a_z\left[\dfrac{H_x^{n+1/2}\left(i,j+\frac{1}{2},k+\frac{1}{2}\right) - H_x^{n+1/2}\left(i,j+\frac{1}{2},k-\frac{1}{2}\right)}{K_z\Delta z}\right] \quad (3.12a)$$

$$\Psi_{eyx}^{n+1/2}\left(i,j+\frac{1}{2},k\right) = b_x\Psi_{eyx}^{n-1/2}\left(i,j+\frac{1}{2},k\right)$$

$$+a_x\left[\dfrac{H_z^{n+1/2}\left(i+\frac{1}{2},j+\frac{1}{2},k\right) - H_z^{n+1/2}\left(i-\frac{1}{2},j+\frac{1}{2},k\right)}{K_x\Delta x}\right] \quad (3.12b)$$

The coefficients a_x and b_x for the electric field E_y and the magnetic field H_x have the same location and value along the x-direction. The coefficients a_z and b_z for the electric field E_y and the magnetic field H_z have the same location and value along the z-direction. The E_z component inside the CPML layers can be written in the following format:

$$E_z^{n+1}\left(i,j,k+\frac{1}{2}\right) = E_z^n\left(i,j,k+\frac{1}{2}\right)$$

$$+\frac{\Delta t}{\varepsilon}\begin{bmatrix} \dfrac{H_y^{n+1/2}\left(i,+\frac{1}{2}j,k+\frac{1}{2}\right) - H_y^{n+1/2}\left(i-\frac{1}{2},j,k+\frac{1}{2}\right)}{K_x\Delta x} \\[2ex] -\dfrac{H_x^{n+1/2}\left(i,j+\frac{1}{2},k+\frac{1}{2}\right) - H_x^{n+1/2}\left(i,j-\frac{1}{2},k+\frac{1}{2}\right)}{K_y\Delta y} \\[2ex] +\Psi_{ezx}^{n+1/2}\left(i,j,k+\frac{1}{2}\right) - \Psi_{ezy}^{n+1/2}\left(i,j,k+\frac{1}{2}\right) \end{bmatrix} \quad (3.13)$$

where $\Psi_{ezx}^{n+\frac{1}{2}}$ and $\Psi_{ezy}^{n+\frac{1}{2}}$ terms can be expressed as follows:

$$\Psi_{ezx}^{n+\frac{1}{2}}\left(i,j,k+\frac{1}{2}\right) = b_x\Psi_{ezx}^{n-\frac{1}{2}}\left(i,j,k+\frac{1}{2}\right)$$
$$+ a_x\left[\frac{H_y^{n+\frac{1}{2}}\left(i+\frac{1}{2},j,k+\frac{1}{2}\right) - H_y^{n+\frac{1}{2}}\left(i-\frac{1}{2},j,k+\frac{1}{2}\right)}{K_x\Delta x}\right] \qquad (3.14a)$$

$$\Psi_{ezy}^{n+1/2}\left(i,j,k+\frac{1}{2}\right) = b_y\Psi_{ezy}^{n-1/2}\left(i,j,k+\frac{1}{2}\right)$$
$$+ a_y\left[\frac{H_z^{n+1/2}\left(i,j+\frac{1}{2},k+1\right) - H_z^{n+1/2}\left(i,j-\frac{1}{2},k+\frac{1}{2}\right)}{K_y\Delta y}\right] \qquad (3.14b)$$

The coefficients a_x and b_x for the electric field E_z and magnetic field H_x have the same location and value along the x-direction. The coefficients a_y and b_y for the electric field E_z and the magnetic field H_y have the same location and value along the y-direction.

3.2 CPML SSE Code Implementation

Because the update inside the CPML region for the electric or magnetic fields is similar to that in the computational domain, the field update inside the CPML region can be carried out together with the field update inside the computational domain, namely, the field update inside the entire domain will be processed together without considering the CPML region separately. We only need to take care of the two Ψ terms inside the CPML region after the updates of regular E and H fields are completed.

It is not necessary to show the complete code inside the CPML region because they are similar in three directions, and here, we only need to show the SSE code in the minimum and the maximum z-direction. The start point in the minimum z-direction always starts from 0; therefore, it has the same processing method as the regular field update inside the computational domain. However, in the maximum CPML region direction, the start position varies with the number of cells in the z-direction and may be different in other simulations. It is worthwhile to mention that the termination point (interface between the CPML region and computational domain) might not provide 128-bit alignment. The four points inside an SSE vector might be located in both the CPML region and the computational domain. In order to avoid overwriting the values inside the computational domain, the increment (two Ψ terms) for the points inside the computational domain during the PML update should be set to zero.

Without the SSE acceleration, the CPML programming is relatively simple. Most important job is to prepare the coefficient distribution in (3.3). Once we get the correct coefficient distributions, the update code inside the CPML region for E_x component is shown as follows:

```
void updatePMLExZMin()
{
int i, j, k;
for (i = Index_E_Boundary[XMIN]; i <= Index_E_Boundary[XMAX] - 1; i ++)
{
    for (j = Index_E_Boundary[YMIN]; j <= Index_E_Boundary[YMAX]; j ++)
    {
        for (k = Index_E_Boundary[ZMIN]; k < Index_E_Boundary[ZMIN] +
            BoundaryLayerNum[ZMIN]; k ++)
        {
            // CoeffE = 1.0 / Eps0
            Pusai_Exy_Zmin[i][j][k] = Beta_PML_ZGrid[k] *
                Pusai_Exy_Zmin[i][j][k] + pEk_PML_Coeff[k] * (Hy[i][j][k]
                - Hy[i][j][k-1]);
            Ex[i][j][k] += - CoeffE * Pusai_Exy_Zmin[i][j][k];
        }
    }
  }
}
```

The E_x component inside the minimum z-direction region with the SSE acceleration is shown below. We will explain the important lines inside the code segment.

```
void updatePMLExZMinSSE()
{
// mask for skip outside PML region
INT_ALN16 mask[4] = {0xFFFFFFFF, 0xFFFFFFFF, 0xFFFFFFFF, 0xFFFFFFFF};
int n = Index_E_Boundary[ZMIN] + BoundaryLayerNum[ZMIN];
int m = n & 3;
for (n = 3; n >= m; n -) mask[n] = 0x0;
```

Declare the variables and arrays as the SSE data type $\_\_m128$.

```
__m128 vCoeffE, *vPusai_Exy_Zmin, *vEx, *vHy, *vBeta_PML_ZGrid,
    *vEk_PML_Coeff, xmm0, xmm1, *vmask;
```

Convert the variables, *Beta_PML_ZGrid* and *Ek_PML_Coeff*, to SSE variable format.

```
vmask = (__m128 *)mask;
vBeta_PML_ZGrid = (__m128 *)Beta_PML_ZGrid;
vEk_PML_Coeff = (__m128 *)pEk_PML_Coeff;
```

Load the *CoeffE* variable and generate four 32-bit variables in the *vCoefffE* vector.

```
vCoeffE = _mm_load1_ps(&CoeffE);

int i, j, k, kk;
for (i = Index_E_Boundary[XMIN]; i <= Index_E_Boundary[XMAX] - 1; i ++)
{
   for (j = Index_E_Boundary[YMIN]; j <= Index_E_Boundary[YMAX]; j ++)
   {
```

Convert the *Pusai_Exy_Zmin* array to the SSE *__m128* format.

```
   vPusai_Exy_Zmin = (__m128 *)Pusai_Exy_Zmin[i][j];
```

Assign the E_x and H_y arrays to the vectors *vEx* and *vHy*, respectively.

```
   vEx = (__m128 *)Ex[i][j];
   vHy = (__m128 *)Hy[i][j];

   k = kk = 0;
```

Since the first element in the *vHy* vector is out of range, replace the first element at index = −1 in the vector with the value at index = 0 using the SSE *shuffle* function, as shown in Fig. 3.3.

```
   xmm0 = _mm_shuffle_ps(vHy[0], vHy[0], _MM_SHUFFLE(2,1,0,0));
```

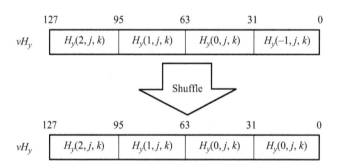

Figure 3.3   Use the shuffle function to initialize the invalid value in an array.

The SSE acceleration can only work on four layers (for a 128-bit vector) inside the CPML region at one time. For a six-layer CPML, the following code segment works on the first four layers, as shown in Fig. 3.4.

```
   while (k + 3 < Index_E_Boundary[ZMIN] + BoundaryLayerNum[ZMIN])
   {
      xmm0 = _mm_sub_ps(vHy[kk], xmm0);
```

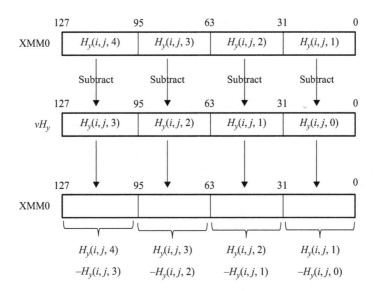

Figure 3.4   Subtraction procedure for two vectors *xmm0* and *vHy*.

Multiply the difference of the magnetic field H_y in the z-direction by its coefficient *vEk_PML_Coeff*.

```
xmm0 = _mm_mul_ps(vEk_PML_Coeff[kk], xmm0);
```

Multiply Ψ by its coefficient *vBeta_PML_ZGrid*.

```
vPusai_Exy_Zmin[kk] = _mm_mul_ps(vBeta_PML_ZGrid[kk],
    vPusai_Exy_Zmin[kk]);
```

Add two Ψ to the *xmm0* vector.

```
vPusai_Exy_Zmin[kk] = _mm_add_ps(vPusai_Exy_Zmin[kk], xmm0);
```

Multiply Ψ by its coefficient *vCoeffE*.

```
xmm1 = _mm_mul_ps(vPusai_Exy_Zmin[kk], vCoeffE);
```

Subtract the contribution of Ψ from the electric field E_x.

```
vEx[kk] = _mm_sub_ps(vEx[kk], xmm1);
```

Move four cells in the z-direction.

```
k += 4;
kk ++;
```

Load the magnetic field H_y to the *xmm0* vector.

```
        xmm0 = _mm_loadu_ps(&Hy[i][j][k-1]);
    }
```

The following code segment works on the remaining two layers. Since the SSE acceleration can only work on four layers at one time, we need to remove the last two numbers in the vector and then add the contributions to the fields using the statement _mm_and_ps (xmm1, vmask[0]). The following code segment is same as the code above; the only difference is the statement _mm_and_ps(xmm1, vmask[0]), which removes the last two numbers in the vector.

```
        if (k < Index_E_Boundary[ZMIN] + BoundaryLayerNum[ZMIN])
        {
            xmm0 = _mm_sub_ps(vHy[kk], xmm0);
            xmm0 = _mm_mul_ps(vEk_PML_Coeff[kk], xmm0);
            vPusai_Exy_Zmin[kk] = _mm_mul_ps(vBeta_PML_ZGrid[kk],
                vPusai_Exy_Zmin[kk]);
            vPusai_Exy_Zmin[kk] = _mm_add_ps(vPusai_Exy_Zmin[kk], xmm0);
                xmm1 = _mm_mul_ps(vPusai_Exy_Zmin[kk], vCoeffE);
            xmm1 = _mm_and_ps(xmm1, vmask[0]); // apply mask
            vEx[kk] = _mm_sub_ps(vEx[kk], xmm1);
        }
    }
  }
}
```

Since it is different from the CPML code in the minimum *z*-direction region, we explain how to use SSE instructions to accelerate the CPML code in the maximum *z*-direction. The CPML code in the C language for the E_x component is relatively simple.

```
void updatePMLExZMax()
{
int i, j, k, k1;
for (i = Index_E_Boundary[XMIN]; i <= Index_E_Boundary[XMAX] - 1; i ++)
{
  for (j = Index_E_Boundary[YMIN]; j <= Index_E_Boundary[YMAX]; j ++)
  {
    for (k = Index_E_Boundary[ZMAX] - BoundaryLayerNum[ZMAX] + 1; k <=
        Index_E_Boundary[ZMAX]; k ++)
    {
        k1 = k - (Index_E_Boundary[ZMAX] - BoundaryLayerNum[ZMAX]);
        // CoeffE = 1.0 / Eps0
        Pusai_Exy_Zmax[i][j][k1] = Beta_PML_ZGrid[k] *
```

```
        Pusai_Exy_Zmax[i][j][k1] + pEk_PML_Coeff[k] * (Hy[i][j][k] -
        Hy[i][j][k-1]);
      Ex[i][j][k] += - CoeffE * Pusai_Exy_Zmax[i][j][k1];
    }
   }
  }
}
```

The E_x component inside the maximum z-direction region with the SSE acceleration is shown below. We next explain the important lines inside the code segment.

```
void updatePMLExZMaxSSE()
{
// mask for skip outside PML region
INT_ALN16 mask[4] = {0xFFFFFFFF, 0xFFFFFFFF, 0xFFFFFFFF, 0xFFFFFFFF};
int n = Index_E_Boundary[ZMAX] - BoundaryLayerNum[ZMAX] + 1;
int m = n & (~3);
int l;
```

If the index at the CPML start point is divided by 4, the reminder may be 0, 1, 2, or 3. We use different schemes to handle the four cases in the SSE implementation using the SSE mask function.

```
for (l = m; l < n; l ++) mask[l-m] = 0x0;
```

```
__m128 vCoeffE, *vPusai_Exy_Zmax, *vEx, *vHy, *vBeta_PML_ZGrid,
   *vEk_PML_Coeff, xmm0, xmm1, *vmask;
```

Convert the variables *Beta_PML_ZGrid* and *pEk_PML_Coeff* to the SSE *__m128* type.

```
vmask = (__m128 *)mask;
vBeta_PML_ZGrid = (__m128 *)Beta_PML_ZGrid;
vEk_PML_Coeff = (__m128 *)pEk_PML_Coeff;
```

Convert the constant floating number *CoeffE* to the constant *vCoeffE* vector.

```
vCoeffE = _mm_load1_ps(&CoeffE);
```

```
int i, j, k, kk, kk1;
for (i = Index_E_Boundary[XMIN]; i <= Index_E_Boundary[XMAX] - 1; i ++)
{
   for (j = Index_E_Boundary[YMIN]; j <= Index_E_Boundary[YMAX]; j ++)
   {
```

Convert the arrays *Pusai_Exy_Zmax*, E_x, and H_y to the SSE *__m128* vectors *vPusai_Exy_Zmax*, *vEx*, and *vHy*, respectively.

```
vPusai_Exy_Zmax = (__m128 *)Pusai_Exy_Zmax[i][j];
vEx = (__m128 *)Ex[i][j];
vHy = (__m128 *)Hy[i][j];
```

Calculate the integer generated from the index k divided by 4.

```
k = m;
kk = k >> 2;
kk1 = 0;
```

Calculate the contribution of H_y to the variable Ψ.

```
xmm0 = _mm_load_ps(&Hy[i][j][k-1]);
xmm0 = _mm_sub_ps(vHy[kk], xmm0);
xmm0 = _mm_mul_ps(vEk_PML_Coeff[kk], xmm0);
```

Calculate the contribution from Ψ at the previous time step.

```
vPusai_Exy_Zmax[kk1] = _mm_mul_ps(vBeta_PML_ZGrid[kk],
    vPusai_Exy_Zmax[kk1]);
```

Multiply Ψ by the coefficient *vCoeffE*.

```
xmm1 = _mm_mul_ps(vCoeffE, vPusai_Exy_Zmax[kk1]);
```

If the number of CPML layers is not a multiple of 4, the mask function helps reset the value outside the CPML region to zero. The reset part is located inside the CPML region.

```
xmm1 = _mm_and_ps(xmm1, vmask[0]);
```

Add the contribution from Ψ to the field E_x inside the CPML region.

```
vEx[kk] = _mm_sub_ps(vEx[kk], xmm1);
```

Move four cells forward in the *z*-direction.

```
k += 4;
kk ++;
kk1 ++;
```

The code segment above is used to handle the exception where the CPML region starts with a number that is not a multiple of 4.

```
while (k <= Index_E_Boundary[ZMAX])
{
   xmm0 = _mm_loadu_ps(&Hy[i][j][k-1]);
   xmm0 = _mm_sub_ps(vHy[kk], xmm0);
```

```
    xmm0 = _mm_mul_ps(vEk_PML_Coeff[kk], xmm0);
    vPusai_Exy_Zmax[kk1] = _mm_mul_ps(vBeta_PML_ZGrid[kk],
        vPusai_Exy_Zmax[kk1]);
    xmm1 = _mm_mul_ps(vCoeffE, vPusai_Exy_Zmax[kk1]);
    vEx[kk] = _mm_sub_ps(vEx[kk], xmm1);

    k += 4;
    kk ++;
    kk1 ++;
   }
  }
 }
}
```

Without SSE acceleration, the CPML programming for the H_x component is relatively easy, and is shown below without further explanation.

```
void updatePMLHxZMin()
{
int i, j, k;

for (i = Index_H_Boundary[XMIN]; i <= Index_H_Boundary[XMAX] + 1; i ++){
    for (j = Index_H_Boundary[YMIN]; j <= Index_H_Boundary[YMAX]; j ++){
        for (k = Index_H_Boundary[ZMIN]; k < Index_H_Boundary[ZMIN] +
            BoundaryLayerNum[ZMIN]; k ++) {

            // CoeffM = 1.0 / Mu0
            Pusai_Hxy_Zmin[i][j][k] = Beta_PML_ZHalf[k] *
                Pusai_Hxy_Zmin[i][j][k] + pHk_PML_Coeff[k] * (Ey[i][j][k+1]
                - Ey[i][j][k]);
            Hx[i][j][k] += CoeffM * Pusai_Hxy_Zmin[i][j][k];
        }
    }
  }
}
```

Now, we describe how to develop the CPML code for the magnetic field H_x calculation based on the SSE instructions. With the SSE acceleration, the PML code for the H_x component in the minimum z-direction is similar to the SSE code for the electric field E_x component. However, we give a complete description to help the reader fully understand the SSE acceleration techniques.

```
void updatePMLHxZMinSSE()
{
// mask to skip the outside PML region
INT_ALN16 mask[4] = {0xFFFFFFFF, 0xFFFFFFFF, 0xFFFFFFFF, 0xFFFFFFFF};
int n = Index_H_Boundary[ZMIN] + BoundaryLayerNum[ZMIN];
int m = n & 3;
```

We assume that the number of CPML layers may change from problem to problem, and we ensure that the SSE vector values outside the computational domain are reset to zero using the SSE mask function. For example, the remainder for a six-layer PML is 2. The case for handling the lower CPML boundary is illustrated in Fig. 3.5.

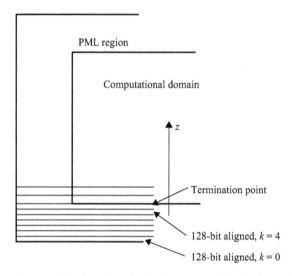

Figure 3.5   Exception handling in the lower boundary in the z-direction.

```
for (n = 3; n >= m; n -) mask[n] = 0x0;
```

Declare the variables to be SSE _*m128* variables.

```
__m128 vCoeffM, *vPusai_Hxy_Zmin, *vHx, *vEy, *vBeta_PML_ZHalf,
*vHk_PML_Coeff, xmm0, xmm1, *vmask;
```

Convert the constants to the constant vectors required by the SSE instructions.

```
vmask = (__m128 *)mask;
vBeta_PML_ZHalf = (__m128 *)Beta_PML_ZHalf;
vHk_PML_Coeff = (__m128 *)pHk_PML_Coeff;
vCoeffM = _mm_load1_ps(&CoeffM);
```

```
int i, j, k, kk;
for (i = Index_H_Boundary[XMIN]; i <= Index_H_Boundary[XMAX] + 1; i ++)
{
    for (j = Index_H_Boundary[YMIN]; j <= Index_H_Boundary[YMAX]; j ++)
    {
```

Convert the arrays to the vectors required by the SSE instructions.

```
vPusai_Hxy_Zmin = (__m128 *)Pusai_Hxy_Zmin[i][j];
vHx = (__m128 *)Hx[i][j];
vEy = (__m128 *)Ey[i][j];

k = kk = 0;

while (k + 3 < Index_H_Boundary[ZMIN] + BoundaryLayerNum[ZMIN])
{
```

Load the E_y array, calculate the difference of $E_y(i, j, k + 1)$ and $E_y(i, j, k)$, and then multiply it by its coefficient.

```
xmm0 = _mm_loadu_ps(&Ey[i][j][k+1]);
xmm0 = _mm_sub_ps(xmm0, vEy[kk]);
xmm0 = _mm_mul_ps(vHk_PML_Coeff[kk], xmm0);
```

Multiply the Ψ variable by its coefficient, add it to the E_y above, multiply it by the coefficient $vCoeffM$, and then add the result to the H_x component.

```
vPusai_Hxy_Zmin[kk] = _mm_mul_ps(vBeta_PML_ZHalf[kk],
   vPusai_Hxy_Zmin[kk]);
vPusai_Hxy_Zmin[kk] = _mm_add_ps(vPusai_Hxy_Zmin[kk], xmm0);
xmm1 = _mm_mul_ps(vCoeffM, vPusai_Hxy_Zmin[kk]);
vHx[kk] = _mm_add_ps(vHx[kk], xmm1);
```

Move forward four cells along the z-direction.

```
    k += 4;
    kk ++;
}
```

The following code segment is designed for exception handling, in which the number of CPML layers is less than 4.

```
if (k < Index_E_Boundary[ZMIN] + BoundaryLayerNum[ZMIN])
{
```

Load the E_y array to the vector $xmm0$, calculate the difference of E_y in the z-direction, and multiply it by its coefficient.

```
xmm0 = _mm_loadu_ps(&Ey[i][j][k+1]);
xmm0 = _mm_sub_ps(xmm0, vEy[kk]);
xmm0 = _mm_mul_ps(vHk_PML_Coeff[kk], xmm0);
```

Multiply Ψ by its coefficient.

```
vPusai_Hxy_Zmin[kk] = _mm_mul_ps(vBeta_PML_ZHalf[kk],
    vPusai_Hxy_Zmin[kk]);
```

Add the contribution of vector *xmm0* from Ψ.

```
vPusai_Hxy_Zmin[kk] = _mm_add_ps(vPusai_Hxy_Zmin[kk], xmm0);
```

Multiply it by its coefficient.

```
xmm1 = _mm_mul_ps(vCoeffM, vPusai_Hxy_Zmin[kk]);
```

Apply the mask function to reset the values outside the CPML region to zero.

```
xmm1 = _mm_and_ps(xmm1, vmask[0]);
```

Add the total contribution from Ψ to the magnetic field H_x inside the CPML region.

```
        vHx[kk] = _mm_add_ps(vHx[kk], xmm1);
      }
    }
  }
}
```

Without the SSE acceleration, the CPML programming for the H_x component is relatively easy, and is shown below without further explanation.

```
void updatePMLHxZMax()
{
int i, j, k, k1;

for (i = Index_H_Boundary[XMIN]; i <= Index_H_Boundary[XMAX] + 1; i ++)
{
   for (j = Index_H_Boundary[YMIN]; j <= Index_H_Boundary[YMAX]; j ++)
   {
      for (k = Index_H_Boundary[ZMAX]-BoundaryLayerNum[ZMAX]+1; k<=
         Index_H_Boundary[ZMAX]; k ++)
      {
         k1 = k - (Index_H_Boundary[ZMAX] - BoundaryLayerNum[ZMAX]);
         // CoeffM = 1.0 / Mu0
         Pusai_Hxy_Zmax[i][j][k1] = Beta_PML_ZHalf[k] *
            Pusai_Hxy_Zmax[i][j][k1] + pHk_PML_Coeff[k] *
            (Ey[i][j][k+1] - Ey[i][j][k]);
         Hx[i][j][k] += CoeffM * Pusai_Hxy_Zmax[i][j][k1];
      }
   }
  }
}
```

We describe how to develop the CPML code for the magnetic field H_x calculation in the maximum z-direction using SSE instructions. With SSE acceleration, the CPML programming for the H_z component in the maximum z-direction is similar to the SSE code for the electric field E_x component. However, we give a complete description to help the reader fully understand the SSE acceleration techniques.

```
void updatePMLHxZMaxSSE()
{
// mask for skip outside PML region
INT_ALN16 mask[4] = {0xFFFFFFFF, 0xFFFFFFFF, 0xFFFFFFFF, 0xFFFFFFFF};
int n = Index_H_Boundary[ZMAX] - BoundaryLayerNum[ZMAX] + 1;
int m = n & (~3);
int l;
```

In the regular computational domain, the termination point of the CPML layer varies from case to case in the practical problems. If the domain is not terminated at a number k that is a multiple of 4, the CPML region must start from the termination point k, which might not be aligned, as shown in Fig. 3.6. We use different ways to handle the four cases in the SSE implementation using the SSE mask function.

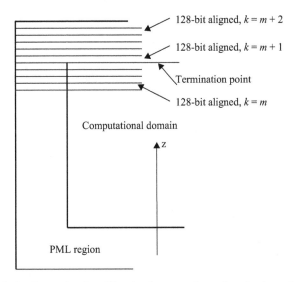

Figure 3.6   Exception handling in the upper boundary in the z-direction.

```
for (l = m; l < n; l ++) mask[l-m] = 0x0;

__m128 vCoeffM, *vPusai_Hxy_Zmax, *vHx, *vEy, *vBeta_PML_ZHalf,
*vHk_PML_Coeff, xmm0, xmm1, *vmask;
vmask = (__m128 *)mask;
vBeta_PML_ZHalf = (__m128 *)Beta_PML_ZHalf;
vHk_PML_Coeff = (__m128 *)pHk_PML_Coeff;
```

```
vCoeffM = _mm_load1_ps(&CoeffM);

int i, j, k, kk, kk1;
for (i = Index_H_Boundary[XMIN]; i <= Index_H_Boundary[XMAX] + 1; i ++)
{
    for (j = Index_H_Boundary[YMIN]; j <= Index_H_Boundary[YMAX]; j ++)
    {
```

Convert the arrays to the vectors required by the SSE instructions.

```
        vPusai_Hxy_Zmax = (__m128 *)Pusai_Hxy_Zmax[i][j];
        vHx = (__m128 *)Hx[i][j];
        vEy = (__m128 *)Ey[i][j];

        k = m;
        kk = k >> 2;
        kk1 = 0;
```

Load the E_y array into the *xmm0* vector, calculate the difference of the two vectors *xmm0* and *vEy*, and multiply by its coefficient.

```
        xmm0 = _mm_loadu_ps(&Ey[i][j][k+1]);
        xmm0 = _mm_sub_ps(xmm0, vEy[kk]);
        xmm0 = _mm_mul_ps(vHk_PML_Coeff[kk], xmm0);
```

Multiply Ψ by its coefficient, and add it to E_y, and then multiply the result by the coefficient *vCoeffM*.

```
        vPusai_Hxy_Zmax[kk1] = _mm_mul_ps(vBeta_PML_ZHalf[kk],
            vPusai_Hxy_Zmax[kk1]);
        vPusai_Hxy_Zmax[kk1] = _mm_add_ps(vPusai_Hxy_Zmax[kk1], xmm0);
        xmm1 = _mm_mul_ps(vCoeffM, vPusai_Hxy_Zmax[kk1]);
```

Apply the mask function to reset the values outside the CPML region to zero.

```
        xmm1 = _mm_and_ps(xmm1, vmask[0]);
```

Add the total contribution from Ψ to the magnetic field H_x inside the CPML region.

```
        vHx[kk] = _mm_add_ps(vHx[kk], xmm1);

        k += 4;
        kk ++;
        kk1 ++;
```

The code segment above is used to handle the exception where the CPML region starts with a number that is not a multiple of 4.

```
    while (k <= Index_H_Boundary[ZMAX])
    {
        xmm0 = _mm_loadu_ps(&Ey[i][j][k+1]);
        xmm0 = _mm_sub_ps(xmm0, vEy[kk]);
        xmm0 = _mm_mul_ps(vHk_PML_Coeff[kk], xmm0);
        vPusai_Hxy_Zmax[kk1] = _mm_mul_ps(vBeta_PML_ZHalf[kk],
            vPusai_Hxy_Zmax[kk1]);
        vPusai_Hxy_Zmax[kk1] = _mm_add_ps(vPusai_Hxy_Zmax[kk1], xmm0);
        xmm1 = _mm_mul_ps(vCoeffM, vPusai_Hxy_Zmax[kk1]);
        vHx[kk] = _mm_add_ps(vHx[kk], xmm1);

        k += 4;
        kk ++;
        kk1 ++;
    }
}
```

References

[1] J. Berenger, "A Perfectly Matched Layer Medium for the Absorption of Electromagnetic Waves," *J. Comput.*, Vol. 114, 1994, pp. 185–200.

[2] S. Gedney, "An Anisotropic Perfectly Matched Layer-Absorbing Medium for the Truncation of FDTD Lattices," *IEEE Transactions on Antennas and Propagation*, Vol. 44, No. 12, 1996, pp. 1630–1639.

[3] W. Chew and W. Wood, "A 3-D Perfectly Matched Medium from Modified Maxwell's Equations with Stretched Coordinates," *Microwave and Optical Technology Letters*, Vol. 7, 1994, pp. 599–604.

[4] W. Chew, J. Jin, and E. Michielssen, "Complex Coordinate Stretching as a Generalized Absorbing Boundary Condition," *Microwave and Optical Technology Letters*, Vol. 15, No. 6, 1997, pp. 363–369.

[5] J. Roden and S. Gedney, "Convolution PML (CPML): An Efficient FDTD Implementation of the CFS-PML for Arbitrary Medium," *Microwave and Optical Technology Letters*, Vol. 27, No. 5, 2000, pp. 334–339.

[6] K. Yee, "Numerical Solution of Initial Boundary Value Problems Involving Maxwell's Equations in Isotropic Media," *IEEE Transactions on Antennas and Propagation*, Vol. 14, No. 5, 1966, pp. 302–307.

[7] A. Taflove and S. Hagness, *Computational Electromagnetics: The Finite-Difference Time-Domain Method*, 3rd ed., Artech House, Norwood, MA, 2005.

[8] W. Yu and R. Mittra, *Conformal Finite-Difference Time-Domain Maxwell's Equations Solver: Software and User's Guide*, Artech House, Norwood, MA, 2004.

CHAPTER 4

Parallel Processing Techniques

Parallel computing [1–5] has become a popular topic today for various engineering applications and scientific researches due to the fast development of computer technologies such as multi-core CPUs, multi-CPU workstations, computer clusters, and high-performance network systems. Traditionally, software written for serial computation:

- Runs on a single computer with a single CPU.
- Breaks the problem into a discrete series of instructions.
- Executes the instructions one after another.

Parallel computing, in the simplest sense, is the simultaneous use of multiple computing resource to solve a computational problem; therefore it:

- Uses multiple CPUs.
- Breaks the problem into discrete parts that can be solved concurrently.
- Breaks each part down to a series of instructions.
- Executes the instructions from each part simultaneously on different CPUs.
- Uses the same code on different CPUs.

The compute resources might be:

- A single computer with multiple processors.
- An arbitrary number of computers connected by a high-performance network.
- A combination of both.

According to the so-called Moore's Dividend, while the number of transistors on a chip is doubling every two years, the gain in the number of transistors can no longer be used to increase individual processor performance due to insufficient instruction level parallelism in a program and a chip power dissipation limit. In 2005, Gordon Moore stated in an interview that his law cannot be sustained indefinitely because transistors would eventually reach the limits of miniaturization at atomic levels. Instead, the gain has been used to increase the number of processors on a chip. Therefore, unless the application itself is highly parallel in nature, the potential performance improvement from increased hardware capacity has reached its limit. Maybe it is time for Koomey's law [6] to replace Moore's law. Koomey says that energy efficiency doubles every 18 months. For fixed computing load, the amount of battery you need will fall by a factor of 2 every year and a half. The parallel computing technique is fast developed with the distributed computing and high-performance network. Following are the incentives for the parallel computing:

- Save time and/or money: Using more resources for a single task will shorten the computing time.
- Solve larger problems: Many problems are so large and/or complex that it is impractical or impossible to solve them on a single computer in a reasonable time.
- Provide concurrency: A single compute resource can only do one thing at a time. Multiple computing resources can work on many things simultaneously.
- Use of non-local resources: Using compute resources on a wide area network, or even the Internet when local compute resources are scarce.
- Limit to serial computing: It is impossible to get a faster serial computer:
  - ○ Transmission speed: The speed of a serial computer is directly dependent upon how fast data can move through hardware.
  - ○ Limit to miniaturization: Processor technology allows an increasing number of transistors to be placed on a chip. However, even with molecular or atomic-level components, a limit will be reached on how small components can be made.
  - ○ Economic limitation: It is increasingly expensive to make a single processor faster. Using a larger number of moderately fast commodity processors to achieve the same (or better) performance is less expensive.
  - ○ Current computer architectures are increasingly relying upon hardware level parallelism to improve performance.

In this chapter, we will introduce parallel processing techniques including OpenMP, MPI (message processing interface), and their combination with SSE. Today, most computers are designed based on single instruction multiple data (SIMD) [7].

4.1 Single Instruction Single Data

Using the single instruction single data (SISD) instruction set, the processor can handle one data at one time. For example, follow the steps below to calculate $A + B$ and $D + E$:

(1) Load the value A;
(2) Load the value B;
(3) Calculate $A + B = C$;
(4) Store the value C;
(5) Load the value E;
(6) Load the value E;
(7) Calculate $D + E = F$;
(8) Store the value F.

4.2 Single Instruction Multiple Data

Unlike the SISD instruction set, the SIMD instruction can handle multiple data in a single instruction; that is, a single instruction can generate multiple results. The VALU accelerations use the SIMD instruction set. For example, follow the steps below to calculate $A[2] + B[2]$:

(1) Load the value A[1] and the value A[2] at the same time;
(2) Load the value B[1] and the value B[2] at the same time;
(3) Calculate $A[1] + B[1]$ and $A[2] + B[2]$ at the same time;
(4) Store the value C[1] and the value C[2] at the same time.

4.3 OpenMP

OpenMP [8] is an API, jointly defined by a group of major computer hardware and software vendors. OpenMP provides a portable and scalable model for developers of shared memory parallel applications. API supports $C/C++$ and FORTRAN on a wide variety of architectures. In the OpenMP parallel processing, the computing resource is shared by the applications dynamically. OpenMP has the following features:

(1) API may be used to explicitly direct the multi-threaded and shared memory parallelism.
(2) It is composed of three primary API components:
   - Compiler directives
   - Runtime library routines
   - Environment variables
(3) Portable
   - API is specified for $C/C++$ and FORTRAN.
   - Most major platforms, including Unix/Linux and Windows, support MPI.
(4) Standardized
   - It is jointly defined and endorsed by a group of major computer hardware and software vendors.
(5) OpenMP
   - Short version: open Multi-Processing
   - Long version: open specifications for multi-processing via collaborative work between interested parties from the hardware and software industry, government, and academia.

OpenMP is a fine-grid parallel processing technique, which is based on the loop statement. For example, a loop in a C code is given as:

```
for (n=0; n<=100; n++)
{
        A[n] = B[n] * C[n];
}
```

Using OpenMP, the code above can be rewritten as follows:

```
#include <omp.h>
#pragma omp parallel private n
for (n=1; n<=100; n++)
```

```
{
        A[n] = B[n] * C[n];
}
```

If the system checks and finds four cores available currently, it will split the loop into four parts equally and assign each part to each core for the calculation. The system also will get a shared space inside the memory to exchange the information. The general structure of an OpenMP code is shown below:

```
#include <omp.h>
main () {
int var1, var2, var3;
Serial code
        .

        .

        .

Beginning of parallel section. Fork a team of threads.
Specify variable scoping
#pragma omp parallel private(var1, var2) shared(var3)
  {
  Parallel section executed by all threads
        .

        .

        .

  All threads join master thread and disband
  }
Resume serial code
        .

        .

        .

}
```

A parallel FDTD code using OpenMP can be written in the following format:

```
//Ex update
#include <omp.h>
#pragma omp parallel private i,j
for( i = 0; i < nx; i++){
    for( j = 0; j < ny; j++) {
        for( k = 0; k < nz; k++) {
            Ex[i][j][k] = Ex[i][j][k] + Dt/Epsilon0((Hz[i][j][k+1]-
                Hz[i][j][k])/Dy - (Hy[i][j+1][k]- Hy[i][j][k])/Dz);
        }
    }
}
```

4.4 MPI

MPI [9, 10] is an international standard library for the message passing, which is proposed as a standard by a broadly based committee of vendors, implementers, and users.

(1) The MPI standard and information on MPI is available to implementers.
(2) MPI is designed for high performance on both massively parallel machines and work-station clusters.
(3) MPI is widely available with both freely available and vendor-supplied implementations.
(4) Test suites for MPI implementations.

MPI provides the parallel hardware vendors with a clearly defined base set of routines that can be efficiently implemented. As a result, hardware vendors can build upon this collection of standard low-level routines to create higher level routines for the distributed-memory communication environment supplied with their parallel machines. MPI provides a simple-to-use portable interface for the basic user, yet powerful enough to allow programmers to use the high-performance message passing operations available on advanced machines.

```
//"Hello World" MPI Test Program
#include <mpi.h>
#include <stdio.h>
#include <string.h>

#define BUFSIZE 128
#define TAG 0

int main(int argc, char *argv[])
{
  char idstr[32], buff[BUFSIZE];
  int numprocs, myid, i;
  MPI_Status stat;

  MPI_Init(&argc,&argv); /*all MPI programs start with MPI_Init; all
                    'N' processes exist thereafter */
  MPI_Comm_size(MPI_COMM_WORLD,&numprocs); /* find out how big the SPMD
                                        world is */
  MPI_Comm_rank(MPI_COMM_WORLD,&myid); /*and this processes' rank is*/

  // At this point, all programs are running equivalently, the rank
  //distinguishes the roles of the programs in the SPMD model, with
  //rank 0 often used specially...
  if(myid == 0){
    printf("%d: We have %d processors\n", myid, numprocs);
```

```
   for(i=1; i<numprocs; i++)
   {
     sprintf(buff, "Hello %d! ", i);
     MPI_Send(buff, BUFSIZE, MPI_CHAR, i, TAG, MPI_COMM_WORLD);
   }
   for(i=1; i<numprocs; i++)
   {
     MPI_Recv(buff, BUFSIZE, MPI_CHAR, i, TAG, MPI_COMM_WORLD, &stat);
     printf("%d: %s\n", myid, buff);
   }
 }
 else
 {
   /* receive from rank 0: */
   MPI_Recv(buff, BUFSIZE, MPI_CHAR, 0, TAG, MPI_COMM_WORLD, &stat);
   sprintf(idstr, "Processor %d ", myid);
   strncat(buff, idstr, BUFSIZE - 1);
   strncat(buff, "reporting for duty\n", BUFSIZE - 1);
   /* send to rank 0: */
   MPI_Send(buff, BUFSIZE, MPI_CHAR, 0, TAG, MPI_COMM_WORLD);
 }
 MPI_Finalize(); /* MPI programs end with MPI Finalize; this is a weak
          synchronization point */
 return 0;
}
```

MPI includes six basic functions, from which other functions can be derived:

MPI_INIT: Initialize the MPI environment.
MPI_FINALIZE: Terminate the MPI environment.
MPI_COMM_SIZE: Determine the number of processes.
MPI_COMM_RANK: Determine the process identifier.
MPI_SEND: Send a message.
MPI_RECV: Receive a message.

MPI has a number of send modes. These represent different choices of *buffering* (where the data kept is until it is received) and *synchronization* (when a send statement is completed). Next, we explain these send functions:

MPI_Send
     MPI_Send will not return until we can use the send buffer.
MPI_Bsend
     MPI_Bsend returns immediately and we can use the send buffer.

MPI_Ssend

    MPI_Ssend will not return until the matching receive is posted.

MPI_Rsend

    MPI_Rsend is used only if the matching receive has been already posted.

MPI_Isend

    MPI_Isend is a non-blocking send, but not necessarily asynchronous. We cannot reuse the send buffer until the message has been received.

MPI_Ibsend

    MPI_Ibsend is a buffered non-blocking send.

MPI_Issend

    MPI_Issend is a synchronous non-blocking send.

MPI_Irsend

    MPI_Irsend is same as MPI_Rsend, but is a non-blocking send.

It is required to exchange magnetic or electric field data between sub-domains when using the MPI library for parallel processing. A typical code to exchange the field data is shown as follows:

```
void transfer_H()
{
    if( id != p - 1 ) {
    MPI_Isend( hy[memory_size - 2][0], 1, new_dtype, id + 1, 0,
        MPI_COMM_WORLD, &req[0]);
    MPI_Isend( hz[memory_size - 2][0], 1, new_dtype, id + 1, 1,
        MPI_COMM_WORLD, &req[1]);
    }
    if( id != 0 ){
        MPI_Irecv( hy[0][0], 1, new_dtype, id - 1, 0, MPI_COMM_WORLD,
            &req[0]);
        MPI_Irecv( hz[0][0], 1, new_dtype, id - 1, 1, MPI_COMM_WORLD,
            &req[1]);
    }
    MPI_Waitall( 2, req, status );
}
void transfer_E()
{
    if( id != 0 ){
        MPI_Isend( ey[1][0], 1, new_dtype, id - 1, 0, MPI_COMM_WORLD,
            &req[0] );
        MPI_Isend( ez[1][0], 1, new_dtype, id - 1, 1, MPI_COMM_WORLD,
            &req[1] );
    }

    if( id != p - 1 ) {
```

```
        MPI_Irecv( ey[memory_size - 1][0], 1, new_dtype, id + 1, 0,
           MPI_COMM_WORLD, &req[0]);
        MPI_Irecv( ez[memory_size - 1][0], 1, new_dtype, id + 1, 1,
           MPI_COMM_WORLD, &req[1]);
    }
MPI_Waitall( 2, req, status );
    }
```

4.5 Three-Level Parallel Architecture

The ordinary parallel FDTD code based on the MPI library or OpenMP is either a one-level or a two-level parallel processing technique [11]. The parallel FDTD code can be constructed as a three-level parallel processing technique in which SSE is involved.

The first-level parallelism is based on the MPI library in which the computational domain is broken into small sub-domains according to the number of cores, CPUs, or nodes. The field update on the interface of each sub-domain is not independent; that is, the field update on the interface requires the information from its neighbors through the MPI functions. However, the internal field updates are independent, which results in the high efficient parallel performance.

The second-level parallelism is based on OpenMP. First, several threads are generated by OpenMP based on the number of available cores, then each thread is assigned to each core for the simulation. The framework of the algorithm is described as follows:

```
#pragma omp parallel private( num_threads, thread_num)
thread_num = omp_get_thread_num();
num_threads = omp_get_num_threads();
float imaxf = (float)imax / (float)num_threads;
for ( i = imin + (int)((float)thread_num * imaxf); i <=
      (int)((float)(thread_num + 1) * imaxf); i ++) {
    for( j = jmin; j <= jmax; j++) {
        for( k = kmin; k <= kmax; k ++ ) {
            E or H field update;
          }
      }
}
```

The third-level parallelism is based on VALU using the SSE instruction set. The length of VALU is either 128 bits in 45-mm lithography or earlier and 256 bits in 32-mm lithography or latter.

References

[1] W. Gropp, E. Lusk, and A. Skjellum, *Using MPI: Portable Parallel Programming with the Message-Passing Interface*, 2nd ed., MIT Press, Cambridge, MA, 1999.

[2] B. Barney, "Introduction to Parallel Computing," https://computing.llnl.gov/tutorials/parallel_comp/

[3] http://www.mathworks.com/products/parallel-computing/index.html

[4] W. Yu, X. Yang, Y. Liu, et al., *Parallel Finite Difference Time Domain Method*, Artech House, Norwood, MA, 2006.

[5] W. Yu, Y. Liu, Z. Su, et al., "A Robust Parallel Conformal Finite Difference Time Domain Processing Package Using MPI Library," *IEEE Antennas and Propagation Magazine*, Vol. 47, No. 3, 2005, pp. 39–59.

[6] J. Koomey, S. Berard, M. Sanchez, and H. Wong, "Implications of Historical Trends in the Electrical Efficiency of Computing," *IEEE Annals of the History of Computing*, Vol. 33, 2011, pp. 46–54.

[7] http://en.wikipedia.org/wiki/SISD

[8] B. Chapman, G. Jost, and R. Pas, *Using OpenMP: Portable Shared Memory Parallel Programming*, MIT Press, Cambridge, MA, 2007.

[9] P. Pacheco, *Parallel Programming with MPI*, Morgan Kaufmann publisher, Burlington, MA, 1996.

[10] http://en.wikipedia.org/wiki/Message_Passing_Interface

[11] L. Zhang, X. Yang, and W. Yu, "Enhanced Parallel FDTD Method Using SSE Instruction Sets," *ACES Journal*, Vol. 27, No. 1, 2012, pp. 1–6.

CHAPTER 5

GPU Acceleration Techniques

Veysel Demir, Atef Elsherbeni and Wenhua Yu

In this chapter, we introduce the basic concept, implementation, and engineering applications of graphics processor unit (GPU) acceleration of parallel FDTD method based on compute unified device architecture (CUDA). Several typical examples are employed to demonstrate the performance of GPU and VALU acceleration techniques.

5.1 Introduction to GPU Architecture

It is a well-known fact that GPU is a specialized processor that is considered as a multi-threaded and massively data parallel co-processor. A general-purpose computation on GPU (GPGPU) is the use of a GPU to perform computation traditionally handled by the CPU. NVIDIA Geforce, Quadro, and Tesla series are capable of general-purpose computing using CUDA. A typical NVIDIA GPU card is shown in Fig. 5.1. CUDA is an integrated host (CPU) and device (GPU) application programming interface based on the C language developed by NVIDIA.

GPUs are similar to multi-core CPUs but with two main differences. CPUs try to improve the execution of a single instruction stream while GPUs take the opposite route obtaining benefits from massively threaded streams of instructions. The second difference is how threads are scheduled. The operating system schedules threads over different cores of a CPU in a pre-emptive fashion. GPUs have dedicated hardware for the cooperative scheduling of threads. Table 5.1 shows the ideal performance and major technical specifications of several typical CPUs and GPUs.

There are three layers, namely, grid, block, and thread, in the GPU programming model. Thread is an execution of a kernel with a given index. Each thread uses its index to access elements in an array such that the collection of all threads cooperatively processes the entire data set of the array. Block is a group of threads, which executes concurrently or serially and yet in no particular order. One can coordinate the threads, somewhat, using the _syncthreads() function that makes a thread stop at a certain point in the kernel until all the other threads in its block reach the same point. Grid is a group of blocks. All threads within a block execute the same kernel via shared memory and barrier synchronization, as shown in Fig. 5.2.

Figure 5.1 A typical NVIDIA GPU card. For example, NVIDIA Tesla C1060 – number of streaming multiprocessors (SMs): 30; number of cores (or streaming processors, SPs) per SM: 8; total number of cores: $30 \times 8 = 240$; clock rate: 1.3 GHz; global memory: 4 GB; shared memory per SM: 16 KB.

5.2 Introduction to GPU Acceleration Techniques

Since the dawn of the computing age, research has relied on the power of CPU to perform a variety of computational tasks. Over the years great progress has been made in harnessing the power of the CPU by introducing faster clock speeds, larger caches, faster memory, multiple processors, and even multiple cores in a single chip. This, however, has also been accompanied by users' need: from browsing the Internet to watching videos and playing games. Due to these needs of the general computer user, the instruction set of the average commercial processor has expanded well past 300 separate instructions in addition to the core instructions of the processor. The CPU has been forced to be a jack-of-all-trades for computing tasks, allowing it to do a greater number of tasks but not specializing in any particular area.

Conversely, GPU is designed to be very narrow in nature in which it only needs to perform relatively few operations. The video card has been designed with only one purpose: to process instructions and data necessary to provide graphics to the user. Over the past few years, advancement in the design of GPUs has occurred at a much greater pace than with CPUs due to the narrow nature in which it was intended to be used. This has led to the development of very powerful processing units for computer graphics. It must be noted that

Table 5.1 Performance and specification of several typical CPUs and GPUs.

Manufacturer and Model	Transistor Count (10^6)	Die Size (mm²)	Shader Cores (ALUs)	Clock Rate (GHz)	RAM Bandwidth (GB/s)	Performance (GFLOPS)	TDP (W)
AMD Opteron 6128	1,200	315	8	2.0	42.7	256	115
AMD A8-3850	758	258	4/400	2.9/0.6	29.8	355	100
Intel Xeon E5540	731	263	4/8	2.53	25.6	40.5/45	80
Intel Core i7 990X	1,170	240	6	3.46–3.7	24.5	107.58	130
Intel Core i7 2600K	995	216	4/48	3.4/0.85	24.5	129.6	95
NVIDIA Tesla C1060	1,400	576	240	1.296	102.4	622.08	187
NVIDIA Tesla C2070	3,100	529	448	1.150	144	1,030.40	238
NVIDIA GeForce GTX 480	3,200	529	480	1.41	177.4	1,345	250
NVIDIA GeForce GTX 580	3,000	520	512	1.544	192.4	1,581.1	244
NVIDIA GeForce GTX 690	2 × 3,540	2 × 294	915	1.019	2 × 192.3	2 × 2,810	300

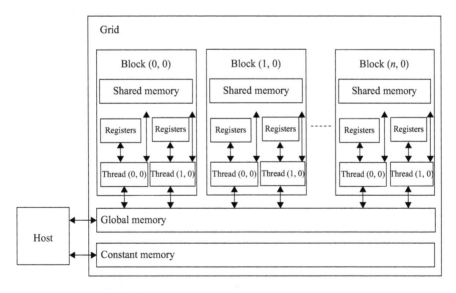

Figure 5.2 Thread relationship with memory in GPU: read/write thread registers; read/write thread local memory; read/write block shared memory; read/write grid global memory; and read-only grid constant memory.

the GPU was designed specifically for rendering graphics, not for doing computational electromagnetics. Luckily, the different processes used in rendering graphics are analogous to many generic vector math operations. Here we look at how to relate the various functions available in the graphics card to various computational electromagnetic applications.

Several implementations of FDTD method have been reported in the literature to run on GPU architecture based on various programming languages. For instance, Brook is used as the programming language in References 1–7, high level shader language (HLSL) is reported in Reference 8, while the FDTD implementations in References 9–11 are based on OpenGL. CUDA [12] development environment from NVIDIA made GPU computing much easier recently, which is a general-purpose parallel computing architecture. To program the CUDA architecture, developers can use C, which can then be run at great performance on a CUDA-enabled processor [13]. CUDA has been reported as the programming environment for implementation of FDTD in a number of publications, while References 14 and 15 illustrate methods to improve the efficiency of FDTD using CUDA. These can be used as guidelines while programming FDTD using CUDA.

CUDA, as other languages or programming platforms, has its advantages and disadvantages. The major advantage is that CUDA is easier to learn compared with other alternatives, and NVIDIA provides extensive support to developers and users. One major disadvantage is that CUDA can run only on CUDA-enabled NVIDIA cards. Although OpenCL and Direct Compute are becoming the new alternatives to CUDA as programming languages on modern GPU-based architectures, CUDA may keep its popularity for scientific computing due to vast learning resources available for developers. In this chapter, we illustrate an implementation of FDTD using CUDA.

In order to start programming with CUDA, one needs to install CUDA drivers and CUDA Toolkit that would include C/C++ compiler, Visual Profiler, and GPU-accelerated BLAS, FFT, Sparse Matrix, and RNG libraries. Another crucial component is GPU computing software development kit (SDK), which includes several tools and code samples. All these components are available at NVIDIA's web portal for Windows, Linux, and Mac OS X operating systems.

In order to program using CUDA, one needs to know the CUDA terminology and architecture. NVIDIA *CUDA Programming Guide*, available at NVIDIA's web portal, is a good resource to learn CUDA.

5.2.1 Performance optimization in CUDA

One should be familiar with the CUDA architecture to some extent in order to develop a program with optimum performance. *CUDA Best Practices Guide* is a good reference for programmers; it provides recommendations for optimization and a list of best practices for programming with CUDA. Although not all of these recommendations are applicable to the case of FDTD programming, the following list of recommendations is taken into consideration while developing an FDTD implementation:

R1) Structure the algorithm in a way that exposes as much data parallelism as possible. Once the parallelism of the algorithm has been exposed, it needs to be mapped to the hardware as efficiently as possible.

R2) Ensure that the global memory accesses are coalesced whenever possible.

R3)   Minimize the use of global memory. Prefer shared memory access where possible.

R4)   Use shared memory to avoid redundant transfers from global memory.

R5)   Hide latency arising from register dependencies, maintain at least 25 percent occupancy on devices with CUDA compute capability 1.1 and lower, and 18.75 percent occupancy on later devices.

R6)   Use a multiple of 32 threads for the number of threads per block as this provides optimal computing efficiency and facilitates coalescing.

5.2.2 Achieving parallelism

At every time iteration of the FDTD loop, new values of three magnetic field components are calculated at every cell simultaneously using the past values of electric and magnetic field components. After magnetic field updates are completed, new values of three electric field components are updated at every cell simultaneously in a separate function using the past values of magnetic and electric field components. Since the calculations for each cell can be performed independently from the other cells, a CUDA algorithm can be developed by assigning each cell calculation to a separate thread, and the highest level of parallelism can be achieved to satisfy the recommendation R1.

5.3 CUDA Implementation of FDTD Method

In this section, we present a CUDA implementation of 2-D FDTD program. CUDA allows the programming of GPUs for parallel processing without any graphics knowledge [16]. The stream processors are fully capable of executing integer and single-precision floating-point arithmetic, with additional cores used for double precision. All multiprocessors have access to global device memory, which is not cached by the hardware.

CUDA arranges threads into thread blocks. All threads in a thread block can read and write any shared memory location assigned to that thread block. Consequently, threads within a thread block can communicate via shared memory, or use shared memory as a user-managed cache, since shared memory latency is two orders of magnitude lower than that of global memory. A barrier primitive is provided so that all threads in a thread block can synchronize their execution.

5.3.1 Coalesced global memory access

In CUDA, memory instructions are the instructions that read from or write to shared, constant, or global memory. When accessing global memory, there are 400–600 clock cycles of memory latency. Much of this global memory latency can be hidden by the thread scheduler if there are sufficient independent arithmetic instructions that can be issued while waiting for the global memory access to complete [17]. Unfortunately in FDTD updates the operations are dominated by memory accesses rather than arithmetic instructions. Hence, the memory access inefficiency is the main bottleneck that reduces efficiency of FDTD on GPU. Global memory bandwidth is used most efficiently when the simultaneous memory accesses by threads in a half-warp (during the execution of a single read or write instruction) can be coalesced into a single memory transaction of 32, 64, or 128 bytes [17].

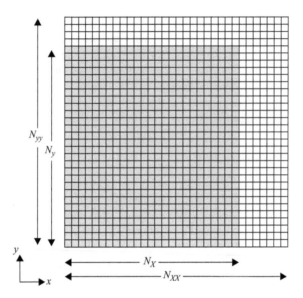

Figure 5.3   An extended computational domain in the x- and y-directions. N_x and N_y are the actual size of the computational domain size. N_{xx} and N_{yy} are the modified domain size with the padded cells.

If the array size, which is the FDTD domain size in number of cells, is a multiple of 16, the coalesced memory access is ensured. In general, an FDTD domain size would be an arbitrary number. In order to achieve coalesced memory access, the FDTD domain can be extended by padding some cells such that the number of cells in each direction is an integer multiple of 16 as illustrated in Fig. 5.3. Although, padding these cells increases the amount of memory needed to store arrays, it improves the efficiency of the kernel functions tremendously. Thus, the recommendation R2 is satisfied.

It should be noted that these padded cells are beyond the boundaries of the original domain and they should be electrically isolated from the original domain. As long as the original domain boundaries are kept as PEC, such as in the case of CPML boundaries, the fields in the original domain will be isolated from the padded cells; thus, padded cells can be assumed to be filled with any type of material. The easiest way is to set these padded cells as free space.

If the original domain size is $N_x \times N_y$, where N_x and N_y are the numbers of cells in the x- and y-directions, respectively, then the modified domain size becomes $N_{xx} \times N_{yy}$, where N_{xx} and N_{yy} are the number of cells of the modified domain. The modified size of the problem space is determined as:

```
% extend the domain and adjust number of cells for gpu
nxx = (floor(nx/16)+1)*16;
nyy = (floor(ny/16)+1)*16;
```

In this way, the actual simulation domain size is extended to $N_{xx} \times N_{yy}$ to improve the CUDA FDTD code performance.

5.3.2 Thread to cell mapping

Arrays are allocated on the CPU memory, and then the coefficient and field data are read into these arrays. These arrays initially reside on the host (CPU) memory and they need to be copied to the device (GPU) global memory. The cudaMalloc() function is used to allocate memory on the device global memory for these arrays, and the cudaMemcpy() function is used to copy the data to the global memory. Once these arrays are ready on the global memory, they are ready for processing on the graphics card by the kernel functions. Next, we will use a 2-D FDTD pseudo-code for transverse magnetic (TM) mode to demonstrate the implementation strategy.

The code segment 1 below shows a function that performs the field update procedure on GPU. Similarly, the code segment 2 shows a function that performs the field update procedure on CPU for the sake of comparison. It is observed from the code segments 1 and 2 that the simulation procedure is the same on GPU and CPU. The essential difference is that fdtdIterationOnGpu() and fdtdIterationOnCpu() are executed on GPU and CPU on the host computer, respectively.

Code segment 1. FDTD iteration for the magnetic field on GPU:

```
bool fdtdIterationOnGpu(){
   update_magnetic_fields_on_gpu();
   update_impressed_magnetic_currents_on_gpu();
   update_magnetic_fields_for_CPML_on_gpu();
   update_electric_fields_on_gpu();
   update_impressed_electric_currents_on_gpu();
   update_electric_fields_for_CPML_on_gpu();
}
```

Code segment 2. FDTD iteration for the electric field on CPU:

```
bool fdtdIterationOnCpu(){

   update_magnetic_fields_on_cpu();
   update_impressed_magnetic_currents_on_cpu();
   update_magnetic_fields_for_CPML_on_cpu();
   update_electric_fields_on_cpu();
   update_impressed_electric_currents_on_cpu();
   update_electric_fields_for_CPML_on_cpu();
}
```

The code segment 3 shows the kernel function that updates the magnetic field components, whereas the code segment 4 shows the kernel function that updates the electric field components. In this implementation for GPU, each cell is processed by an associated thread. The CUDA internal variables threadIdx and blockIdx are used to identify the threads and data elements, which they will update. The variable blockIdx is used to identify the thread blocks as illustrated in Fig. 5.4. Similarly, the variable `threadIdx` is used to identify threads within a thread block as shown in Fig. 5.5. Thus, one can identify any thread, and also cell, in a 2-D array with indices i and j such that:

```
int i = blockIdx.x * blockDim.x + threadIdx.x;
int j = blockIdx.y * blockDim.y + threadIdx.y;
```

At this point, it should be noted that although the arrays that are being processed are 2-D, they are stored in device (GPU) global memory as 1-D arrays and elements of these arrays

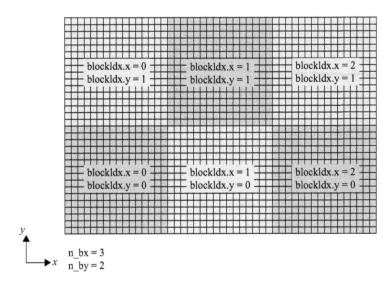

Figure 5.4   A grid of thread blocks that spans a 48 × 32 cell's 2-D problem space.

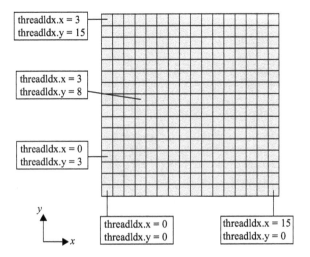

Figure 5.5   Threads in a thread block.

are accessed in kernel functions in a linear fashion. Thus, a conversion from i and j indices to the linear index, denoted as "ci" in the code segment 1, is required. Index i runs faster than index j, i.e., the data stored at (i, j) is adjacent to $(i + 1, j)$ on the physical memory; thus, the conversion to linear index can be done simply as:

```
int ci = j * nxx + i;
```

Code segment 3. update_electric_fields_on_gpu:

```
__global__ void  //declares a function as being a kernel
update_magnetic_fields_on_kernel(float* Chxh, float* Chxez, float*
Chyh, float* Chyez, float* Hx,  float* Hy, float* Ez, int nxx)
{
    __shared__ float sEz[TILE_SIZE][2*TILE_SIZE+1];
    int tx = threadIdx.x;
    int ty = threadIdx.y;
    int i = blockIdx.x * blockDim.x + tx;
    int j = blockIdx.y * blockDim.y + ty;
    int ci = j*nxx + i;
    sEz[ty][tx] = Ez[ci];
    sEz[ty][tx+TILE_SIZE] = Ez[ci+TILE_SIZE];
    __syncthreads();
    Hx[ci] = Chxh[ci]*Hx[ci]+Chxez[ci]*(Ez[ci+nxx]-sEz[ty][tx]);
    Hy[ci] = Chyh[ci]*Hy[ci]+Chyez[ci]*(sEz[ty][tx+1]-sEz[ty][tx]);
}
```

where Chxh and Chyh are the coefficients of electric and magnetic fields in the FDTD magnetic field update equations. The declaration __shared__ in the CUDA kernel places a floating type of array sEz[TILE_SIZE][2*TILE_SIZE+1] into shared memory.

Function __syncthreads() is used to make all the threads in a block to be at the same point even if warps are being executed in parallel. The actual execution in hardware may not be parallel because the number of cores within a stream multiprocessor (SM) can be less than 32. This function acts as a barrier to all the threads in that particular thread block. No thread can continue past that block until all threads have reached that location. While this may seem to slowdown execution because threads will be idle if they reach it before other threads, it is absolutely necessary to synchronize the threads here. By using __syncthreads(), we can guarantee that all threads are in the same iteration of the while loop at the same time, thus ensuring that all threads are reading the correct values from shared memory.

Code segment 4. update_electric_fields_on_gpu:

```
__global__ void //declares a function as being a kernel
update_electric_fields_on_kernel(float* Cexe, float*
Cexhz, float* Ceye, float* Ceyhz,  float* Ex, float* Ey, float* Hz, int nxx)
```

```
{
    __shared__ float sHz[TILE_SIZE][2*TILE_SIZE+1];
    int tx = threadIdx.x;
    int ty = threadIdx.y;
    int i = blockIdx.x * blockDim.x + tx;
    int j = blockIdx.y * blockDim.y + ty;
    int ci = j*nxx + i;
    sHz[ty][tx] = Hz[ci-TILE_SIZE];
    sHz[ty][tx+TILE_SIZE] = Hz[ci];
    __syncthreads();
    Ex[ci] = Cexe[ci]*Ex[ci]+Cexhz[ci]*(Hz[ci]-Hz[ci-nxx]);
    Ey[ci] = Ceye[ci]*Ey[ci]+Ceyhz[ci]*(sHz[ty][tx+TILE_SIZE]-
            sHz[ty][tx+TILE_SIZE-1]);
}
```

where `Cexe` and `Ceye` are the coefficients of electric and magnetic fields in the FDTD electric field update equations.

5.3.3 Use of shared memory

Because shared memory is on GPU chip, access to it is much faster than that to the local and global memory. Parameters that reside in the shared memory space of a thread block have the lifetime of the block, and are accessible from all the threads within the block [18]. Therefore, if a data block on the global memory has to be used frequently in a kernel, it is better to load the data to the shared memory and reuse the data from the shared memory. Here it should be reminded that shared memory is available only through the lifetime of a thread; thus, the relevant field data have to be reloaded to the shared memory every time a kernel function is called.

Shared memory is especially useful when threads need access to unaligned data. For instance, in order to calculate $H_y(i,j)$, a thread mapped to the cell (i,j) needs E_z at (i,j) as well as E_z at $(i+1,j)$. In the kernel code, the index of a thread that is processing the cell (i,j) is indexed as "ci". A cell with index $(i+1,j)$ can be accessed by `ci+1`, while a cell with index $(i,j+1)$ can be accessed by `ci+nxx`. Access to $(i,j+1)$ is coalesced, but that to $(i+1,j)$ is not. If access to a field component at a neighboring cell in the x-direction is needed, i.e., $(i+1,j)$, then shared memory can be used to load the data block mapped by the thread block, and then the neighboring field value can be accessed from the shared memory. At this point one needs to use the CUDA function `__syncthreads()` to ensure that all threads in the block are synchronized; thus, all necessary data are loaded to the shared memory before they are used by the neighboring threads.

As discussed above, uncoalesced memory accesses can be prevented by using shared memory. However, a problem arises when the data of the neighboring cells are accessed through shared memory. While loading the shared memory, each thread copies one element from the global memory to the shared memory. If the thread on the boundary of the thread block needs to access the data in the neighboring cell, this data will not be available since it has not been loaded to the shared memory. One way to overcome this problem is to load another set of data, which includes the data from the neighboring cell, to the shared memory. In the presented implementation shown in the code segment 3, two square blocks of data are copied from the global memory to the shared memory as:

```
sEz[ty][tx]  = Ez[ci];
sEz[ty][tx+TILE_SIZE]=Ez[ci+TILE_SIZE];
```

Then E_z at $(i+1,j)$ is safely accessed from the shared memory to update $H_y(i,j)$ as:

```
Hy[ci]=Chyh[ci]*Hy[ci]+Chyez[ci]*(sEz[ty][tx+1]-sEz[ty][tx]);
```

A similar treatment is shown in the code segment 4, where $E_y(i,j)$ is updated by $H_z(i-1,j)$ through an effective use of shared memory: First two blocks of data are from the global memory to the shared memory as:

```
sHz[ty][tx]  = Hz[ci-TILE_SIZE];
sHz[ty][tx+TILE_SIZE]  = Hz[ci];
```

Then $E_y(i,j)$ is updated as:

```
Ey[ci]=Ceye[ci]*Ey[ci]+Ceyhz[ci]*(sHz[ty][tx+TILE_SIZE]-
sHz[ty][tx+TILE_SIZE-1]);
```

5.3.4 Optimization of number of threads

As pointed out in the recommendations R5 and R6, occupancy of the microprocessors and number of threads in a block are two other important parameters that affect the performance of a CUDA program. Number of threads and occupancy are tightly connected. It is possible to set the number of threads as a desired value, but it may be impossible to control the occupancy, which is a function of number of threads, number of registers used in the kernel, amount of shared memory used by the kernel, compute capability of the device, etc. A good practice is to optimize the number of threads while keeping the occupancy at a reasonable value. As a rule of thumb, it is better to keep kernel functions small such that they do not use many registers.

CUDA Visual Profiler is a GUI-based profiling tool provided by NVIDIA that can be used to measure performance and find potential opportunities for optimization in order to achieve maximum performance of kernels in a CUDA program. It can show information such as the total GPU and CPU times of a thread, memory read-write throughputs, global memory load and store efficiencies, occupancy, etc. Therefore, the kernel functions can be profiled using the Visual Profiler and, if not satisfactory, their efficiencies can be improved.

Although the block size is chosen as $16 \times 16 = 256$ here, one can choose a different configuration and test with Visual Profiler to evaluate its efficiency. It should also be noted that the presented grid scheme, i.e., 2-D array of square thread blocks, is not the only way to map threads to cells. It is possible to use other grid configurations, such as 1-D thread blocks, develop algorithms based on these configurations, and evaluate if the developed algorithms are superior.

5.4 Engineering Applications

In this section, we use the CUDA FDTD code and the parallel FDTD code enhanced by the VALU acceleration techniques to simulate several typical antenna problems and demonstrate their performance based on two available GPU and CPU platforms. Since different mesh strategies in the FDTD simulations will significantly affect the simulation performance, it is hard to compare the performance of GPU and CPU. It may be of no meaning to directly compare two results in this section, although they are plotted in the same figure. In this section, we demonstrate how to employ GPU and VALU acceleration techniques to accelerate the parallel FDTD method.

5.4.1 Introduction to hardware platforms

The VALU acceleration platform is based on a customized 4-CPU workstation, and the configuration is:

- Processor: AMD Opteron 6128 2.0 GHz
- Memory: 64-GB DDR3 1333 MHz
- Memory Bandwidth: 47 GB/s
- NUMA Architecture: Yes
- Operating System: Linux CentOS version 5.2

The GPU configuration is:

- NVIDIA GPU Model: GTX480
- Number of CUDA Cores: 480
- Graphics Clock: 700 MHz
- Processor Clock Tester: 1,401 MHz
- Texture Fill Rate: 42 billion/s
- Memory Clock: 1,848 MHz (3,696 data rate)
- Standard Memory Config.: 1,536 MB
- Memory Interface: GDDR5
- Memory Interface Width: 384-bit
- Memory Bandwidth: 177.4 GB/s

Configuration of the host computer for GTX480 GPU is:

- Processor: Intel(R) Core^{TM} 2 Quad CPU Q9550, 2.83 GHz
- Memory: 8-GB DDR3
- Operating system: 64-bit Windows 7

Next, we use the FDTD method on GPU and VALU platforms described above to simulate typical antenna problems. The mesh distributions, boundary selection, and white buffer space in the GPU and VALU simulations are selected based on authors' experience without special optimization.

5.4.2 Loop microstrip antenna

The configuration of loop microstrip antenna [19] is described in Fig. 5.6, in which the microstrip loop is mounted on the top surface of the dielectric slab and the ground plane is located at the bottom surface of the dielectric slab.

In the CUDA FDTD simulation, the cell sizes are chosen to be 0.25 mm in the x-, y-, and z-directions. The total number of cells including the PML layers in the x-, y-, and z-directions is 241, 241, and 51, respectively. The absorbing boundary is chosen to be CPML and the

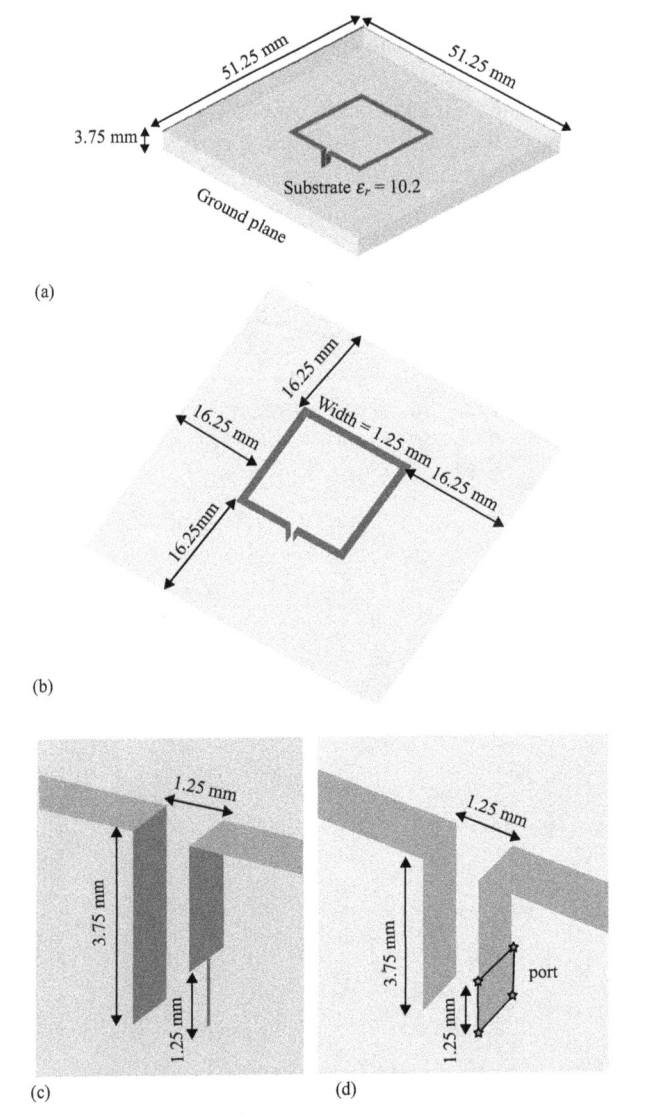

Figure 5.6 Loop antenna configuration and feed structure: (a) dielectric slab dimensions and parameter, (b) loop relative location and width, (c) feed structure in the VALU simulation, (d) feed structure in the GPU simulation.

number of CPML layers is 8 in the six directions. The white buffer space in the six directions includes 10 uniform cells. It takes 57 s for 15,000 time steps on the NVIDIA GeFore GTX480 GPU platform. The simulation result is S_{11} only, which is shown in Fig. 5.7.

For the same problem on CPU, the non-uniform cell size (the adjacent cell ratio is 1.05) is selected to be 0.25 mm, and the number of cells is 146, 147, and 47 in the x-, y-, and z-directions, respectively. The parallel partition is $4 \times 2 \times 1$, namely, the number of sub-domains is 4, 2, and 1 in the x-, y-, and z-directions, respectively. The absorbing boundary is CPML and the number of CPML layers is 6 in the six directions. The white buffer space in the six directions includes 10 uniform cells. It takes 31 s for 15,000 time steps on the VALU platform to complete the simulation. The simulation result is also plotted in Fig. 5.7 for the sake of comparison.

Since the problem sizes in the two simulations described above are different, it is hard to compare their performance. We define the simulation performance as the number of million cells processed per second (NMCPS) [18]:

$$\text{NMCPS} = \frac{N_x \times N_y \times N_z \times \text{number of time steps}}{\text{simulation time in seconds} \times 10^6} \tag{5.1}$$

where N_x, N_y, and N_z are the number of cells in the x-, y-, and z-directions, respectively. Using the definition in (5.1), the GPU and VALU performances are 778 NMCPS and 517 NMCPS, respectively. Namely, one NVIDIA GeFore GTX480 is as fast as six AMD Opteron 6128 CPUs (2.0 GHz) for this example, assuming that the parallel efficiency of four CPUs is 100%.

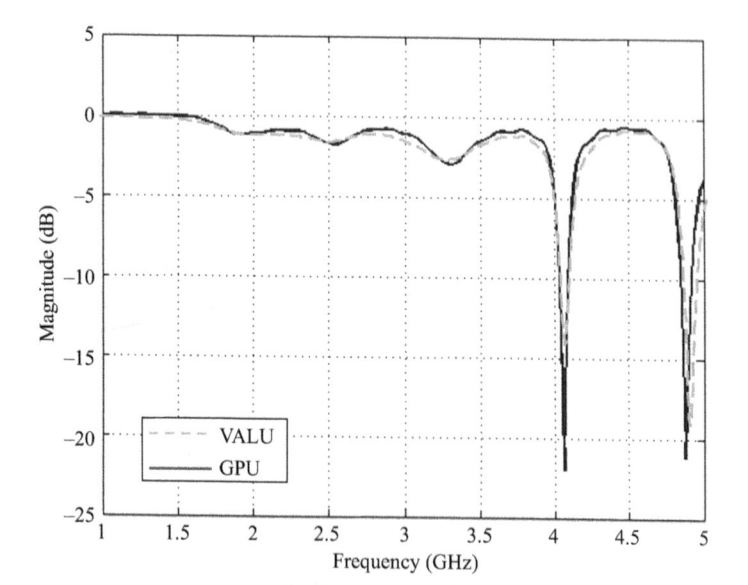

Figure 5.7 S_{11} variation of the loop antenna with frequency obtained by using the GP‍‌ VALU acceleration techniques.

5.4.3 Electromagnetic band gap structure

The electromagnetic band gap (EBG) configuration is described in Fig. 5.8 in which the *artificial magnetic conductor (AMC)* ground, as shown in Fig. 5.9, is inset inside the dielectric slab. Other than the AMC ground, the loop antenna, dielectric slab, and PEC ground remain same as the dimensions in Fig. 5.6(a).

In the CUDA FDTD simulation, the cell sizes are chosen to be 0.20833 mm in the x-, y-, and z-directions. The total number of cells including the PML layers in the x-, y-, and z-directions is 282, 282, and 74, respectively. The absorbing boundary is CPML and the number of CPML layers is 8 in the six directions. The white buffer space in the six directions includes 10 uniform cells. It takes 10 min and 30 s for 100,000 time steps on the NVIDIA GeFore GTX480 GPU platform. The simulation result is S_{11} only, which is shown in Fig. 5.10.

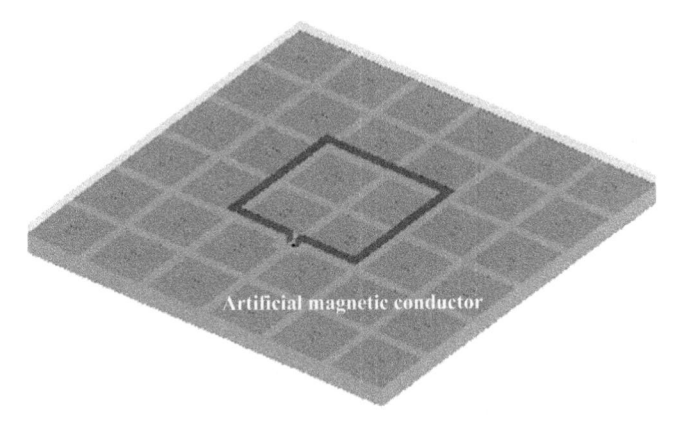

Figure 5.8   EBG configuration in which EBG is used to improve the return loss.

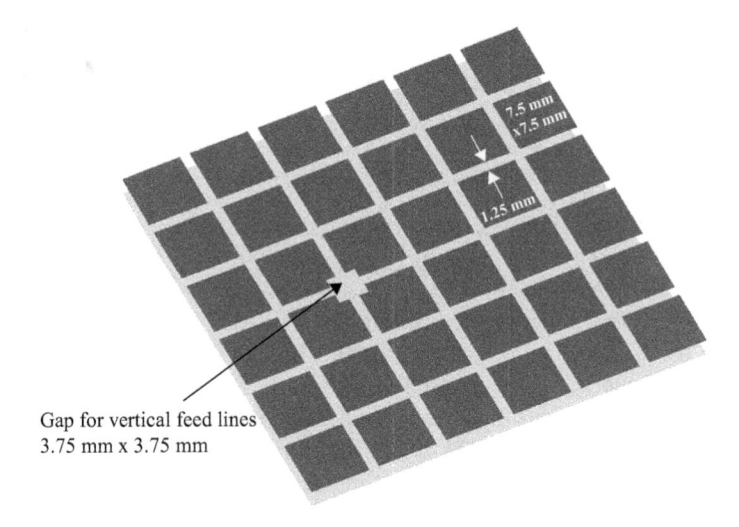

Figure 5.9   Dimensions in the AMC structure and feed gap.

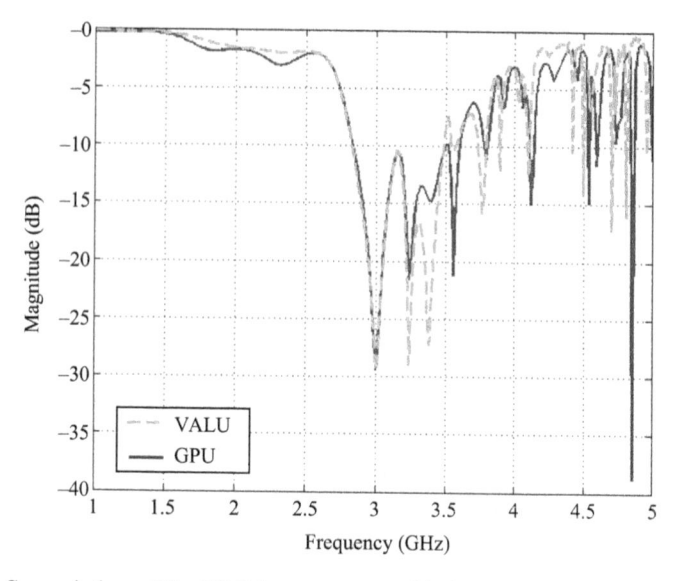

Figure 5.10 S_{11} variation of the EBG loop antenna with frequency obtained by using the GPU and VALU acceleration techniques.

For the same problem, the non-uniform cell size (the adjacent cell ratio is 1.2) is selected to be 0.26 mm, 0.256 mm, and 0.23 mm, respectively, and the number of cells is 146, 157, and 47 in the x-, y-, and z-directions, respectively. The parallel partition is $4 \times 2 \times 1$, namely, the number of sub-domains is 4, 2, and 1 in the x-, y- and z-directions, respectively. The absorbing boundary is CPML and the number of CPML layers is 6 in the six directions. The white buffer space in the six directions includes 10 uniform cells. It takes 3 min and 24 s for 100,000 time steps on the VALU platform. The simulation result is also plotted in Fig. 5.10 for the sake of comparison.

The GPU and VALU performances are 933 NMCPS and 524 NMCPS, respectively. Namely, one NVIDIA GeFore GTX480 is as fast as 7.12 AMD Opteron 6128 CPUs (2.0 GHz) for this example.

5.4.4 Stripfed dielectric resonator antenna

The dimensions of stripfed dielectric resonator antenna are described in Fig. 5.11(a), and the stripfed structure is shown in Fig. 5.11(b).

In the CUDA FDTD simulation, the cell size is chosen to be 0.3575 mm, 0.5 mm, and 0.5 mm in the x-, y-, and z-directions, respectively. The total number of cells including the PML layers in the x-, y-, and z-directions is 120, 110, and 88, respectively. The absorbing boundary is CPML and the number of CPML layers is 8 in the six directions. The white buffer space in the six directions includes 10 uniform cells. It takes 21 s for 10,000 time steps on the NVIDIA GeFore GTX480 GPU platform with far-field pattern outputs at two frequencies. The simulation result is S_{11} only, which is shown in Fig. 5.12.

For the same problem, the non-uniform cell size (the adjacent cell ratio is 1.05) is selected to be 0.3 mm, and the number of cells is 124, 100, and 88 in the x-, y-, and

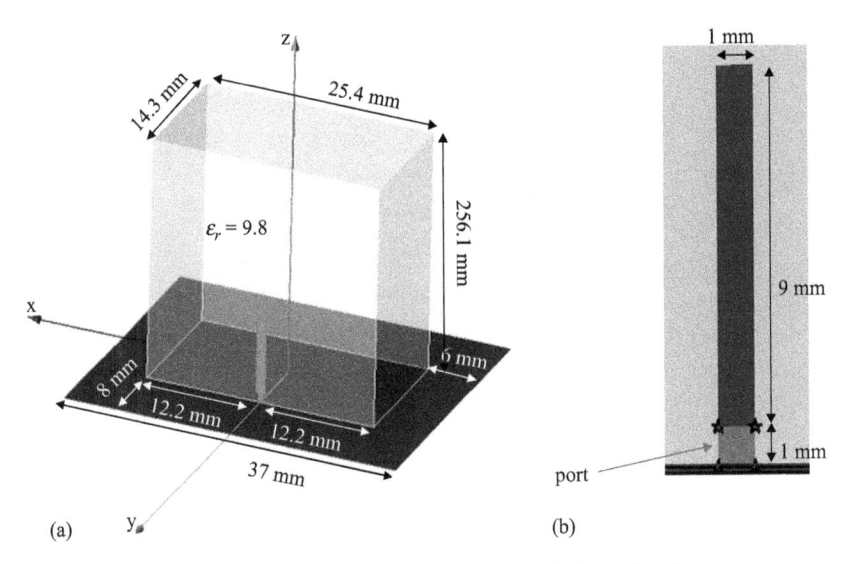

Figure 5.11 Dimensions of dielectric resonator antenna and the stripfed structure: (a) dimensions of dielectric block and ground, (b) stripfed structure.

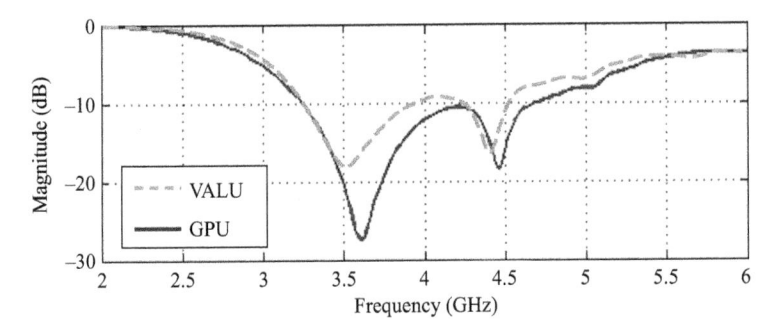

Figure 5.12 S_{11} variation of stripfed dielectric resonator antenna with frequency.

z-directions, respectively. The parallel partition is $2 \times 2 \times 2$, namely, the number of sub-domains is 2 in the x-, y-, and z-directions. The absorbing boundary is CPML and the number of CPML layers is 6 in the six directions. The white buffer space in the six directions includes 10 uniform cells. It takes 32 s for 10,000 time steps on the VALU platform. The simulation result is also plotted in Fig. 5.12.

The GPU and VALU performances are 550 NMCPS and 320 NMCPS, respectively. Namely, one NVIDIA GeFore GTX480 is as fast as 6.8 AMD Opteron 6128 CPUs (2.0 GHz) for this example.

5.4.5 Square-ring patch antenna

Dimensions of square-ring patch antenna [20] are described in Fig. 5.13. Dielectric substrate is finite and its dielectric constant and conductivity are 4.4 and 0.01, respectively.

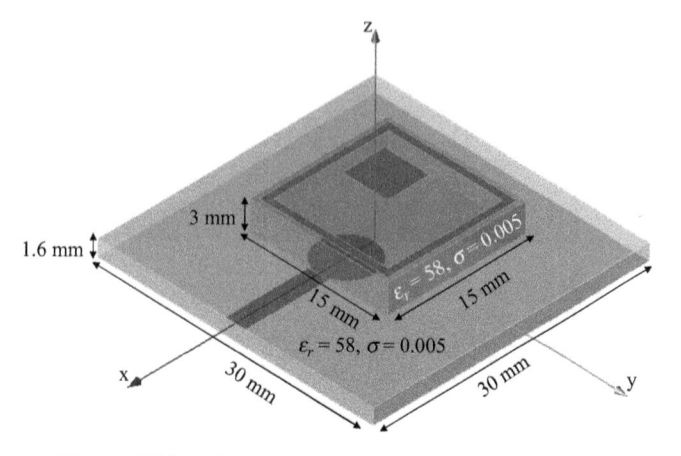

Figure 5.13   Dimensions of square-ring patch antenna.

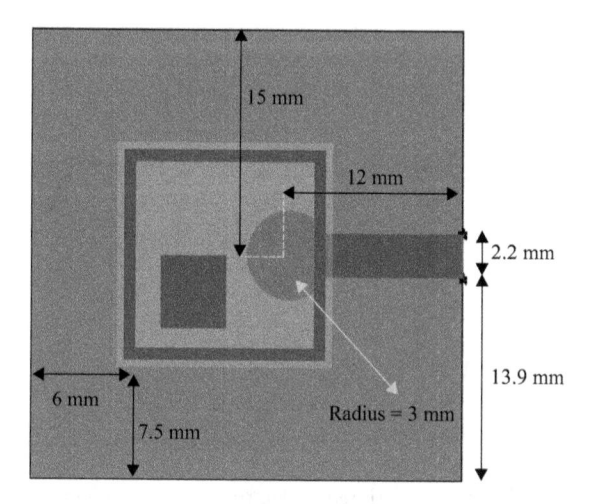

Figure 5.14   Square-ring location and feed structure and dimensions.

The ring location on the top surface of the substrate is shown in Fig. 5.14. The feed structure and dimensions are also shown in the same figure.

The square patch location on the top surface of the substrate is shown in Fig. 5.15. The ring width is also shown in the same figure.

In the CUDA FDTD simulation, the cell size is chosen to be 0.1 mm in the x-, y-, and z-directions. The total number of cells including the PML layers in the x-, y-, and z-directions is 356, 356, and 106, respectively. The absorbing boundary is CPML and the number of CPML layers is 8 in the six directions. The white buffer space in the six directions includes 10 uniform cells. It takes 242 min for 1,000,000 time steps on the NVIDIA GeFore GTX480 GPU platform. The simulation result is S_{11} only, which is shown in Fig. 5.16.

For the same problem, the non-uniform cell size (the adjacent cell ratio is 1.05) is selected to be 0.2 mm, and the number of cells is 142, 149, and 53 in the x-, y-, and

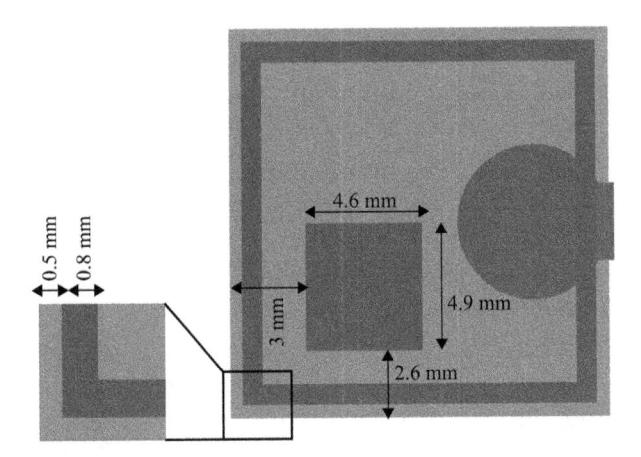

Figure 5.15 Patch dimensions and locations.

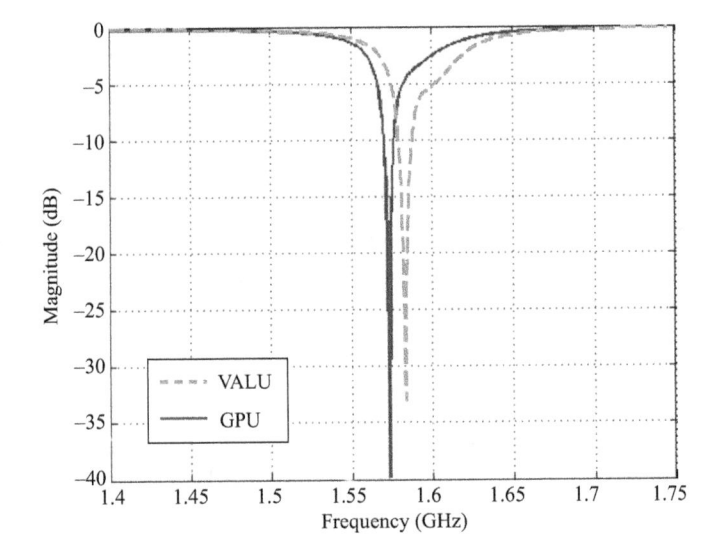

Figure 5.16 S_{11} variation of square-ring patch antenna with frequency.

z-directions, respectively. The parallel partition is $4 \times 2 \times 1$, namely, the number of sub-domains is 4, 2, and 1 in the x-, y-, and z-directions, respectively. The absorbing boundary is CPML and the number of CPML layers is 6 in the six directions. The white buffer space in the six directions includes 10 uniform cells. It takes 11 min and 32 s for 300,000 time steps on the VALU platform. The simulation result is also plotted in Fig. 5.16 for the sake of comparison.

The GPU and VALU performances are 925 NMCPS and 485 NMCPS, respectively. Namely, one NVIDIA GeFore GTX480 is as fast as 7.6 AMD Opteron 6128 CPUs (2.0 GHz) for this example.

References

[1] M. Inman, A. Elsherbeni, and C. Smith, "GPU Programming for FDTD Calculations," *The Applied Computational Electromagnetics Society (ACES) Conference*, 2005.

[2] M. Inman and A. Elsherbeni, "Programming Video Cards for Computational Electromagnetics Applications," *IEEE Antennas and Propagation Magazine*, Vol. 47, No. 6, December 2005, pp. 71–78.

[3] M. Inman and A. Elsherbeni, "Acceleration of Field Computations Using Graphical Processing Units," *The Twelfth Biennial IEEE Conference on Electromagnetic Field Computation CEFC 2006*, April 30–May 3, 2006.

[4] M. Inman, A. Elsherbeni, J. Maloney, and B. Baker, "Practical Implementation of a CPML Absorbing Boundary for GPU Accelerated FDTD Technique," *The 23rd Annual Review of Progress in Applied Computational Electromagnetics Society*, March 2007, pp. 19–23.

[5] M. Inman, A. Elsherbeni, J. Maloney, and B. Baker, "Practical Implementation of a CPML Absorbing Boundary for GPU Accelerated FDTD Technique," *Applied Computational Electromagnetics Society Journal*, Vol. 23, No. 1, 2008, pp. 16–22.

[6] M. Inman and A. Elsherbeni, "Optimization and Parameter Exploration Using GPU Based FDTD Solvers," *IEEE MTT-S International Microwave Symposium Digest*, June 2008, pp. 149–152.

[7] M. Inman, A. Elsherbeni, and V. Demir, "Graphics Processing Unit Acceleration of Finite Difference Time Domain," Ch. 12, in *The Finite Difference Time Domain Method for Electromagnetics (with MATLAB Simulations)*, SciTech Publishing, 2009.

[8] N. Takada, N. Masuda, T. Tanaka, Y. Abe, and T. Ito, "A GPU Implementation of the 2-D Finite-Difference Time-Domain Code Using High Level Shader Language," *Applied Computational Electromagnetics Society Journal*, Vol. 23, No. 4, 2008, pp. 309–316.

[9] S. Krakiwsky, L. Turner, and M. Okoniewski, "Graphics Processor Unit (GPU) Acceleration of Finite-Difference Time-Domain (FDTD) Algorithm," *Proceedings of the 2004 International Symposium on Circuits and Systems*, Vol. 5, May 2004, pp. V-265–V-268.

[10] S. Krakiwsky, L. Turner, and M. Okoniewski, "Acceleration of Finite-Difference Time-Domain (FDTD) Using Graphics Processor Units (GPU)," *2004 IEEE MTT-S International Microwave Symposium Digest*, Vol. 2, June 2004, pp. 1033–1036.

[11] S. Adams, J. Payne, and R. Boppana, "Finite Difference Time Domain (FDTD) Simulations Using Graphics Processors," *Proceedings of the 2007 DoD High Performance Computing Modernization Program Users Group (HPCMP) Conference*, 2007, pp. 334–338.

[12] NVIDIA CUDA zone, http://www.nvidia.com/object/cuda_home.html

[13] *CUDA 2.1 Quickstart Guide*, http://www.nvidia.com/object/cuda_develop.html

[14] P. Sypek, A. Dziekonski, and M. Mrozowski, "How to Render FDTD Computations More Effective Using a Graphics Accelerator," *IEEE Transactions on Magnetics*, Vol. 45, No. 3, 2009, pp. 1324–1327.

[15] V. Demir and A. Elsherbeni, "Compute Unified Device Architecture (CUDA) Based Finite-Difference Time-Domain (FDTD) Implementation," *Journal of the Applied Computational Electromagnetics Society (ACES)*, Vol. 25, No. 4, April 2010, pp. 303–314.

[16] P. Micikevicius, "3D Finite Difference Computation on GPUs Using CUDA," *GPGPU-2 Proceedings of 2nd Workshop on General Purpose Processing on Graphics Processing Units*, 2009, pp. 79–84.

[17] *CUDA 2.1 Programming Guide*, http://www.nvidia.com/object/cuda_develop.html

[18] V. Demir and A. Elsherbeni, "Utilization of CUDA-OpenGL Interoperability to Display Electromagnetic Fields Calculated by FDTD," *Computational Electromagnetics International Workshop (CEM'11)*, Izmir, Turkey, August 10–13, 2011.

[19] B. Li and K. Leung, "Strip-fed Rectangular Dielectric Resonator Antennas with/without a Parasitic Patch," *IEEE Transactions on Antennas and Propagation*, Vol. 53, No. 7, 2005, pp. 2200–2207.

[20] H. Chen, Y. Wang, Y. Lin, et al., "Microstrip-Fed Circularly Polarized Square-Ring Patch Antenna for GPS Applications," *IEEE Transactions on Antennas and Propagation*, Vol. 57, No. 4, 2009, pp. 264–1267.

Engineering Applications

In this chapter, we apply the FDTD method advanced by the parallel processing and SSE acceleration techniques [1–9] in solutions to a variety of practical engineering problems and demonstrate its advantages over other electromagnetic simulation techniques. We first introduce the hardware platform configuration and then apply the parallel FDTD code enhanced by the SSE technique to solve the problems. The performance of VALU acceleration is associated not only with the hardware configuration and code structure but also with the problem model, excitation type, and output options. The parallel FDTD code used in this chapter has been optimized for the best performance in terms of the VALU acceleration, mesh generation, model handling, excitation, and output processing. The examples include a helix antenna array, dielectric lens, electromagnetic analysis of an automobile and a helicopter, finite-sized frequency selective surface (FSS), curved FSS, microwave filter, reverberation chamber, airplane wireless fidelity (WIFI) analysis, low-pass filter, microwave divider, and waveguide slot antenna array.

6.1 Hardware Platform Description

Here, we introduce the basic configuration of hardware platforms used in examples. Hardware parts of the workstation, as indicated in Fig. 6.1, are available from popular online stores. The system is optimized by the authors to achieve the best simulation performance.

All simulations in the chapter, except when explicitly specified otherwise, are carried out on either a 4-CPU workstation with 64-GB memory or a 4-workstation cluster with a total of eight CPUs and 128-GB memory. The configuration in Fig. 6.1 is detailed in Table 6.1.

We first look at an ideal case to investigate the performance of the parallel FDTD code with and without the VALU acceleration option. We have demonstrated that the VALU performance is almost four times faster than that of the ALU in the ideal test case [2]. When a practical FDTD code is applied to solve engineering problems, the VALU performance varies with the involved models and simulation options. Here, we employ a simple example as the test case in which we can isolate the FDTD update from other options such as the PML boundary, dispersive medium, far-field transformation, material distribution generation, mesh generation, and output options, which enables us to investigate the VALU performance for the FDTD update alone.

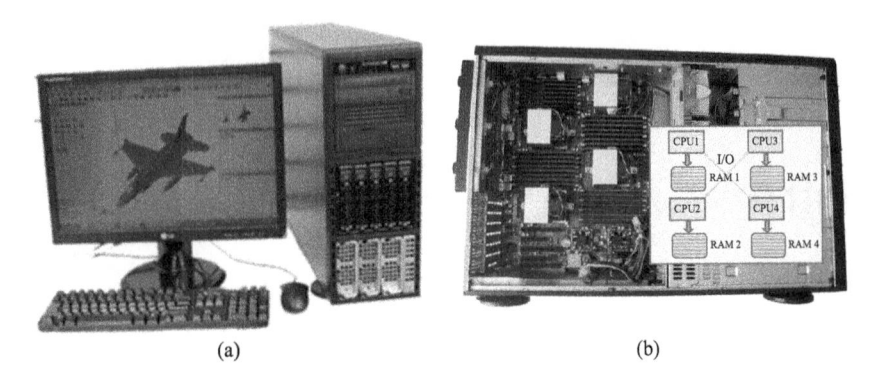

(a)   (b)

Figure 6.1 Optimized workstation for electromagnetic simulations: (a) main setup and
(b) 4-CPU configuration with NUMA architecture. The operating system can be
either Windows or Linux.

Table 6.1 Hardware configuration of the workstation in Fig. 6.1.

Option	Description
CPU	AMD Opteron 6168 1.9 GHz
Memory	64 GB DDR3 1333 MHz
Motherboard	SuperMicro
Operating system	Linux (CentOS 5.2)
Hard drive	500GB 7200 turns/min

The test structure is an empty cubical computational domain truncated by a PEC
boundary over all six sides of the cube and discretized into a uniform mesh with different
numbers of cells in each test case, namely, with 300, 400, 500, 600, 800, and 1000 million
cells, respectively. Each case is run twice, with and without the VALU acceleration option.
The performance comparison of the two options is plotted in Fig. 6.2. Again, the parallel
FDTD code used is a practical code that is fully optimized for both options. It is worth
mentioning that the Intel compiler partially uses VALU in the reference code without VALU
acceleration. In principle, if the processor is sufficiently fast and the memory bandwidth is a
bottleneck, continued improvement of the CPU performance is not relevant. The code performance improvement and memory optimization techniques that result in the data discontinuity inside memory have a major conflict with the requirements of VALU
acceleration. Therefore, in the parallel FDTD code development, a trade-off must be made
between the code performance and memory usage.

Next, we test the parallel FDTD code on a workstation cluster including 16 workstations, and the configuration of each workstation is described in Table 6.1, as shown in
Fig. 6.3. The Infiniband network system is used to link 16 workstations together. The size
of test examples varies from 27 MB to 10,000 MB. In each test case, we use a different
number of nodes and the simulation performance is summarized in Fig. 6.4. It is observed
from the figure that the simulation performance on one 16-workstation cluster can reach up
to 11,500 Mcells/s.

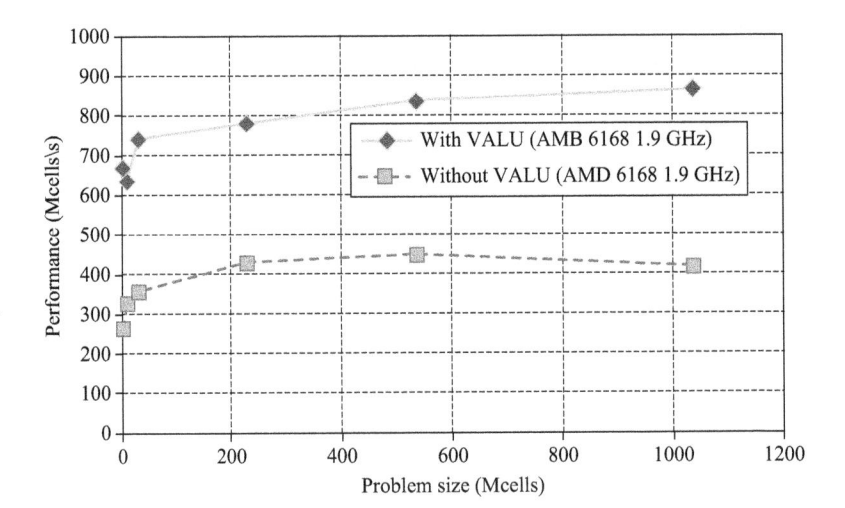

Figure 6.2   Performance comparison of the FDTD code with and without VALU acceleration option on a 4-CPU AMD workstation vs. the number of cells in the mesh of an empty cubical computational domain (ideal test case).

Figure 6.3   A 16-workstation cluster for the parallel FDTD benchmark.

6.2 Performance Investigation of VALU Acceleration Technique

Before proceeding to practical examples, we consider a large realistic problem to investigate the VALU performance on different hardware platforms with different operating systems. The hardware platforms are listed as follows:

(1) 2-CPU workstation installed with Windows operating system
- 2 AMD Opteron 6128 2.0 GHz CPUs
- Total number of cores: 16

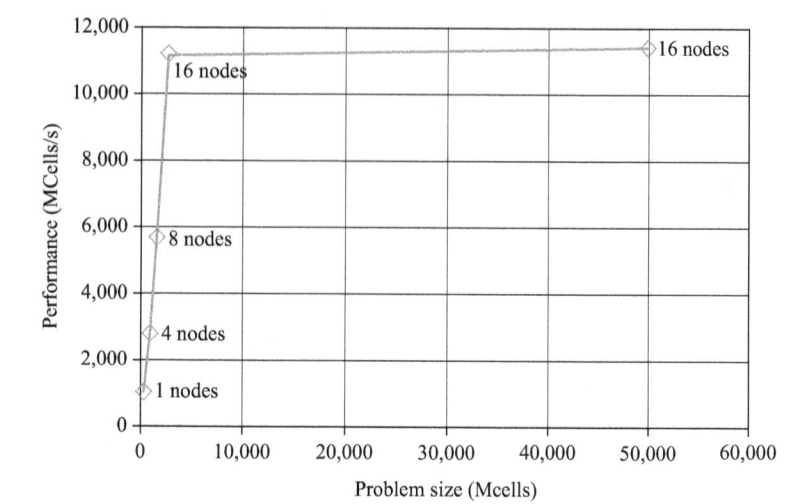

Figure 6.4 Performance of the parallel FDTD code on the 16-workstation cluster in Fig. 6.3.

- Memory: 64-GB DDR3 1,333 MHz
- Hard drive: 7,200 turns/min
- NUMA architecture
- Windows XP

(2) 2-CPU workstation installed with Linux operating system
- 2 AMD Opteron 6128 2.0 GHz CPUs
- Total number of cores: 16
- Linux CentOS version 5.2
- Memory: 64-GB DDR3 1,333 MHz
- Hard drive: 7,200 turns/min
- NUMA architecture

(3) 4-CPU workstation installed with Windows operating system
- 4 AMD Opteron 6128 2.0 GHz CPUs
- Total number of cores: 32
- Memory: 64-GB DDR3 1,333 MHz
- Hard drive: 7,200 turns/minute
- NUMA architecture
- Windows XP

(4) 4-CPU workstation installed with Linux operating system
- 4 AMD Opteron 6168 1.9 GHz CPUs
- Total number of cores: 48
- Memory: 64-GB DDR3 1,333 MHz
- Hard drive: 7,200 turns/min
- NUMA architecture
- Linux CentOS version 5.2

(5) 4-workstation cluster installed with Linux operating system
- 8 AMD Opteron 6128 2.0 GHz CPUs
- Total number of cores: 64

- Memory: 128-GB DDR3 1,333 MHz
- Hard drive: 7,200 turns/min
- NUMA architecture
- Infiniband network system
- Linux CentOS version 5.2

Since each AMD CPU includes two physical CPUs, to achieve a better parallel performance, we partition the domain into sub-domains, the number of which is equal to twice the number of physical CPUs.

We present two examples, a microwave connector with S-parameter outputs only and a scattering problem with the output of conformal surface current distributions on the electric conductor, and investigate the performance of VALU acceleration.

In the first example, the microwave connector has eight ports, as shown in Fig. 6.5. The connector includes two pieces that are mounted on two separate plastic parts and are used to realize the connection between components. We use the differential Gaussian pulse to excite one port at the time, with the remaining ports being terminated by 50-Ω matching loads. The outputs are the port voltage, current, impedance, and S-parameter matrix. We use the platforms listed above to simulate this connector. S_{11}, S_{21}, and the impedance at the excitation port are plotted in Figs. 6.6 and 6.7, respectively.

Data continuity inside memory is a very important factor that affects the performance of the VALU acceleration. For the microwave connector problem, the main bottleneck is the conformal implementation, which results in the data discontinuity inside memory. If the

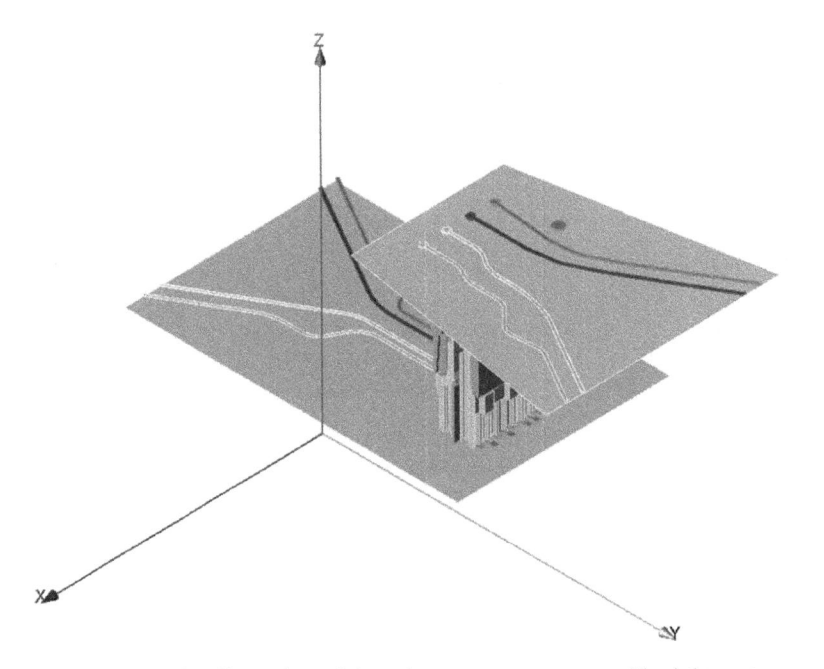

Figure 6.5 Configuration of the microwave connector with eight ports.

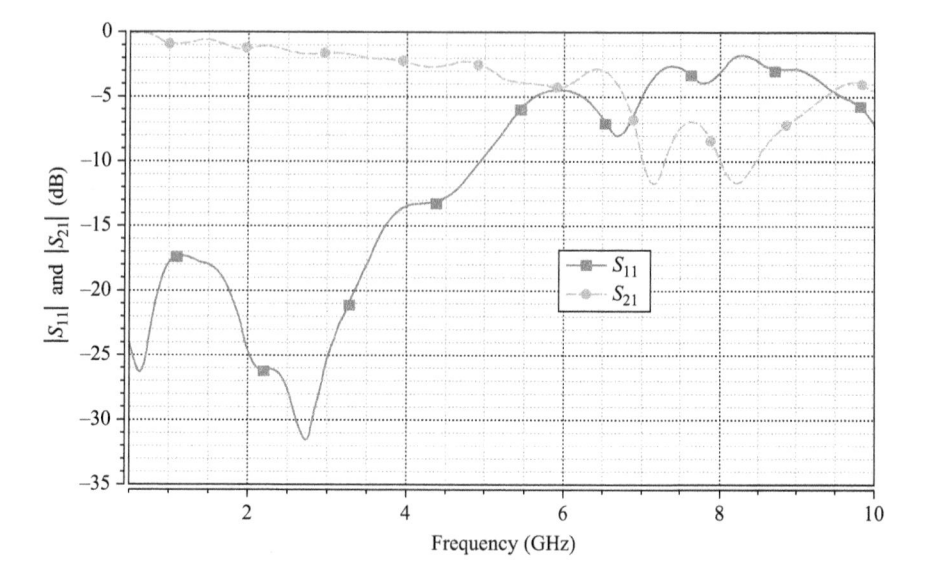

Figure 6.6   Variation of S_{11} and S_{21} parameters of the microwave connector in Fig. 6.5 vs. frequency.

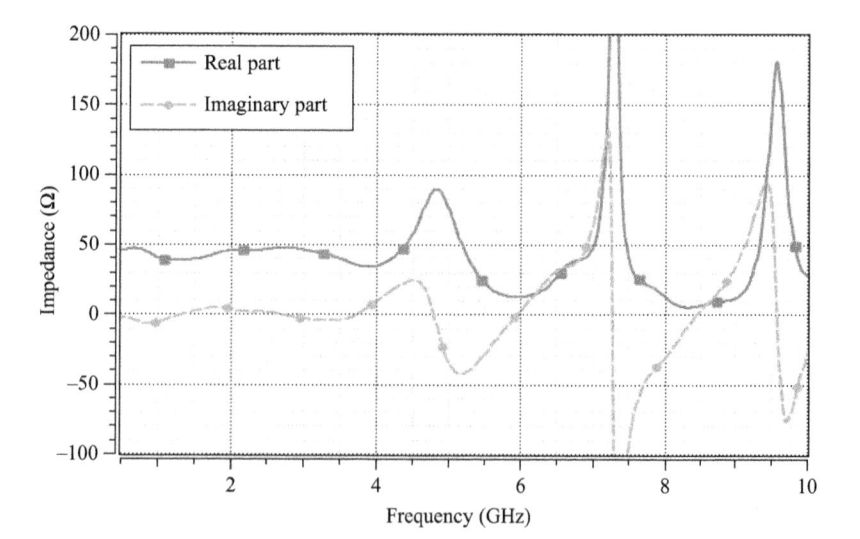

Figure 6.7   Impedance at the excitation port of the microwave connector in Fig. 6.5 vs. frequency.

Table 6.2 Performance summary for the microwave connector in Fig. 6.5 with dispersive media.

Hardware Platform	OS	CPU	Simulation Time
2-CPU workstation (VALU)	Windows XP	2 AMD 6128 2.0 GHz	221 min
2-CPU workstation (no VALU)	Windows XP	2 AMD 6128 2.0 GHz	313 min
4-CPU workstation (VALU)	Linux CentOS	4 AMD 6128 2.0 GHz	52 min
4-CPU workstation (no VALU)	Linux CentOS	4 AMD 6128 2.0 GHz	71 min
4-CPU workstation (VALU)	Linux CentOS	4 AMD 6168 1.9 GHz	46 min
4-CPU workstation (no VALU)	Linux CentOS	4 AMD 6168 1.9 GHz	62 min
4-Node cluster (VALU)	Linux CentOS	8 AMD 6128 2.0 GHz	52 min
4-Node cluster (no VALU)	Linux CentOS	8 AMD 6168 2.0 GHz	68 min

dielectric substrate is a dispersive medium, it will further deteriorate the performance of the VALU acceleration. The simulation performance for different cases on different platforms is summarized in Table 6.2.

Next, we investigate the performance of VALU on the conformal technique and dispersive medium implementation in the parallel FDTD code. The distribution of the deformed cells inside the computational domain varies from case to case. Usually, we use the small size of arrays to describe the discontinuous data distributed in the computational domain, instead of using a large array that has the same size as the computational domain. The issue in this case is that the data in the specified array are not continuous any more. Therefore, the parallel FDTD code may not benefit from the VALU acceleration. For a large curved PEC body, we may not observe much advantage of the VALU acceleration over the traditional parallel FDTD code. In addition, even for a traditional parallel FDTD code, today's Intel compilers partially use VALU to improve the simulation performance. The parallel FDTD code used in this text has been fully optimized by an Intel compiler.

Fig. 6.8 shows the magnetic field distribution inside a deformed cell obtained by the conformal FDTD method [3]. The magnetic field is located at the center of the cell, as in the traditional FDTD method. The electric fields are located at the same sides as in the regular FDTD method, but have non-zero values only outside the PEC conductor. The magnetic field inside the deformed cell can be expressed as shown in Fig. 6.8.

$$H_z^{n+1/2}(i+1/2,j+1/2,k) = H_z^{n-1/2}(i+1/2,j+1/2,k)$$

$$+\frac{\Delta t}{\mu_z}\left[\begin{array}{c} \dfrac{\Delta x_0 E_x^n(i+1/2,j+1,k) - \Delta x E_x^n(i+1/2,j,k)}{\Delta x_0 \Delta y_0} \\ -\dfrac{\Delta y_0 E_y^n(i+1,j+1/2,k) - \Delta y E_y^n(i,j+1/2,k)}{\Delta x_0 \Delta y_0} \end{array}\right]$$

$$(6.1)$$

It is observed from (6.1) that the update formulation inside deformed cells is different from the regular FDTD update. In order to accelerate the simulation, we mark and index the deformed cells, and then carry out the regular FDTD update in the entire domain. After the regular simulation is completed, we go back to use (6.1) to recalculate the magnetic field

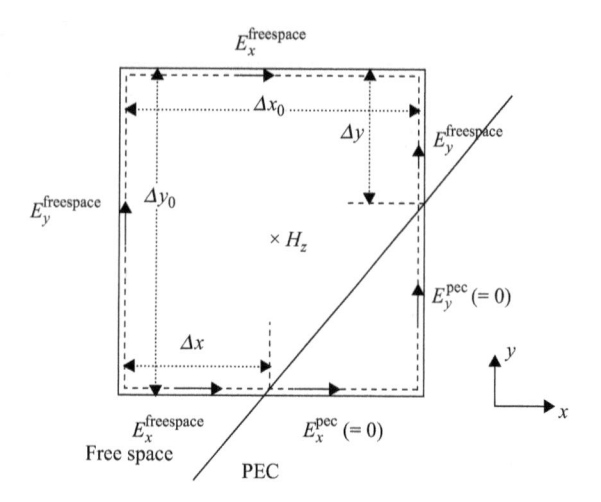

Figure 6.8   Distribution of electric and magnetic fields inside a deformed cell.

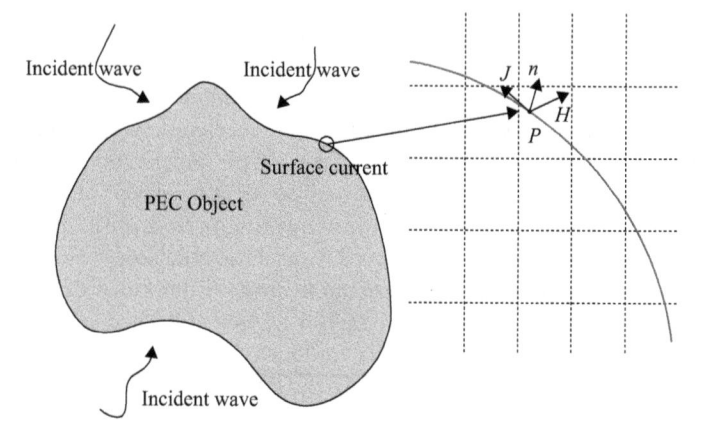

Figure 6.9   Description for the general conformal surface current problems.

inside these cells. In this case, the magnetic and electric fields inside these cells are not continuous in any direction. For problems that include a large number of deformed cells, the VALU acceleration will be slower than for those without deformed cells.

6.3 Surface Current Calculation Technique

When compared to the method of moments (MoM) and finite element method (FEM) methods, one of the major drawbacks of the parallel FDTD method is a lack of conformal surface current information on the arbitrary shaped conductors. In this section, we describe a way to calculate the conformal surface current distribution in the FDTD simulation [10–12]. The mesh shape in the FDTD update is rectangular and the PEC geometry may be arbitrary, as shown in Fig. 6.9.

In order to calculate the conformal surface current on the surface of an arbitrary PEC geometry, we need the following information:

(1) Normal direction information at the surface of PEC body.
(2) Tangential magnetic field at the same point.

After generating the mesh and material distributions, we do not have the pieces of information above in the FDTD simulation since they are not required by the FDTD update. To this end, we need to generate a surface mesh that intersects with the FDTD mesh, and the normal direction at each point is included in the surface mesh. The tangential component of the magnetic field on the PEC surface will be generated by the nearby magnetic fields in the FDTD meshes through the spatial interpolation. Using the electromagnetic field boundary conditions on the PEC surface, the electric surface current at the point P can be expressed as:

$$\vec{J} = \hat{n} \times \vec{H} \tag{6.2}$$

where $\hat{n}$ and $\vec{H}$ are the normal unit vector on the surface and the magnetic field vector at the observation point P, respectively. Using the triangular surface mesh to approximate the PEC surface is a conventional choice in electromagnetic simulation techniques. The triangular mesh information includes the three-node coordinates and the index of each triangular mesh, which is standard in the 3-D mesh generation. The surface current located at the vertex of each triangle can be obtained by the interpolation method. The normal unit vector at each vertex can be expressed as follows:

$$\hat{n}_{\text{center}} = \sum_{i=1}^{N} a_i \hat{n}^i_{\text{center}} \tag{6.3}$$

where $\hat{n}^i_{\text{center}}$ is the normal unit vector for the ith triangle at the considered vertex, and a_i is the ith angle related to the vertex point, as shown in Fig. 6.10. Also, $\hat{n}_{\text{center}}$ and α can be obtained by the three-node coordinates given by the triangular mesh information in the surface modeling process:

$$n_{\text{center}} = (x_3 - x_2, y_3 - y_2, z_3 - z_2) - (x_1 - x_2, y_1 - y_2, z_1 - z_2) \tag{6.4a}$$

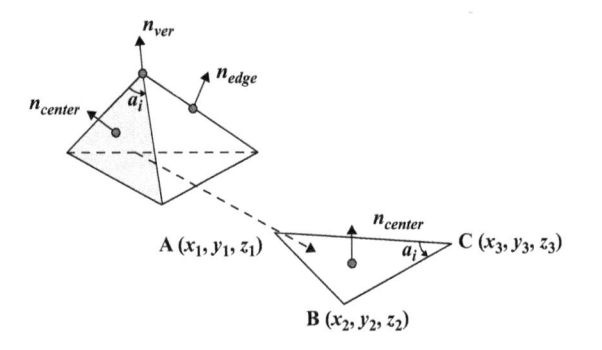

Figure 6.10 Calculation of the vertex normal vector.

$$\alpha = \arccos\left(\frac{a^2 + b^2 - c^2}{2ab}\right)$$ (6.4b)

where x_u, y_u, and z_u ($u = 1, 2,$ and 3) are the vertex coordinates of the triangle; parameters a, b, and c are lengths of the triangle edges. In cases of triangles with one edge being too small compared to the other two, the formulation should be modified by removing such weak triangles.

To calculate the magnetic field H at the chosen point, we need to first identify the corresponding points in the FDTD mesh, as shown in Fig. 6.11.

The magnetic field H at the observation point P can be calculated by using the magnetic field components in the x-, y-, and z-directions in the related FDTD cells. The points P_1, P_2, and P_3 are the projection positions of the point P on three coordinate system planes. The magnetic field H at each point can be calculated as follows:

$$H_{R1} = \frac{d_{z1}}{\Delta z} H_x(Q_{11}) + \frac{d_{z2}}{\Delta z} H_x(Q_{12})$$ (6.5a)

$$H_{R2} = \frac{d_{z1}}{\Delta z} H_x(Q_{21}) + \frac{d_{z2}}{\Delta z} H_x(Q_{22})$$ (6.5b)

$$H_x(P_1) = \frac{d_{y1}}{\Delta y} H_{R1} + \frac{d_{y2}}{\Delta y} H_{R2}$$ (6.5c)

$$H_x(P_1) = \frac{d_{y1}}{\Delta y}\left(\frac{d_{z1}}{\Delta z} H_x(Q_{11}) + \frac{d_{z2}}{\Delta z} H_x(Q_{12})\right) + \frac{d_{y2}}{\Delta y}\left(\frac{d_{z1}}{\Delta z} H_x(Q_{21}) + \frac{d_{z2}}{\Delta z} H_x(Q_{22})\right)$$ (6.5d)

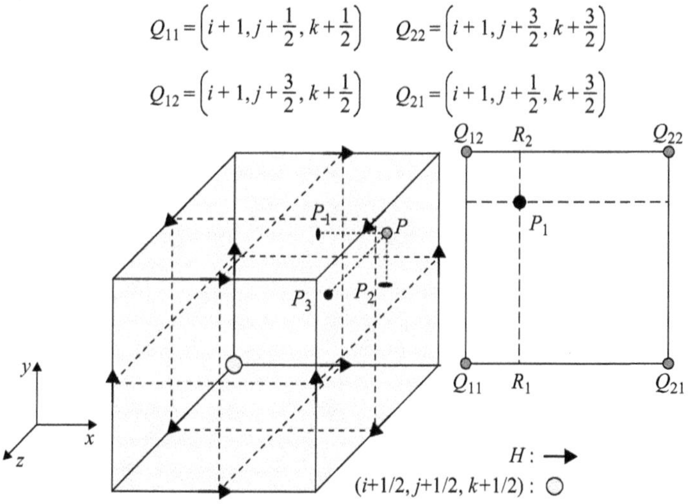

$$Q_{11} = \left(i+1, j+\frac{1}{2}, k+\frac{1}{2}\right) \quad Q_{22} = \left(i+1, j+\frac{3}{2}, k+\frac{3}{2}\right)$$

$$Q_{12} = \left(i+1, j+\frac{3}{2}, k+\frac{1}{2}\right) \quad Q_{21} = \left(i+1, j+\frac{1}{2}, k+\frac{3}{2}\right)$$

Figure 6.11   Vertex in the surface mesh and the associated points in the FDTD mesh.

where d_y and d_z are the distances between P_1 and the observation location of the magnetic field H_x in the y- and z-directions, respectively, and Δy and Δz are the corresponding cell sizes. The interpolation formulas need to be modified for some special cases. If any H fields in one direction are located inside the PEC body but are outside the PEC body in the staircasing approximation, their values at these points should be forced to be zero. If all the four H fields are equal to zero, the interpolation formula becomes invalid and should be modified accordingly. One improved scheme is to extend the interpolation domain that includes 27 cells (16 cells in one direction). The interpolation formula can be modified to the following format:

$$H_x(P) = \left(1 - \frac{d_u}{\sum_{u=0}^{N} d_u}\right) H_x(Q_u) + \cdots + \left(1 - \frac{d_N}{\sum_{u=0}^{N} d_u}\right) H_x(Q_N) \qquad (6.6)$$

where N is the number of H_x fields that are not equal to zero and d_u is the distance between the location of the uth H_x field and the point P. To get the current value at the chosen point P, such points are placed at the vertices of the triangular mesh. Furthermore, the current at P can be calculated using the boundary condition formula based on the H field information and the normal vector obtained at the previous steps. The current in the frequency domain can be given by:

$$\vec{J}(\vec{P}, \omega_0) = \hat{n}(\vec{P}) \times \vec{H}(\vec{P}, \omega_0) = \begin{bmatrix} \hat{e}_x & \hat{e}_y & \hat{e}_z \\ \hat{n}_x(\vec{P}) & \hat{n}_y(\vec{P}) & \hat{n}_z(\vec{P}) \\ \vec{H}_x(\vec{P}, \omega_0) & \vec{H}_y(\vec{P}, \omega_0) & \vec{H}_z(\vec{P}, \omega_0) \end{bmatrix} \qquad (6.7)$$

where e_u and $n_u(P)$ ($u = x$, y, and z) are the coordinate unit vectors and normal vector components, respectively. As a demonstration example, we calculate the surface current on the surface of a PEC partial sphere with the radius of 1 m illuminated by a plane wave, as shown in Fig. 6.12.

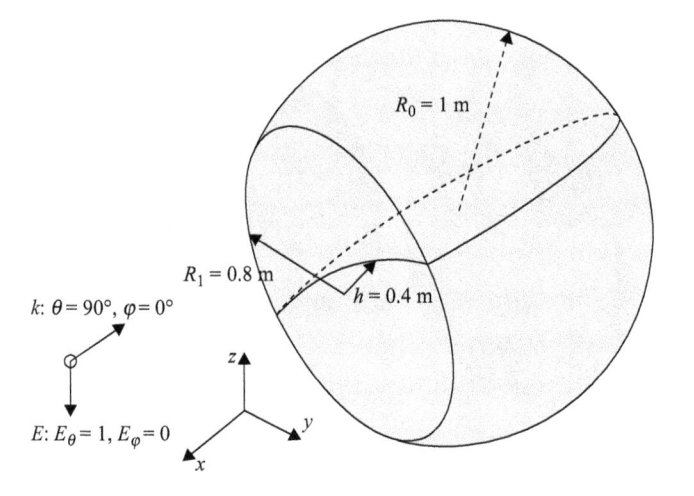

Figure 6.12 A PEC partial sphere illuminated by a plane wave.

To calculate the surface current, we generate a surface triangle mesh for the PEC structure, which only exists on the surface of PEC objects inside the computational domain and is independent from the regular rectangular FDTD mesh. The surface mesh for the surface current is shown in Fig. 6.13. The propagation of the incident plane wave is set in the x-direction with the z-polarization.

Figure 6.14 shows the surface current distributions at frequencies of 300 MHz and 900 MHz, respectively. The electric surface current distribution on the surface mesh is calculated by using the nearby magnetic field information on the regular FDTD cells via the interpolation technique described above.

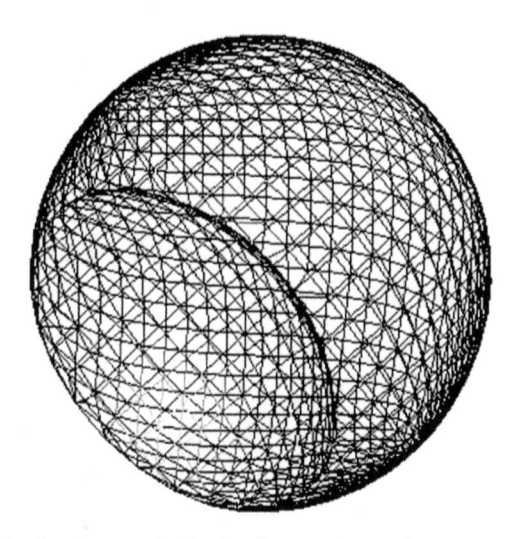

Figure 6.13 Surface mesh distribution on the partial sphere in Fig. 6.12.

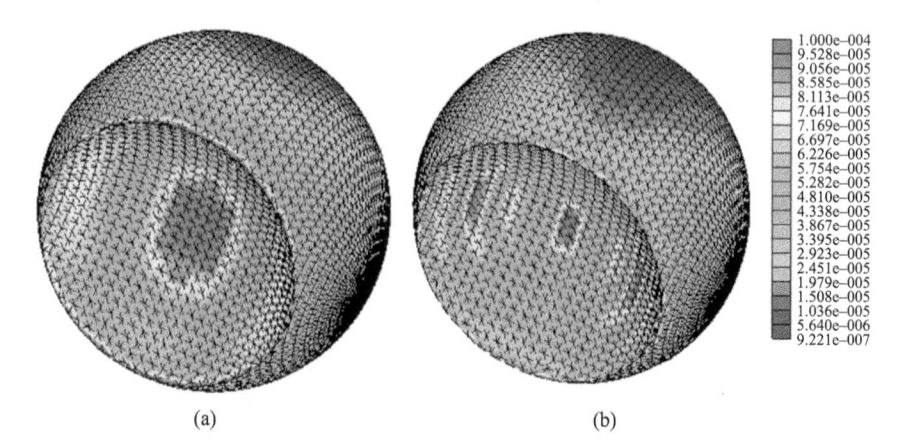

Figure 6.14 Surface current distributions on the partial sphere in Fig. 6.12 at (a) 300 MHz and (b) 900 MHz.

6.4 Helix Antenna Array

The next example is an antenna array consisting of 32 helixes, which are 3 mm × 3 mm in cross section, and are supported by dielectric cores, as shown in Figs. 6.15 and 6.16. Due to the dielectric cores, the FEM- and MoM-based methods may not be efficient enough in handling such a large problem. However, with the parallel FDTD method, we can simulate this structure on the workstation in Fig. 6.1 to calculate the S-parameter matrix and far-field patterns. The parallel FDTD method based on the traditional Yee's grids does not provide the surface information to calculate the conformal surface current distribution on the helix surface. Thus, we use a new conformal technique described in Section 6.3 to calculate the surface current distribution.

In order to validate the conformal parallel FDTD method against the results by the MoM method, we remove the dielectric support cores from the computational domain and simulate the helix array with the PEC plate. The directivity patterns obtained by the two methods are plotted in Fig. 6.17 [6, 9], and we observe a good agreement of the two sets of results. The surface current on the entire helix antenna array is plotted in Fig. 6.18. To calculate the surface current, the surface mesh must be generated before the FDTD simulation, as shown in Fig. 6.19. The surface current distribution on a single helix is shown in Fig. 6.20.

Figure 6.15 A single helix element with a dielectric support core.

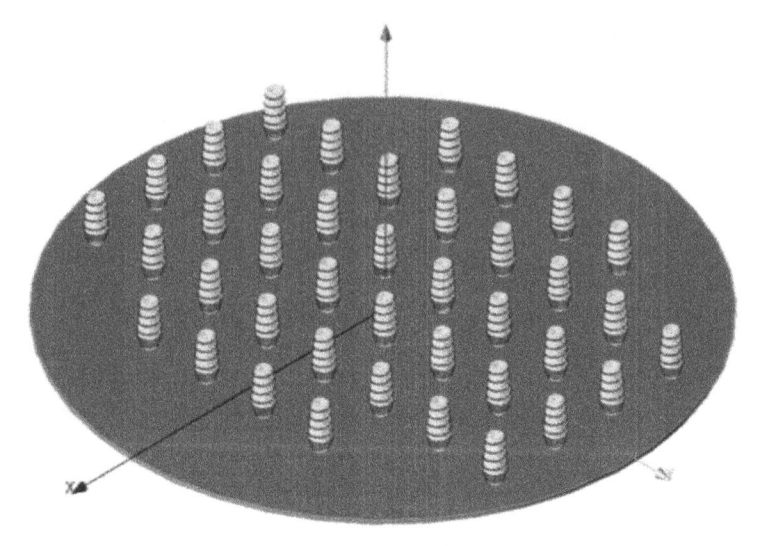

Figure 6.16   A helix antenna array composed of elements in Fig. 6.15, mounted on a circular PEC plate.

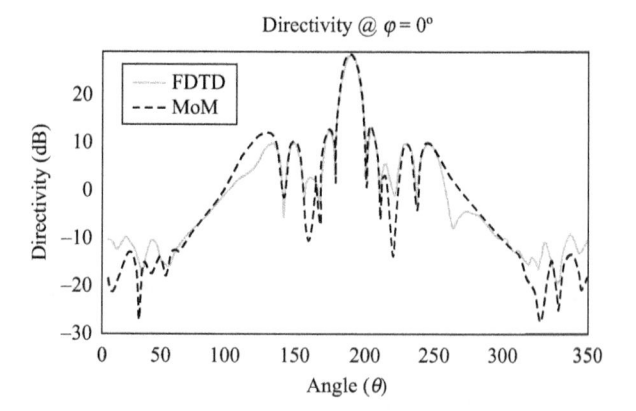

Figure 6.17   Comparison of the directivity patterns at 10 GHz of the antenna array in Fig. 6.16 with dielectric cores omitted using the parallel FDTD and MoM methods.

Simulation summary

- Hardware platform: 4-CPU workstation
- Number of time steps: 7,700
- Convergence: below −30 dB
- Total memory usage: 2.8 GB
- Number of unknowns: 67 Mcells
- Total simulation time: 16 min

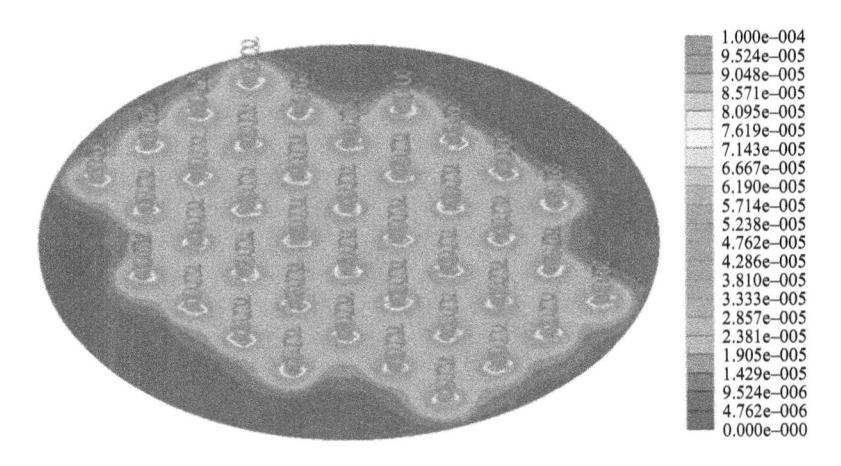

Figure 6.18   Surface current distribution at 10 GHz on the antenna array in Fig. 6.16 (with dielectric cores included).

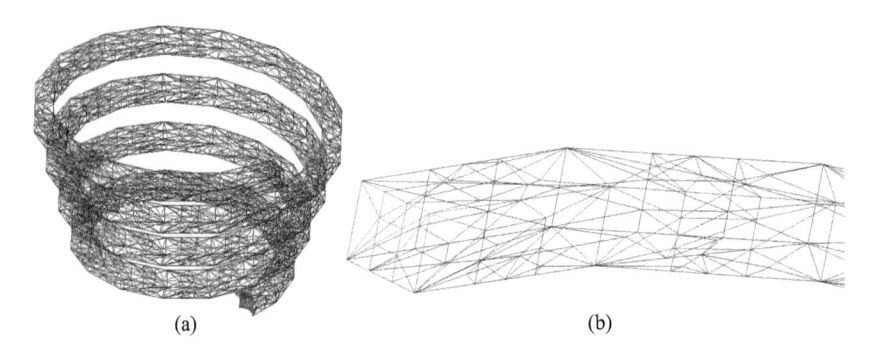

(a)   (b)

Figure 6.19   Conformal surface mesh distribution on the helix in Fig. 6.15: (a) surface mesh at the lower part of the helix and (b) local detail of the mesh.

6.5 Dielectric Lens

The basic concept embedded in the design procedure for the flat lenses is to mimic the phase characteristics of conventional lenses that are composed of homogenous dielectric materials and have specific curved profiles. We take advantage of the symmetric nature of the geometry and reduce the design problem to that of an equivalent 2-D flat lens, as shown in Fig. 6.21. Let D be the diameter of the lens, F the focal length, and r the distance along the radial direction measured from the center of the lens ($0 \leq r < D/2$).

For the 2-D case, our objective is to transform the cylindrical wavefront into a planar one. The phase delay function caused by the path differences can be expressed as [13–18]:

$$\varphi(\theta) = \frac{2\pi F}{\lambda} \frac{1 - \cos\theta}{\cos\theta} \tag{6.8}$$

Figure 6.20   Conformal current distribution at 10 GHz on a single helix in Fig. 6.15 based on the conformal mesh.

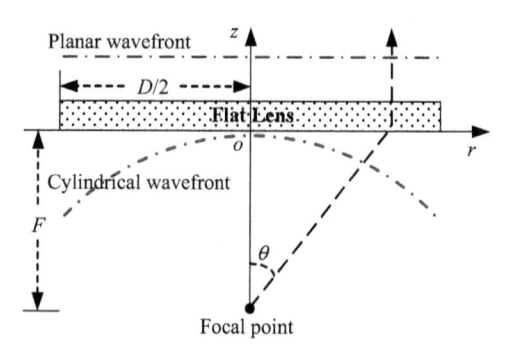

Figure 6.21   2-D schematic diagram of the flat lens.

The required radial phase shift function of the lens is given by:

$$PD_r(\theta) = P_r - \varphi(\theta) \tag{6.9}$$

with the incident angle θ, measured from the focal axis, defined as:

$$\theta = \tan^{-1}(r/F) \tag{6.10}$$

where λ is the wavelength in free space. P_r denotes the reference phase and its value can be chosen as needed to adjust the required phase shift. We observe that the required phase shift function complements the phase delay function. The operating frequency of 30 GHz is selected as our target, while F is chosen to be 6λ and $F/D = 0.5$. The phase delay function is plotted in Fig. 6.22(a) for θ ranging from $-45°$ to $45°$ with P_r equaling $0°$. We notice that the required phase shift has a maximum value on the order of $900°$. Since such a large value is difficult to achieve by using a planar structure, we modify the design to that of a zone plate to cap the required phase shift function to $360°$ and achieve the *desired* phase shift in five sections, as shown in Fig. 6.22(b). The extension of the 2-D analysis to the 3-D case is accomplished by changing the definition of the incident angle expression, given by:

$$\theta = \tan^{-1}(\sqrt{(x^2 + y^2)}/F) \tag{6.11}$$

to the one given below, where we assume that the flat surface of the lens is in the *x-y* plane, and its center is located at the origin of the coordinate system.

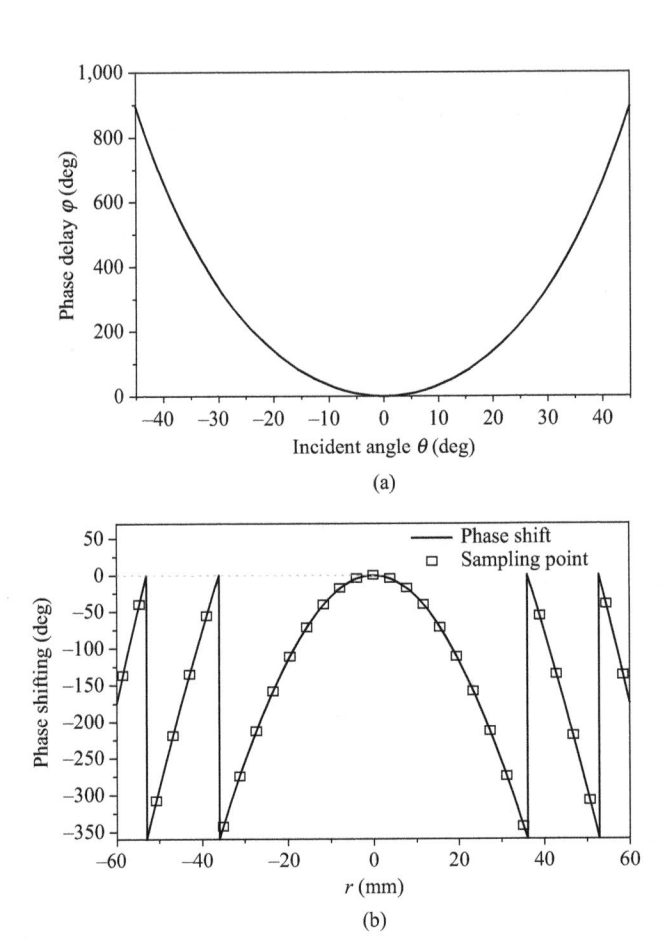

(a)

(b)

Figure 6.22   (a) Phase shift delay function vs. the incident angle θ and (b) zone-plate phase shift function vs. radius.

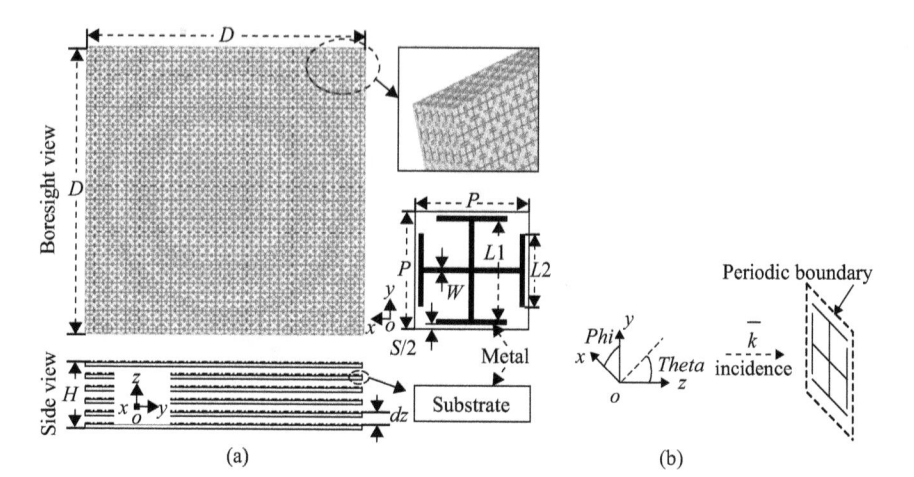

Figure 6.23   Flat lens composed of the JC/FSS: (a) geometry and dimensions ($D = 120.9$ mm, $H = 10.508$ mm, $P = 3.9$ mm, $W = 0.2$ mm, $L1 = 3.2$ mm, $dz = 2.0$ mm, $S = 0.3$ mm, $L2 = 1.6$–2.6 mm) and (b) model of the structure.

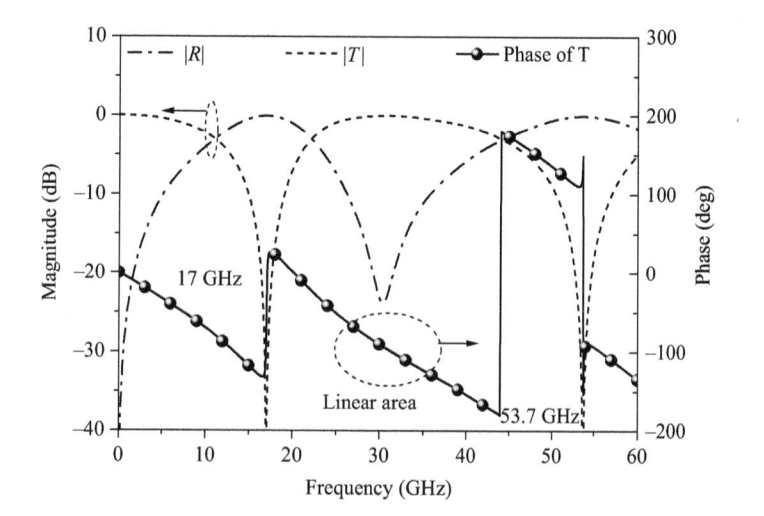

Figure 6.24   Transmission performance of the JC/FSS in Fig. 6.23 for $L2 = 2.2$ mm.

The configuration and dimensions of a Jerusalem cross-frequency selective surface (JC/FSS) are shown in Fig. 6.23. The transmission performance of the JC/FSS is plotted in Fig. 6.24.

Next, we use the parallel FDTD method enhanced with the VALU acceleration to simulate the dielectric lens [13] with six-layer PEC striplines that is illuminated by a rectangular horn antenna. The parallel FDTD code is employed to simulate the dielectric lens system including the feed horn and lens, as shown in Fig. 6.25. Before simulating the

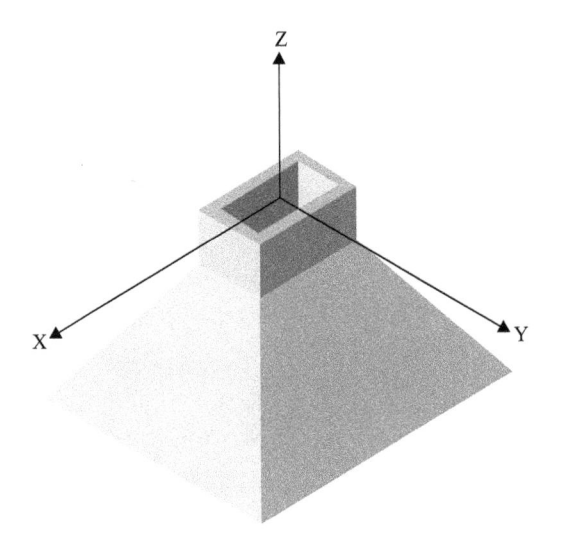

Figure 6.25   Rectangular feed horn excited by a TE_{10} mode.

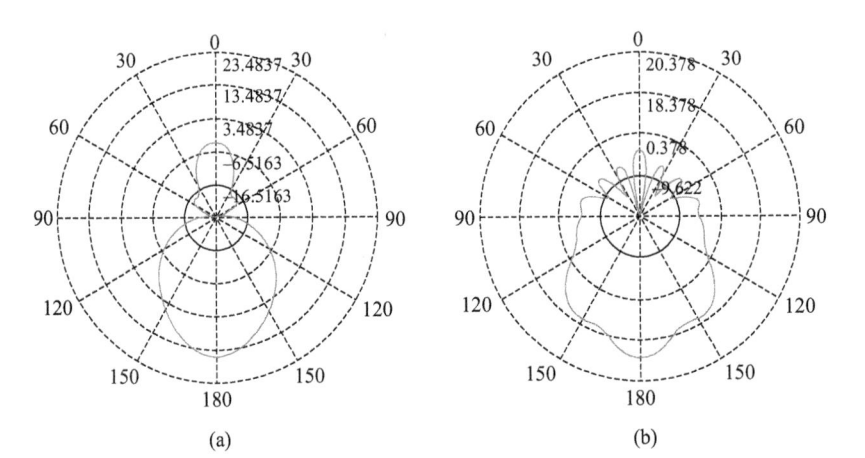

Figure 6.26   Directivity patterns of the feed horn in Fig. 6.25 at 30 GHz in (a) the x-z plane and (b) the y-z plane.

antenna system, we first simulate the feed horn alone to check its directivity, as shown in Fig. 6.26; it turns out to be 13.9 dB.

Since the feed horn, dielectric lens, and excitation source pattern are symmetric about the x-z and y-z planes, we do not need to simulate the entire structure, instead we only need to simulate a quarter of the structure, as shown in Fig. 6.27. The simulation results should be same as for the original problem. The PEC and PMC boundaries are used to truncate the domain in the x- and y-directions, respectively, and such selection is determined by the polarization of the excitation source. If the polarization is E_y, on the other hand, the PEC boundary should be used in the y-direction and the PMC boundary should be used in the x-direction.

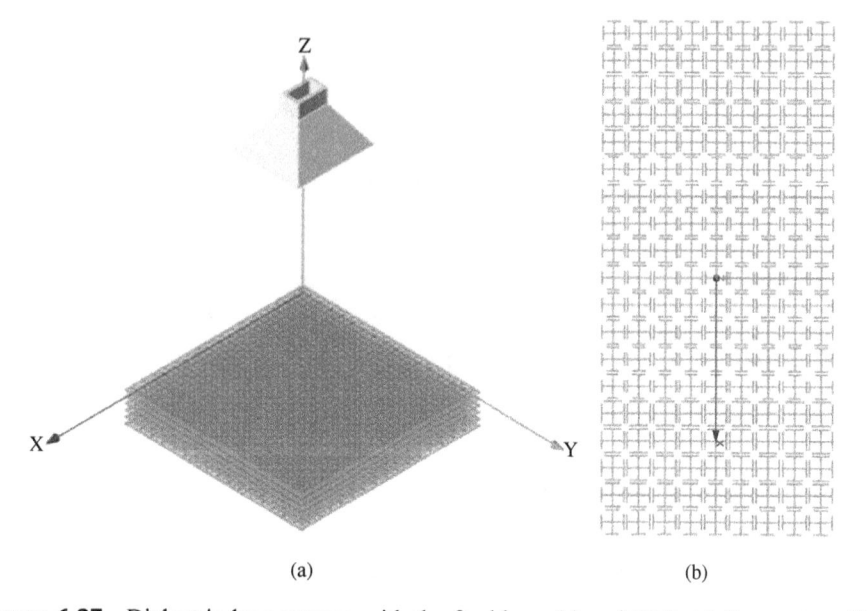

(a)   (b)

Figure 6.27   Dielectric lens antenna with the feed horn (a) and PEC stripline pattern (b).

We choose the JC element for the FSS because of its good phase shift characteristics, good matching (low reflection) properties, and relatively stable frequency behavior over a wide frequency range for both the TE (transverse electric) and TM (transverse magnetic) polarizations. The lens configuration, realized by using JC/FSS, as shown in Fig. 6.27(b), consists of cross-shaped, conducting JC elements printed on dielectric substrates. To achieve the desired phase shift level, that is, a maximum of 360°, as well as relatively wideband low loss, we need a total of six equally spaced layers. The JC geometrical parameters are also noted in Fig. 6.27. Each JC has a fixed cell size of P, and the gap between adjacent JCs is noted as S. Only $L2$ varies for achieving the desired phase shift and all the remaining parameters are fixed as given in the footprint of Fig. 6.27. To consider a realistic model, the substrate is chosen to be Rogers Duroid RT5880 with $\varepsilon_r = 2.2$ and $\tan\sigma = 0.0009$, and a thickness of 0.508 mm. The JC patterns are assumed to be 0.02-mm copper strips with an electric conductivity of $\sigma = 5.8 \times 10^7$ S/m. These parameters including the conductivity value and the loss tangent are considered in the following simulations to thoroughly assess the loss of the lens. The directivity of the entire dielectric antenna system is shown in Fig. 6.28; it is 26.9 dB, that is, 13 dB higher than the feed horn alone.

To get an idea how the dielectric lens system works, we plot the phase distribution in the x-z and y-z planes when the feed horn is excited by the TE_{10} mode, as shown in Fig. 6.29. We can observe from the figure that the cylindrical wave above the dielectric lens becomes a plane wave below the dielectric lens. For the same reason, if a plane wave illuminates the dielectric lens, it will form a focal point on the other side of the dielectric lens.

To validate the parallel FDTD results, we measure the gain pattern and plot the measured and simulated results together, as shown in Fig. 6.30. We observe a good agreement of the two sets of results.

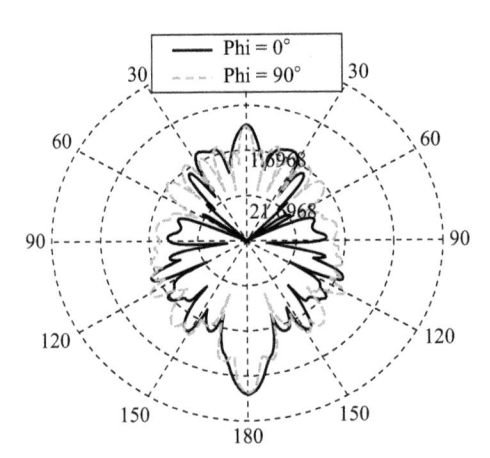

Figure 6.28   Directivity patterns of the antenna system in Fig. 6.27 at 30 GHz.

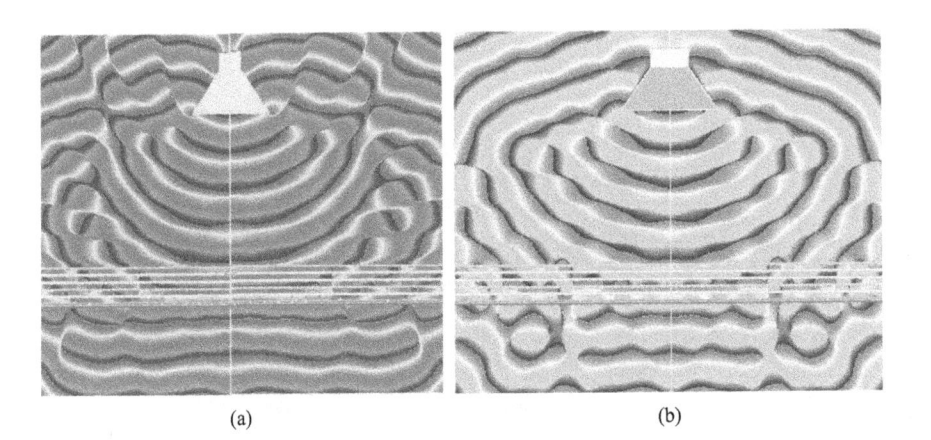

Figure 6.29   Phase patterns at 30 GHz of the antenna system in Fig. 6.27 in (a) the *x-z* plane and (b) the *y-z* plane.

Simulation summary

- Platform: 4-CPU workstation
- Number of time steps: 85,900
- Convergence criterion: −30 dB
- Memory usage: 25 GB
- Number of unknowns: 554 Mcells
- Total simulation time: 5 h 26 min

6.6 Vehicle Electromagnetic Analysis

In this section, we use the parallel FDTD code to simulate a vehicle model [19–21], which is generated originally in AutoCAD, as shown in Fig. 6.31. Although the simulation of a

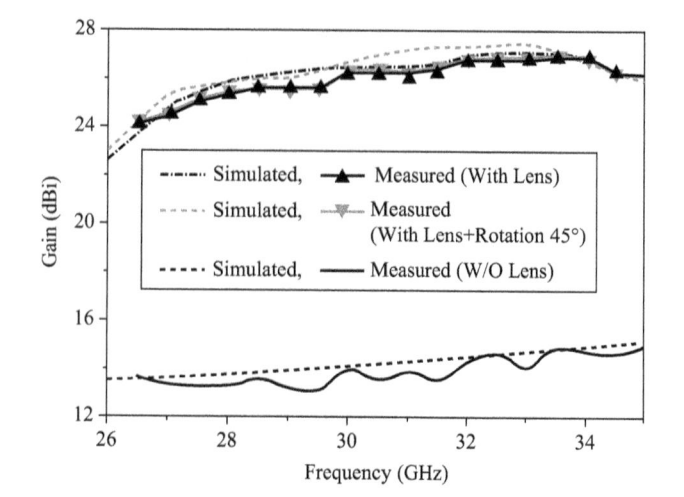

Figure 6.30 Variation of measured and simulated gain patterns of the antenna in Fig. 6.27 with frequency.

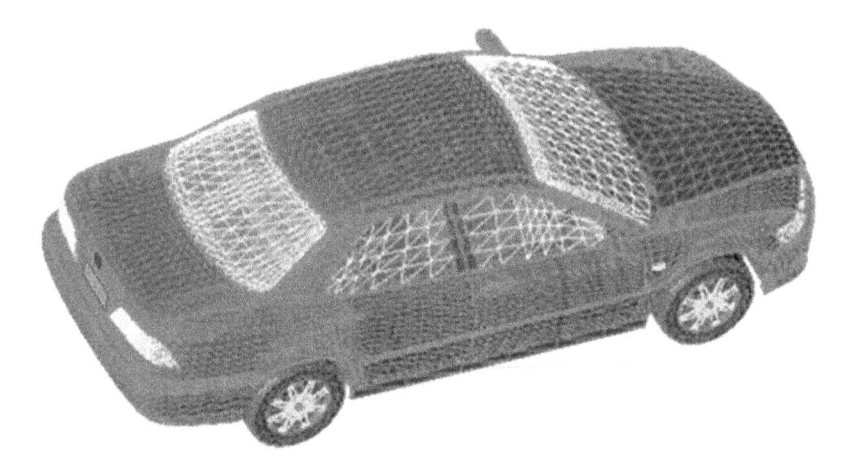

Figure 6.31 A vehicle model in the AutoCAD triangle mesh format.

complete vehicle is difficult for the traditional FDTD method on a regular computer, and not so for the parallel FDTD method, the challenging issue is how to import the vehicle model into the parallel FDTD code. First, we need a DXF (drawing interchange format) reader that can identify the surface mesh format of AutoCAD. The requirements for the mechanical manufacturing and electromagnetic simulation are different, in that the electromagnetic simulation software additionally requires a continuous surface and continuity of its derivatives. If we import it into the parallel FDTD code, the material distribution may be incorrect. Therefore, it is important for us to check if the model is correct before we simulate it using the parallel FDTD code. One simple method is to check if its material distributions such as the conductivity distribution is correct. Since the material distribution is generated at the beginning of the simulation, if the material distribution is not correct, we can terminate the FDTD simulation, fix the model, and make sure that the model is correct.

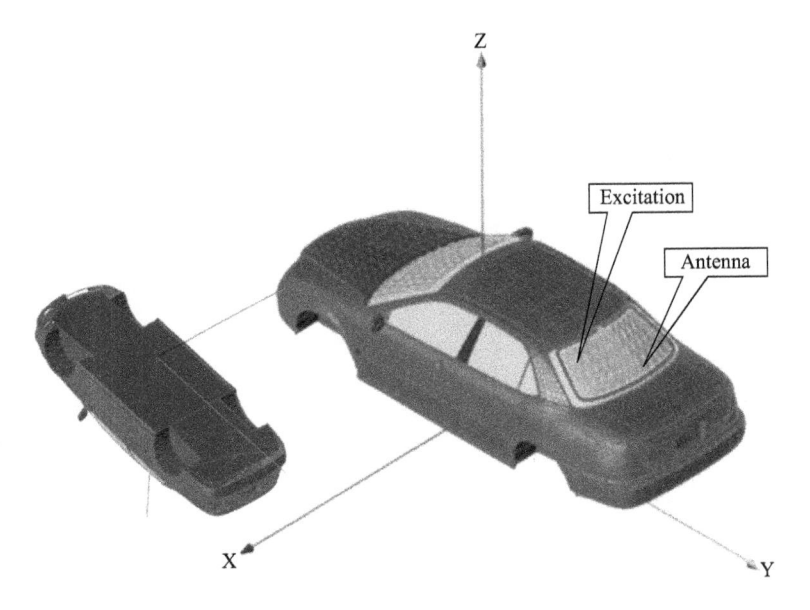

Figure 6.32   A vehicle model without wheels and with an excitation antenna.

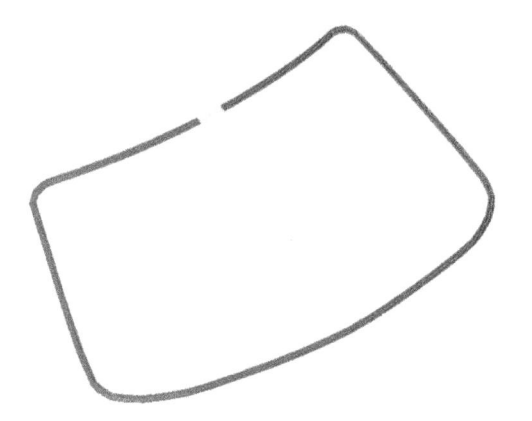

Figure 6.33   A loop antenna model mounted on the rear glass of the car in Fig. 6.32.

When the vehicle model is imported into the parallel FDTD code, its parts are separate from each other and can be edited separately. For example, we can remove four wheels from the computational domain since they do not affect the far-field pattern and reflection coefficient substantially. The vehicle model with the wheels removed is shown in Fig. 6.32. A 3-D curved loop antenna is mounted on the rear windshield. A small gap is located at the upper center and a voltage source is employed to excite the antenna. It is worth mentioning that this antenna is used only to demonstrate the parallel FDTD code performance.

The loop antenna configuration is shown in Fig. 6.33. The current distribution on the loop at 2.5 GHz is shown in Fig. 6.34 when a voltage source is used to excite the antenna. The directivity pattern at 2.5 GHz is plotted in Fig. 6.35.

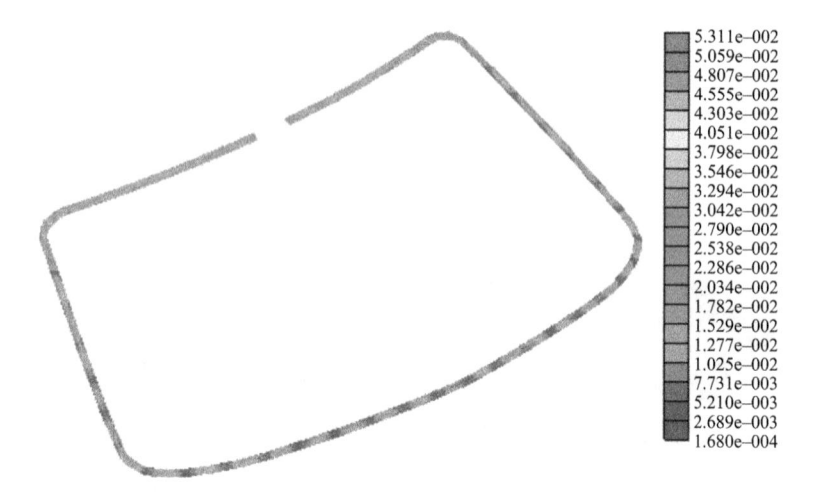

Figure 6.34   Surface current distribution at 2.5 GHz on the loop antenna in Fig. 6.33.

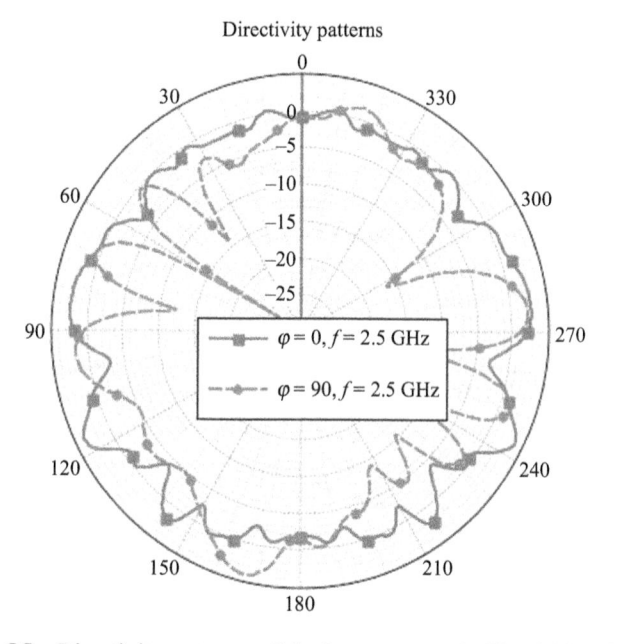

Figure 6.35   Directivity patterns of the loop antenna in Fig. 6.33 at 2.5 GHz.

To calculate the surface current, we need the surface mesh first, then we calculate the magnetic field on the surface of the vehicle. For the infinitely thin conductor, the surface current can flow only in one layer. However, for a conductor of a finite thickness, the surface current can flow on both sides of the conductor. The surface current distribution at 2.5 GHz on the surface of the vehicle is shown in Fig. 6.36. The directivity pattern at 2.5 GHz is shown in Fig. 6. 37.

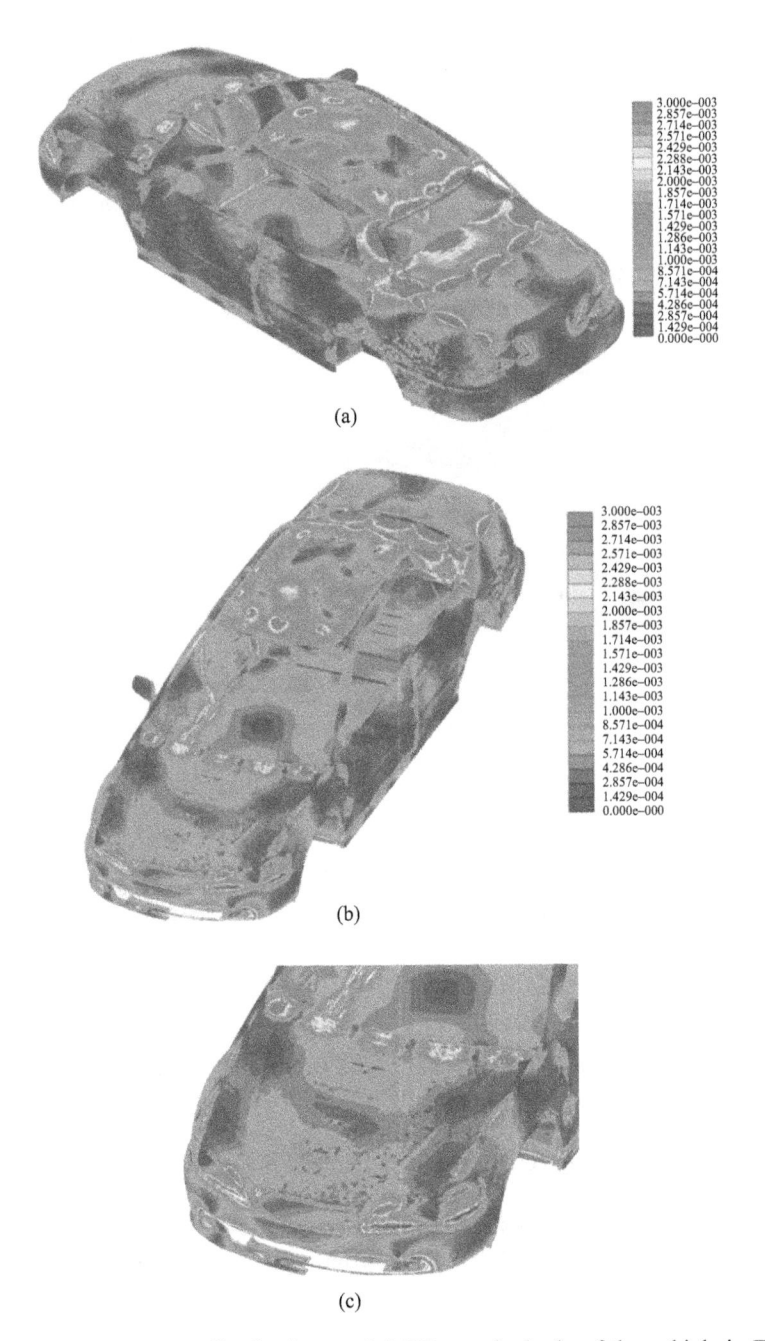

Figure 6.36   Surface current distributions at 2.5 GHz on the body of the vehicle in Fig. 6.22:
(a) side view, (b) front view, and (c) magnified detail of the front view.

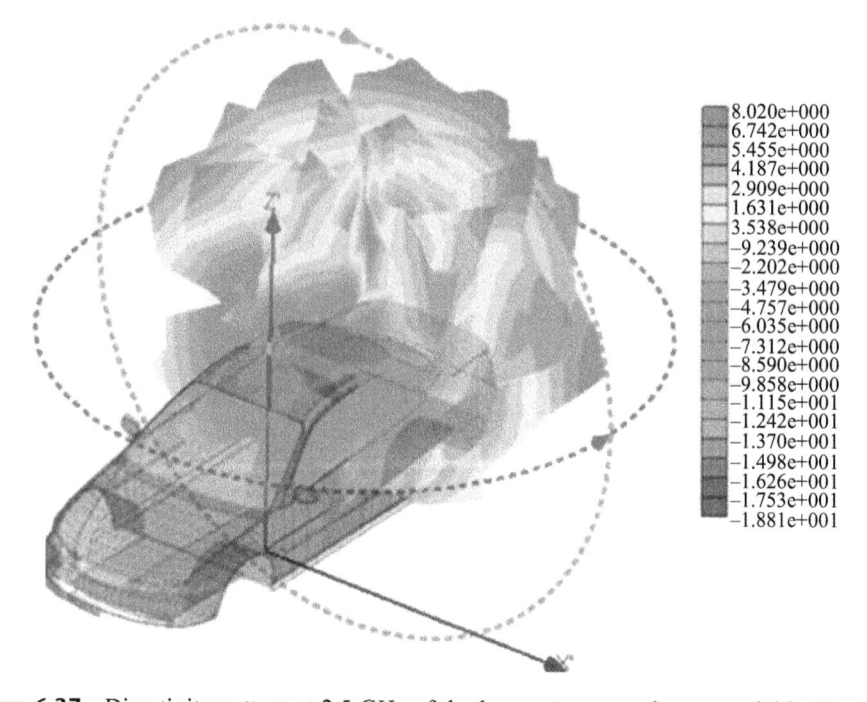

8.020e+000
6.742e+000
5.455e+000
4.187e+000
2.909e+000
1.631e+000
3.538e+000
−9.239e+000
−2.202e+000
−3.479e+000
−4.757e+000
−6.035e+000
−7.312e+000
−8.590e+000
−9.858e+000
−1.115e+001
−1.242e+001
−1.370e+001
−1.498e+001
−1.626e+001
−1.753e+001
−1.881e+001

Figure 6.37 Directivity pattern at 2.5 GHz of the loop antenna on the car model in Fig. 6.22.

Simulation summary

- Hardware platform: 4-CPU workstation
- Number of time steps: 15,000
- Convergence: below −30 dB
- Total memory usage: 22 GB
- Number of unknowns: 1,441 Mcells
- Total simulation time: 3 h 38 min

A BMW-850 vehicle model shown in Fig. 6.38 is downloaded from a public domain, and it is used to demonstrate an application of the parallel FDTD method to calculate the surface current distribution and far-field pattern.

The BMW model in Fig. 6.38 is ill-conditioned; that is, if we generate the material distribution in the parallel FDTD code, we will find that the model is incorrect. For example, we can see the symmetric features in the vehicle model; however, using the original model, the surface current distribution will be totally different. To fix the ill-conditioned model, we replace it using the correct symmetric pieces. In addition, to avoid generating another ill-conditioned problem, we cannot unite two pieces together if they do not have a finite thickness. The surface current distribution at 3 GHz on the vehicle body is plotted in Fig. 6.39. The directivity pattern at 3 GHz is plotted in Fig. 6.40.

Simulation summary

- Hardware platform: 4-CPU workstation
- Number of time steps: 14,200

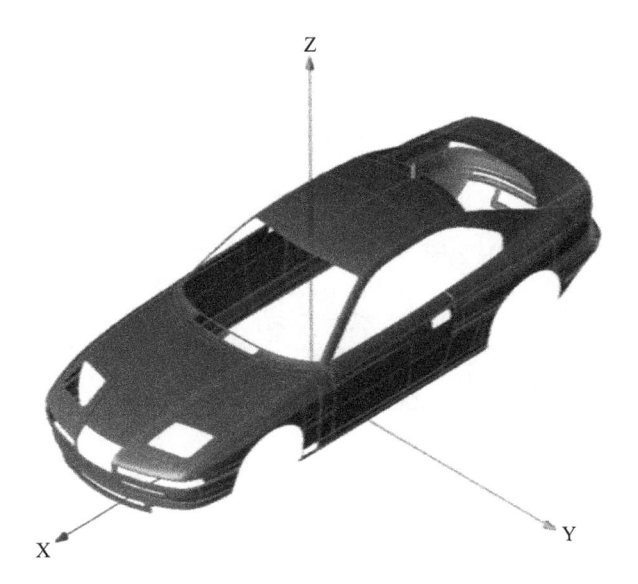

Figure 6.38   A simplified BMW-850 car model.

- Convergence: below –30 dB
- Total memory usage: 21.7 GB
- Number of unknowns: 618 Mcells
- Total simulation time: 3 h 38 min

6.7 Helicopter Electromagnetic Analysis

An infinitely thin PEC structure can support surface current distribution in only one layer. For example, we pick one piece of surface from the helicopter model that has no thickness, as shown in Fig. 6.41.

To calculate the surface current at one point on the surface, we need to identify its normal direction from the surface mesh information, and then calculate the tangential direction. If the PEC structure has no thickness, the magnetic fields on two sides may be totally different since they may be located in the different domains. We can calculate the surface current based on the following formulation:

$$J = \frac{I}{L} = \frac{1}{L} \oint \vec{H} \cdot \vec{dl} = \frac{1}{L}(LH_1 + LH_3) = H_1 + H_3 \tag{6.12}$$

In the derivation above, it is assumed that the two tangential components of magnetic fields are zero. The magnetic fields H_1 and H_3 are calculated from their neighbors at their own side, respectively. If the PEC structure has a finite thickness, one of magnetic fields H_1 and H_3 is zero.

A helicopter model is shown in Fig. 6.42. In its original model, the double layers look very good. For the sake of simplicity, we delete the inner layer and keep only the outer layer so that the surface current calculation will be efficient. Although this model is downloaded from a public domain, it turns out to be well-conditioned.

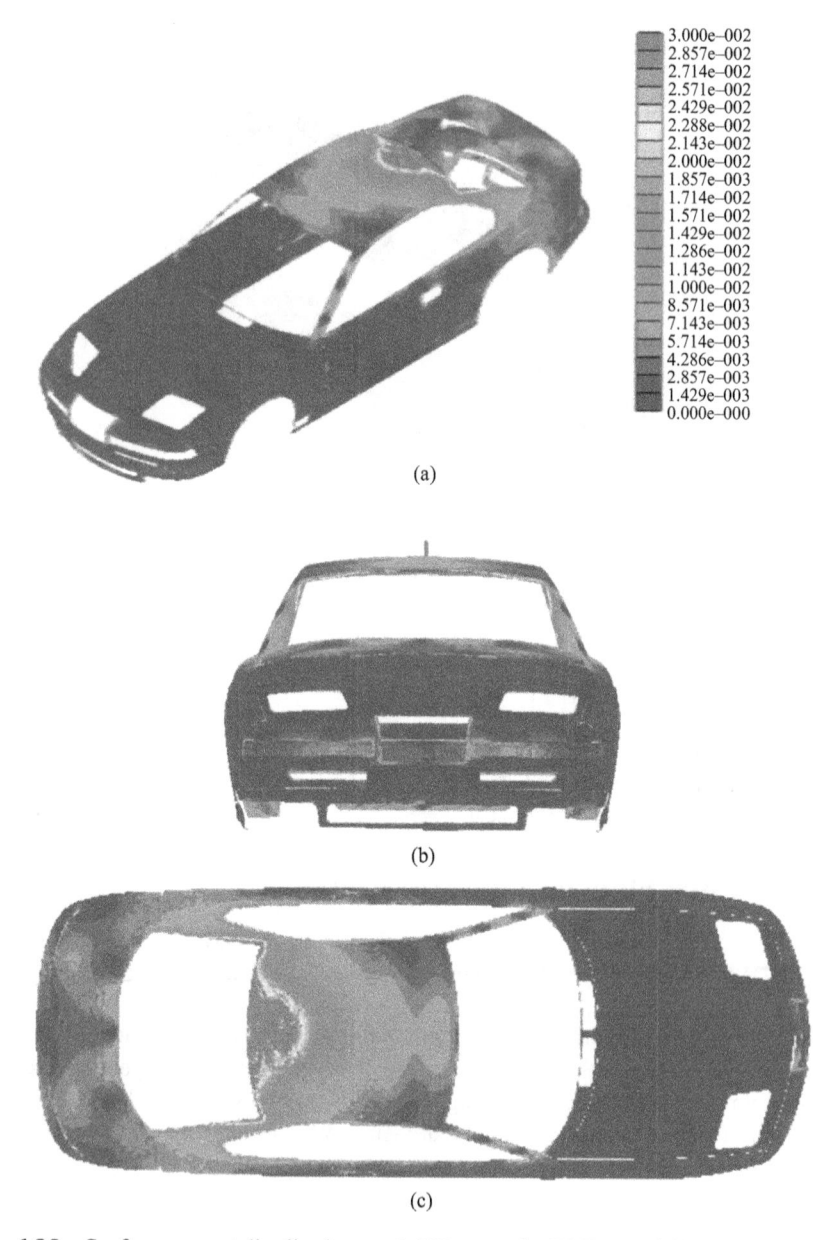

3.000e–002
2.857e–002
2.714e–002
2.571e–002
2.429e–002
2.288e–002
2.143e–002
2.000e–002
1.857e–003
1.714e–002
1.571e–002
1.429e–002
1.286e–002
1.143e–002
1.000e–002
8.571e–003
7.143e–003
5.714e–003
4.286e–003
2.857e–003
1.429e–003
0.000e–000

(a)

(b)

(c)

Figure 6.39   Surface current distributions at 3 GHz over the BMW model in Fig. 6.38 excited by a monopole antenna: (a) side view, (b) back view, and (c) top view.

If we generate the conductivity distribution before the parallel FDTD update, as shown in Fig. 6.43, it is correct. It is worth mentioning that even if the material distribution is correct, that does not necessarily mean that we can generate the correct surface current distribution on the conductor body. For example, to generate the correct surface current distribution, the

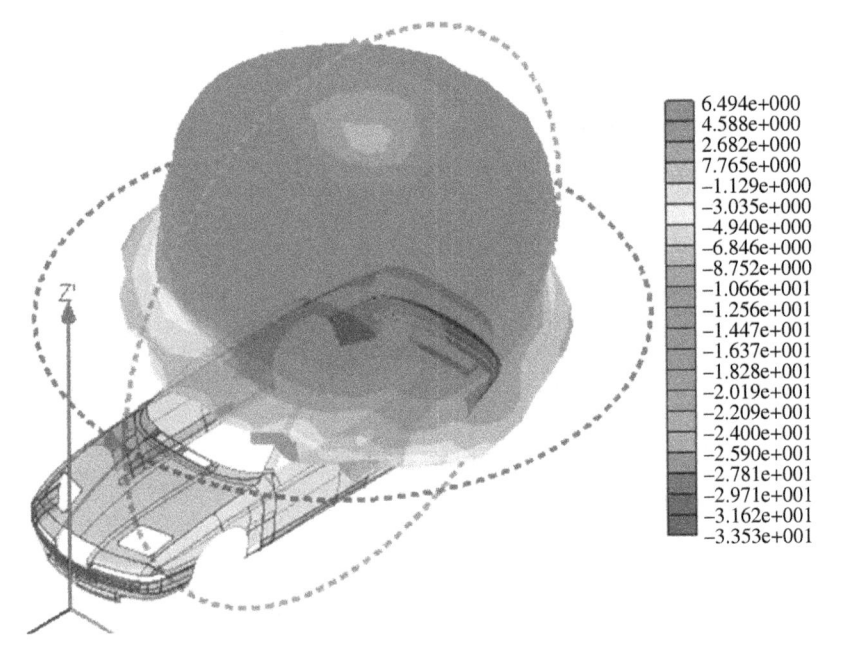

Figure 6.40   3-D directivity pattern at 3 GHz of a monopole antenna attached to the BMW model in Fig. 6.38.

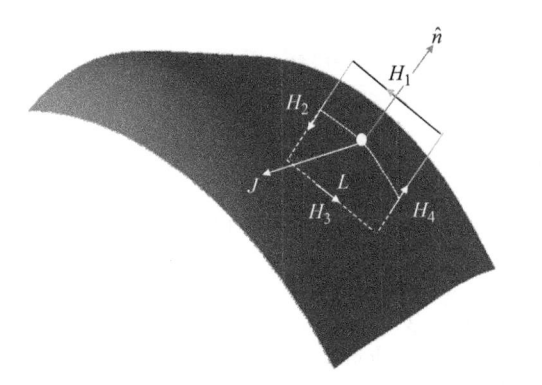

Figure 6.41   Calculation scheme of surface current on the infinitely thin structure.

normal direction on the surface of the conductor surface must be correct. However, it can be corrected in most cases. The conformal surface current distribution on the helicopter body is shown in Fig. 6.44.

Simulation summary

- Hardware platform: 4-CPU workstation
- Number of time steps: 10,100

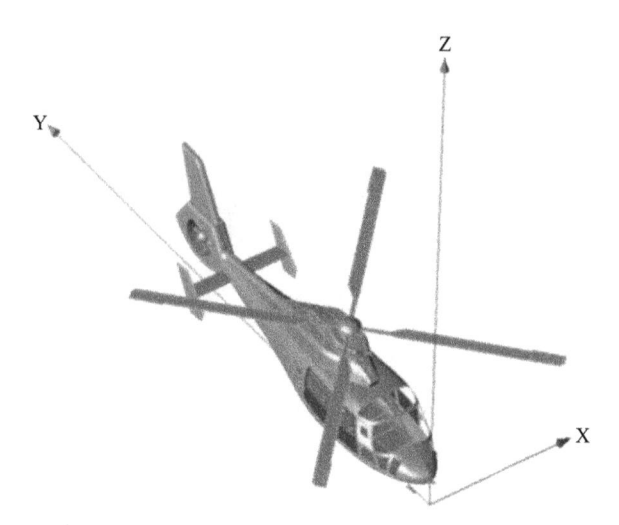

Figure 6.42 A simplified helicopter model.

Figure 6.43 Conductivity distribution of the simplified helicopter model.

- Convergence: below −30 dB
- Total memory usage: 56 GB
- Number of unknowns: 1,565 Mcells
- Total simulation time: 4 h 18 min

6.8 Finite FSS Analysis

For periodic structures, we only need to simulate one element to obtain the solution of the original problem. Although the original problem may be extremely large, the problem domain that we need to simulate can be relatively small. From the solution of one element simulation, we can get the solution of the original problem through the periodic property. Unlike the periodic structures, the finite FSS [22–27], as shown in Fig. 6.45, requires simulating the complete problem geometry since the edge effect and coupling must be taken

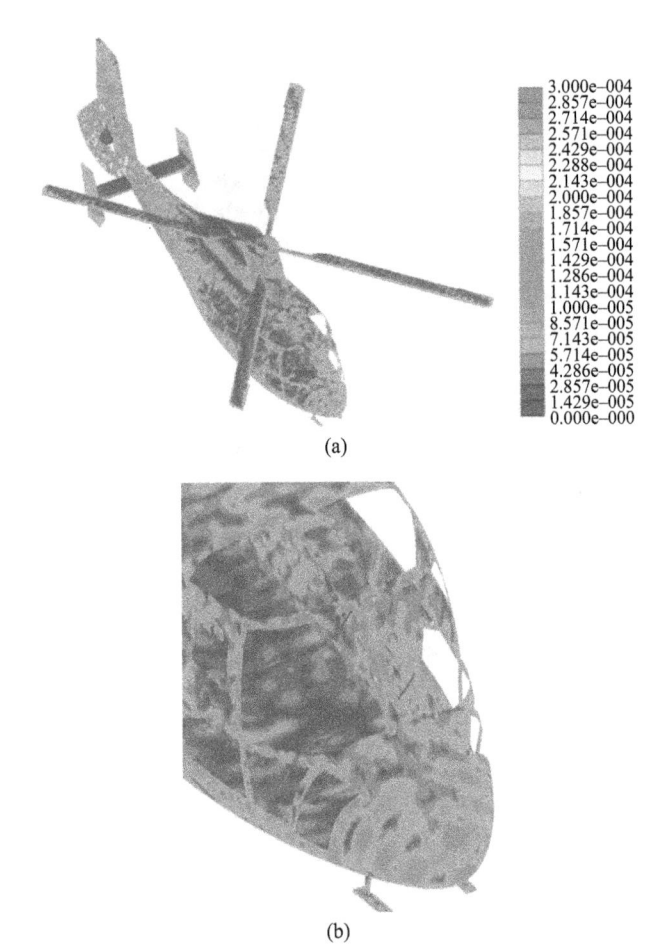

3.000e–004
2.857e–004
2.714e–004
2.571e–004
2.429e–004
2.288e–004
2.143e–004
2.000e–004
1.857e–004
1.714e–004
1.571e–004
1.429e–004
1.286e–004
1.143e–004
1.000e–005
8.571e–005
7.143e–005
5.714e–005
4.286e–005
2.857e–005
1.429e–005
0.000e–000

(a)

(b)

Figure 6.44 Conformal surface current distribution at 1.5 GHz on the body of the helicopter model in Fig. 6.42: (a) 3-D view and (b) magnified detail at the front of the helicopter.

Figure 6.45 Finite FSS configuration with six-layer dielectric slabs and three-layer FSS screens.

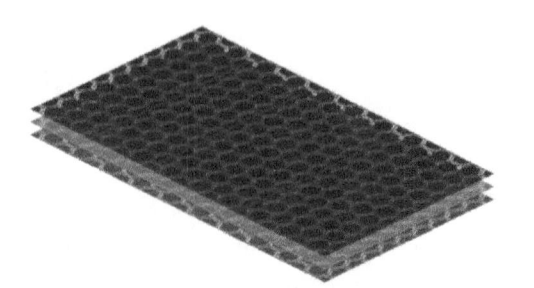

Figure 6.46   Three-layer 20×10 element FSS screens.

Figure 6.47   Element configuration in the finite FSS structure.

into account in the simulation. A six-layer dielectric slab with three-layer FSS screens (20×10) and the element configuration are shown in Figs. 6.46 and 6.47, respectively. There are two ways to calculate the transmitted power through the FSS structure: (1) using the plane wave as the excitation source and (2) using the Gaussian beam as the excitation source. In both cases, we need to use a PEC plate to split the domain into two separate sub-domains: the incident sub-region and the transmitted sub-region.

The PEC plate that encloses the finite FSS structure should be large enough and should touch the PML boundary for the plane wave excitation, as shown in Fig. 6.48. The plane wave will be truncated by the CPML boundary, which, in turn, will introduce an error into the transmitted power calculation. If the PEC plate is sufficiently large, the error can be ignored. To calculate the transmitted power or transmission coefficient, we need to run the simulation twice, one simulation for the incident power and the other for the total power. The transmitted power can be calculated from the incident and total powers.

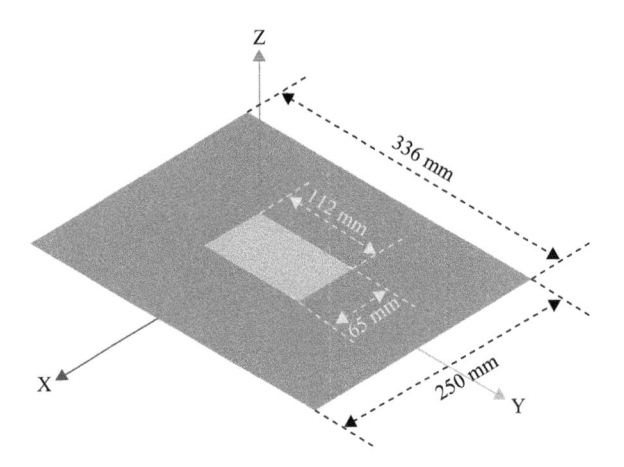

Figure 6.48   Simulation setting for the transmission coefficient of finite FSS structure.

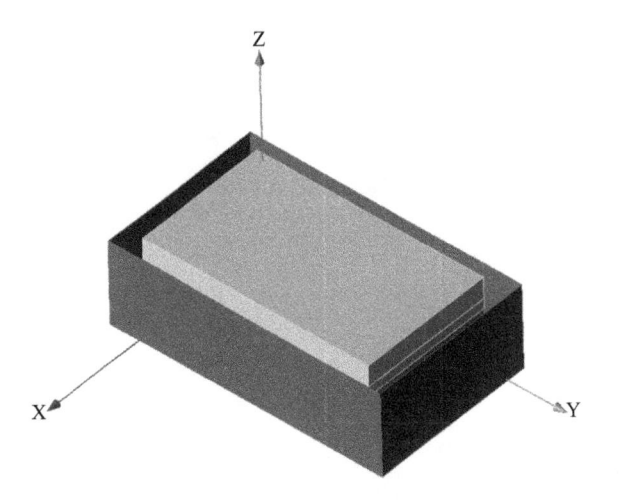

Figure 6.49   Power calculation configuration of finite FSS structure.

The transmitted power is measured at the five walls that surround the FSS structure, as shown in Fig. 6.49. The power calculation through the five walls is based on the following formulation:

$$\text{Power} = \frac{1}{2}\text{Re}\left(\int_S \vec{E}^* \times \vec{H} \cdot d\vec{s} \right) \tag{6.13}$$

The transmitted power through the FSS structure is plotted in Fig. 6.50. It is evident from the figure that the finite FSS structure has a good performance in the band pass from 7 GHz to 12 GHz. A similar conclusion can be drawn from the power density distribution shown in Fig. 6.51.

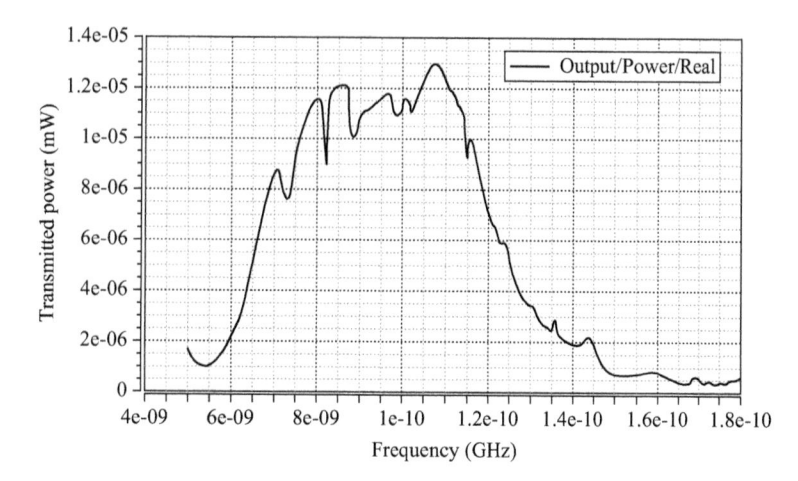

Figure 6.50 Transmitted power through the finite FSS structure.

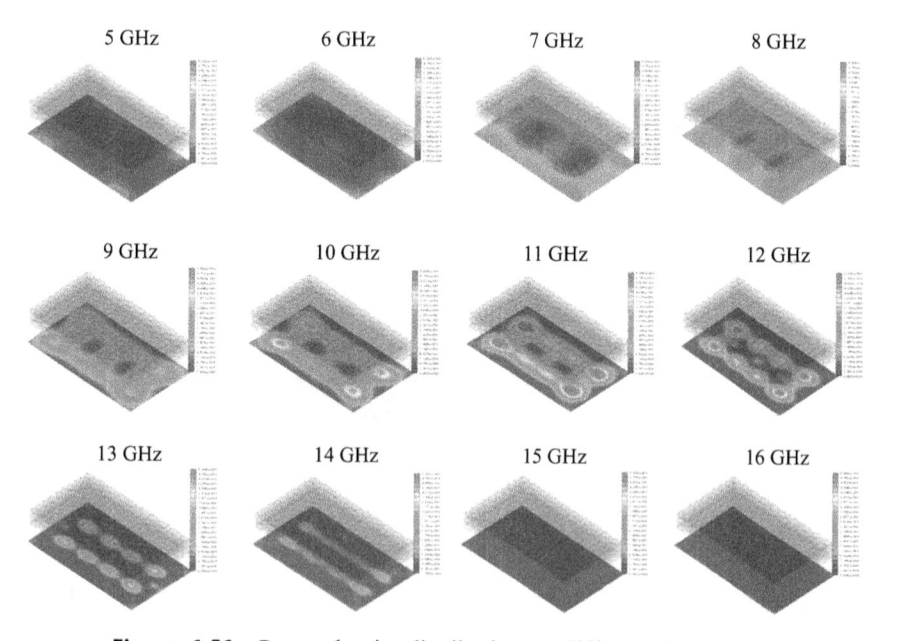

Figure 6.51 Power density distributions at different frequencies.

We can also use the Gaussian beam [28, 29] as the excitation source to calculate the transmitted power. The parameters of the Gaussian beam are shown in Fig. 6.52.

The definition of the Gaussian beam is expressed as follows:

$$E(r,z) = E_0 \frac{w_0}{w(z)} \exp\left(\frac{-r^2}{w^2(z)}\right) \exp\left(-ikz - ik\frac{r^2}{2R(z)} + i\zeta(z)\right) \qquad (6.14)$$

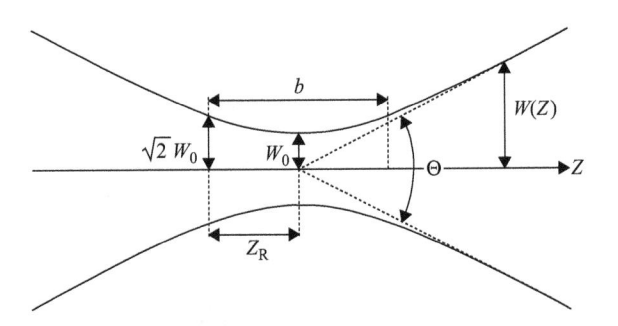

Figure 6.52 Parameter definitions in the Gaussian beam.

where r is the radial distance from the central axis of the beam, z is the axial distance from the beam's narrowest point, I is the imaginary unit, $k = 2\pi/\lambda$ is the wave number (in radians per meter), $E_0 = |E(0,0)|$, $w(z)$, is the radius at which the field amplitude and power drop to $1/e$ and $1/e^2$ of their axial values, respectively, $w_0 = w(0)$ is the waist size, $R(z)$ is the radius of curvature of the beam's wave fronts, and $\zeta(z)$ is the Gouy phase shift, an extra contribution to the phase that is seen in Gaussian beams.

In the parallel FDTD simulation, we ignore the dependence of the Gaussian beam on the frequency and the variation along the z-direction. The Gaussian beam is simplified as follows:

$$E(r) = E_0 e^{-r^2/w^2} \tag{6.15}$$

where E_0 is the amplitude of the plane wave, w is the width of the Gaussian beam, and r is the distance from the beam axis, as shown in Fig. 6.53. The spot of Gaussian beam should be larger than the area of the FSS structure. If the spot of the beam is smaller, we will not count the contribution from the edge of the FSS structure.

Simulation summary

- Hardware platform: 4-CPU workstation
- Number of time steps: 33,700
- Convergence: below −30 dB
- Total memory usage: 17.3 GB
- Number of unknowns: 357 Mcells
- Total simulation time: 9 h 43 min

6.9 Curved FSS Analysis

In reality, a finite FSS is usually a curved structure, as shown in Fig. 6.54. The curved FSS structure is obtained by transforming the structure through the formulation $z = z + 0.001(x^2 + y^2)$. The three FSS screens in the curved FSS structure are shown in Fig. 6.55. Most traditional FSS analysis tools are not good any more for the curved FSS structures. For the parallel FDTD method, of course, the fine cell sizes must be adapted to

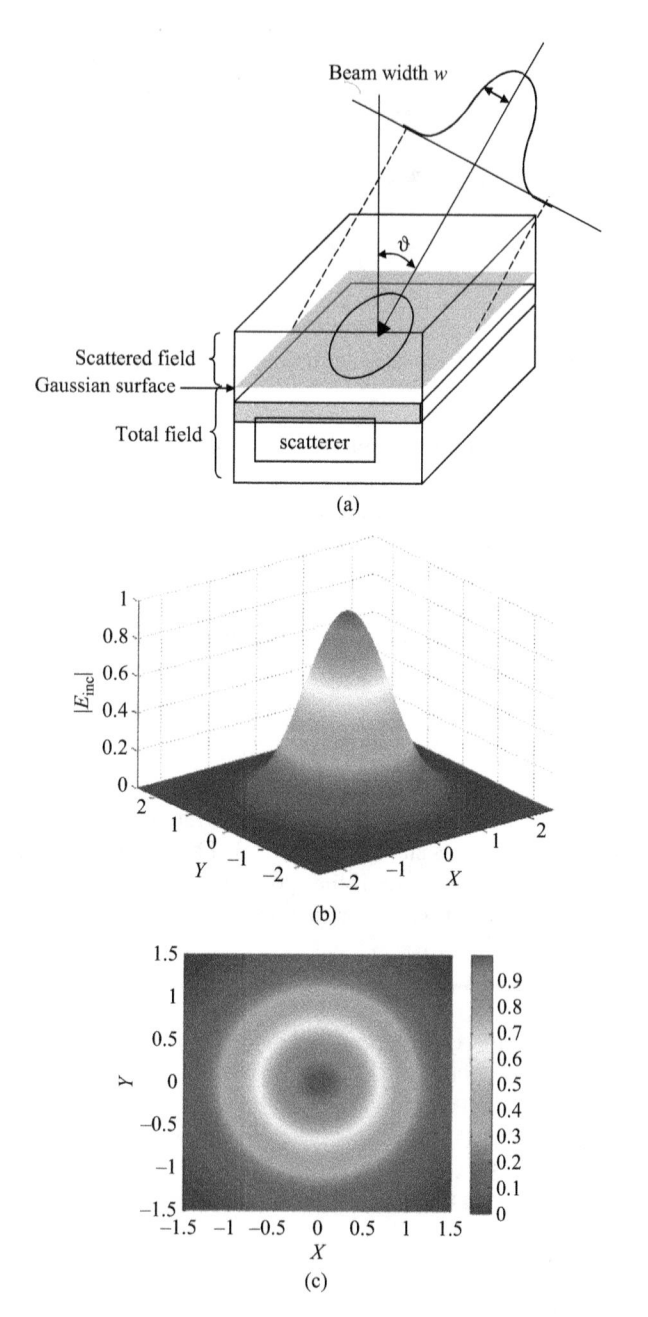

Figure 6.53 Gaussian beam excitation in the parallel FDTD simulation: (a) configuration of the excitation setup, (b) 3-D incident field distribution on the Gaussian surface, and (c) 2-D cut in the horizontal plane of the incident field distribution.

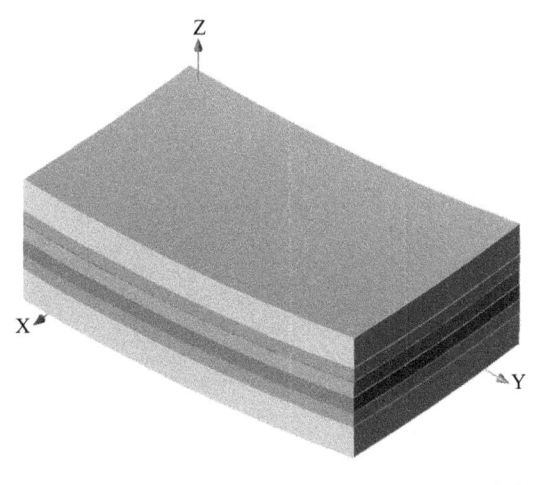

Figure 6.54   Curved FSS configuration with six-layer dielectrics and three-layer FSS screens.

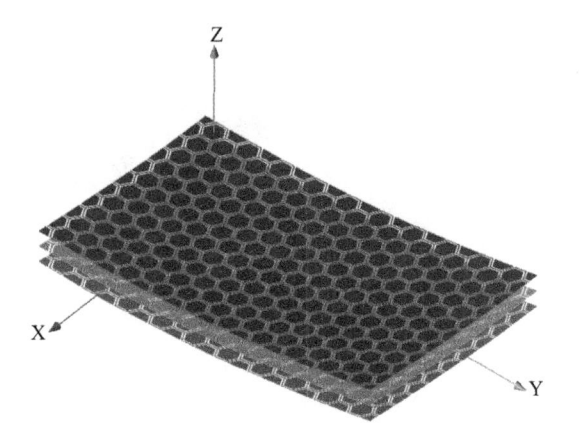

Figure 6.55   Three FSS screens inside the curved FSS structure.

describe the field variation in the curved slots, as well as coupling and edge effects. For the planar structure, the FSS structure is enclosed by a large PEC plate that forces the plane wave through the FSS structure. Then, we calculate the incident and transmitted power through the FSS area. For the curved FSS structures, we need to design a specially shaped PEC plate to enclose the FSS structure, as shown in Fig. 6.56.

The transmitted power and the power density are plotted in Figs. 6.57 and 6.58, respectively, when a plane wave is incident on the curved FSS structure.

Simulation summary

- Hardware platform: 4-CPU workstation
- Number of time steps: 70,000
- Convergence: below −30 dB

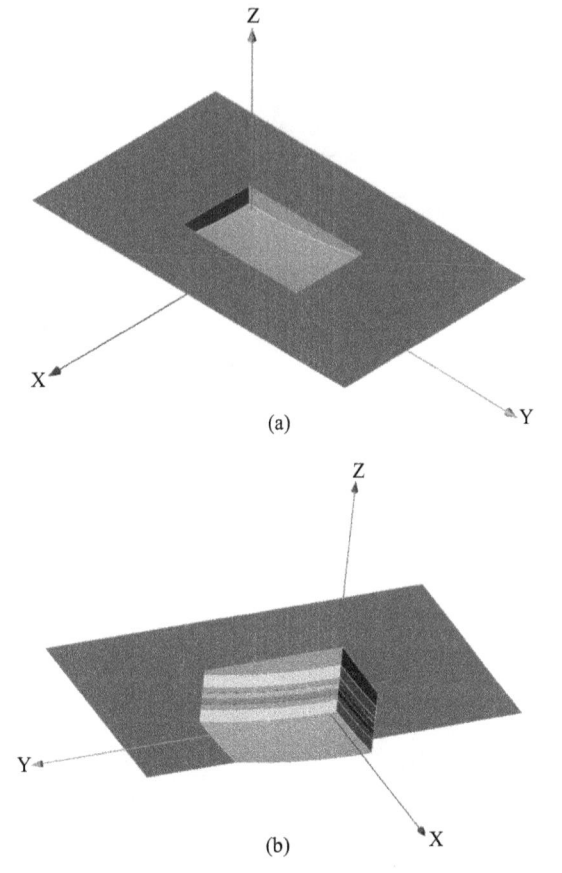

(a)

(b)

Figure 6.56   Configuration for the transmitted power calculation on the curved FSS structure: (a) front view and (b) back view.

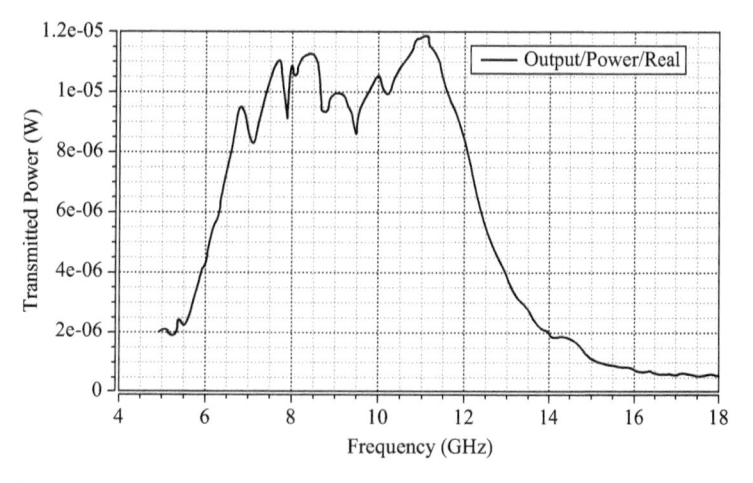

Figure 6.57   Transmitted power when a plane wave is incident on the curved FSS structure.

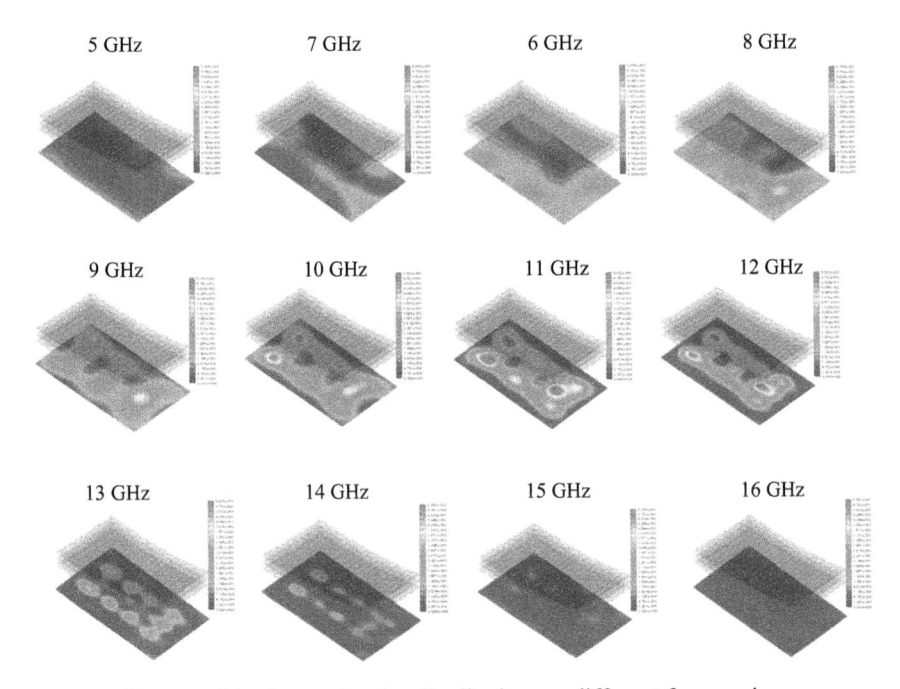

Figure 6.58   Power density distributions at different frequencies.

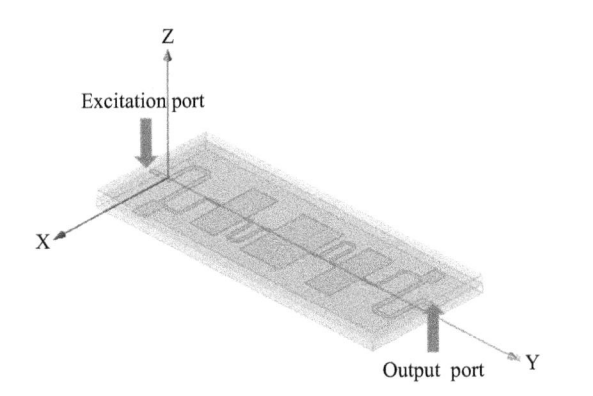

Figure 6.59   Low-pass filter configuration with two ports.

- Total memory usage: 15.6 GB
- Number of unknowns: 282 Mcells
- Total simulation time: 8 h 36 min

6.10 Microwave Filter Analysis

In this section, we use the parallel FDTD method to simulate a low-pass filter [30, 31], as shown in Fig. 6.59. To calculate the conformal surface current distribution, we need to mesh the filter structure using the conformal mesh, as shown in Fig. 6.60. The mesh size will affect the accuracy of the surface current distribution.

The reflection and transmission coefficients of the low-pass filter are plotted in Fig. 6.61 when one port is excited and the other port is terminated by using a 50-Ω

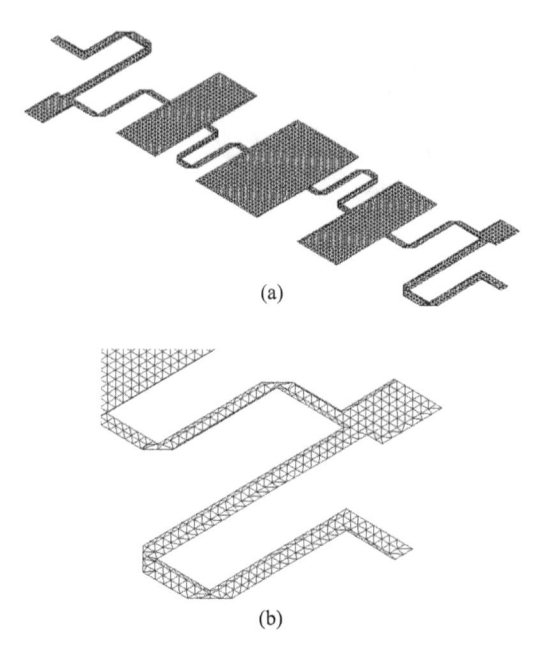

(a)

(b)

Figure 6.60   Conformal mesh distribution for the conformal current distribution calculation on the low-pass microwave filter in Fig. 6.59: (a) complete mesh distribution and (b) partial mesh distribution.

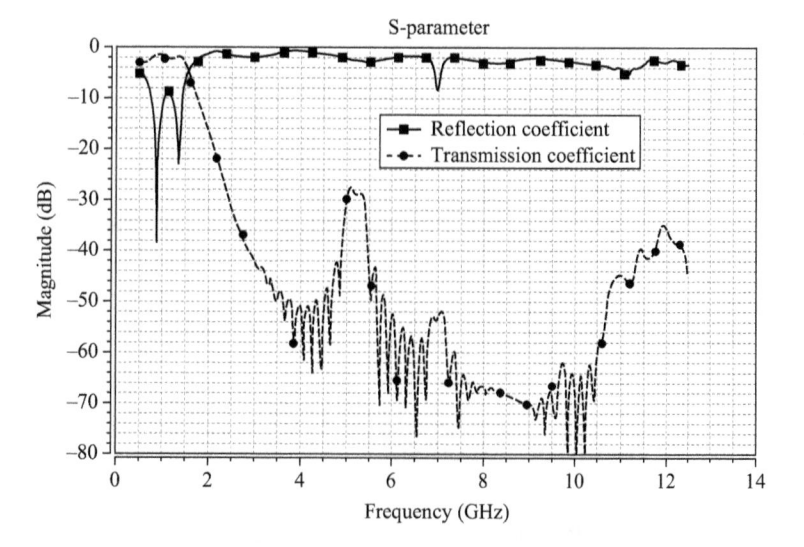

Figure 6.61   Reflection and transmission coefficients of the low-pass filter in Fig. 6.59.

matching load. The surface current distributions at different frequencies are shown in Fig. 6.62, where we observe that the filter passes at the low frequency band and stops at the high frequency band.

6.11 Planar Power Divider

The planar power divider [32–34], shown in Fig. 6.63, is a popular microwave component used to divide the power to two ports equally (in the ideal case). In this case, one port is excited and the other three ports are terminated using 50-Ω matching loads. Since the power is coupled from one strip line to another one, the simulation will take a long time to reach the convergence, as shown in Fig. 6.64.

The S-parameters computed at different ports are plotted in Fig. 6.65. The level of transmission coefficients is about –3 dB, that is, the incident power is divided into two equal parts.

In order to calculate the conformal surface current, we mesh the stripline using the surface mesh, as shown in Fig. 6.66(a). The current distribution is calculated through the magnetic fields computed in the FDTD update. The zoomed surface mesh is shown in Fig. 6.66(b). The surface current distribution on the striplines at 15 GHz is plotted in Fig. 6.67.

Figure 6.62 Conformal current distributions on the filter structure in Fig. 6.59 at (a) 1 GHz, (b) 5 GHz, and (c) 10 GHz.

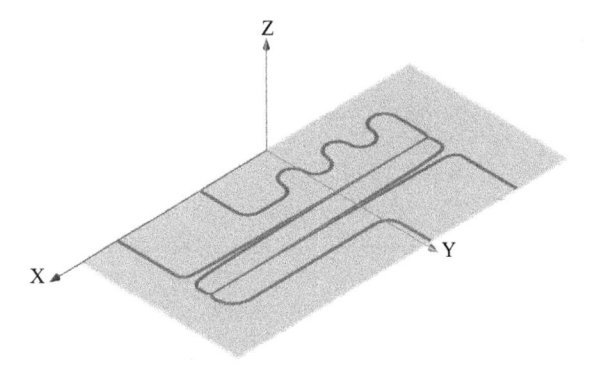

Figure 6.63 Power divider configuration.

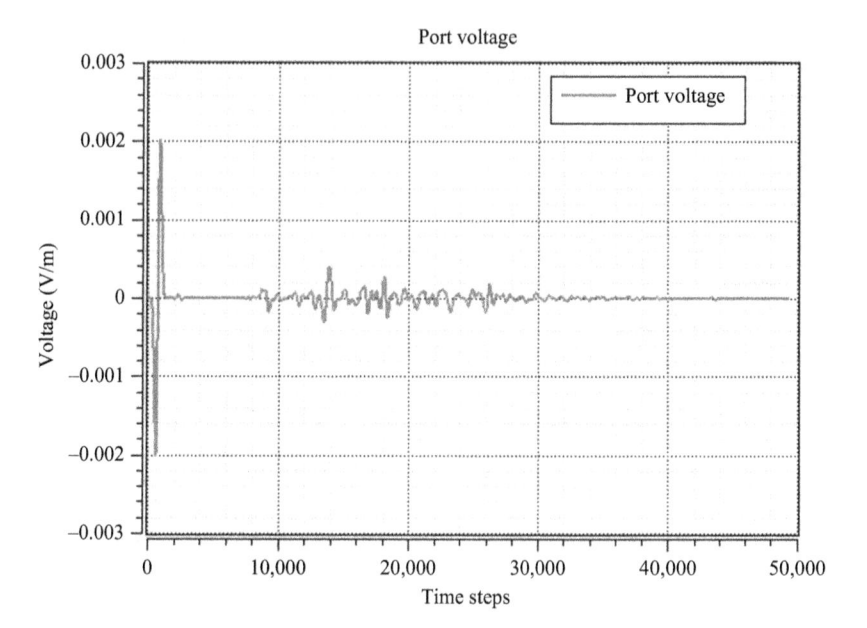

Figure 6.64   Time domain port voltage measured at the excitation port in the structure in Fig. 6.63.

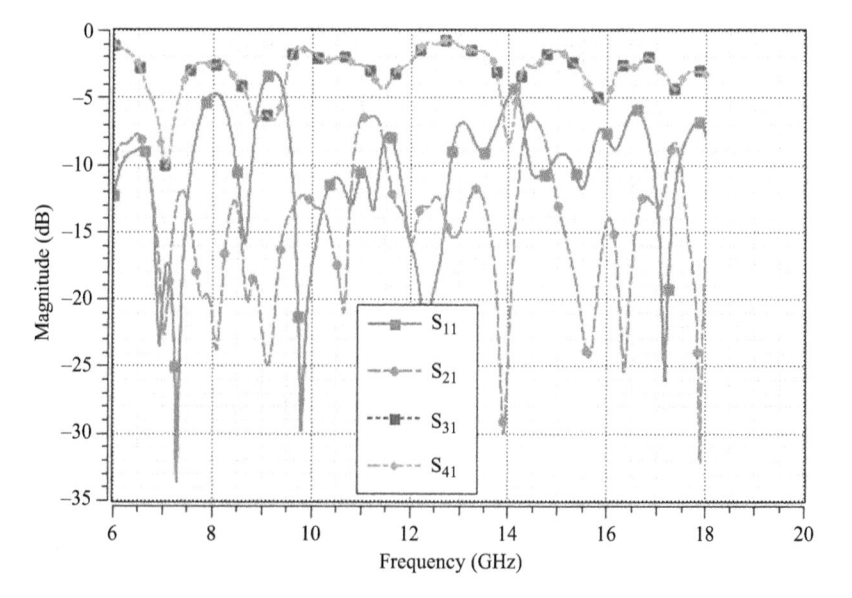

Figure 6.65   S-parameters computed at each of the ports of the power divider in Fig. 6.63.

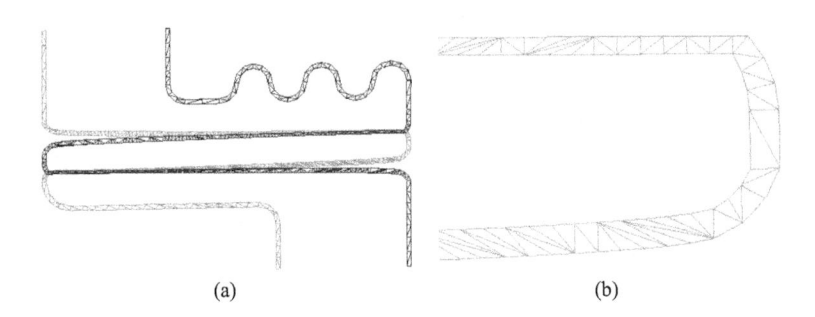

(a)   (b)

Figure 6.66   Surface mesh on the strip lines of the power divider in Fig. 6.63: (a) overall mesh distribution and (b) zoomed detail of the mesh.

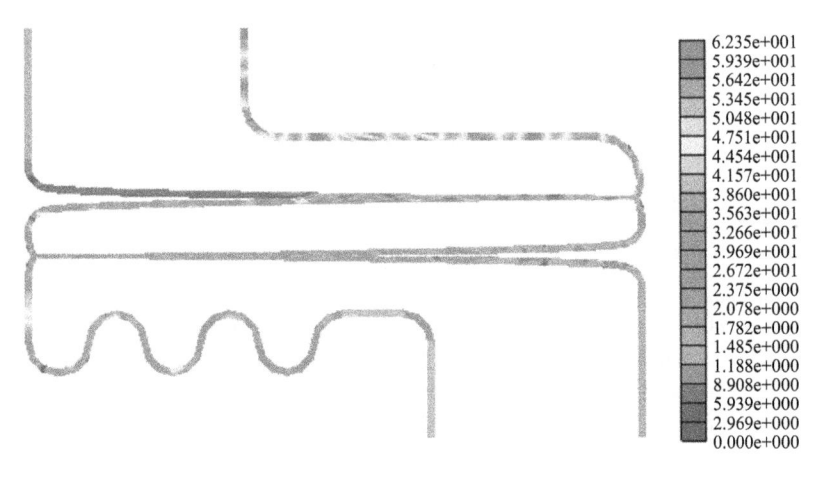

Figure 6.67   Surface current distribution on the mesh in Fig. 6.66 at 15 GHz.

Simulation summary

- Hardware platform: 4-CPU workstation
- Number of time steps: 49,400
- Convergence: below −30 dB
- Memory usage: 136 MB
- Number of unknowns: 3.2 Mcells
- Total simulation time: 13 min

6.12 Reverberation Chamber

The reverberation chamber [35–40], shown in Fig. 6.68, is an important piece of test equipment for the electromagnetic compatibility (EMC) and electromagnetic interference (EMI) problems. It is used to generate the sufficient types of modes and check if the electronic devices work well in the complicated environment. One of the most challenging issues

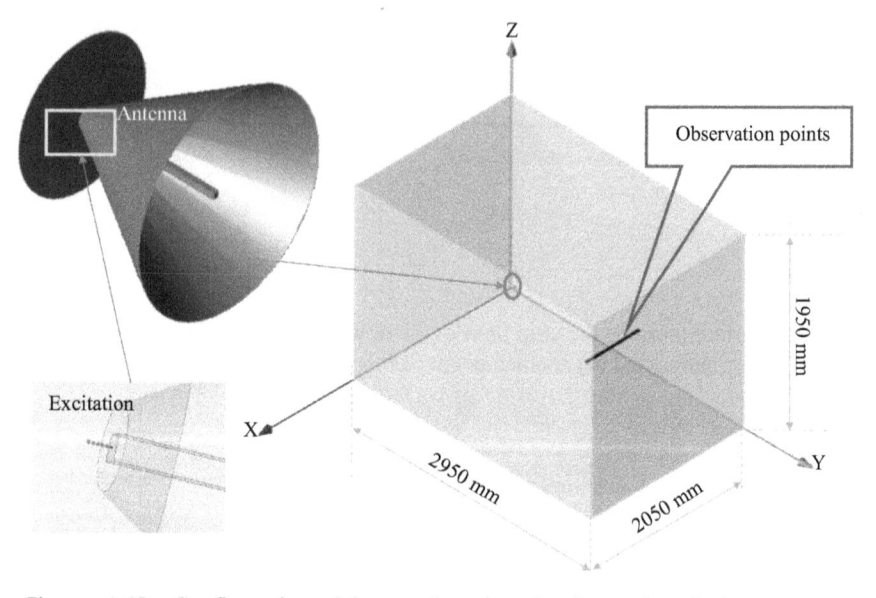

Figure 6.68 Configuration of the reverberation chamber and excitation antenna.

related to reverberation chamber is how to terminate the simulation to get the smooth frequency domain result since the power inside the chamber is held forever for a lossless system. We use the window function, for example, Hamming window, to add on the time domain signature to force the signal convergence to zero. The width of the Hamming window will be determined by the highest frequency of interest.

Spectral leakage is the result of the assumption in the fast Fourier transform (FFT) algorithm that the time signature in the FFT transformation is exactly repeated throughout all time and that signals contained in the transformation are thus periodic at intervals that correspond to the length of the transformation. If the time signature in the FFT transformation has a non-integer number of cycles, this assumption is violated and spectral leakage occurs. Spectral leakage distorts the measurement in such a way that energy from a given frequency component spreads to adjacent frequencies. If we cannot run a high-Q system until its time signature is convergent to zero, we need to choose a window function correctly to suppress the spectral leakage for a certain measurement.

To choose a proper window function, we must know the highest frequency of interest in the solution. If the signal contains the strong interfering frequency components distant from the frequency of interest, we should choose a window function with a high side lobe. If there is a strong interfering signal near the frequency of interest, we should choose a window function with a low side lobe. If the frequency of interest contains two or more signals very near to each other, then the frequency resolution is very important. It is best to choose a window function with a very narrow main lobe. If the amplitude accuracy of a single frequency component is more important than the exact location of the component in a given frequency band, we should choose a window function with a wide main lobe. If the signal spectrum is rather flat or broadband in the frequency content, we can use the rectangle window.

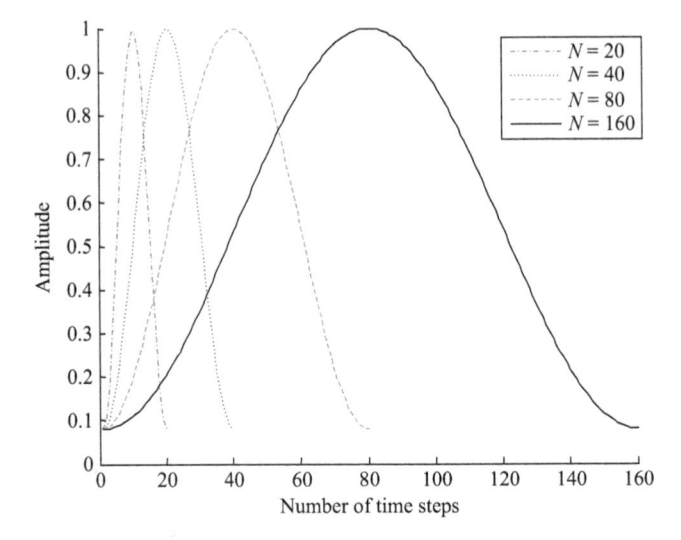

Figure 6.69 Signature of the Hamming window function with different widths.

For the reverberation chamber problems, since the computational domain is surrounded by the perfect electric conductor, the power will be limited inside the chamber. The time signature measured inside the chamber will not be convergent, and the frequency domain response will not be smooth. In order to get the smooth frequency response, we usually apply a window function, for example, Hamming window, in the time domain signature. If the simulation time is sufficiently long, we will get an accurate and smooth frequency response. A typical Hamming window function is expressed as follows:

$$\omega(n) = 0.54 - 0.46\cos\left(\frac{2\pi n}{N-1}\right) \tag{6.16}$$

where n is the time step in the FDTD simulation and N is the total number of time steps. The time signature of the Hamming window function and its frequency response are plotted in Figs. 6.69 and 6.70, respectively. It is observed from Fig. 6.70 that the application of the Hamming window in the time domain signature is a filter and removes the contributions from the noise generated by the higher frequencies.

The field variation along the observation line at 3 GHz is plotted in Fig. 6.71. The field distribution at 3 GHz inside the chamber is shown in Fig. 6.72.

Simulation summary

- Hardware platform: 4-CPU workstation
- Number of time steps: 102,704
- Convergence: below −30 dB with window function
- Memory usage: 5.6 GB
- Number of unknowns: 174 Mcells
- Total simulation time: 6 h 21 min

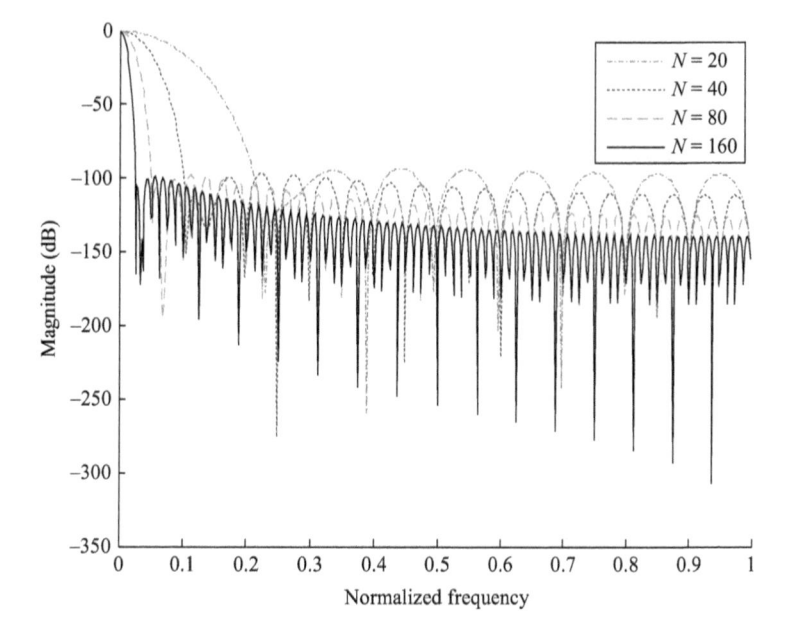

Figure 6.70 Frequency response of the Hamming window function with different widths.

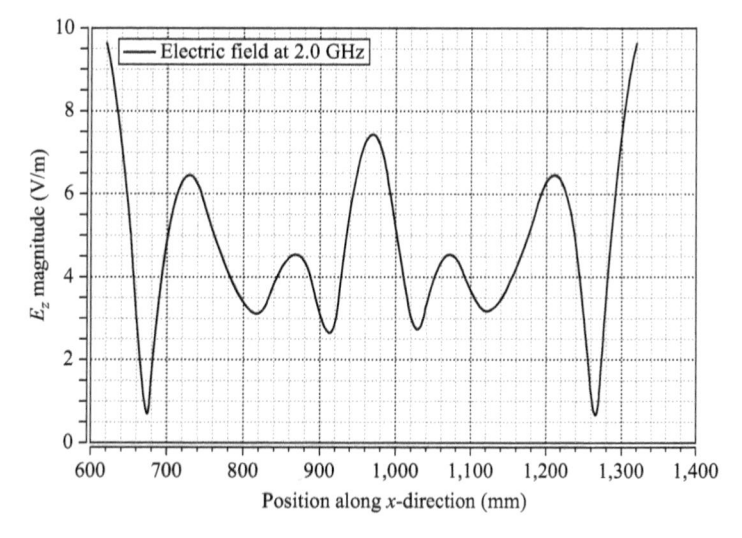

Figure 6.71 Field variation along the observed line at 3 GHz.

6.13 Airplane WIFI Analysis

In this section, we use the parallel FDTD method to simulate the WIFI application inside a simplified airplane model, as shown in Fig. 6.73. If the thickness of the airplane body is finite, we have to use the small cells to describe the thickness. Otherwise, for the infinitely

Figure 6.72   Field distribution at 3 GHz inside the chamber.

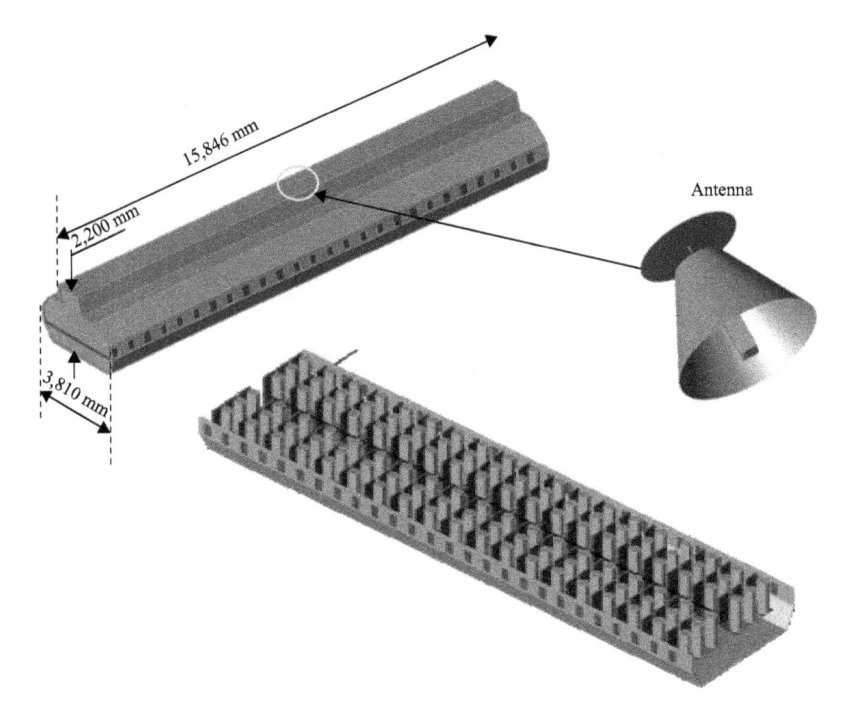

Figure 6.73   Simplified airplane model with a WIFI antenna.

thin PEC shell, the cell size can be large since the PEC shell will not be leaking. If a human body inside the aircraft is taken into account, a very fine mesh must be used because of high relative dielectric constants of biological tissues. The WIFI antenna is a PEC discone antenna, which is a dipole backed by a circular PEC plate.

We first check the characteristics of the antenna, as shown in Fig. 6.74, before we simulate the real WIFI problem. The antenna alone is a relatively small problem. The surface current distribution on the PEC surface is plotted in Fig. 6.75 when a voltage source is used to excite the antenna. The reflection coefficient and far-field patterns at 3 GHz are shown in Figs. 6.76 and 6.77, respectively.

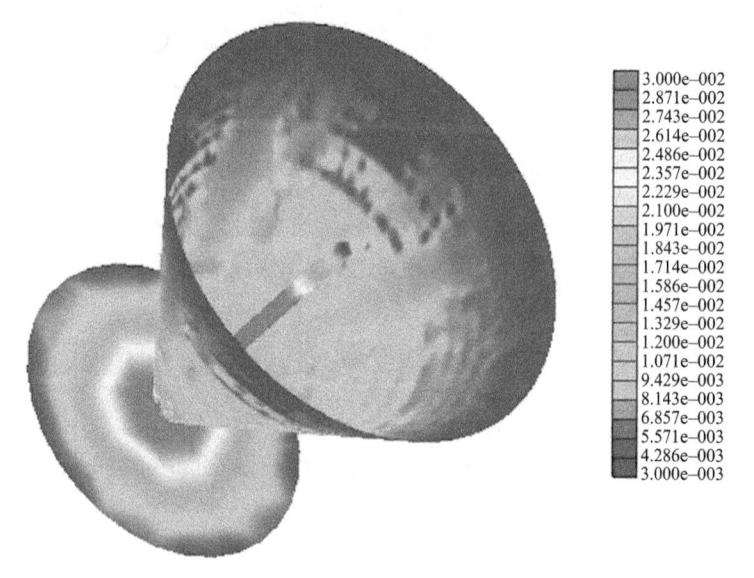

	3.000e–002
	2.871e–002
	2.743e–002
	2.614e–002
	2.486e–002
	2.357e–002
	2.229e–002
	2.100e–002
	1.971e–002
	1.843e–002
	1.714e–002
	1.586e–002
	1.457e–002
	1.329e–002
	1.200e–002
	1.071e–002
	9.429e–003
	8.143e–003
	6.857e–003
	5.571e–003
	4.286e–003
	3.000e–003

Figure 6.74   Surface current distribution at 3 GHz on the PEC surface of the WIFI discone antenna.

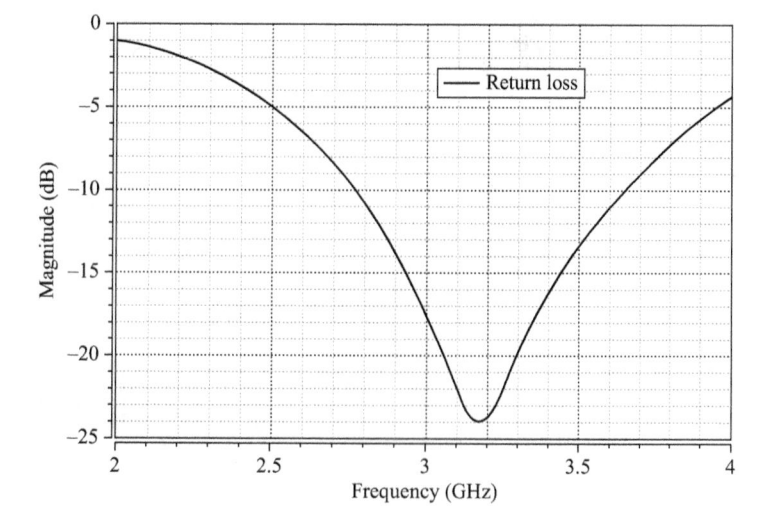

Figure 6.75   Reflection coefficient of the WIFI discone antenna in Fig. 6.73.

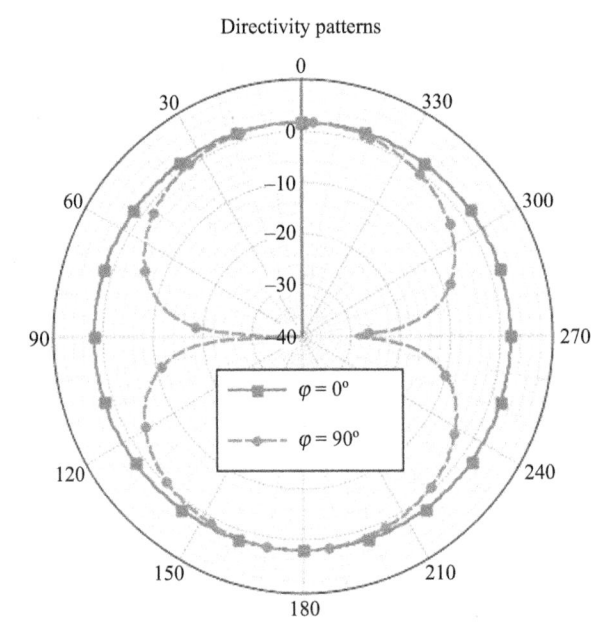

Figure 6.76 2-D directivity patterns of the discone antenna in Fig. 6.73 at 3 GHz.

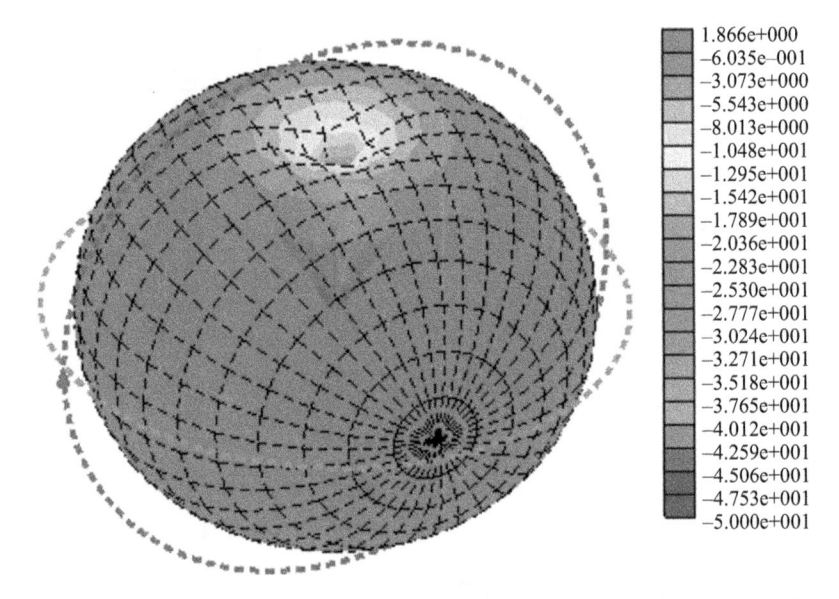

Figure 6.77 3-D directivity pattern of the discone antenna in Fig. 6.73 at 3 GHz.

Then we simulate the system with the WIFI antenna placed inside the aircraft. The surface current distribution and field distribution inside the aircraft at 3 GHz are shown in Figs. 6.78 and 6.79, respectively.

The field distribution at 3 GHz at a height of 500 mm in the vertical direction is plotted in Fig. 6.80. It is observed from the figure that the strong signal is located in the area below the antenna.

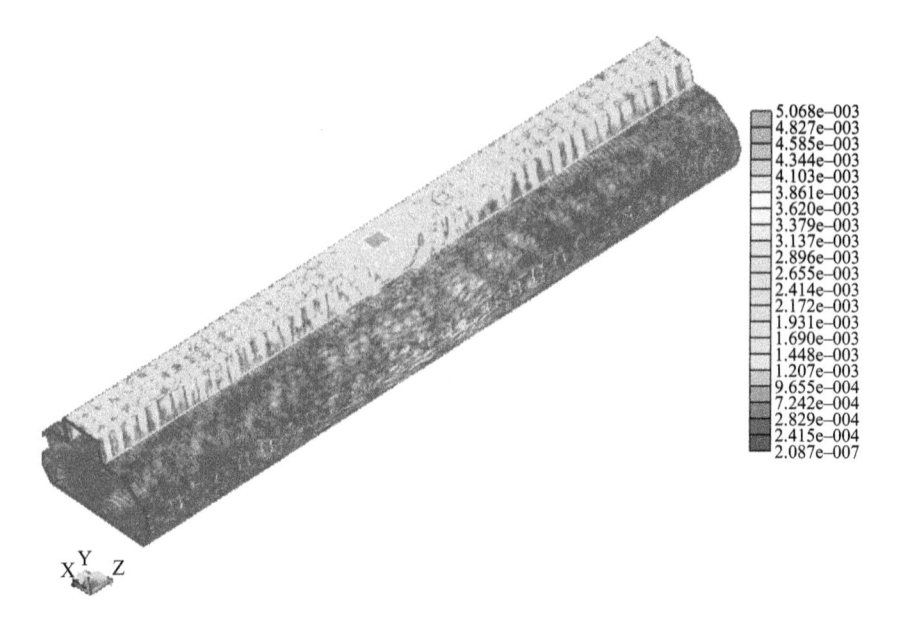

Figure 6.78 Surface current distribution on the airplane body at 3 GHz.

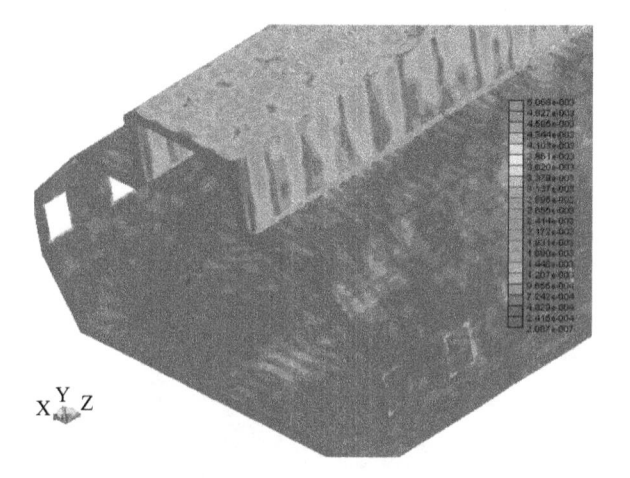

Figure 6.79 Zoomed conformal surface current distribution on the airplane body at 3 GHz.

6.14 Waveguide Slot Antenna

In this section, we use the parallel FDTD method to simulate a waveguide slot antenna consisting of an array of slanted slots fed by a waveguide [41–43], as shown in Figs. 6.81 and 6.82. The coupled slots are slanted and require the fine mesh to describe the power transmission from the waveguide feed to the slot array. The output parameters include the directivity pattern at the specified frequencies and reflection coefficient.

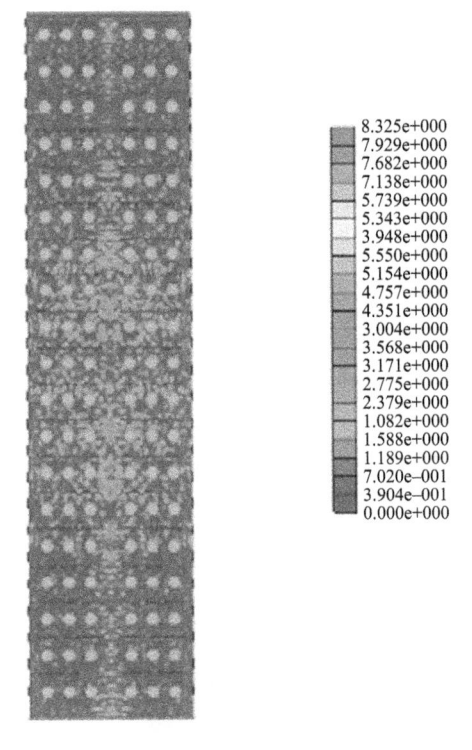

8.325e+000
7.929e+000
7.682e+000
7.138e+000
5.739e+000
5.343e+000
3.948e+000
5.550e+000
5.154e+000
4.757e+000
4.351e+000
3.004e+000
3.568e+000
3.171e+000
2.775e+000
2.379e+000
1.082e+000
1.588e+000
1.189e+000
7.020e–001
3.904e–001
0.000e+000

Y X
Z

Figure 6.80 Field distribution in the horizontal plane (height = 500 mm) inside the airplane at 3 GHz.

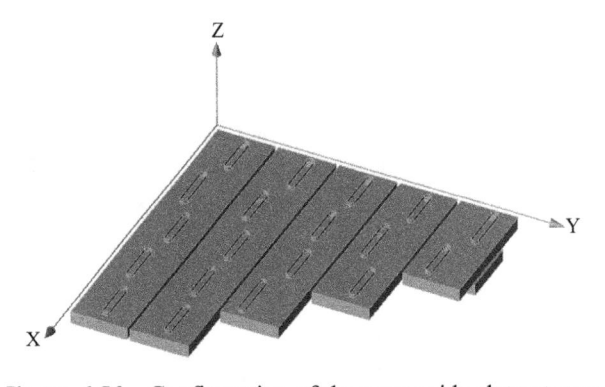

Figure 6.81 Configuration of the waveguide slot antenna.

In this waveguide slot antenna problem, the key point is to accurately simulate the slanted feed slots that determine the transmitted power. Next, we introduce a modified diagonal approximation technique [1] to accurately simulate the slanted slots. It is a well-known fact that for a slot oriented at 45° with respect to the coordinate system axis, we can use the diagonal approximation with the uniform mesh to accurately simulate the slanted slot, as

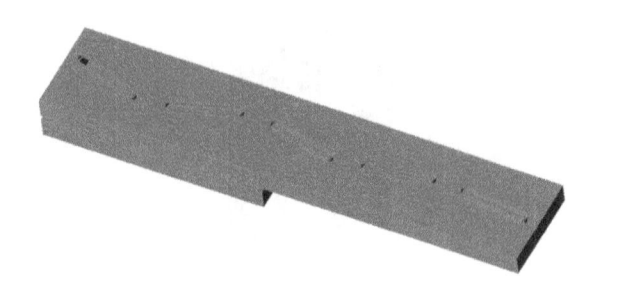

Figure 6.82   Feed array of slanted slots excited by a waveguide.

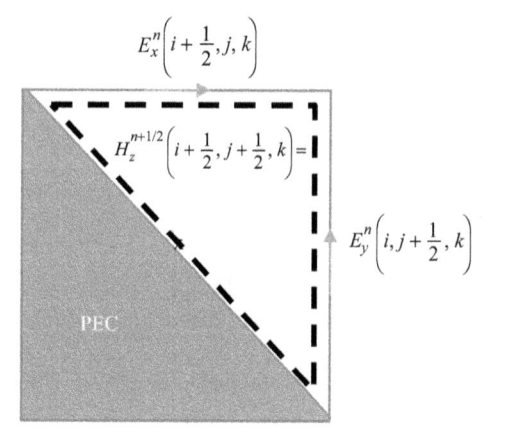

Figure 6.83   Configuration of the diagonal approximation in the FDTD method.

shown in Fig. 6.83. Here, two electric fields in the deformed cell are located inside the PEC structure and the other two electric fields are located outside the PEC structure. In the diagonal approximation, the magnetic field update inside the deformed cell can be expressed as:

$$H_z^{n+1/2}\left(i+\frac{1}{2},j+\frac{1}{2},k\right)$$

$$= H_z^{n-1/2}\left(i+\frac{1}{2},j+\frac{1}{2},k\right) + \frac{\Delta t}{\mu_z}\left[\frac{\Delta x E_x^n\left(i+\frac{1}{2},j,k\right)}{0.5\Delta x\Delta y} - \frac{\Delta y E_y^n\left(i,j+\frac{1}{2},k\right)}{0.5\Delta x\Delta y}\right] \quad (6.17)$$

In practical problems, the slot orientation may be arbitrary, and hence the uniform mesh may not be a good approximation to simulate a slot problem, as illustrated in Fig. 6.84. If we

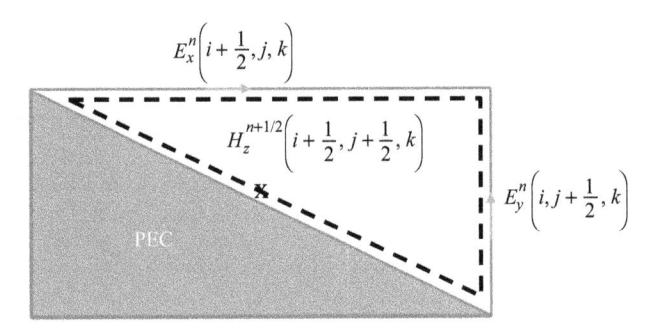

Figure 6.84 Configuration of the improved diagonal approximation in the FDTD method.

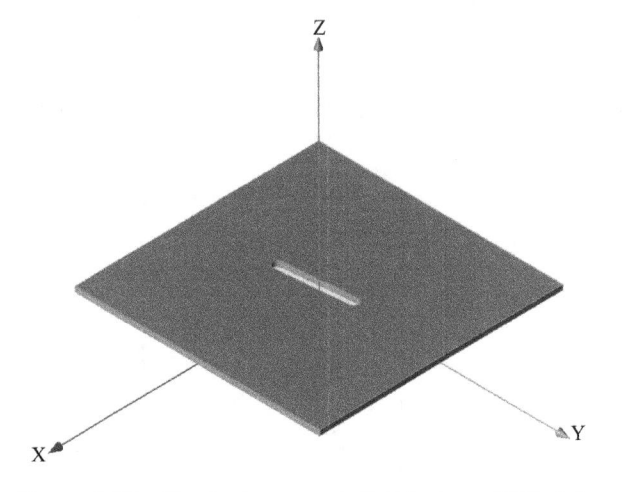

Figure 6.85 Single slot on an infinitely large PEC plate.

properly select the cell sizes in different directions, we can significantly improve the simulation results by using the diagonal approximation.

Now, we investigate the case with a single slot on an infinitely large PEC plate, as shown in Fig. 6.85. The slot is slanted for a small angle of 5.7° with respect to the x-axis. The polarization of an incident plane wave is along the x-axis. As a reference, we use the fine cell size of 0.01 mm in all three directions. We assume that the result generated by using the fine mesh is accurate. If the frequency of interest is about 10 GHz, the cell size of 0.01 mm corresponds to 300 cells per wavelength, which is sufficient for the accurate result. In numerical experiments, we use the uniform mesh first, that is, the cell dimensions are the same in all three directions ($\Delta x = \Delta y = \Delta z = 0.2$ mm). When we change the mesh cell sizes, the results vary accordingly. However, when we select the cell size to be $\Delta x = 0.1$ mm, $\Delta y = 0.5$ mm, the simulation result is closer to that obtained by using the

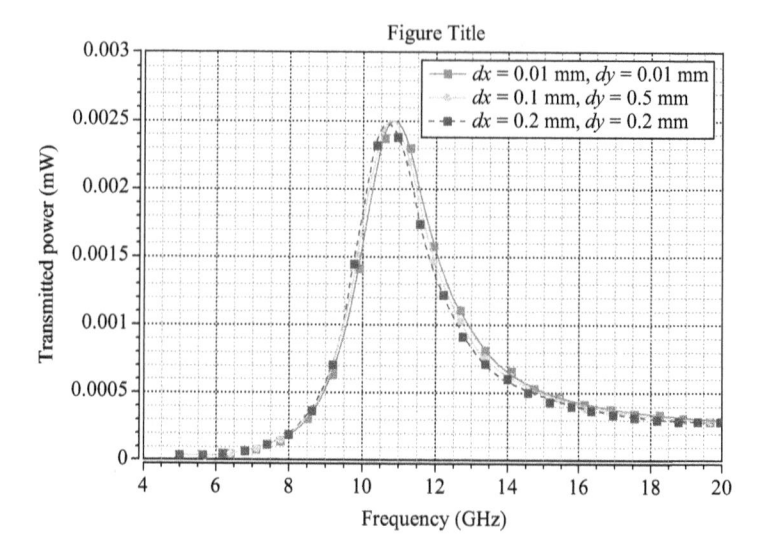

Figure 6.86   Comparison of results using different cell sizes in the x- and y-directions for the structure in Fig. 6.85.

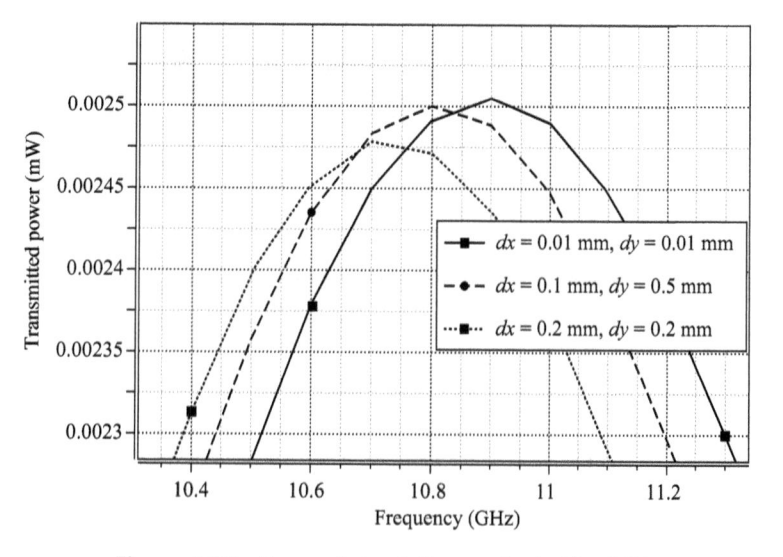

Figure 6.87   Zoomed simulation results in Fig. 6.86.

fine mesh, as shown in Fig. 6.86. The zoomed figure is shown in Fig. 6.88. At the beginning, we set the cell size in the x-direction to 0.2 mm, and increase the cell size in the y-direction from 0.2 mm to 0.5 mm. We find that the large cell size makes the result closer to that obtained by using the fine mesh. When we set the cell size in the y-direction to 0.5 mm and decrease the cell size in the x-direction from 0.5 mm to 0.1 mm, we find that the small cell size makes the result closer to that obtained by using the fine mesh.

It is evident from Fig. 6.87 that the properly selected mesh shape will significantly improve the simulation results with less computing resources as shown in Table 6.3.

The simulation results are also summarized in Table 6.4. The advantage of the rectangular mesh over the square mesh is summarized in Table 6.4.

We use the method described above to simulate the waveguide slot array antenna, and the reflection coefficient and 2-D and 3-D directivity patterns are shown in Figs. 6.88–6.90. Note that the simulation results are in a good agreement with the measurement data, which are not shown here.

Table 6.3 Problem sizes and memory requirements for different mesh types in the analysis of the structure in Fig. 6.85.

Mesh Type	Problem Size	Memory Requirement
Fine mesh	31.69 Mcells	2.15 GB
Regular mesh	0.15 Mcells	31.17 MB
Rectangular mesh	0.117 Mcells	26.06 MB

Table 6.4 Simulation result summary.

Mesh Type	Resonant Frequency	Transmitted Power
Fine mesh	10.9 GHz	0.002504 mW
Regular mesh	10.8 GHz	0.0025 mW
Rectangular mesh	10.7 GHz	0.002476 mW

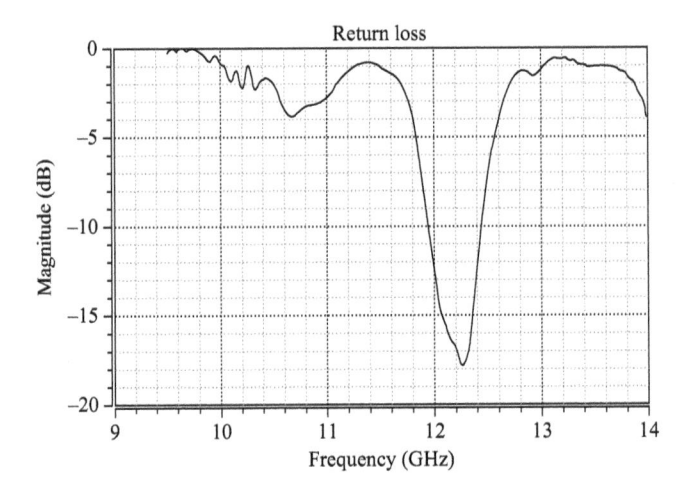

Figure 6.88 Reflection coefficient of the waveguide slot antenna array in Fig. 6.81.

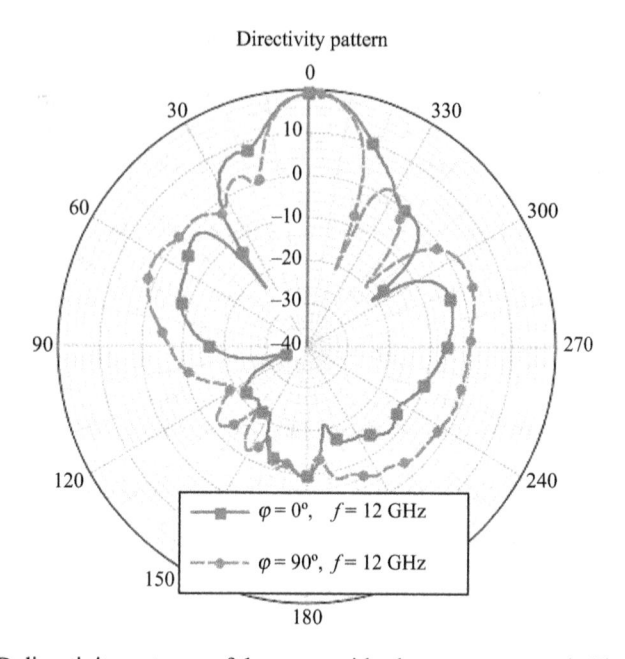

Figure 6.89 2-D directivity patterns of the waveguide slot antenna array in Fig. 6.81 at 12 GHz.

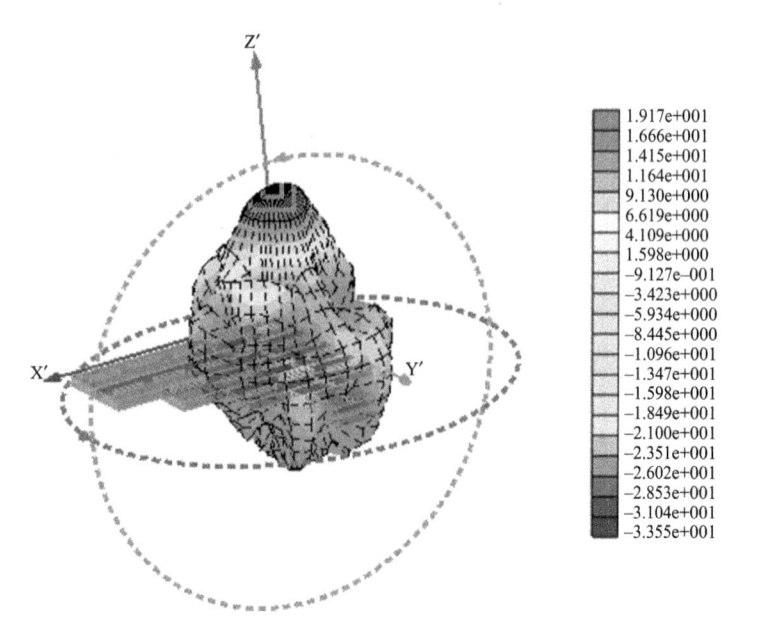

Figure 6.90 3-D directivity pattern of the waveguide slot antenna array in Fig. 6.81 at 12 GHz.

References

[1] A. Taflove and S. Hagness, *Computational Electromagnetics: The Finite-Difference Time-Domain Method*, 3rd ed., Artech House, Norwood, MA, 2005.

[2] W. Yu, X. Yang, Y. Liu, et al., *Advanced FDTD Method: Parallelization, Acceleration and Engineering Applications*, Artech House, Norwood, MA, 2011.

[3] W. Yu, X. Yang, Y. Liu, et al., *Parallel Finite Difference Time Domain Method*, Artech House, Norwood, MA, 2006.

[4] W. Yu, X. Yang, Y. Liu, et al., "New Development of Parallel Conformal FDTD Method in Computational Electromagnetics Engineering," *IEEE Antennas and Propagation Magazine*, Vol. 53, No. 3, 2011, pp. 15–41.

[5] W. Yu, X. Yang, Y. Liu, et al., "High Performance Conformal FDTD Method," *IEEE Microwave Magazine*, Vol. 11, No. 3, 2010, pp. 42–55.

[6] W. Yu, Y. Liu, Z. Su, et al., "A Robust Parallel Conformal Finite Difference Time Domain Processing Package Using MPI Library," *IEEE Antennas and Propagation Magazine*, Vol. 47, No. 3, 2005, pp. 39–59.

[7] W. Yu, X. Yang, Y. Liu, et al., "A New Conformal Mesh Generating Technique for Conformal Finite-Difference Time-Domain (CFDTD) Method," *IEEE Antennas and Propagation Magazine*, Vol. 46, No. 1, 2004, pp. 37–49.

[8] A. Elsherbeni and V. Demir, *The Finite Difference Time Domain Method for Electromagnetics: With MATLAB Simulations*, SciTech, Raleigh, NC, 2009.

[9] W. Yu and R. Mittra, "A Conformal FDTD Software Package for Modeling of Antennas and Microstrip Circuit Components," *IEEE Antennas and Propagation Magazine*. Vol. 42, No. 5, 2000, pp. 28–39.

[10] J. Nadobny, D. Sullivan, P. Wust, et al., "A High-Resolution Interpolation at Arbitrary Interfaces for the FDTD Method," *IEEE Transactions on Microwave Theory and Techniques*, Vol. 46, No. 11, 1998, pp. 1759–1766.

[11] W. Yu, X. Yang, Y. Liu, et al., "Advanced Features to Enhance the FDTD Method in GEMS Simulation Software Package," *2011 IEEE International Symposium on Antennas and Propagation* (APSURSI), Spokane, WA, July 2011, pp. 2728–2731.

[12] J. Wang, W. Yu, W. Yin, et al., "A Novel Conformal Surface Current Technique Based on High Performance Parallel FDTD Method," *IEEE Transactions on Electromagnetic Compatibility*, Pittsburg, 2011, pp. 1–4.

[13] Y. Zhang, R. Mittra, W. Hong, "Systematic design of planar lenses using artificial dielectrics," *IEEE Antennas and Propagation Society International Symposium (APS/URSI)*, Toronto Canada, 2010, pp. 1–4.

[14] Y. Zhang, R. Mittra, and W. Hong, "Systematic Design of Planar Lenses Using Artificial Dielectrics," *2010 AP-S International Symposium on Antennas and Propagation and 2010 USUN/CNC/URSI Meeting*, Toronto, ON, Canada, July 11–17, 2010, pp. 1–4.

[15] R. Liu, Q. Cheng, J. Y. Chin, et al., "Broadband Gradient Index Microwave Quasi-Optical Elements Based on Non-resonant Metamaterials," *Optics Express*, Vol. 17, No. 23, 2009, pp. 21030–21041.

[16] N. Gagnon, A. Petosa, and D. Mcnamara, "Comparison Between Conventional Lenses and an Electrically Thin Lens Made Using a Phase Shifting Surface (PSS) at Ka Band," *Loughborough Antenna Propagation Conference*, 2009, Loughborough, UK, November 2009, pp. 1–4.

[17] N. Gagnon, A. Petosa, and D. Mcnamara, "Thin Microwave Quasi-Transparent Phase-Shifting Surface (PSS)," *IEEE Transactions on Antennas and Propagation.*, Vol. 58, No. 4, 2010, pp. 1193–1201.

[18] N. Gagnon, A. Petosa, and D. McNamara, "Phase-Correcting Lens Antennas Made Using a Three-Layer Phase Shifting Surface (PSS) at Ka Band," *Proceedings of the 14th International Symposium on Antenna Technology and Applied Electromagnetics (ANTEM 2010)*, Ottawa, Canada, July 2010.

[19] X. Bunlon, P. Borderies, J. R. Poirier, et al., "Simulation of Radiation from an Antenna Mounted on a Vehicle by a Multilevel QR Compression Algorithm," *IEEE Microwave and Wireless Components Letters*, Vol. 15, No. 3, 2005, pp. 177–179.

[20] J. Huang and A. Densmore, "Microstrip Yagi Array Antenna for Mobile Satellite Vehicle Application," *IEEE Transactions on Antennas and Propagation*, Vol. 39, No. 7, 1991, pp. 1024–1030.

[21] R. Kronberger, A. Stephan, and M. Daginnus, "3D Antenna Measurement and Electromagnetic Simulation for Advanced Vehicle Antenna Development," *IEEE Antennas and Propagation Society International Symposium*, Vol. 3, Boston, USA, 2001, pp. 342–345.

[22] B. Philips, E. Parker, R. J. Langley, "Ray Tracing Analysis of the Transmission Performance of Curved FSS," *IEE Proceedings – Microwaves, Antennas and Propagation*, Vol. 142, No. 3, 1995, pp. 193–200.

[23] B. Philips, E. Parker, R. J. Langley, "Finite Curved Frequency Selective Surfaces," *Electronics Letters*, Vol. 29, No. 10, 1993, pp. 882–883.

[24] Y. Rahmat-Samii and A. Tulintseff, "Diffraction Analysis of Frequency Selective Reflector Antennas," *IEEE Transactions on Antennas and Propagation*, Vol. 41, No. 4, 1993, pp. 476–487.

[25] B. Stupfel and Y. Pion, "Impedance Boundary Conditions for Finite Planar and Curved Frequency Selective Surfaces," *IEEE Transactions on Antennas and Propagation*, Vol. 53, No. 4, 2005, pp. 1415–1425.

[26] B. Sanz-Izquierdo, E. Parker, J. B. Robertson, et al., "Singly and Dual Polarized Convoluted Frequency Selective Structures," *IEEE Transactions on Antennas and Propagation*, Vol. 58, No. 3, 2010, pp. 690–696.

[27] S. Savia, E. Parker, and B. Philips, "Finite Planar- and Curved-Ring-Element Frequency-Selective Surfaces," *IEEE Transactions on Antennas and Propagation*, Vol. 39, No. 2, 1991, pp. 211–217.

[28] http://en.wikipedia.org/wiki/Gaussian_beam

[29] L. Ma and R. Mittra, "Implementation of Gaussian Beam Sources in FDTD for Scattering Problems," *IEEE Antennas and Propagation Society International Symposium*, June 2007, Honololo, Hawaii, pp. 1665–1668.

[30] F. He, K. Wu, and W. Hong, "A Wideband Bandpass Filter by Integrating a Section of High Pass HMSIW with a Microstrip Low Pass Filter," *GSMM Global Symposium on Millimeter Waves*, Nanjing, 2008, pp. 282–284.

[31] J. Gu and X. Sun, "Compact Low Pass Filter Using Spiral Compact Microstrip Resonant Cells," *Electronics Letters*, Vol. 41, No. 19, 2005, pp. 1065–1066.

[32] Y. Wu, Y. Liu, Q. Xue, et al., "Analytical Design Method of Multiway Dual-Band Planar Power Dividers with Arbitrary," *IEEE Transactions on Power Division Microwave Theory and Techniques*, Vol. 58, No. 12, 2010, pp. 3832–3841.

[33] C. Leung and Q. Xue, "A Parallel-Strip Ring Power Divider with High Isolation and Arbitrary Power-Dividing Ratio," *IEEE Transactions on Microwave Theory and Techniques*, Vol. 5, No. 11, 2007, pp. 2419–2426.

[34] G. Mikucki and A. Agrawal, "A Broad-band Printed Circuit Hybrid Ring Power Divider," *IEEE Transactions on Microwave Theory and Techniques*, Vol. 37, No. 1, 1989, pp. 112–117.

[35] http://en.wikipedia.org/wiki/Window_function

[36] H. Albert, "Some Windows with Very Good Sidelobe Behavior," *IEEE Transactions on Acoustics, Speech, and Signal Processing*, Vol. 29, No. 1, 1981, pp. 84–91.

[37] F. Harris, "On the Use of Windows for Harmonic Analysis with the Discrete Fourier Transform", *Proceedings of the IEEE*, Vol. 66, No. 1, 1978, pp. 51–83.

[38] http://www.virtins.com/doc/D1003/Evaluation_of_Various_Window_Functions_using_Multi-Instrument_D1003.pdf

[39] L. Arnaut, "Compound Exponential Distributions for Undermoded Reverberation Chambers," *IEEE Transactions on Electromagnetic Compatibility*, Vol. 44, No. 3, 2002, pp. 442–457.

[40] C. Bruns and R. Vahldieck, "A Closer Look at Reverberation Chambers – 3-D Simulation and Experimental Verification," *IEEE Transactions on Electromagnetic Compatibility*, Vol. 47, No. 3, 2005, pp. 612–626.

[41] Y. Wang and S. Chung, "A Short Open-End Slot Antenna with Equivalent Circuit Analysis," *IEEE Transactions on Antennas and Propagation*, Vol. 58, No. 5, 2010, pp. 1771–1775.

[42] J. Li and L. Li, "Analysis of Omnidirectional Waveguide Slots Array Antennas," *2003 6th International Symposium on Antennas, Propagation and EM Theory*, Singapore, 2003.

[43] Y. Ding and K. Wu, "T-Type Folded Substrate Integrated Waveguide (TFSIW) Slot Array Antenna," *IEEE Microwave and Guided Wave Letters*, Vol. 8, No. 5, 1998, pp. 205–207.

Cloud Computing Techniques

Cloud computing is one type of service combination of software and hardware that does not require the end user to have knowledge of physical locations and configurations of computing systems, as illustrated in Fig. 7.1. A similar concept is used in the electricity grid and the water supplying system, where the end users consume power and water without needing to understand the component devices or infrastructure required to provide the service. Cloud computing is not a new concept as it has been used for many years in various engineering applications and scientific researches. Today, it is popular because many large companies are involved in it with advanced technologies and huge number of computer nodes available.

Cloud computing describes a new supplement, consumption, and delivery model for the software and hardware services based on the Internet protocols, and it typically involves provisioning of dynamically scalable and often virtualized resources. It is a byproduct and consequence of the ease-of-access to remote computing sites provided by the Internet. This may take the form of web-based tools or applications that the end users can access and use through a web browser as if the programs were installed locally on their own computers. Therefore, the end users may not need to install any application software on their local computers. All the computations and data processing happen in the remote resource.

Cloud computing provides the delivery of applications via the Internet, which are accessed from web browsers, desktop, or handheld devices, while the application software and data are stored on servers at the remote locations. In some cases, the applications are delivered via screen-sharing technology, while the computing resources are consolidated at the remote data centers; in other cases, the entire applications are coded using web-based technologies.

At the foundation of cloud computing is the broader concept of infrastructure convergence and shared services. This type of data center environment allows the end users to get their applications up and running faster, with less investment, easier manageability, and less maintenance, and enables the end users to more rapidly adjust the computing resources to meet fluctuating and unpredictable business demand.

Most cloud computing infrastructures consist of services delivered through shared data centers and appearing as a single point of access for the consumer computing requirement. Commercial offerings may be required to meet service-level agreements, which especially allow the smaller companies to access the large computing resources in a short time at a small cost.

Figure 7.1   Cloud computing is the delivery of computing as a service.

The tremendous impacts of cloud computing have prompted many governments world-wide to consider cloud computing as their infrastructure and to increase their spending budgets. Many countries and regions focus on cloud computing and consider it as the new and next economic growth point.

The term "cloud" means that the computing resources are huge and far away from where we can reach and are distributed in different areas [1]. We can only feel their existence through the Internet. Since the cloud computing is closely related to the mobile communication and applications in our daily lives, we always connect the cloud computing to the cell phone communication and bank account access; however, it is a broad concept and has been used in many areas.

Cloud computing is a natural evolution of the widespread adoption of virtualization, service-oriented architecture, autonomic, and utility computing. Details are abstracted from the end users who no longer have need for expertise in, or control over, the technology infrastructure "in the cloud" that supports them.

The underlying concept of cloud computing dates back to the 1960s with an idea that "computation may someday be organized as a public utility." Almost all the modern-day characteristics of cloud computing, the comparison to the electricity industry, and the use of public, private, government, and community forms were thoroughly explored in Douglas Parkhill's 1966 book [2]. The cloud computing concept also goes back to the 1950s when Herb Grosch, a computer scientist at IBM, postulated that the entire world would operate on dumb terminals powered by about 15 large data centers.

The actual term "cloud" borrows from telephony in which the telecommunication companies, which offered primarily dedicated point-to-point data circuits, began offering virtual private network (VPN) services with comparable quality of service (QoS) but at a much lower cost. By switching traffic to the balance utilization, they were able to utilize their overall network bandwidth more effectively. The cloud symbol was used to denote the demarcation point for the responsibility between the provider and the end users. Cloud computing extends this boundary to cover servers as well as the network infrastructure.

Amazon played a key role in the development of cloud computing by modernizing their data centers, which were using as little as 10 percent of their capacity at any one time, just to leave room for occasional spikes. Having found that the new cloud architecture resulted in the significant internal efficiency improvements that could add new features faster and more easily, Amazon initiated a new product development effort to provide cloud computing to external customers, and launched Amazon web service (AWS) [3] on a utility computing basis in 2006.

In early 2008, Eucalyptus [4] became the first open-source, AWS API-compatible platform for deploying private clouds. In the same time period, OpenNebula, enhanced in the RESERVOIR [5] European Commission-funded project, became the first open-source software for deploying private and hybrid clouds, and for the federation of clouds. In the same year, efforts were focused on providing QoS guarantees to cloud-based infrastructures, in the framework of the IRMOS [6] European Commission-funded project, resulting in a real-time cloud environment.

7.1 Basic Terminologies in Cloud Computing

Basic characteristics of cloud computing include but are not limited to the following three:

- The storing and accessing of applications and computer data often through a web browser rather than by running the installed software on the user personal computers or office servers.
- Internet-based computing provided to computers and mobile devices on demand.
- Using the Internet to access web-based applications and web services as a service.

Basic terminologies in the cloud computing include:

Off-site: A basic principle of cloud computing is that the end users are accessing the computing resources that are in a data center far away from them. That means the end users do not buy the servers and storage, but the service providers do.

Virtual: The computing resources in the cloud can be assembled with drag-and-drop ease. Employing virtualization, the cloud service providers let the end users assemble software stacks of databases, web servers, operating systems, storage, and networking, and then manage them as virtual servers.

On demand: In the cloud, the end users can add and subtract resources, including number and type of computing processors, amount of memory, network bandwidth, gigabytes of storage, and 32-bit or 64-bit architectures. The end users can dial up when they need more, and dial down when they need less.

Subscription style: These tend to be month-to-month deals, often payable by credit card, rather than annual contacts. For example, Amazon charges in intervals of 10 cents per hour for their EC2, which stands for "Elastic Compute Cloud." Amazon allows the users to use their cloud computing in either the pay-by-the-hour or the pay-by-the-gigabyte.

Shared: For economies of scale, many service providers use a multitenant architecture to squeeze workloads from multiple customers onto the same physical machines. It is just one of the things that distinguish cloud computing from outsourcing and from hosted data centers.

Simple: Many of the cloud services providers – whether they specialize in application hosting, storage, or compute cycles – let the end users sign up and configure resources in a few minutes, using an interface that the end users do not have to be a system administrator to understand.

Web based: The computing resources can be accessed through web browsers without requiring the end users installing any application software. For example, the end users cannot install any electromagnetic application software on a smartphone or other handheld devices today.

In addition, the following terminologies are also important:

Public cloud: It is the one based on the standard cloud computing model, in which a service provider makes resources, such as applications and storage, available to the general public over the Internet. Public cloud services may be free or offered on a pay-per-usage model. The main benefits of using a public cloud service are:

- Easy and inexpensive setup because hardware, application, and bandwidth costs are covered by the provider.
- Scalability to meet needs.
- No wasted resources because the end users pay for what they use.

Private cloud: It is a proprietary network or a data center that supplies the hosted services to a limited number of users. When a service provider uses public cloud resources to create their private cloud, the result is called a virtual private cloud. Regardless of private or public cloud, the goal of cloud computing is to provide easy, scalable access to computing resources.

Private cloud is relative to the public cloud, and limits the users inside a local network or VPN certification. For example, today the most cloud computing systems inside companies or universities belong to the private cloud. The main benefits of a private cloud service are as follows:

- Data security is guaranteed since all the users are behind the firewall.
- The known details of cloud resource help increase the usage efficiency.
- Software and hardware upgrade are faster and more efficient.

7.2 Electromagnetic Cloud Example

In the electromagnetic simulations [7], use of the most public clouds today on the market is charged based on the number of the compute cores. Due to the NUMA architecture in the popular servers and multi-CPU workstations, the job division in terms of CPUs has much higher parallel efficiency than that based on the compute cores. Most vendors do not like to charge based on the number of CPUs because the hardware cost of the modern servers increases with the number of cores. Therefore, for a private cloud, the company can decide the rental policy to achieve the best system performance.

7.2.1 Electromagnetic cloud example

Suppose that an electromagnetic software package has been installed on a cloud and we have an account to access the cloud resources; now we can use the web browser to login the cloud system, as shown in Fig. 7.2. We can access the files on clouds just like on the local computer, as shown in Fig. 7.3, submit jobs to the clouds without requiring installation of any electromagnetic software packages, as shown in Fig. 7.4, monitor the simulation progress, as shown in Fig. 7.5, and check the simulation results, as shown in Fig. 7.6.

Cloud computing includes two key techniques: (1) virtual machines and (2) web-based applications. In the electromagnetic cloud computing, the cloud computing system will select the machines according to the users' requirements. Since the large amount of data has to be exchanged from one node to another, the electromagnetic cloud computing requires that the nodes in one cloud must be connected through a high-performance network. The electromagnetic cloud computing has a web-based environment that allows the users to modify (and even create) the project model, excitation and output options, mesh distribution, and all the data post-processing on the cloud.

7.2.2 Rocks cluster management software

Electromagnetic simulation software is one of the applications on the Rocks cluster management software. Rocks cluster distribution (originally called NPACI Rocks) [8] is a widely used cluster operating system and a Linux distribution intended for high-performance

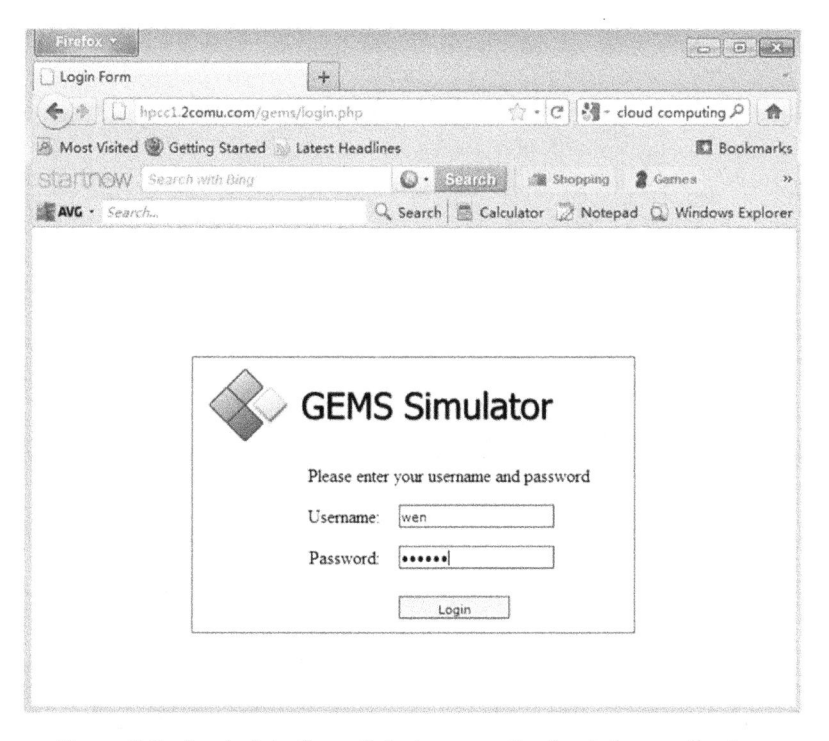

Figure 7.2 Login interface of electromagnetic simulation application.

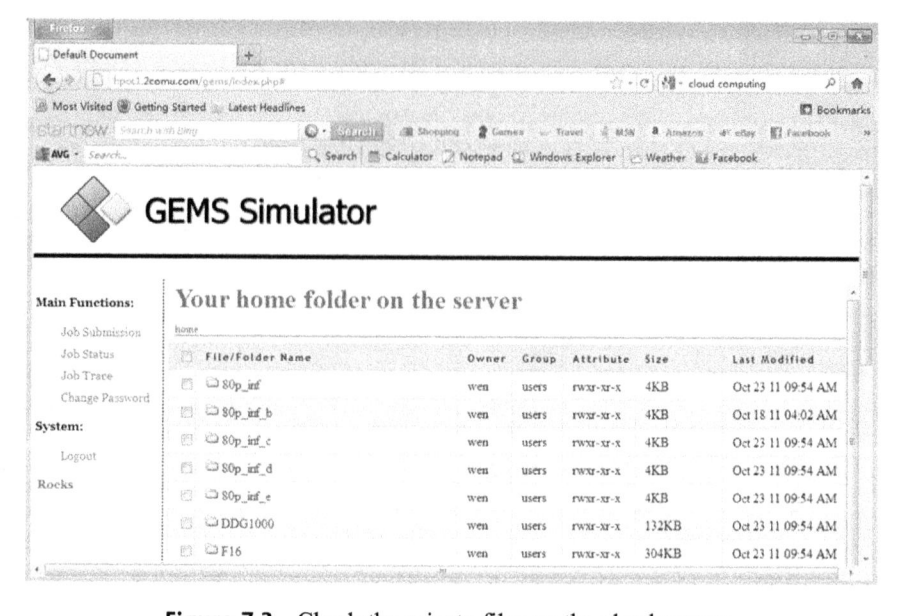

Figure 7.3   Check the private files on the cloud servers.

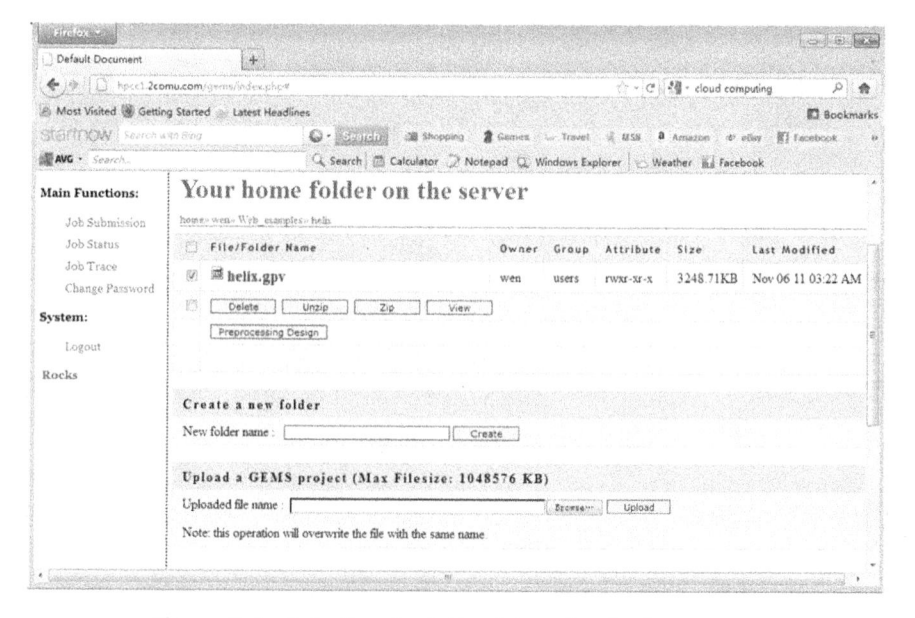

Figure 7.4   Submit a simulation job to the cloud resources.

computing clusters. It was started by National Partnership for Advanced Computational Infrastructure and San Diego Supercomputer Center in 2000 and was initially funded in part by a National Science Foundation (NSF) grant (2000–2007) but is currently funded by the follow-up NSF grant. Rocks was initially based on the Red Hat Linux distribution. However,

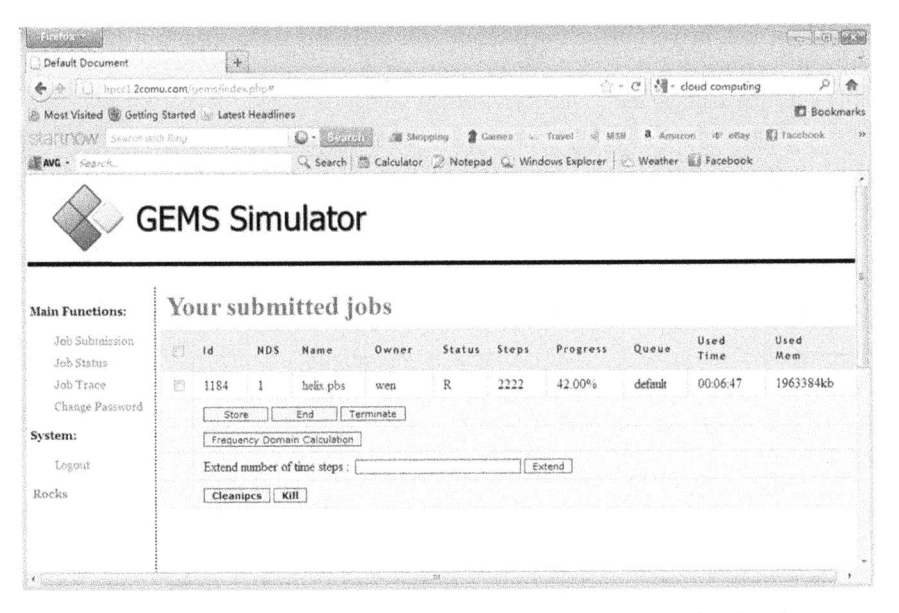

Figure 7.5   Monitor the simulation status and job list on the cloud.

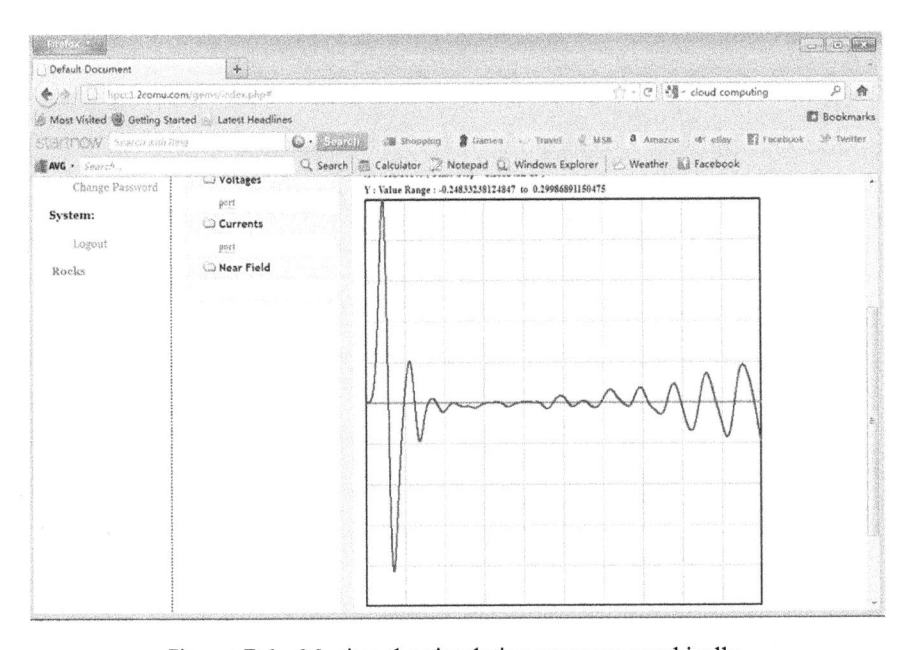

Figure 7.6   Monitor the simulation progress graphically.

the modern versions of Rocks are now based on CentOS, with a modified Anaconda installer that simplifies mass installation onto many computers. Rocks includes many tools (such as MPI) which are not part of CentOS but are integral components that make a group of computers into a cluster.

Installations can be customized with additional software packages at install time by using special user-supplied "Roll CDs" extend the system by integrating seamlessly and automatically into the management and packaging mechanisms used by base software, simplifying installation and configuration of large numbers of computers. Over a dozen of rolls have been created, including the SUN Grid Engine (SGE) roll, the Condor roll, the Lustre roll, the Java roll, and the Ganglia roll.

7.3 Scientific Cloud Computing

Cloud computing emerges as a new computing paradigm, which aims to provide reliable, customized, and qualified service, and guaranteed dynamic computing environments for the end users. This section introduces the basic concepts and applications in the engineering projects [9].

7.3.1 Introduction

The cloud computing proposed in late 2007 currently emerges as a hot topic due to its abilities to offer flexible dynamic IT infrastructures, QoS guaranteed computing environments and configurable software services. There are still no widely accepted definitions for the cloud computing albeit the cloud computing practice has attracted much attention. Several reasons lead to this situation:

● Cloud computing involves researchers and engineers from various backgrounds, for instance, grid computing, software engineering, and databases. They work on cloud computing from different viewpoints.
● Technologies that enable the cloud computing are still evolving and progressing, for example, Web 2.0 [10] and service oriented computing (SOC).
● Existing computing clouds still lack large-scale deployment and usage, which would finally justify the concept of cloud computing.

The examples and concepts are based on the engineering computing, which is different from the general cloud computing due to the following reasons:

● Electromagnetic simulation requires a large amount of data exchanging during simulation. Therefore, the computing resource must be located at the same place and connected through the high-performance network.
● To efficiently use the multi-CPU servers or workstations, the job division must be based on the number of CPUs, instead of compute cores like in the most cloud system.
● The users require checking the simulation status and intermediate results during the simulation, and hence the backup nodes must be available to do the data post-processing.
● The users often need the view and modification of the simulation models, which may require a large amount of data communication and the faster graphical functions.
● The users require that their data be secure in any cases. Most time, people compare it to the credit card system; however, the value of data leaking cannot be easily evaluated.

7.3.2 Cloud computing service

Conceptually, the users acquire computing platforms from computing clouds and then run their applications inside. Therefore, computing clouds render users with services to access hardware, software, and data resources, thereafter an integrated computing platform as a service, in a transparent way:

- Hardware as a service: As the result of rapid advances in hardware virtualization, the users could buy hardware as a pay-as-you-go subscription service. A typical example could be found at Amazon EC2.
- Software as a service: The users can get the service across the Internet. This model eliminates the need to install and run the application on the customer's local computers. However, the users may need to keep the original result data, so the users need to install the data post-processing software to generate the results later on. For example, the users want to change the frequency range of interest or derive the new output parameters based on the simulation results.
- Data as a service: The data usually have two types of formats, namely, the raw data and graphical results. The users usually download the raw data to their local computer and view the graphical result through network from regular computer or handheld devices such as smartphones or tablets.

Amazon storage service provides a simple web services interface that can be used to store and retrieve, declared by Amazon, any amount of data, at any time, from anywhere on the web. Cloud computing offers the development platform, and the users can develop their own data post-processing code on the cloud platform. And then, the users can run the code and generate the results from anywhere and at any time through network without requiring any local real data processing.

7.3.3 Features in cloud computing

The cloud computing is different from other computing paradigms in the following aspects:

- User-centric interfaces
  The users obtain and employ computing platforms in computing clouds as easily as they access a traditional public utility (such as electricity, water, natural gas, or telephone network), for instance:
  - The cloud interfaces do not force users to change their working habits and environments, for example, programming language, compiler, and operating system.
  - The cloud client software installed locally is relatively simple. For example, the users can install the result visualization software in their local computer or no software at all on their local handheld devices.
  - The cloud interfaces are location independent and can be accessed by the popular Internet browser.
- On-demand service provisioning
  The computing clouds provide resources and services for users on demand. The users can customize and personalize their computing environments.

- QoS guaranteed offer
  The computing environments provided by computing clouds can guarantee QoS for the users, for instance, hardware performance like CPU speed, I/O (input/output) bandwidth, and memory amount.
- Autonomous system
  The computing cloud is an autonomous system and it is managed transparently to users. Hardware, software, and data inside clouds can be automatically reconfigured to present a single platform image.
- Scalability and flexibility
  The scalability and flexibility are the most important features that drive the emergence of the cloud computing. Cloud services and computing platforms offered by computing clouds could be scaled across various parameters, such as geographical locations, hardware performance, and software configurations.

7.3.4 Advanced technologies in cloud computing

A number of advanced technologies in cloud computing include:

- Virtualization technology
  The virtual machine techniques, such as VMware [11] for Windows and Linux systems and Xen [12] for Linux system, offer the virtualized simulation and system configuration results on demand. The virtual network advances support users with a customized network environment to access cloud resources.
- Web service
  The web service is normally exposed as the web browser services, which follow the industry standards such as WSDL [13], SOAP [14], and UDDI [15]. A set of cloud services furthermore could be used in an application environment, thus making them available on various distributed platforms and could be further accessed across the Internet.
- Web 2.0
  Web 2.0 is an emerging technology describing the innovative trends of using World Wide Web technology and web design that aims to enhance creativity, information sharing, collaboration, and functionality. Web 2.0 applications typically include the following features:
  - Rich Internet application: It defines the experience brought from desktop to browser whether it is from a graphical point of view or usability point of view.
  - Web-oriented architecture – It is a key piece in Web 2.0, which defines how Web 2.0 applications expose their functionality so that other applications can leverage and integrate the functionality providing a set of much richer applications.
  - Social web – It defines how Web 2.0 tends to interact much more with the end users and make the end users an integral part.

  The essential idea behind Web 2.0 is to improve the interconnectivity and interactivity of web applications. The new paradigm to develop and access web applications enables users to access the web more easily and efficiently. The cloud computing services in nature are web applications that render desirable computing services on demand.

- Worldwide distributed storage system – A cloud storage model should foresee:
  - A network storage system, which is backed by the distributed storage providers, offers the storage capacity for the users to lease. The data storage could be migrated, merged, and managed transparently to the end users for whatever data formats.

- A distributed data system, which provides the data sources accessed in a semantic way. The users could locate their data sources in a large distributed environment by the logical name instead of the physical locations.
- Programming model

The users drive into the computing cloud with data and applications. Some cloud programming models should be proposed for users to adapt to the cloud infrastructure. For the simplicity and easy access of cloud services, the cloud programming model, however, should not be too complex or too innovative for the end users. The MapReduce [16–18] is a programming model and an associated implementation for processing and generating large data sets across the Google worldwide infrastructures.

7.4 Cloud Computing and Grid Computing

This section is devoted to comparing the cloud computing and the grid computing [19–21] in various aspects, such as definitions, infrastructures, middleware, and applications. It is of interest to develop computing clouds on the existing grid infrastructures to get advantages of grid middleware and applications.

- Definition

The grid computing, originating from high-performance distributed computing, aims to share distributed computing resource for remote job execution and for the large-scale problem-solving. The grid computing emphasizes the resource side by making huge efforts to build an independent and complete distributed system. The cloud computing provides the user-centric functionalities and services for the users to build the customized computing environments. The cloud computing, which is oriented toward the industry service, follows an application-driven model.

- Infrastructure

Grid infrastructure has the following features:

- Grid infrastructure in nature is a decentralized system, which spans across geographically distributed sites.
- Grid infrastructure normally contains heterogeneous resources, such as hardware/software configurations, access interfaces, and management policies.

On the contrary, from the viewpoint of users, the computing clouds operate like a central compute server with single access point. The cloud infrastructures could span several computing centers, like Google and Amazon, and in general contain homogeneous resources, operated under central control.

- Middleware

The grid community has established well-defined industry standards for grid middleware, for example, WSRF [22]. The middleware for cloud computing, or the cloud operating system, is still underdeveloped and lacks standards. A number of research issues remain unsolved, for example, distributed virtual machine management, cloud service orchestration, and distributed storage management.

- Accessibility and application

The grid computing has an ambitious objective to offer dependable, consistent, pervasive, and inexpensive access to high-end computational capabilities. However, the inexperienced users still find difficulties to adapt their applications to grid computing. Furthermore, it is not easy to get a performance guarantee from computational grids. The cloud computing, on the contrary, could offer customized, scalable, and QoS guaranteed computing environments for users with an easy and pervasive access. The grid computing has gained numerous success stories in many application fields.

References

[1] en.Wikipedia.org/wiki/cloud_computing

[2] D. Parkhill, *The Challenge of the Computer Utility*, Addison-wesley, Upper Saddle River, NJ, 1st edition, 1966.

[3] http://aws.typepad.com/aws/2006/08/amazon_ec2_beta.html

[4] Eucalyptus Project, http://eucalyptus.cs.ucsb.edu/

[5] Eucalyptus Project, http://www-03.ibm.com/press/us/en/pressrelease/23448.wss

[6] http://www.youtube.com/watch?v=zLn_D3_d4sI

[7] http://www.2comu.com, State College, PA

[8] http://en.wikipedia.org/wiki/Rocks_Cluster_Distribution

[9] L. Wang and G. Laszewski, "Scientific Cloud Computing: Early Definition and Experience," *10th IEEE International Conference on High Performance Computing and Communications*, 2008, Dalian, China.

[10] Web 2.0 definition, http://en.wikipedia.org/wiki/web 2/

[11] VMware virtualization technology, http://www.vmware.com

[12] http://www.xen.org/

[13] Web Service Description Language (WSDL), http://www.w3.org/tr/wsdl/

[14] Simple Object Access Protocol (SOAP), http://www.w3.org/tr/soap/

[15] OASIS UDDI Specification, http://www.oasisopen.org/committees/uddi-spec/doc/ tcspecs.htm

[16] J. Dean and S. Ghemawat, MapReduce: Simplified Data Processing on Large Clusters, *Communications of the ACM*, 2008.

[17] M. Olson, "HADOOP: Scalable, Flexible Data Storage and Analysis," *IQT Quarterly*, pp. 14–18, Spring 2010.

[18] J. Lin and C. Dyer, "Data -Intensive Text Processing with MapReduce," *Morgan and Claypool*, San Rafael, CA, 2010.

[19] F. Lelli, E. Frizziero, M. Gulmini, et al., "The Many Faces of the Integration of Instruments and the Grid," *International Journal of Web and Grid Services*, Vol. 3, No. 3, 2007, pp. 239–266.

[20] http://www.redbooks.ibm.com/redpapers/pdfs/redp3613.pdf

[21] http://arxiv.org/ftp/arxiv/papers/0901/0901.0131.pdf

[22] http://en.wikipedia.org/wiki/Web_Services_Resource_Framework

3-D Parallel FDTD Source Code

In this appendix, we present a 3-D parallel FDTD demonstration code enhanced by the VALU acceleration, which can be used for general electromagnetic problems. The source code includes the electric and magnetic field updates, CPML update, 3-D parallel processing, VALU acceleration, OpenMp, and MPI. The code is programmed in the C language. The readers can modify it for different applications by adding different subroutines and functions.

Appendix 1: Input Parameters

(1) Cell size: *dx*, *dy*, *dz*
(2) Time factor: 0.995
(3) Source position: source_position_x, source_position_y, source_position_z
(4) Number of time steps: time_steps
(5) Number of cells: *nx*, *ny*, *nz*
(6) Excitation pulse: $\exp(-0.5 * ((20.0 - n) / 6.0)^2)$

Appendix 2: Output Parameters

(1) Field at point: electric field
(2) Field on surface: electric field
(3) Elapsed time: simulation time
(4) Intermediate CPML parameters: number of layers, *a* and *b* values

Appendix 3: Functions

(1) 3-D parallel FDTD code with the CPML absorbing boundary condition
(2) Gaussian pulse excitation
(3) Field outputs at point and on surface

Appendix 4: Code Requirements

(1) Hardware:
   o CPU: Intel Pentium IV, AMD Athlon 64, or newer CPUs.
(2) Compiler: Microsoft VC 2005 or higher versions, Intel C 9.0 or higher versions, GCC 4.0 or higher versions.
(3) MPI environment: MPI2: In the MPICH2 under Windows system, the default installation of MPICH2 is in C:\Program Files\MPICH2. Three sub-directories are in the installation directory: *include*, *bin*, and *lib*. The *include* and *lib* directories contain the header files and libraries necessary to compile MPI applications. The bin directory contains the process manager, smpd.exe, and the MPI job launcher, mpiexec.exe. The *dll*s that implement MPICH2 are copied to the Windows System32 directory.

   The libraries in the *lib* directory were compiled with Microsoft Visual Studio NET 2003 and Intel Fortran 8.1. These compilers and any others that can link with the Microsoft *.lib files can be used to create user applications. Both gcc and g77 for Cygwin (Unix-like environment and command line interface for Microsoft Windows) can be used with the libmpich*.a libraries.

For MS Developer Studio users: Create a project and add [1]

"C:\Program Files\MPICH2\include"

to the *include* path and

"C:\Program Files\MPICH2\lib"

to the library path. Add mpi.lib and cxx.lib to the link command. Add cxxd.lib to the Debug target link instead of cxx.lib.

Appendix 5: Subroutine List in the FDTD Code

In this part, we explain the major subroutines used in the parallel FDTD code to help the readers understand the FDTD code, PML, parallel processing, and VALU acceleration techniques. Six micros that help in structure optimization are used in the FDTD code. These six micros are:

#define h_update_nonmagnetic	for the magnetic field update (this code is designed for the nonmagnetic material).
#define e_update_nonelectric:	for the electric field update (this code is designed for the nonelectric material).
#define e_update_nonelectric_pml_add:	for the electric field addition operation inside the PML region.
#define e_update_nonelectric_pml_sub:	for the electric field subtraction operation inside the PML region.
#define h_update_nonmagnetic_pml_sub:	for the magnetic field subtraction operation inside the PML region.
#define h_update_nonmagnetic_pml_add:	for the magnetic field addition operation inside the PML region.

We list the major subroutines in the parallel FDTD code and briefly explain them. Since the "main" routine reflects the structure of the parallel FDTD code and the relationship of each subroutine, we explain each line in this routine.

main: controls the main structure of the FDTD code, and its subroutines are:

MPI_Init:	initialize MPI environment
MPI_Comm_size:	number of sub-domains
MPI_Comm_rank:	position of the current sub-domain
size:	size of sub-domain in the x-direction
low_value:	start position of the sub-domain in the x-direction
high_value:	end position of the sub-domain in the x-direction
source_owner:	excitation source inside the current sub-domain
source_left_owner:	left position of the excitation source inside the current sub-domain
source_right_owner:	right position of the excitation source inside the current sub-domain
memory_size:	memory used by the current sub-domain
source_position_x_local:	local position of the excitation source in the sub-domain
Index_E_Boundary[X_MIN]:	initial electric field boundary position in the x-direction
Index_E_Boundary[Y_MIN]:	initial electric field boundary position in the y-direction
Index_E_Boundary[Z_MIN]:	initial electric field boundary position in the z-direction
Index_E_Boundary[X_MAX]:	end electric field boundary position in the x-direction
Index_E_Boundary[Y_MAX]:	end electric field boundary position in the y-direction
Index_E_Boundary[Z_MAX]:	end electric field boundary position in the z-direction
Index_H_Boundary[X_MIN]:	initial magnetic field boundary position in the x-direction
Index_H_Boundary[Y_MIN]:	initial magnetic field boundary position in the y-direction
Index_H_Boundary[Z_MIN]:	initial magnetic field boundary position in the z-direction
Index_H_Boundary[X_MAX]:	end magnetic field boundary position in the x-direction
Index_H_Boundary[Y_MAX]:	end magnetic field boundary position in the y-direction
Index_H_Boundary[Z_MAX]:	end magnetic field boundary position in the z-direction
BoundaryLayerNum[X_MIN]:	number of PML layers in the minimum x-direction
BoundaryLayerNum[X_MAX]:	number of PML layers in the maximum x-direction
BoundaryLayerNum[Y_MIN]:	number of PML layers in the minimum y-direction
BoundaryLayerNum[Y_MAX]:	number of PML layers in the maximum y-direction
BoundaryLayerNum[Z_MIN]:	number of PML layers in the minimum z-direction
BoundaryLayerNum[Z_MAX]:	number of PML layers in the maximum z-direction
initialize_array:	initialize the arrays
initialize_CPML:	initialize the arrays inside the PML region

MPI_Type_vector:	define the MPI data type
MPI_Type_commit:	submit the new data type
compute:	field update
MPI_Finalize:	finish the MPI process
memory_malloc_1D:	allocate memory for 1-D array
memory_malloc_3D:	convert 1-D array to 3-D array
initialize_array:	initialize the arrays
initialize_CPML:	initialize the PML coefficients
Compute:	field update including the PML and computational domain
MPI_Barrier:	wait each other among the sub-domains
elapsed_time:	start recording the simulation time
compute_MPI_PEC:	use the PEC boundary to truncate the domain
compute_MPI_CPML:	use the CPML boundary to truncate the domain
compute_SSE_PEC:	PEC boundary accelerated by SSE
compute_SSE_CPML:	CPML boundary accelerated by SSE
data_collect:	collect the output data
elapsed_time:	stop recording simulation time
output_Ez:	output the simulation result
output_ElaspedTime:	output the simulation time
output_ElaspedTime:	output the simulation time
compute_MPI_PEC:	PEC boundary in the six sides
compute_MPI_CPML:	PML boundary in the six sides
compute_H:	compute the magnetic fields for the PEC boundary inside the computational domain
compute_H_PUSAI:	compute the magnetic fields for the PML boundary inside the computational domain
compute_H_SSE:	compute the magnetic fields for the PEC boundary with the SSE acceleration inside the computational domain
compute_H_PUSAI_SSE:	compute the magnetic fields for the PML boundary with the SSE acceleration inside the computational domain
compute_E:	compute the electric fields for the PEC boundary inside the computational domain
compute_E_PUSAI:	compute the electric fields for the PML boundary inside the computational domain
compute_E_SSE:	compute the electric fields for the PEC boundary with the SSE acceleration inside the computational domain
compute_E_PUSAI_SSE:	compute the electric fields for the PML boundary with the SSE acceleration inside the computational domain

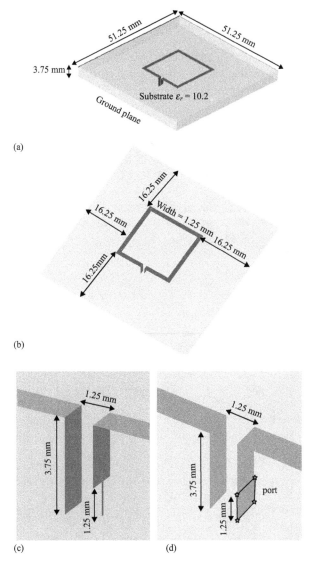

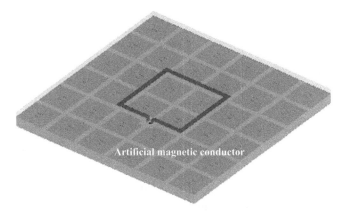

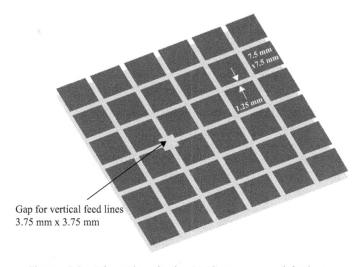

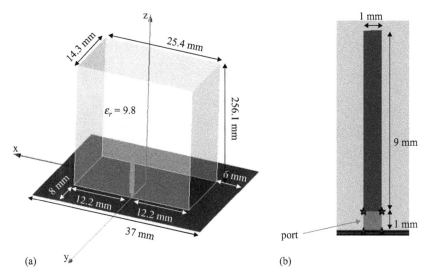

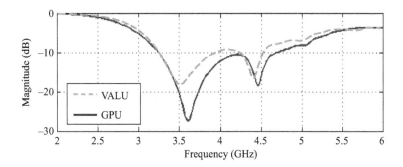

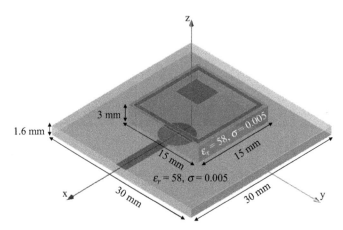

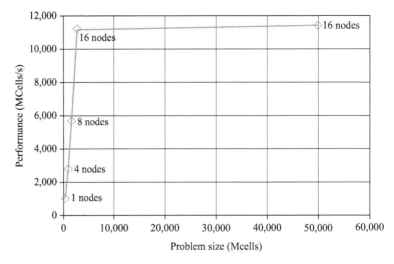

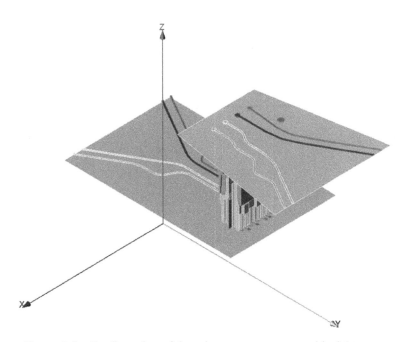

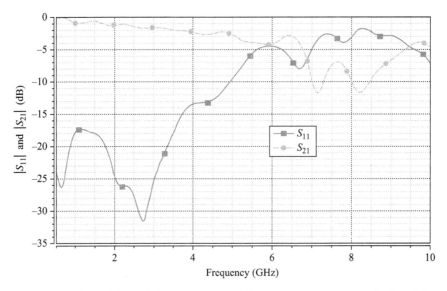

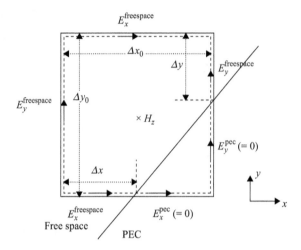

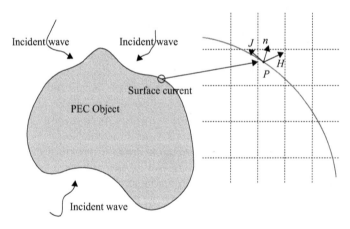

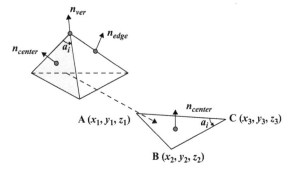

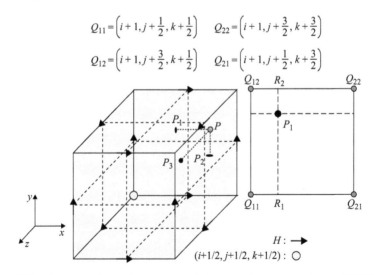

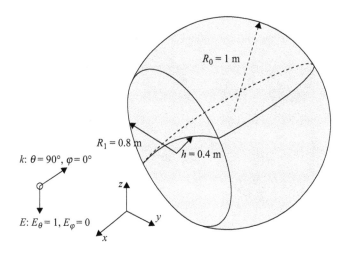

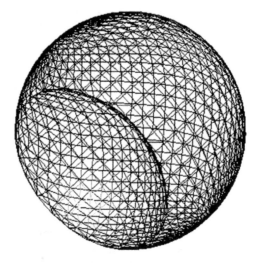

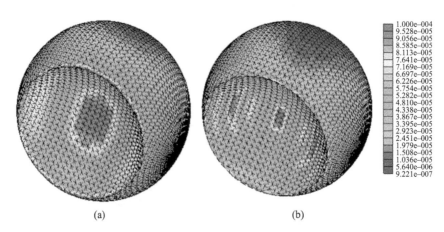

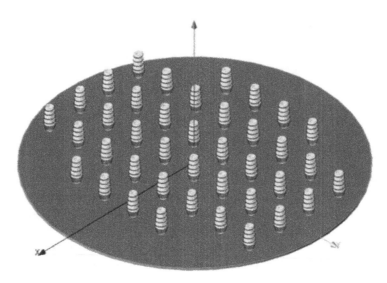

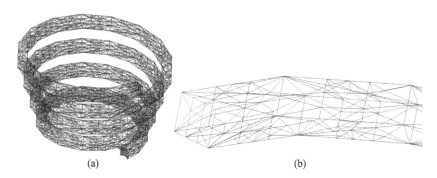

$$\theta = \tan^{-1}\left(\sqrt{(x^2 + y^2)}/F\right) \tag{6.11}$$

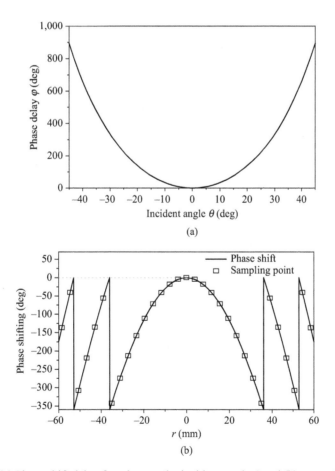

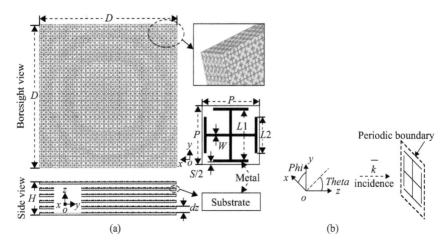

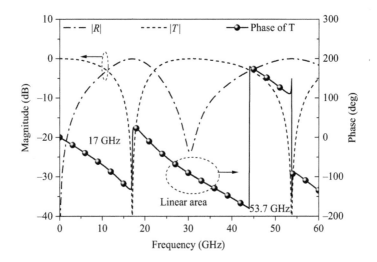

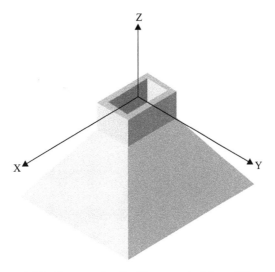

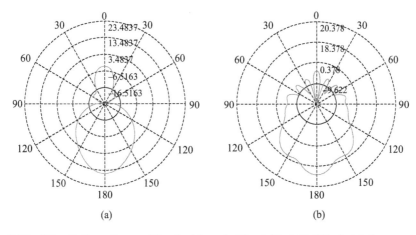

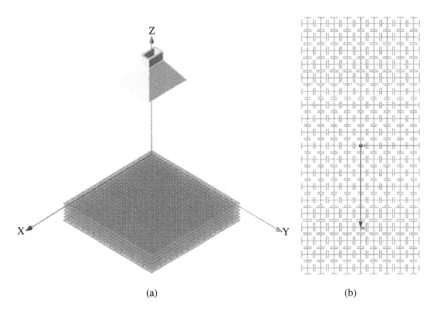

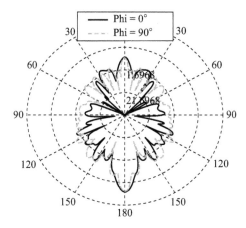

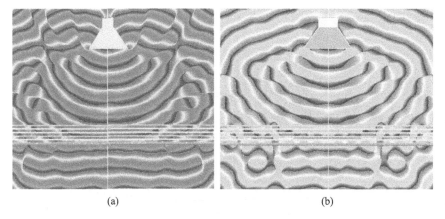

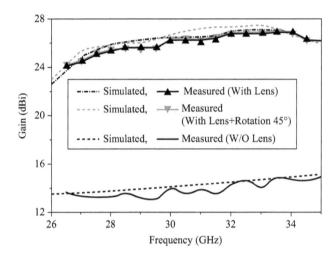

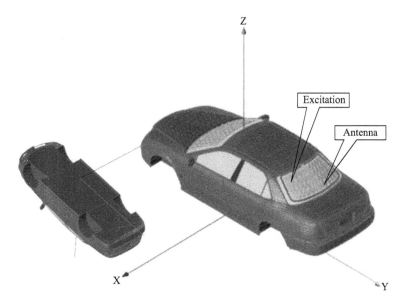

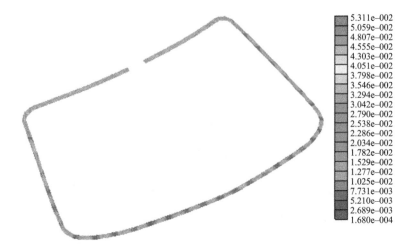

	5.311e–002
	5.059e–002
	4.807e–002
	4.555e–002
	4.303e–002
	4.051e–002
	3.798e–002
	3.546e–002
	3.294e–002
	3.042e–002
	2.790e–002
	2.538e–002
	2.286e–002
	2.034e–002
	1.782e–002
	1.529e–002
	1.277e–002
	1.025e–002
	7.731e–003
	5.210e–003
	2.689e–003
	1.680e–004

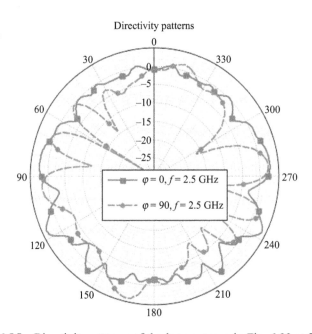

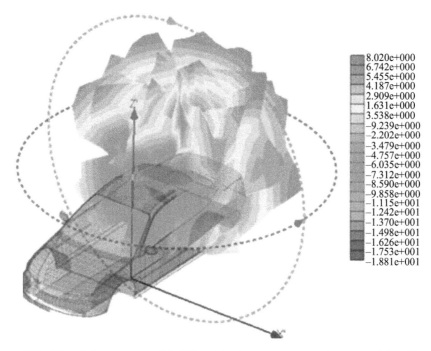

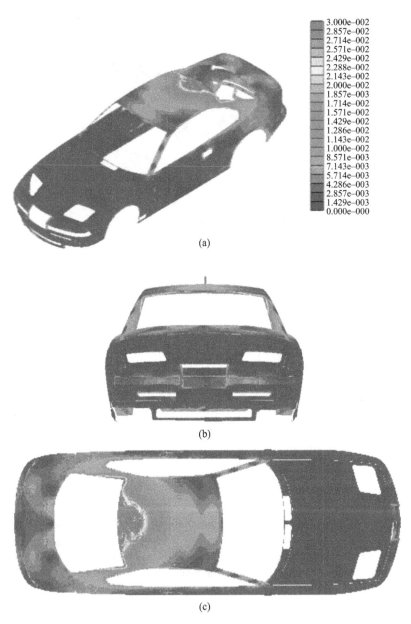

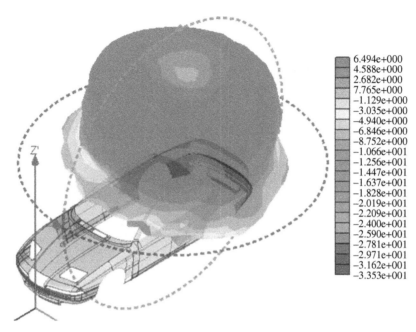

6.494e+000	
4.588e+000	
2.682e+000	
7.765e+000	
−1.129e+000	
−3.035e+000	
−4.940e+000	
−6.846e+000	
−8.752e+000	
−1.066e+001	
−1.256e+001	
−1.447e+001	
−1.637e+001	
−1.828e+001	
−2.019e+001	
−2.209e+001	
−2.400e+001	
−2.590e+001	
−2.781e+001	
−2.971e+001	
−3.162e+001	
−3.353e+001	

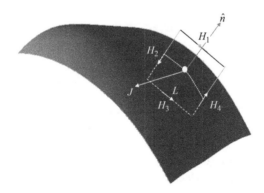

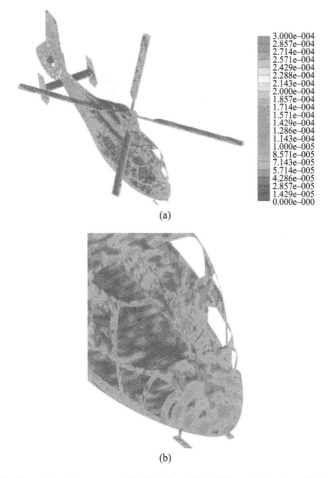

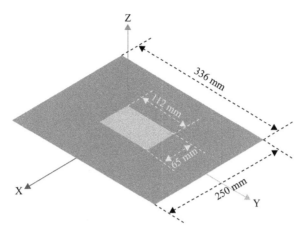

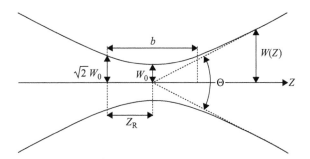

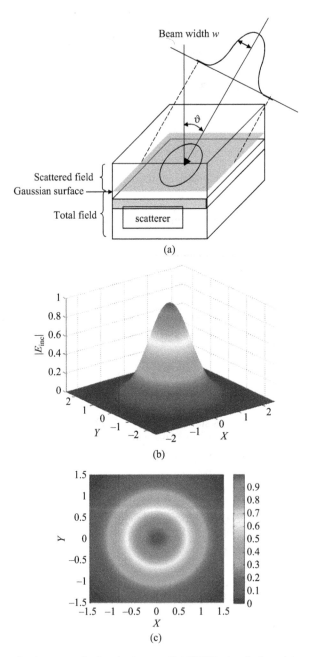

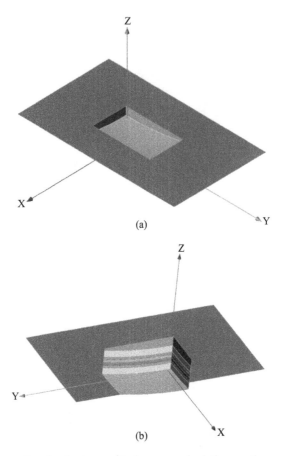

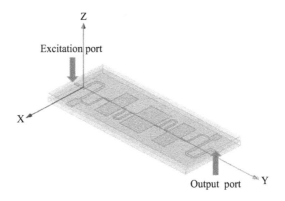

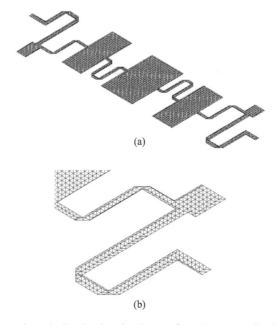

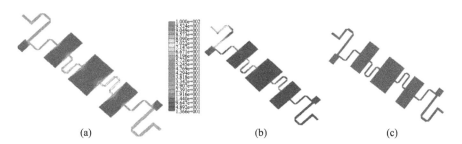

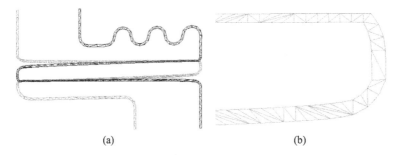

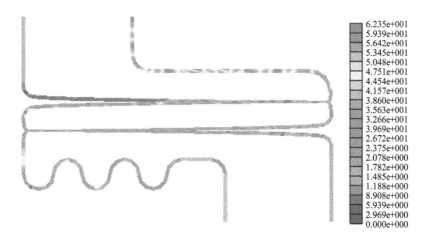

6.235e+001
5.939e+001
5.642e+001
5.345e+001
5.048e+001
4.751e+001
4.454e+001
4.157e+001
3.860e+001
3.563e+001
3.266e+001
3.969e+001
2.672e+001
2.375e+000
2.078e+000
1.782e+000
1.485e+000
1.188e+000
8.908e+000
5.939e+000
2.969e+000
0.000e+000

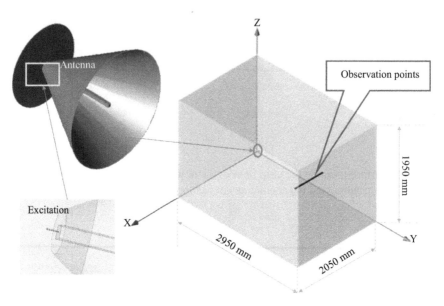

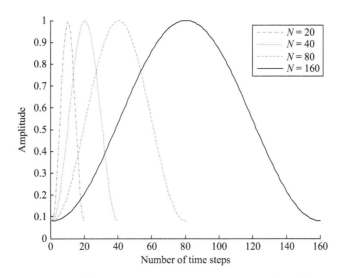

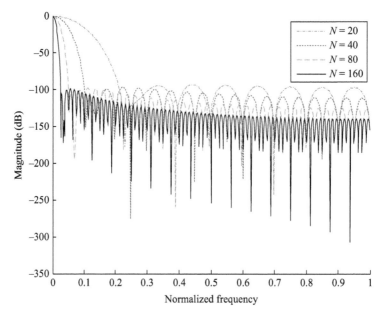

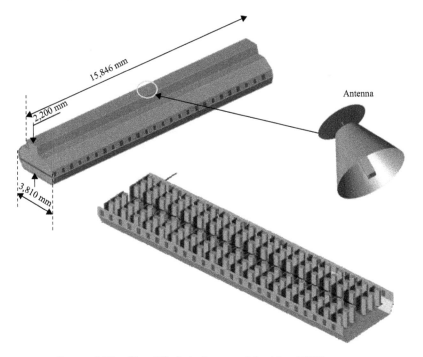

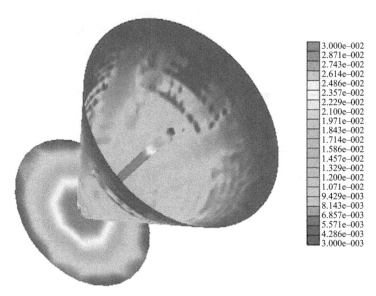

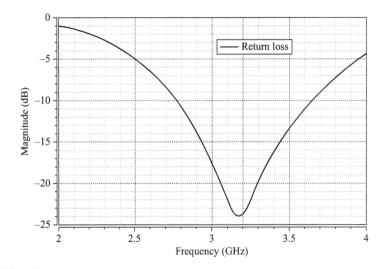

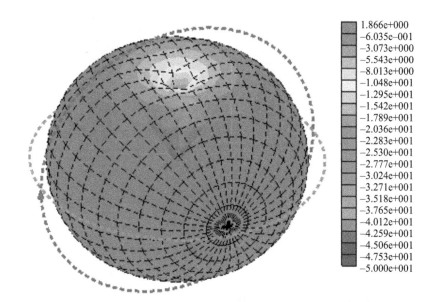

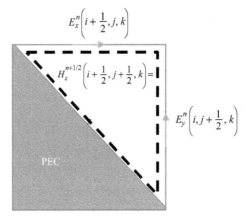

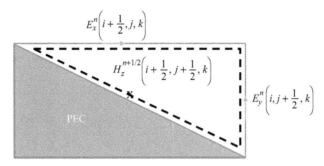

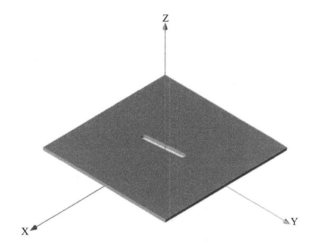

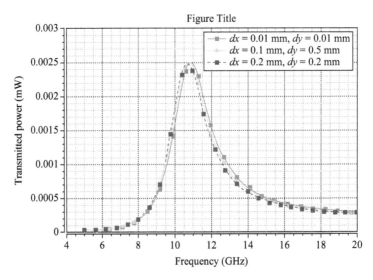

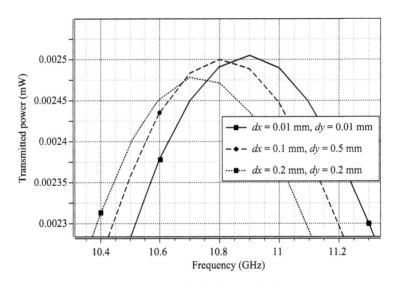

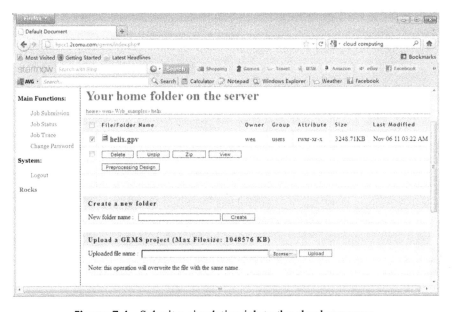

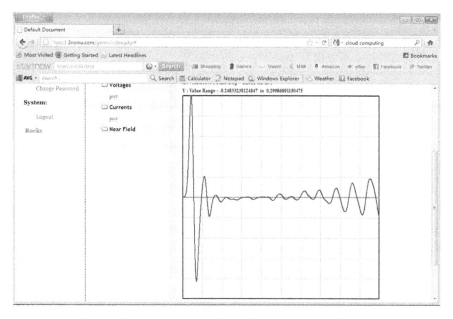

#pragma omp parallel private:	split and assign the job to multiple cores
transfer_H:	exchange the magnetic fields on the interface between the adjacent domains
transfer_E:	exchange the electric fields on the interface between the adjacent domains
add_source:	add the excitation source
source:	implementation of the excitation source
data_collect:	collect the simulation results
output_Ez:	output the simulation results

Appendix 6: Source Code

```
//*********************************************************************
// 3-D Parallel FDTD code with CPML absorbing boundary conditions [2,3]
//*********************************************************************

#include<stdio.h>
#include<math.h>
#include<string.h>
#include<stdlib.h>

#include "mpi.h"
#include "MyMPI.h"

#include "omp.h"

#include "xmmintrin.h"

typedef __m128 Vec4f;

#define h_update_nonmagnetic(co0,h,co1,e1max,e1,co2,e2max,e2,xmm) do {
      xmm = _mm_sub_ps(_mm_mul_ps(co0, h), _mm_sub_ps(_mm_mul_ps(co1,
      _mm_sub_ps(e1max, e1)), _mm_mul_ps(co2, _mm_sub_ps(e2max, e2))));
} while (0)

#define e_update_nonelectric(co0,e,co1,h1,h1min,co2,h2,h2min,xmm) do {
      xmm = _mm_add_ps(_mm_mul_ps(co0, e), _mm_sub_ps(_mm_mul_ps(co1,
      _mm_sub_ps(h1, h1min)), _mm_mul_ps(co2, _mm_sub_ps(h2, h2min))));
} while (0)

#define e_update_nonelectric_pml_add(beta,pusai,co0,h1,h1min,e,cb,xmm) do {
      pusai = _mm_add_ps(_mm_mul_ps(beta, pusai), _mm_mul_ps(co0,
      _mm_sub_ps(h1, h1min)));
      xmm = _mm_add_ps(e, _mm_mul_ps(cb, pusai));
} while (0)

#define e_update_nonelectric_pml_sub(beta,pusai,co0,h1,h1min,e,cb,xmm) do {
      pusai = _mm_add_ps(_mm_mul_ps(beta, pusai), _mm_mul_ps(co0,
      _mm_sub_ps(h1, h1min)));
      xmm = _mm_sub_ps(e, _mm_mul_ps(cb, pusai));
} while (0)

#define h_update_nonmagnetic_pml_sub(beta,pusai,co0,e1max,e1,h,db,xmm) do {
      pusai = _mm_add_ps(_mm_mul_ps(beta, pusai), _mm_mul_ps(co0,
      _mm_sub_ps(e1max, e1)));\
```

```
        xmm = _mm_sub_ps(h, _mm_mul_ps(db, pusai));
} while (0)

#define h_update_nonmagnetic_pml_add(beta,pusai,co0,e1max,e1,h,db,xmm) do {\
        pusai = _mm_add_ps(_mm_mul_ps(beta, pusai), _mm_mul_ps(co0,
        _mm_sub_ps(e1max, e1)));
        xmm = _mm_add_ps(h, _mm_mul_ps(db, pusai));
} while (0)
float PI = 3.141592653589793f;
float C0 = (float)2.99792458E+8;
float Mu0 = (float)( 4.0 * PI * 1.0E-7 );
float Eps0 = (float)( 1.0 / (Mu0 * C0 * C0) );

int i, j, k, n;
FILE* fp;
int time_steps = 100;
int save_steps = time_steps;

int nx= 119, ny = 79, nz = 79;

float ***ex, ***ey, ***ez, ***hx, ***hy, ***hz;
float *ex_tmp, *ey_tmp, *ez_tmp, *hx_tmp, *hy_tmp, *hz_tmp;
int low_tag;

float ***Ez_save;
float *Ez_save_tmp;

float ***pusai_eyz_X_MIN, *pusai_eyz_X_MIN_tmp;
float ***pusai_ezy_X_MIN, *pusai_ezy_X_MIN_tmp;
float ***pusai_hyz_X_MIN, *pusai_hyz_X_MIN_tmp;
float ***pusai_hzy_X_MIN, *pusai_hzy_X_MIN_tmp;

float ***pusai_exz_Y_MIN, *pusai_exz_Y_MIN_tmp;
float ***pusai_hxz_Y_MIN, *pusai_hxz_Y_MIN_tmp;
float ***pusai_ezx_Y_MIN, *pusai_ezx_Y_MIN_tmp;
float ***pusai_hzx_Y_MIN, *pusai_hzx_Y_MIN_tmp;

float ***pusai_exy_Z_MIN, *pusai_exy_Z_MIN_tmp;
float ***pusai_eyx_Z_MIN, *pusai_eyx_Z_MIN_tmp;
float ***pusai_hxy_Z_MIN, *pusai_hxy_Z_MIN_tmp;
float ***pusai_hyx_Z_MIN, *pusai_hyx_Z_MIN_tmp;

float ***pusai_eyz_X_MAX, *pusai_eyz_X_MAX_tmp;
float ***pusai_hyz_X_MAX, *pusai_hyz_X_MAX_tmp;
float ***pusai_ezy_X_MAX, *pusai_ezy_X_MAX_tmp;
float ***pusai_hzy_X_MAX, *pusai_hzy_X_MAX_tmp;

float ***pusai_exz_Y_MAX, *pusai_exz_Y_MAX_tmp;
float ***pusai_hxz_Y_MAX, *pusai_hxz_Y_MAX_tmp;
float ***pusai_ezx_Y_MAX, *pusai_ezx_Y_MAX_tmp;
float ***pusai_hzx_Y_MAX, *pusai_hzx_Y_MAX_tmp;

float ***pusai_exy_Z_MAX, *pusai_exy_Z_MAX_tmp;
float ***pusai_hxy_Z_MAX, *pusai_hxy_Z_MAX_tmp;
float ***pusai_eyx_Z_MAX, *pusai_eyx_Z_MAX_tmp;
float ***pusai_hyx_Z_MAX, *pusai_hyx_Z_MAX_tmp;

float *pEi_PML_Coeff, *pEj_PML_Coeff, *pEk_PML_Coeff;
float *pHi_PML_Coeff_M_Lossless, *pHj_PML_Coeff_M_Lossless,
*pHk_PML_Coeff_M_Lossless;
```

```
float *pEi_Coeff, *pEj_Coeff, *pEk_Coeff;
float *pHi_Coeff_M_Lossless, *pHj_Coeff_M_Lossless,
*pHk_Coeff_M_Lossless;

//.....................................................
// Declare enumeration types and initialize the parameters
//.....................................................

enum {X_MIN, Y_MIN, Z_MIN, X_MAX, Y_MAX, Z_MAX};
int Index_E_Boundary[6], Index_H_Boundary[6];

int m_iNumOfLayers = 7;

//6-layer CPML
int BoundaryLayerNum[6];

int imin, imax, jmin, jmax, kmin, kmax;
int ishift, jshift, kshift;

float dx = 0.001f;     //Input parameter
float dy = dx;         //Input parameter
float dz = dx;         //Input parameter

float dx_Inv = 1 / dx;
float dy_Inv = 1 / dy;
float dz_Inv = 1 / dz;
float ma = 1.0;
float m = 4;
float sigma_max = 0.75f;

float sgmax1 = (float)( sigma_max * (m + 1) / (150.0 * PI * dx) );
float sgmay1 = (float)( sigma_max * (m + 1) / (150.0 * PI * dy) );
float sgmaz1 = (float)( sigma_max * (m + 1) / (150.0 * PI * dz) );
float sgmax2 = (float)( sigma_max * (m + 1) / (150.0 * PI * dx) );
float sgmay2 = (float)( sigma_max * (m + 1) / (150.0 * PI * dy) );
float sgmaz2 = (float)( sigma_max * (m + 1) / (150.0 * PI * dz) );

float k_pml = 1.0;
float alpha_pml = 0.0;
float maxFreq_Source = 1e6;
float deltaT = (float)( 0.995 * 1.0 / (C0 * sqrt(1.0 / (dx * dx) +
1.0  (dy * dy) + 1.0 / (dz * dz))) );
float m_deltaT = deltaT;
float factor = PI * maxFreq_Source;

float alpha_pmlx1 = alpha_pml * Eps0 * factor;
float alpha_pmly1 = alpha_pml * Eps0 * factor;
float alpha_pmlz1 = alpha_pml * Eps0 * factor;
float alpha_pmlx2 = alpha_pml * Eps0 * factor;
float alpha_pmly2 = alpha_pml * Eps0 * factor;
float alpha_pmlz2 = alpha_pml * Eps0 * factor;

float k0_pmlx1 = k_pml;
float k0_pmly1 = k_pml;
float k0_pmlz1 = k_pml;
float k0_pmlx2 = k_pml;
float k0_pmly2 = k_pml;
float k0_pmlz2 = k_pml;
```

```
//Holllow domain
float CA = 1.0;
float CB = deltaT / Eps0;
float DA = 1.0;
float DB = deltaT / Mu0;

float x, x1, x2;
float y, y_1, y2, z, z1, z2, sgma, temp, temp_ma;

float *K_PML_XGrid, *K_PML_YGrid, *K_PML_ZGrid,
*K_PML_XGrid_Inv,*K_PML_YGrid_Inv, *K_PML_ZGrid_Inv;
float *K_PML_XHalf, *K_PML_YHalf, *K_PML_ZHalf, *K_PML_XHalf_Inv,
*K_PML_YHalf_Inv, *K_PML_ZHalf_Inv;

float *Beta_PML_XGrid, *Beta_PML_YGrid, *Beta_PML_ZGrid,
*Beta_PML_XHalf, *Beta_PML_YHalf, *Beta_PML_ZHalf;

float *Alpha_PML_XGrid, *Alpha_PML_YGrid, *Alpha_PML_ZGrid,
*Alpha_PML_XHalf, *Alpha_PML_YHalf, *Alpha_PML_ZHalf;

int id, p, size, low_value, high_value;
int memory_size;

//int source_position_x = nx / 2, source_position_y = ny / 2,
source_position_z = nz / 2;
int source_position_x = (nx + 1) / 2, source_position_y = (ny + 1) / 2,
source_position_z = (nz + 1) / 2;

int source_owner, source_left_owner, source_right_owner;
int source_position_x_local;

MPI_Request req[2];
MPI_Status status[2];
MPI_Datatype new_dtype;

double elapsed_time;

float* memory_malloc_1D();

float*** memory_malloc_3D();

void initialize_array();

void initialize_CPML();

void output_Function();

void output_Parameters();

void compute_E();
void compute_E_PUSAI();
void compute_E_SSE();
void compute_E_PUSAI_SSE();

void compute_H();
void compute_H_PUSAI();
void compute_H_SSE();
void compute_H_PUSAI_SSE();

void compute();
void compute_MPI_PEC();
void compute_MPI_CPML();
```

```
void compute_SSE_PEC();
void compute_SSE_CPML();

void transfer_H();

void transfer_E();

void source();

void add_source();

void data_collect();

void output_Ez();

void output_ElaspedTime();

int main( int argc, char* argv[] )
{
   MPI_Init( &argc, &argv);
   MPI_Comm_size( MPI_COMM_WORLD, &p );
   MPI_Comm_rank( MPI_COMM_WORLD, &id );

   size = BLOCK_SIZE( id, p, nx + 1 );
   low_value = BLOCK_LOW( id, p, nx + 1 );
   high_value = BLOCK_HIGH( id, p, nx + 1 );

   source_owner = BLOCK_OWNER( source_position_x, p, nx + 1 );
   source_left_owner = BLOCK_OWNER( source_position_x - 1, p, nx + 1 );
   source_right_owner = BLOCK_OWNER( source_position_x + 1, p, nx + 1 );

   source_right_owner = %d\n\n", source_left_owner, source_owner,
     source_right_owner);

   memory_size = size + 2;

   source_position_x_local = source_position_x - low_value + 1;

   Index_E_Boundary[X_MIN] = 1;
   Index_E_Boundary[Y_MIN] = 1;
   Index_E_Boundary[Z_MIN] = 1;
   Index_E_Boundary[X_MAX] = nx - 1;
   Index_E_Boundary[Y_MAX] = ny - 1;
   Index_E_Boundary[Z_MAX] = nz - 1;

   Index_H_Boundary[X_MIN] = 1;
   Index_H_Boundary[Y_MIN] = 1;
   Index_H_Boundary[Z_MIN] = 1;
   Index_H_Boundary[X_MAX] = nx - 2;
   Index_H_Boundary[Y_MAX] = ny - 2;
   Index_H_Boundary[Z_MAX] = nz - 2;

   BoundaryLayerNum[X_MIN] = 6;
   BoundaryLayerNum[X_MAX] = 6;
   BoundaryLayerNum[Y_MIN] = 6;
   BoundaryLayerNum[Y_MAX] = 6;
   BoundaryLayerNum[Z_MIN] = 6;
   BoundaryLayerNum[Z_MAX] = 6;

   initialize_array();

   initialize_CPML();

   //output_Parameters();
```

```
    MPI_Type_vector( 1, (ny + 1) * (nz + 1), (ny + 1) * (nz + 1),
       MPI_FLOAT, &new_dtype );
    MPI_Type_commit( &new_dtype );

    compute();

    MPI_Finalize();
}

float* memory_malloc_1D( float* array_name, int array_size, float
initialize_value )
{
        //initialize_value
        array_name = (float*)_aligned_malloc(sizeof(float)*array_size,16);
        for( i = 0; i < array_size; i++)
        {
                array_name[i] = initialize_value;
        }
        return array_name;
}

float*** memory_malloc_3D( float*** array_name, float* array_name_tmp,
int array_size_x, int array_size_y, int array_size_z, float
initialize_value )
{
    array_name_tmp = memory_malloc_1D( array_name_tmp, array_size_x *
       array_size_y * array_size_z, initialize_value);
    array_name = (float ***)_aligned_malloc(sizeof(float**)*array_size_x,16);
    for( i = 0; i < array_size_x; i++)
    {
        array_name[i] = (float **)_aligned_malloc(sizeof(float*)*array_size_y,16);
        for( j = 0; j < array_size_y; j++)
        {
            low_tag = i * array_size_y * array_size_z + j * array_size_z;
            array_name[i][j] = &array_name_tmp[low_tag];
            for( k = 0; k < array_size_z; k++)
            {
                array_name[i][j][k] = initialize_value;
            }
        }
    }
    return array_name;
}

void initialize_array()
{
    while ((nz + 1) % 4 != 0)
    {
            nz ++;
    }

    ex = memory_malloc_3D( ex, ex_tmp, memory_size, ny+1, nz+1, 0.0);
    ey = memory_malloc_3D( ey, ey_tmp, memory_size, ny+1, nz+1, 0.0);
    ez = memory_malloc_3D( ez, ez_tmp, memory_size, ny+1, nz+1, 0.0);
    hx = memory_malloc_3D( hx, hx_tmp, memory_size, ny+1, nz+1, 0.0);
    hy = memory_malloc_3D( hy, hy_tmp, memory_size, ny+1, nz+1, 0.0);
    hz = memory_malloc_3D( hz, hz_tmp, memory_size, ny+1, nz+1, 0.0);
```

```
Ez_save=memory_malloc_3D( Ez_save,Ez_save_tmp,nx+1,ny+1,nz+1,0.0);

//^^^^^^^^^^^^^^^^^^^^^^^^^^^^^^^^^^^^^^^^^^^^^^^^^^^^^^^^^^^^^^^^^
//              pusai_MIN
//^^^^^^^^^^^^^^^^^^^^^^^^^^^^^^^^^^^^^^^^^^^^^^^^^^^^^^^^^^^^^^^^^
//pusai_X_Direction
pusai_eyz_X_MIN = memory_malloc_3D( pusai_eyz_X_MIN,
    pusai_eyz_X_MIN_tmp, m_iNumOfLayers+1, ny+1, nz+1, 0.0);
pusai_hyz_X_MIN = memory_malloc_3D( pusai_hyz_X_MIN,
    pusai_hyz_X_MIN_tmp, m_iNumOfLayers+1, ny+1, nz+1, 0.0);
pusai_ezy_X_MIN = memory_malloc_3D( pusai_ezy_X_MIN,
    pusai_ezy_X_MIN_tmp, m_iNumOfLayers+1, ny+1, nz+1, 0.0);
pusai_hzy_X_MIN = memory_malloc_3D( pusai_hzy_X_MIN,
    pusai_hzy_X_MIN_tmp, m_iNumOfLayers+1, ny+1, nz+1, 0.0);

//pusai_Y_Direction
pusai_exz_Y_MIN = memory_malloc_3D( pusai_exz_Y_MIN,
    pusai_exz_Y_MIN_tmp, memory_size, m_iNumOfLayers+1, nz+1, 0.0);
pusai_hxz_Y_MIN = memory_malloc_3D( pusai_hxz_Y_MIN,
    pusai_hxz_Y_MIN_tmp, memory_size, m_iNumOfLayers+1, nz+1, 0.0);
pusai_ezx_Y_MIN = memory_malloc_3D( pusai_ezx_Y_MIN,
    pusai_ezx_Y_MIN_tmp, memory_size, m_iNumOfLayers+1, nz+1, 0.0);
pusai_hzx_Y_MIN = memory_malloc_3D( pusai_hzx_Y_MIN,
    pusai_hzx_Y_MIN_tmp, memory_size, m_iNumOfLayers+1, nz+1, 0.0);

//pusai_Z_Direction
pusai_exy_Z_MIN = memory_malloc_3D( pusai_exy_Z_MIN,
    pusai_exy_Z_MIN_tmp, memory_size, ny+1, m_iNumOfLayers+1, 0.0);
pusai_hxy_Z_MIN = memory_malloc_3D( pusai_hxy_Z_MIN,
    pusai_hxy_Z_MIN_tmp, memory_size, ny+1, m_iNumOfLayers+1, 0.0);
pusai_eyx_Z_MIN = memory_malloc_3D( pusai_eyx_Z_MIN,
    pusai_eyx_Z_MIN_tmp, memory_size, ny+1, m_iNumOfLayers+1, 0.0);
pusai_hyx_Z_MIN = memory_malloc_3D( pusai_hyx_Z_MIN,
    pusai_hyx_Z_MIN_tmp, memory_size, ny+1, m_iNumOfLayers+1, 0.0);

//^^^^^^^^^^^^^^^^^^^^^^^^^^^^^^^^^^^^^^^^^^^^^^^^^^^^^^^^^^^^^^^^^
//              pusai_MAX
//^^^^^^^^^^^^^^^^^^^^^^^^^^^^^^^^^^^^^^^^^^^^^^^^^^^^^^^^^^^^^^^^^
//pusai_X_Direction
pusai_eyz_X_MAX = memory_malloc_3D( pusai_eyz_X_MAX,
    pusai_eyz_X_MAX_tmp, m_iNumOfLayers+1, ny+1, nz+1, 0.0);
pusai_hyz_X_MAX = memory_malloc_3D( pusai_hyz_X_MAX,
    pusai_hyz_X_MAX_tmp, m_iNumOfLayers+1, ny+1, nz+1, 0.0);
pusai_ezy_X_MAX = memory_malloc_3D( pusai_ezy_X_MAX,
    pusai_ezy_X_MAX_tmp, m_iNumOfLayers+1, ny+1, nz+1, 0.0);
pusai_hzy_X_MAX = memory_malloc_3D( pusai_hzy_X_MAX,
    pusai_hzy_X_MAX_tmp, m_iNumOfLayers+1, ny+1, nz+1, 0.0);

//pusai_Y_Direction
pusai_exz_Y_MAX = memory_malloc_3D( pusai_exz_Y_MAX,
    pusai_exz_Y_MAX_tmp, memory_size, m_iNumOfLayers+1, nz+1, 0.0);
pusai_hxz_Y_MAX = memory_malloc_3D( pusai_hxz_Y_MAX,
    pusai_hxz_Y_MAX_tmp, memory_size, m_iNumOfLayers+1, nz+1, 0.0);
pusai_ezx_Y_MAX = memory_malloc_3D( pusai_ezx_Y_MAX,
    pusai_ezx_Y_MAX_tmp, memory_size, m_iNumOfLayers+1, nz+1, 0.0);
pusai_hzx_Y_MAX = memory_malloc_3D( pusai_hzx_Y_MAX,
    pusai_hzx_Y_MAX_tmp, memory_size, m_iNumOfLayers+1, nz+1, 0.0);
```

```
//pusai_Z_Direction
pusai_exy_Z_MAX = memory_malloc_3D( pusai_exy_Z_MAX,
    pusai_exy_Z_MAX_tmp, memory_size, ny+1, m_iNumOfLayers+1, 0.0);
pusai_hxy_Z_MAX = memory_malloc_3D( pusai_hxy_Z_MAX,
    pusai_hxy_Z_MAX_tmp, memory_size, ny+1, m_iNumOfLayers+1, 0.0);
pusai_eyx_Z_MAX = memory_malloc_3D( pusai_eyx_Z_MAX,
    pusai_eyx_Z_MAX_tmp, memory_size, ny+1, m_iNumOfLayers+1, 0.0);
pusai_hyx_Z_MAX = memory_malloc_3D( pusai_hyx_Z_MAX,
    pusai_hyx_Z_MAX_tmp, memory_size, ny+1, m_iNumOfLayers+1, 0.0);

//CPL coefficients
K_PML_XGrid = memory_malloc_1D( K_PML_XGrid, memory_size, 1.0);
K_PML_YGrid = memory_malloc_1D( K_PML_YGrid, ny + 1, 1.0);
K_PML_ZGrid = memory_malloc_1D( K_PML_ZGrid, nz + 1, 1.0);

K_PML_XGrid_Inv = memory_malloc_1D(K_PML_XGrid_Inv,memory_size,1.0);
K_PML_YGrid_Inv = memory_malloc_1D( K_PML_YGrid_Inv, ny + 1, 1.0);
K_PML_ZGrid_Inv = memory_malloc_1D( K_PML_ZGrid_Inv, nz + 1, 1.0);

K_PML_XHalf = memory_malloc_1D( K_PML_XHalf, memory_size, 1.0);
K_PML_YHalf = memory_malloc_1D( K_PML_YHalf, ny + 1, 1.0);
K_PML_ZHalf = memory_malloc_1D( K_PML_ZHalf, nz + 1, 1.0);

K_PML_XHalf_Inv = memory_malloc_1D(K_PML_XHalf_Inv,memory_size,1.0);
K_PML_YHalf_Inv = memory_malloc_1D( K_PML_YHalf_Inv, ny + 1, 1.0);
K_PML_ZHalf_Inv = memory_malloc_1D( K_PML_ZHalf_Inv, nz + 1, 1.0);

Beta_PML_XGrid = memory_malloc_1D( Beta_PML_XGrid, memory_size, 0.0);
Beta_PML_YGrid = memory_malloc_1D( Beta_PML_YGrid, ny + 1, 0.0);
Beta_PML_ZGrid = memory_malloc_1D( Beta_PML_ZGrid, nz + 1, 0.0);
Beta_PML_XHalf = memory_malloc_1D( Beta_PML_XHalf, memory_size, 0.0);
Beta_PML_YHalf = memory_malloc_1D( Beta_PML_YHalf, ny + 1, 0.0);
Beta_PML_ZHalf = memory_malloc_1D( Beta_PML_ZHalf, nz + 1, 0.0);

Alpha_PML_XGrid = memory_malloc_1D(Alpha_PML_XGrid,memory_size,0.0);
Alpha_PML_YGrid = memory_malloc_1D(Alpha_PML_YGrid, ny + 1, 0.0);
Alpha_PML_ZGrid = memory_malloc_1D(Alpha_PML_ZGrid, nz + 1, 0.0);
Alpha_PML_XHalf = memory_malloc_1D(Alpha_PML_XHalf,memory_size,0.0);
Alpha_PML_YHalf = memory_malloc_1D( Alpha_PML_YHalf, ny + 1, 0.0);
Alpha_PML_ZHalf = memory_malloc_1D( Alpha_PML_ZHalf, nz + 1, 0.0);

pEi_PML_Coeff = memory_malloc_1D( pEi_PML_Coeff, memory_size, 0.0);
pEj_PML_Coeff = memory_malloc_1D( pEj_PML_Coeff, ny+1, 0.0);
pEk_PML_Coeff = memory_malloc_1D( pEk_PML_Coeff, nz+1, 0.0);
pHi_PML_Coeff_M_Lossless =
  memory_malloc_1D( pHi_PML_Coeff_M_Lossless, memory_size, 0.0);
pHj_PML_Coeff_M_Lossless =
  memory_malloc_1D( pHj_PML_Coeff_M_Lossless, ny+1, 0.0);
pHk_PML_Coeff_M_Lossless =
  memory_malloc_1D( pHk_PML_Coeff_M_Lossless, nz+1, 0.0);

pEi_Coeff = memory_malloc_1D( pEi_Coeff, memory_size, 0.0);
pEj_Coeff = memory_malloc_1D( pEj_Coeff, ny+1, 0.0);
pEk_Coeff = memory_malloc_1D( pEk_Coeff, nz+1, 0.0);
pHi_Coeff_M_Lossless = memory_malloc_1D( pHi_Coeff_M_Lossless,
memory_size, 0.0);
pHj_Coeff_M_Lossless=memory_malloc_1D(pHj_Coeff_M_Lossless,ny+1,0.0);
pHk_Coeff_M_Lossless=memory_malloc_1D(pHk_Coeff_M_Lossless,nz+1,0.0);
}
```

```
void initialize_CPML()
{
//~~~~~~~~~~~~~~~~~~~~~~~~~~~~~~~~~~~~~~~~~~~~~~~~~~~~~~~~~~~~~~~~~~
//                      E-field coefficients
//~~~~~~~~~~~~~~~~~~~~~~~~~~~~~~~~~~~~~~~~~~~~~~~~~~~~~~~~~~~~~~~~~~
//X_MIN

if( id == 0)
{
    x1 = 2;
    x2 = 2 + BoundaryLayerNum[X_MIN];
    for( i = 2; i < 2 + BoundaryLayerNum[X_MIN]; i++)
    {
        x = i;
        temp = pow( fabs(x2 - x) / BoundaryLayerNum[X_MIN], m);

        factor£¬ËùÒÔ temp_ma == 0
        temp_ma = alpha_pmlx1 * pow( fabs(x - x1) /
            BoundaryLayerNum[X_MIN], ma);

        K_PML_XGrid[i] = 1.0 + (k0_pmlx1 - 1.0) * temp;

        sgma = sgmax1 * temp;
        K_PML_XGrid_Inv[i] = 1.0 / K_PML_XGrid[i];
        Beta_PML_XGrid[i] = exp(-(sgma / K_PML_XGrid[i] + temp_ma) * m_deltaT / Eps0);
        Alpha_PML_XGrid[i] = (Beta_PML_XGrid[i] - 1.0) * sgma /
            ((sgma + K_PML_XGrid[i] * temp_ma) * K_PML_XGrid[i]);
    }
  }

//X_MAX

if( id == p - 1 )
{
    x1 = memory_size - 3 - BoundaryLayerNum[X_MAX];
    x2 = memory_size - 3;

    for (i = memory_size - 3 - BoundaryLayerNum[X_MAX] + 1; i <=
        memory_size - 3; i ++)
    {
        x = i;
        temp = pow( fabs(x - x1) / BoundaryLayerNum[X_MAX], m);
        temp_ma = alpha_pmlx2 * pow( fabs(x2 - x) /
            BoundaryLayerNum[X_MAX], ma);
        K_PML_XGrid[i] = 1.0 + (k0_pmlx2 - 1.0) * temp;
        sgma = sgmax2 * temp;
        K_PML_XGrid_Inv[i] = 1.0 / K_PML_XGrid[i];
        Beta_PML_XGrid[i] = exp(-(sgma / K_PML_XGrid[i] + temp_ma) *
            m_deltaT / Eps0);
        Alpha_PML_XGrid[i] = (Beta_PML_XGrid[i] - 1.0) * sgma /
            ((sgma + K_PML_XGrid[i] * temp_ma) * K_PML_XGrid[i]);
    }
}

//Y_MIN
y_1 = Index_E_Boundary[Y_MIN];
```

```
y2 = Index_E_Boundary[Y_MIN] + BoundaryLayerNum[Y_MIN];
for (j = Index_E_Boundary[Y_MIN]; j < Index_E_Boundary[Y_MIN] +
  BoundaryLayerNum[Y_MIN]; j ++)
{
  y = j;
  temp = pow( fabs(y2 - y ) / BoundaryLayerNum[Y_MIN], m);
  temp_ma = alpha_pmly1 * pow( fabs(y - y_1) / BoundaryLayerNum[Y_MIN], ma);
  K_PML_YGrid[j] = 1.0 + (k0_pmly1 - 1.0) * temp;
  sgma = sgmay1 * temp;
  K_PML_YGrid_Inv[j] = 1.0 / K_PML_YGrid[j];
  Beta_PML_YGrid[j] = exp(-(sgma / K_PML_YGrid[j] + temp_ma) *
    m_deltaT / Eps0);
  Alpha_PML_YGrid[j] = (Beta_PML_YGrid[j] - 1.0) * sgma / ((sgma +
    K_PML_YGrid[j] * temp_ma) * K_PML_YGrid[j]);
}

// Y_MAX
y_1 = Index_E_Boundary[Y_MAX] - BoundaryLayerNum[Y_MAX];
y2 = Index_E_Boundary[Y_MAX];
for (j = Index_E_Boundary[Y_MAX] - BoundaryLayerNum[Y_MAX] + 1;
  j <= Index_E_Boundary[Y_MAX]; j ++)
{
  y = j;
  temp = pow( fabs(y - y_1) / BoundaryLayerNum[Y_MAX], m);
  temp_ma = alpha_pmly2 * pow( fabs( y2 - y ) /
    BoundaryLayerNum[Y_MAX], ma);
  K_PML_YGrid[j] = 1.0 + (k0_pmly2 - 1.0) * temp;
  sgma = sgmay2 * temp;
  K_PML_YGrid_Inv[j] = 1.0 / K_PML_YGrid[j];
  Beta_PML_YGrid[j] = exp(-(sgma / K_PML_YGrid[j] + temp_ma) *
    m_deltaT / Eps0);
  Alpha_PML_YGrid[j] = (Beta_PML_YGrid[j] - 1.0) * sgma / ((sgma +
    K_PML_YGrid[j] * temp_ma) * K_PML_YGrid[j]);
 }

// Z_MIN
z1 = Index_E_Boundary[Z_MIN];
z2 = Index_E_Boundary[Z_MIN] + BoundaryLayerNum[Z_MIN];
for (k = Index_E_Boundary[Z_MIN]; k < Index_E_Boundary[Z_MIN] +
  BoundaryLayerNum[Z_MIN]; k ++)
{
  z = k;
  temp = pow( fabs(z2 - z) / BoundaryLayerNum[Z_MIN], m);
  temp_ma = alpha_pmlz1*pow( fabs(z - z1)/BoundaryLayerNum[Z_MIN],ma);
  K_PML_ZGrid[k] = 1.0 + (k0_pmlz1 - 1.0) * temp;
  sgma = sgmaz1 * temp;
  K_PML_ZGrid_Inv[k = 1.0/K_PML_ZGrid[k];
  Beta_PML_ZGrid[k]=exp(-(sgma/K_PML_ZGrid[k]+temp_ma)*m_deltaT/Eps0);
  Alpha_PML_ZGrid[k] = (Beta_PML_ZGrid[k] - 1.0) * sgma / ((sgma +
    K_PML_ZGrid[k] * temp_ma) * K_PML_ZGrid[k]);
}

// Z_MAX
z1 = Index_E_Boundary[Z_MAX] - BoundaryLayerNum[Z_MAX];
z2 = Index_E_Boundary[Z_MAX];
```

```
      for(k = Index_E_Boundary[Z_MAX] - BoundaryLayerNum[Z_MAX] + 1; k <=
         Index_E_Boundary[Z_MAX]; k ++)
{
   Z = k;
   temp = pow( fabs(z - z1) / BoundaryLayerNum[Z_MAX], m);
      temp_ma = alpha_pmly2 * pow( fabs(z2 - z) /
      BoundaryLayerNum[Z_MAX], ma);
   K_PML_ZGrid[k] = 1.0 + (k0_pmlz2 - 1.0) * temp;
   sgma = sgmaz2 * temp;
   K_PML_ZGrid_Inv[k] = 1.0 / K_PML_ZGrid[k];
   Beta_PML_ZGrid[k] = exp(-(sgma / K_PML_ZGrid[k] + temp_ma) *
      m_deltaT / Eps0);
   Alpha_PML_ZGrid[k] = (Beta_PML_ZGrid[k] - 1.0) * sgma / ((sgma +
      K_PML_ZGrid[k] * temp_ma) * K_PML_ZGrid[k]);
}

//~~~~~~~~~~~~~~~~~~~~~~~~~~~~~~~~~~~~~~~~~~~~~~~~~~~~~~~~~~~~~~~~~
//                     H-field coefficients
//~~~~~~~~~~~~~~~~~~~~~~~~~~~~~~~~~~~~~~~~~~~~~~~~~~~~~~~~~~~~~~~~~
// X_MIN

if( id == 0 )
{
   x1 = 2;
   x2 = 2 + BoundaryLayerNum[X_MIN];
   for (i = 2; i < 2 + BoundaryLayerNum[X_MIN]; i ++)
   {
     x = i + 0.5;
     temp = pow( fabs(x2 - x) / BoundaryLayerNum[X_MIN], m);

     BoundaryLayerNum[X_MIN], ma);

     K_PML_XHalf[i] = 1.0 + (k0_pmlx1 - 1.0) * temp;

     sgma = sgmax1 * temp;
     K_PML_XHalf_Inv[i] = 1.0 / K_PML_XHalf[i];
     Beta_PML_XHalf[i]=exp(-sgma/K_PML_XHalf[i]+temp_ma)*m_deltaT/Eps0);
     Alpha_PML_XHalf[i] = (Beta_PML_XHalf[i] - 1.0) * sgma / ((sgma +
        K_PML_XHalf[i] * temp_ma) * K_PML_XHalf[i]);
   }
}

// X_MAX

if( id == p - 1 )
{
   x1 = memory_size - 4 - BoundaryLayerNum[X_MAX] + 1;
   x2 = memory_size - 4;
   for (i = memory_size - 4 - BoundaryLayerNum[X_MAX] + 1; i <=
     memory_size - 4; i ++)
   {
      x = i + 0.5;
      temp = pow(fabs(x-x1)/ BoundaryLayerNum[X_MAX],m);
      temp_ma = alpha_pmlx2 * pow( fabs(x2 - x) /
         BoundaryLayerNum[X_MAX], ma);
      K_PML_XHalf[i] = 1.0 + (k0_pmlx2 - 1.0) * temp;
      sgma = sgmax2 * temp;
      K_PML_XHalf_Inv[i] = 1.0 / K_PML_XHalf[i];
```

```
            Beta_PML_XHalf[i] = exp(-(sgma / K_PML_XHalf[i] + temp_ma ) *
                m_deltaT / Eps0);
            Alpha_PML_XHalf[i] = (Beta_PML_XHalf[i] - 1.0) * sgma /
                ((sgma + K_PML_XHalf[i] * temp_ma) * K_PML_XHalf[i]);
        }
}

// Y_MIN
y_1 = Index_H_Boundary[Y_MIN];
y2 = Index_H_Boundary[Y_MIN] + BoundaryLayerNum[Y_MIN];
for(j = Index_H_Boundary[Y_MIN]; j < Index_H_Boundary[Y_MIN] +
    BoundaryLayerNum[Y_MIN]; j++)
{
    y = j + 0.5;
    temp = pow( fabs(y2 - y) / BoundaryLayerNum[Y_MIN], m);
    temp_ma = alpha_pmly1 * pow( fabs(y - y_1) / BoundaryLayerNum[Y_MIN], ma);
    K_PML_YHalf[j] = 1.0 + (k0_pmly1 - 1.0) * temp;
    sgma = sgmay1 * temp;
    K_PML_YHalf_Inv[j] = 1.0 / K_PML_YHalf[j];
    Beta_PML_YHalf[j] = exp(-(sgma / K_PML_YHalf[j] + temp_ma) *
        m_deltaT / Eps0);
    Alpha_PML_YHalf[j] = (Beta_PML_YHalf[j] - 1.0) * sgma / ((sgma +
        K_PML_YHalf[j] * temp_ma) * K_PML_YHalf[j]);
}

// Y_MAX
y_1 = Index_H_Boundary[Y_MAX] - BoundaryLayerNum[Y_MAX] + 1;
y2 = Index_H_Boundary[Y_MAX];
for (j = Index_H_Boundary[Y_MAX] - BoundaryLayerNum[Y_MAX] + 1;
    j <= Index_H_Boundary[Y_MAX]; j ++)
{
    y = j + 0.5;
    temp = pow( fabs(y - y_1) / BoundaryLayerNum[Y_MAX], m);
    temp_ma = alpha_pmly2*pow(fabs(y2-y)/BoundaryLayerNum[Y_MAX],ma);
    K_PML_YHalf[j] = 1.0 + (k0_pmly2 - 1.0) * temp;
    sgma = sgmay2 * temp;
    K_PML_YHalf_Inv[j] = 1.0 / K_PML_YHalf[j];
    Beta_PML_YHalf[j] = exp(-(sgma / K_PML_YHalf[j] + temp_ma) *
        m_deltaT / Eps0);
    Alpha_PML_YHalf[j] = (Beta_PML_YHalf[j] - 1.0) * sgma / ((sgma +
        K_PML_YHalf[j] * temp_ma) * K_PML_YHalf[j]);
}

// Z_MIN
z1 = Index_H_Boundary[Z_MIN];
z2 = Index_H_Boundary[Z_MIN] + BoundaryLayerNum[Z_MIN];
for (k = Index_H_Boundary[Z_MIN]; k < Index_H_Boundary[Z_MIN] +
    BoundaryLayerNum[Z_MIN]; k ++)
{
    z = k + 0.5;
    temp = pow( fabs(z2 - z) / BoundaryLayerNum[Z_MIN], m);
    temp_ma = alpha_pmlz1*pow(fabs(z-z1)/BoundaryLayerNum[Z_MIN], ma);
    K_PML_ZHalf[k] = 1.0 + (k0_pmlz1 - 1.0) * temp;
    sgma = sgmaz1 * temp;
    K_PML_ZHalf_Inv[k] = 1.0 / K_PML_ZHalf[k];
    Beta_PML_ZHalf[k] = exp(-(sgma / K_PML_ZHalf[k] + temp_ma) *
        m_deltaT / Eps0);
```

```
    Alpha_PML_ZHalf[k] = (Beta_PML_ZHalf[k] - 1.0) * sgma / ((sgma +
        K_PML_ZHalf[k] * temp_ma) * K_PML_ZHalf[k]);
}

// Z_MAX
z1 = Index_H_Boundary[Z_MAX] - BoundaryLayerNum[Z_MAX] + 1;
z2 = Index_H_Boundary[Z_MAX];
for (k = Index_H_Boundary[Z_MAX] - BoundaryLayerNum[Z_MAX] + 1;
    k <= Index_H_Boundary[Z_MAX]; k ++)
{
    z = k + 0.5;
    temp = pow( fabs(z - z1) / BoundaryLayerNum[Z_MAX], m);
    temp_ma = alpha_pmlz2*pow( fabs(z2-z)/BoundaryLayerNum[Z_MAX], ma);
    K_PML_ZHalf[k] = 1.0 + (k0_pmlz2 - 1.0) * temp;
    sgma = sgmaz2 * temp;
    K_PML_ZHalf_Inv[k] = 1.0 / K_PML_ZHalf[k];
    Beta_PML_ZHalf[k] = exp(-(sgma / K_PML_ZHalf[k] + temp_ma )
        * m_deltaT / Eps0);
    Alpha_PML_ZHalf[k] = (Beta_PML_ZHalf[k] - 1.0) * sgma /
        ((sgma + K_PML_ZHalf[k] * temp_ma) * K_PML_ZHalf[k]);
}

//~~~~~~~~~~~~~~~~~~~~~~~~~~~~~~~~~~~~~~~~~~~~~~~~~~~~~~~~~~~~~~~~~
//Simplified coefficients
//~~~~~~~~~~~~~~~~~~~~~~~~~~~~~~~~~~~~~~~~~~~~~~~~~~~~~~~~~~~~~~~~~
//pusai

for (i = 1; i <= memory_size - 2; i ++)
{
    pEi_PML_Coeff[i] = Alpha_PML_XGrid[i] / dx;
}

for (j = Index_E_Boundary[Y_MIN]; j <= Index_E_Boundary[Y_MAX]; j ++)
{
    pEj_PML_Coeff[j] = Alpha_PML_YGrid[j] / dy;
}

for (k = Index_E_Boundary[Z_MIN]; k <= Index_E_Boundary[Z_MAX]; k ++)
        {
                pEk_PML_Coeff[k] = Alpha_PML_ZGrid[k] / dz;
        }

        for (i = 1; i <= memory_size - 2; i ++)
        {
                pHi_PML_Coeff_M_Lossless[i] = Alpha_PML_XHalf[i] / dx;
        }

for (j = Index_H_Boundary[Y_MIN]; j <= Index_H_Boundary[Y_MAX] + 1; j ++)
        {
                pHj_PML_Coeff_M_Lossless[j] = Alpha_PML_YHalf[j] / dy;
        }

for (k = Index_H_Boundary[Z_MIN]; k <= Index_H_Boundary[Z_MAX] + 1; k ++)
        {
                pHk_PML_Coeff_M_Lossless[k] = Alpha_PML_ZHalf[k] / dz;
        }
```

```
        //domain
        for (i = 1; i <= memory_size - 2; i ++)
        {
                pEi_Coeff[i] = CB * K_PML_XGrid_Inv[i] / dx;
        }

for (j = Index_E_Boundary[Y_MIN]; j <= Index_E_Boundary[Y_MAX]; j ++)
        {
                pEj_Coeff[j] = CB * K_PML_YGrid_Inv[j] / dy;
        }

for (k = Index_E_Boundary[Z_MIN]; k <= Index_E_Boundary[Z_MAX]; k ++)
        {
                pEk_Coeff[k] = CB * K_PML_ZGrid_Inv[k] / dz;
        }

        for (i = 1; i <= memory_size - 2; i ++)
        {
                pHi_Coeff_M_Lossless[i] = DB * K_PML_XHalf_Inv[i] / dx;
        }

for (j = Index_H_Boundary[Y_MIN]; j <= Index_H_Boundary[Y_MAX] + 1; j ++)
        {
                pHj_Coeff_M_Lossless[j] = DB * K_PML_YHalf_Inv[j] / dy;
        }

for (k = Index_H_Boundary[Z_MIN]; k <= Index_H_Boundary[Z_MAX] + 1; k ++)
        {
                pHk_Coeff_M_Lossless[k] = DB * K_PML_ZHalf_Inv[k] / dz;
        }

}

void compute()
{
   MPI_Barrier(MPI_COMM_WORLD);

   elapsed_time = - MPI_Wtime();
   for( n = 1; n <= time_steps; n++)
   {
      //PEC boundary condition for regular FDTD update
      compute_MPI_PEC();

      //PML boundary condition for regular FDTD update
      //compute_MPI_CPML();

      // PEC boundary condition for SSE FDTD update
      //compute_SSE_PEC();

      //PEC boundary condition for SSE FDTD update
      //compute_SSE_CPML();

    }

    data_collect();
    elapsed_time += MPI_Wtime();

    if( id == 0 )
    {
       output_Ez();
```

```
      output_ElaspedTime();
   }
}

void output_ElaspedTime()
{
   fp = fopen("output\\elapsed_time ","a");
   ny + 1, nz + 1, elapsed_time );
   fprintf(fp,"MPI + OpenMP + PML: %d Time steps, %d Process, %d * %d * %d,
      number of grids, Time: %f\n", time_steps, p, nx + 1, ny + 1, nz + 1,
      elapsed_time );
   fclose(fp);
}

void compute_MPI_PEC()
{
   compute_H();
   transfer_H();
   compute_E();
   source();
   transfer_E();
}

void compute_MPI_CPML()
{
   compute_H_PUSAI();
   transfer_H();
   compute_E_PUSAI();
   source();
   transfer_E();
}

void compute_SSE_PEC()
{
   compute_H_SSE();
   transfer_H();
   compute_E_SSE();
   source();
   transfer_E();
}

void compute_SSE_CPML()
{
   compute_H_PUSAI_SSE();
   transfer_H();
   compute_E_PUSAI_SSE();
   source();
   transfer_E();
}

void compute_H()
{
   int thread_num, num_threads;

   #pragma omp parallel private(num_threads, thread_num)
   {
```

```
        thread_num = omp_get_thread_num();

        num_threads = omp_get_num_threads();

        int i, j, k;
        imin = 1;
        imax = memory_size - 2;
        jmin = Index_H_Boundary[Y_MIN];
        jmax = Index_H_Boundary[Y_MAX] + 1;
        kmin = Index_H_Boundary[Z_MIN];
        kmax = Index_H_Boundary[Z_MAX] + 1;

        float imaxf = (float)imax / (float)num_threads;

        for (i = imin + (int)((float)thread_num * imaxf); i <=
            (int)((float)(thread_num + 1) * imaxf); i ++)
        {
            for( j = jmin; j <= jmax; j++)
            {
                for( k = kmin; k <= kmax; k ++ )
                {
                    hx[i][j][k] = DA * hx[i][j][k] - ( pHj_Coeff_M_Lossless[j]
                        * ( ez[i][j+1][k] - ez[i][j][k] ) -
                    pHk_Coeff_M_Lossless[k] * ( ey[i][j][k+1] -
                        ey[i][j][k] ) );

                    hy[i][j][k] = DA * hy[i][j][k] - ( pHk_Coeff_M_Lossless[k]
                        * ( ex[i][j][k+1] - ex[i][j][k] ) - pHi_Coeff_M_Lossless[i]
                        * ( ez[i+1][j][k] - ez[i][j][k] ) );

                    hz[i][j][k] = DA * hz[i][j][k] - ( pHi_Coeff_M_Lossless[i]
                        * ( ey[i+1][j][k] - ey[i][j][k] ) - pHj_Coeff_M_Lossless[j]
                        * ( ex[i][j+1][k] - ex[i][j][k] ) );
                }
            }
        }
    }
}

void compute_H_PUSAI()
{
int thread_num, num_threads;

#pragma omp parallel private(num_threads, thread_num)
{
    thread_num = omp_get_thread_num();

    num_threads = omp_get_num_threads();

    int i, j, k;
    imin = 1;
    imax = memory_size - 2;
    jmin = Index_H_Boundary[Y_MIN];
    jmax = Index_H_Boundary[Y_MAX] + 1;
    kmin = Index_H_Boundary[Z_MIN];
    kmax = Index_H_Boundary[Z_MAX] + 1;

    float imaxf = (float)imax / (float)num_threads;
```

```
for (i = imin + (int)((float)thread_num * imaxf);
     i <= (int)((float)(thread_num + 1) * imaxf); i ++)
{
    for( j = jmin; j <= jmax; j++)
    {
        for( k = kmin; k <= kmax; k ++ )
        {
            hx[i][j][k] = DA * hx[i][j][k] -
                ( pHj_Coeff_M_Lossless[j] * ( ez[i][j+1][k] -
                ez[i][j][k] ) - pHk_Coeff_M_Lossless[k] *
                ( ey[i][j][k+1] - ey[i][j][k] ) );

            hy[i][j][k] = DA * hy[i][j][k] -
                ( pHk_Coeff_M_Lossless[k] * ( ex[i][j][k+1] -
                ex[i][j][k] ) - pHi_Coeff_M_Lossless[i] *
                ( ez[i+1][j][k] - ez[i][j][k] ) );

            hz[i][j][k] = DA * hz[i][j][k] -
                ( pHi_Coeff_M_Lossless[i] * ( ey[i+1][j][k] -
                ey[i][j][k] ) - pHj_Coeff_M_Lossless[j]
                * ( ex[i][j+1][k] - ex[i][j][k] ) );

            //pusai_Z_MIN

            if( (k >= Index_H_Boundary[Z_MIN]) && ( k <= Index_H_Boundary
            [Z_MIN] + BoundaryLayerNum[Z_MIN] - 1) )
            {

                pusai_hxy_Z_MIN[i][j][k] = Beta_PML_ZHalf[k] *
                    pusai_hxy_Z_MIN[i][j][k] + pHk_PML_Coeff_M_Lossless[k]
                    * ( ey[i][j][k+1] - ey[i][j][k] );

                hx[i][j][k] = hx[i][j][k] + DB *
                    pusai_hxy_Z_MIN[i][j][k];

                pusai_hyx_Z_MIN[i][j][k] = Beta_PML_ZHalf[k]
                    * pusai_hyx_Z_MIN[i][j][k] + pHk_PML_Coeff_M_Lossless[k]
                    * ( ex[i][j][k+1] - ex[i][j][k] );

                hy[i][j][k] = hy[i][j][k] - DB *
                    pusai_hyx_Z_MIN[i][j][k];
            }

            //pusai_Z_MAX

            if( (k >= Index_H_Boundary[Z_MAX] -
                BoundaryLayerNum[Z_MAX] + 1 ) &&
                ( k <= Index_H_Boundary[Z_MAX]) )
            {

                kshift = Index_H_Boundary[Z_MAX] -
                    BoundaryLayerNum[Z_MAX] + 1;

                pusai_hxy_Z_MAX[i][j][k-kshift] = Beta_PML_ZHalf[k]
                    * pusai_hxy_Z_MAX[i][j][k-kshift] +
                    pHk_PML_Coeff_M_Lossless[k]
                    * ( ey[i][j][k+1] - ey[i][j][k] );
```

```
            hx[i][j][k] = hx[i][j][k] + DB *
                pusai_hxy_Z_MAX[i][j][k-kshift];

        pusai_hyx_Z_MAX[i][j][k-kshift] = Beta_PML_ZHalf[k]
            * pusai_hyx_Z_MAX[i][j][k-kshift] +
            pHk_PML_Coeff_M_Lossless[k] * ( ex[i][j][k+1]
            - ex[i][j][k] );

        hy[i][j][k] = hy[i][j][k] - DB *
            pusai_hyx_Z_MAX[i][j][k-kshift];
        }
    }

    //pusai_Y_MIN
    if( j >= Index_H_Boundary[Y_MIN] && j <=
        (Index_H_Boundary[Y_MIN]+BoundaryLayerNum[Y_MIN]-1))
    {
        for( k = kmin; k <= kmax; k++)
        {
            pusai_hxz_Y_MIN[i][j][k] = Beta_PML_YHalf[j]
                * pusai_hxz_Y_MIN[i][j][k] +
            pHj_PML_Coeff_M_Lossless[j] * ( ez[i][j+1][k] -
                ez[i][j][k] );
            hx[i][j][k] = hx[i][j][k] - DB *
                pusai_hxz_Y_MIN[i][j][k];
            pusai_hzx_Y_MIN[i][j][k] = Beta_PML_YHalf[j] *
                pusai_hzx_Y_MIN[i][j][k] +
                pHj_PML_Coeff_M_Lossless[j] * ( ex[i][j+1][k] -
                ex[i][j][k] );
            hz[i][j][k] = hz[i][j][k] + DB *
                pusai_hzx_Y_MIN[i][j][k];
        }
    }


    //pusai_Y_MAX
    if( j >= (Index_H_Boundary[Y_MAX] -
    BoundaryLayerNum[Y_MAX] + 1) && j <=
    Index_H_Boundary[Y_MAX] )
    {
        jshift = Index_H_Boundary[Y_MAX] - BoundaryLayerNum[Y_MAX] + 1;
        for( k = kmin; k <= kmax; k++)
        {
            pusai_hxz_Y_MAX[i][j-jshift][k] = Beta_PML_YHalf[j]
                * pusai_hxz_Y_MAX[i][j-jshift][k] +
                pHj_PML_Coeff_M_Lossless[j] * ( ez[i][j+1][k] -
                ez[i][j][k] );

            hx[i][j][k] = hx[i][j][k] - DB *
                pusai_hxz_Y_MAX[i][j-jshift][k];

            pusai_hzx_Y_MAX[i][j-jshift][k] = Beta_PML_YHalf[j]
                * pusai_hzx_Y_MAX[i][j-jshift][k] +
            pHj_PML_Coeff_M_Lossless[j] * ( ex[i][j+1][k] -
                ex[i][j][k] );
```

```
                    hz[i][j][k] = hz[i][j][k] + DB *
                        pusai_hzx_Y_MAX[i][j-jshift][k];
                }
            }
        }

        //pusai_X_MIN
        if( i >= 2 && i <= ( 2 + BoundaryLayerNum[X_MIN] - 1 ) )
        {
            if( id == 0)
            {
                for( j = jmin; j <= jmax; j++)
                {
                    for( k = kmin; k <= kmax;k++)
                    {
                        pusai_hyz_X_MIN[i][j][k] = Beta_PML_XHalf[i] *
                            pusai_hyz_X_MIN[i][j][k] +
                            pHi_PML_Coeff_M_Lossless[i] * ( ez[i+1][j][k] -
                            ez[i][j][k] );

                        hy[i][j][k] = hy[i][j][k] + DB *
                            pusai_hyz_X_MIN[i][j][k];

                        pusai_hzy_X_MIN[i][j][k] = Beta_PML_XHalf[i] *
                            pusai_hzy_X_MIN[i][j][k] +
                        pHi_PML_Coeff_M_Lossless[i] *
                            ( ey[i+1][j][k] - ey[i][j][k] );

                        hz[i][j][k] = hz[i][j][k] - DB *
                            pusai_hzy_X_MIN[i][j][k];

                    }
                }
            }
        }

        //pusai_X_MAX
        if( i >= ( memory_size - 4 - BoundaryLayerNum[X_MAX] + 1 )
            && i <= memory_size - 4 )
        {
            if( id == p - 1 )
            {
                ishift = memory_size - 4 - BoundaryLayerNum[X_MAX] + 1;
                for( j = jmin; j <= jmax; j++)
                {
                    for( k = kmin; k <= kmax; k++)
                    {
                        pusai_hyz_X_MAX[i-ishift][j][k] = Beta_PML_XHalf[i]
                        * pusai_hyz_X_MAX[i-ishift][j][k] +
                            pHi_PML_Coeff_M_Lossless[i] * ( ez[i+1][j][k]
                            - ez[i][j][k] );

                        hy[i][j][k] = hy[i][j][k] + DB *
                            pusai_hyz_X_MAX[i-ishift][j][k];

                        pusai_hzy_X_MAX[i-ishift][j][k] = Beta_PML_XHalf[i]
                            * pusai_hzy_X_MAX[i-ishift][j][k] +
                        pHi_PML_Coeff_M_Lossless[i] * ( ey[i+1][j][k] -
                            ey[i][j][k] );
```

```c
                            hz[i][j][k] = hz[i][j][k] - DB *
                                pusai_hzy_X_MAX[i-ishift][j][k];
                    }
                }
            }
        }
    }
}
}

void compute_H_SSE()
{
int thread_num, num_threads;

    #pragma omp parallel private(num_threads, thread_num)
    {

        thread_num = omp_get_thread_num();

        num_threads = omp_get_num_threads();
        int i, j, k, vk;
        imin = 1;
        imax = memory_size - 2;
        jmin = Index_H_Boundary[Y_MIN];
        jmax = Index_H_Boundary[Y_MAX] + 1;
        kmin = Index_H_Boundary[Z_MIN];
        kmax = Index_H_Boundary[Z_MAX] + 1;

        float imaxf = (float)imax / (float)num_threads;

        int vkmax = kmax >> 2;

        Vec4f xmm0, xmm1, xmm2;
//0x0: false, %doutput is 0

            __declspec( align( 16 ) ) int mask1[4] = {0x0, 0x0, 0x0, 0x0},
                mask2[4] = {0x0, 0x0, 0x0, 0x0};

        Vec4f *pMask1 = (Vec4f *)&mask1;
        Vec4f *pMask2 = (Vec4f *)&mask2;

        // setup mask
        int r = (kmax + 1) % 4;
        if (r == 0) r = 4;
        for (i = 0; i < r - 1; i ++)

        {
            mask1[i] = mask2[i] = 0xFFFFFFFF;
        }

        mask2[i] = 0xFFFFFFFF;

        Vec4f *vhx, *vhy, *vhz;
            Vec4f *vex, vex_max_hy, *vex_max_hz, *vey, vey_max_hx,
            *vey_max_hz, *vez, *vez_max_hx, *vez_max_hy;
            Vec4f vpHi_Coeff_M_Lossless, vpHj_Coeff_M_Lossless,
```

```
        vpHk_Coeff_M_Lossless;

Vec4f vDA = _mm_load1_ps( &DA );

for (i = imin + (int)((float)thread_num * imaxf); i <=
     (int)((float)(thread_num + 1) * imaxf); i ++)
{
   vpHi_Coeff_M_Lossless =
          _mm_load1_ps( &pHi_Coeff_M_Lossless[i] );

   for( j = jmin; j <= jmax; j++)
   {
     vpHj_Coeff_M_Lossless =
          _mm_load1_ps( &pHj_Coeff_M_Lossless[j] );

     vhx = ( Vec4f * )hx[i][j];
     vhy = ( Vec4f * )hy[i][j];
     vhz = ( Vec4f * )hz[i][j];

     vex = ( Vec4f * )ex[i][j];
     vex_max_hz = ( Vec4f * )ex[i][j+1];

     vey = ( Vec4f * )ey[i][j];
     vey_max_hz = ( Vec4f * )ey[i+1][j];

     vez = ( Vec4f * )ez[i][j];
     vez_max_hx = ( Vec4f * )ez[i][j+1];
     vez_max_hy = ( Vec4f * )ez[i+1][j];

     k = vk = 0;

     vey_max_hx=_mm_loadu_ps(&ey[i][j][k+1]);

     vex_max_hy=_mm_loadu_ps(&ex[i][j][k+1]);
     vpHk_Coeff_M_Lossless =
        _mm_load_ps(&pHk_Coeff_M_Lossless[k]);

     while (vk < vkmax)
     {

        h_update_nonmagnetic(vDA, vhx[vk],
            vpHj_Coeff_M_Lossless, vez_max_hx[vk], vez[vk],
            vpHk_Coeff_M_Lossless, vey_max_hx, vey[vk], xmm0);
            h_update_nonmagnetic(vDA, vhy[vk],
            vpHk_Coeff_M_Lossless, vex_max_hy, vex[vk],
            vpHi_Coeff_M_Lossless, vez_max_hy[vk], vez[vk],
            xmm1);

        h_update_nonmagnetic(vDA, vhz[vk],
            vpHi_Coeff_M_Lossless, vey_max_hz[vk], vey[vk],
            vpHj_Coeff_M_Lossless, vex_max_hz[vk], vex[vk],
            xmm2);

        vhx[vk] = xmm0;
        vhy[vk] = xmm1;
        vhz[vk] = xmm2;

        k += 4;
        vk ++;
```

```
                    vey_max_hx=_mm_loadu_ps(&ey[i][j][k+1]);

                    vex_max_hy=_mm_loadu_ps(&ex[i][j][k+1]);
                        vpHk_Coeff_M_Lossless =
                        _mm_load_ps(&pHk_Coeff_M_Lossless[k]);
                }

            h_update_nonmagnetic(vDA, vhx[vk], vpHj_Coeff_M_Lossless,
                vez_max_hx[vk], vez[vk], vpHk_Coeff_M_Lossless,
                vey_max_hx, vey[vk], xmm0);

            h_update_nonmagnetic(vDA, vhy[vk], vpHk_Coeff_M_Lossless,
                vex_max_hy, vex[vk], vpHi_Coeff_M_Lossless, vez_max_hy[vk],
                vez[vk], xmm1);

            h_update_nonmagnetic(vDA, vhz[vk], vpHi_Coeff_M_Lossless,
                vey_max_hz[vk], vey[vk], vpHj_Coeff_M_Lossless,
                vex_max_hz[vk], vex[vk], xmm2);


            xmm0 = _mm_and_ps(xmm0, *pMask2);
            xmm1 = _mm_and_ps(xmm1, *pMask2);
            xmm2 = _mm_and_ps(xmm2, *pMask2);

            vhx[vk] = xmm0;
            vhy[vk] = xmm1;
            vhz[vk] = xmm2;
        }
      }
    }
}

void compute_H_PUSAI_SSE()
{
    int thread_num, num_threads;

    #pragma omp parallel private(num_threads, thread_num)
    {
        thread_num = omp_get_thread_num();

        num_threads = omp_get_num_threads();
        int i, j, k, vk;
        imin = 1;
        imax = memory_size - 2;
        jmin = Index_H_Boundary[Y_MIN];
        jmax = Index_H_Boundary[Y_MAX] + 1;
        kmin = Index_H_Boundary[Z_MIN];
        kmax = Index_H_Boundary[Z_MAX] + 1;

        float imaxf = (float)imax / (float)num_threads;

        int vkmax = kmax >> 2;

        Vec4f xmm0, xmm1, xmm2;

        __declspec( align( 16 ) ) int mask1[4] = {0x0, 0x0, 0x0, 0x0},
            mask2[4] = {0x0, 0x0, 0x0, 0x0};
```

```
        mask1[i]);
        mask2[i]);

        Vec4f *pMask1 = (Vec4f *)&mask1;
        Vec4f *pMask2 = (Vec4f *)&mask2;

        // setup mask
        int r = (kmax + 1) % 4;
        if (r == 0) r = 4;

        for (i = 0; i < r - 1; i ++)
        {
                mask1[i] = mask2[i] = 0xFFFFFFFF;
        }

        mask2[i] = 0xFFFFFFFF;

        Vec4f *vhx, *vhy, *vhz;
        Vec4f *vex, vex_max_hy, *vex_max_hz, *vey, vey_max_hx,
           *vey_max_hz, *vez, *vez_max_hx, *vez_max_hy;
        Vec4f vpHi_Coeff_M_Lossless, vpHj_Coeff_M_Lossless,
           vpHk_Coeff_M_Lossless;
        Vec4f vDA = _mm_load1_ps( &DA );

        //pusai_Y_MIN
        Vec4f xmm0_Y_MIN, xmm1_Y_MIN;
        Vec4f vBeta_PML_YHalf, vpHj_PML_Coeff_M_Lossless;
        Vec4f vDB = _mm_load1_ps( &DB );
        Vec4f *vpusai_hxz_Y_MIN, *vpusai_hzx_Y_MIN;

        //pusai_Y_MAX
        Vec4f xmm0_Y_MAX, xmm1_Y_MAX;
        Vec4f *vpusai_hxz_Y_MAX, *vpusai_hzx_Y_MAX;

        //pusai_X_MIN
        Vec4f xmm0_X_MIN, xmm1_X_MIN;
        Vec4f *vpusai_hyz_X_MIN, *vpusai_hzy_X_MIN;
        Vec4f vBeta_PML_XHalf, vpHi_PML_Coeff_M_Lossless;

        //pusai_X_MAX
        Vec4f xmm0_X_MAX, xmm1_X_MAX;
        Vec4f *vpusai_hyz_X_MAX, *vpusai_hzy_X_MAX;

        //pusai_Z_MIN
        Vec4f xmm0_Z_MIN, xmm1_Z_MIN, xmmo_0_Z_MIN, xmmo_1_Z_MIN;

        int vkmax_Z_MIN = (Index_H_Boundary[Z_MIN] +
           BoundaryLayerNum[Z_MIN] - 1) >> 2;

        __declspec( align( 16 ) ) int mask2_Z_MIN[4] = {0x0, 0x0, 0x0,
           0x0}, mask3_Z_MIN[4] = {0xFFFFFFFF, 0xFFFFFFFF, 0xFFFFFFFF,
           0xFFFFFFFF};

        // setup mask
        int r_Z_MIN = (Index_H_Boundary[Z_MIN] + BoundaryLayerNum[Z_MIN]
           - 1 + 1) % 4;
        if (r_Z_MIN == 0) r_Z_MIN = 4;
        for (i = 0; i < r_Z_MIN - 1; i ++)
        {
```

```
mask2_Z_MIN[i] = 0xFFFFFFFF;
        mask3_Z_MIN[i] = 0x0;
 }
 mask2_Z_MIN[i] = 0xFFFFFFFF;
 mask3_Z_MIN[i] = 0x0;

 Vec4f *pMask2_Z_MIN = (Vec4f *)&mask2_Z_MIN;
 Vec4f *pMask3_Z_MIN = (Vec4f *)&mask3_Z_MIN;

 Vec4f *vpusai_hxy_Z_MIN, *vpusai_hyx_Z_MIN;
 Vec4f vey_max, vex_max;
 Vec4f *vBeta_PML_ZHalf = (Vec4f *)Beta_PML_ZHalf;
 Vec4f *vpHk_PML_Coeff_M_Lossless = (Vec4f
        *)pHk_PML_Coeff_M_Lossless;

 //pusai_Z_MAX
 int kshift, vkshift;
 kshift = Index_H_Boundary[Z_MAX] - BoundaryLayerNum[Z_MAX] + 1;
 int kmin_aligned = (Index_H_Boundary[Z_MAX] -
     BoundaryLayerNum[Z_MAX] + 1) & (~3);

 Vec4f xmm0_Z_MAX, xmm1_Z_MAX, xmmo_0_Z_MAX, xmmo_1_Z_MAX;

 __declspec( align( 16 ) ) int mask1_Z_MAX[4] = {0x0, 0x0, 0x0,
    0x0}, mask3_Z_MAX[4] = {0xFFFFFFFF, 0xFFFFFFFF, 0xFFFFFFFF,
    0xFFFFFFFF}, mask4_Z_MAX[4] = {0x0, 0x0, 0x0, 0x0};

 Vec4f *pMask1_Z_MAX = (Vec4f *)&mask1_Z_MAX;
 Vec4f *pMask3_Z_MAX = (Vec4f *)&mask3_Z_MAX;
 Vec4f *pMask4_Z_MAX = (Vec4f *)&mask4_Z_MAX;

 int vkmax_Z_MAX = Index_H_Boundary[Z_MAX] >> 2;

 // setup mask
 int r_Z_MAX = (Index_H_Boundary[Z_MAX] +1 ) % 4;
 if (r_Z_MAX == 0) r_Z_MAX = 4;
 for (i = 0; i < r_Z_MAX - 1; i ++) {
        mask1_Z_MAX[i] = 0xFFFFFFFF;
 }
 mask1_Z_MAX[i] = 0xFFFFFFFF;
 for (i = 0; i < kmin - kmin_aligned; i ++) {
        mask3_Z_MAX[i] = 0x0;
        mask4_Z_MAX[i] = 0xFFFFFFFF;
 }

 Vec4f *vpusai_hxy_Z_MAX, *vpusai_hyx_Z_MAX;
 Vec4f vey_max_Z_MAX, vex_max_Z_MAX;

 for (i = imin + (int)((float)thread_num * imaxf); i <=

     (int)((float)(thread_num + 1) * imaxf); i ++)
 {
   vpHi_Coeff_M_Lossless =
   _mm_load1_ps( &pHi_Coeff_M_Lossless[i] );

   for( j = jmin; j <= jmax; j++)
   {
       vpHj_Coeff_M_Lossless =
            _mm_load1_ps( &pHj_Coeff_M_Lossless[j] );
```

```
vhx = ( Vec4f * )hx[i][j];
vhy = ( Vec4f * )hy[i][j];
vhz = ( Vec4f * )hz[i][j];

vex = ( Vec4f * )ex[i][j];
vex_max_hz = ( Vec4f * )ex[i][j+1];

vey = ( Vec4f * )ey[i][j];
vey_max_hz = ( Vec4f * )ey[i+1][j];

vez = ( Vec4f * )ez[i][j];
vez_max_hx = ( Vec4f * )ez[i][j+1];
vez_max_hy = ( Vec4f * )ez[i+1][j];

k = vk = 0;

vey_max_hx=_mm_loadu_ps(&ey[i][j][k+1]);

vex_max_hy=_mm_loadu_ps(&ex[i][j][k+1]);
vpHk_Coeff_M_Lossless =
        _mm_load_ps(&pHk_Coeff_M_Lossless[k]);

while (vk < vkmax)
{
   h_update_nonmagnetic(vDA, vhx[vk],
         vpHj_Coeff_M_Lossless, vez_max_hx[vk], vez[vk],
         vpHk_Coeff_M_Lossless, vey_max_hx, vey[vk], xmm0);

   h_update_nonmagnetic(vDA, vhy[vk],
   vpHk_Coeff_M_Lossless, vex_max_hy, vex[vk],
   vpHi_Coeff_M_Lossless, vez_max_hy[vk], vez[vk], xmm1);

   h_update_nonmagnetic(vDA, vhz[vk],
   vpHi_Coeff_M_Lossless, vey_max_hz[vk], vey[vk],
   vpHj_Coeff_M_Lossless, vex_max_hz[vk], vex[vk], xmm2);

   vhx[vk] = xmm0;
   vhy[vk] = xmm1;
   vhz[vk] = xmm2;

   k += 4;
   vk ++;

   vey_max_hx=_mm_loadu_ps(&ey[i][j][k+1]);

   vex_max_hy=_mm_loadu_ps(&ex[i][j][k+1]);

   vpHk_Coeff_M_Lossless =
         _mm_load_ps(&pHk_Coeff_M_Lossless[k]);
 }

h_update_nonmagnetic(vDA, vhx[vk], vpHj_Coeff_M_Lossless,
   vez_max_hx[vk], vez[vk], vpHk_Coeff_M_Lossless,
   vey_max_hx, vey[vk], xmm0);
h_update_nonmagnetic(vDA, vhy[vk], vpHk_Coeff_M_Lossless,
   vex_max_hy, vex[vk], vpHi_Coeff_M_Lossless,
   vez_max_hy[vk], vez[vk], xmm1);
h_update_nonmagnetic(vDA, vhz[vk], vpHi_Coeff_M_Lossless,
   vey_max_hz[vk], vey[vk], vpHj_Coeff_M_Lossless,
   vex_max_hz[vk], vex[vk], xmm2);
```

```
xmm0 = _mm_and_ps(xmm0, *pMask2);
xmm1 = _mm_and_ps(xmm1, *pMask2);
xmm2 = _mm_and_ps(xmm2, *pMask2);

vhx[vk] = xmm0;
vhy[vk] = xmm1;
vhz[vk] = xmm2;

//pusai_Y_MIN
if( j >= Index_H_Boundary[Y_MIN] && j <=
(Index_H_Boundary[Y_MIN] + BoundaryLayerNum[Y_MIN]-1))
{
   vBeta_PML_YHalf = _mm_load1_ps(&Beta_PML_YHalf[j]);
   vpHj_PML_Coeff_M_Lossless =
      _mm_load1_ps(&pHj_PML_Coeff_M_Lossless[j]);
   vpusai_hxz_Y_MIN = (Vec4f *)pusai_hxz_Y_MIN[i][j];
   vpusai_hzx_Y_MIN = (Vec4f *)pusai_hzx_Y_MIN[i][j];

   vk = 0;
   while (vk < vkmax)
   {

     h_update_nonmagnetic_pml_sub(vBeta_PML_YHalf,
        vpusai_hxz_Y_MIN[vk], vpHj_PML_Coeff_M_Lossless,
        vez_max_hx[vk], vez[vk], vhx[vk], vDB, xmm0_Y_MIN);

     h_update_nonmagnetic_pml_add(vBeta_PML_YHalf,
        vpusai_hzx_Y_MIN[vk], vpHj_PML_Coeff_M_Lossless,
        vex_max_hz[vk], vex[vk], vhz[vk], vDB, xmm1_Y_MIN);

     vhx[vk] = xmm0_Y_MIN;
     vhz[vk] = xmm1_Y_MIN;

     vk ++;
    }
   h_update_nonmagnetic_pml_sub(vBeta_PML_YHalf,
      vpusai_hxz_Y_MIN[vk], vpHj_PML_Coeff_M_Lossless,
      vez_max_hx[vk], vez[vk], vhx[vk], vDB, xmm0_Y_MIN);

   h_update_nonmagnetic_pml_add(vBeta_PML_YHalf,
      vpusai_hzx_Y_MIN[vk], vpHj_PML_Coeff_M_Lossless,
      vex_max_hz[vk], vex[vk], vhz[vk], vDB, xmm1_Y_MIN);

   xmm0_Y_MIN = _mm_and_ps(xmm0_Y_MIN, *pMask2);
      xmm1_Y_MIN = _mm_and_ps(xmm1_Y_MIN, *pMask2);
      vhx[vk] = xmm0_Y_MIN;
      vhz[vk] = xmm1_Y_MIN;
}

//pusai_Y_MAX
if( j >= (Index_H_Boundary[Y_MAX] - BoundaryLayerNum[Y_MAX]
   + 1) && j <= Index_H_Boundary[Y_MAX] )
{
   jshift = Index_H_Boundary[Y_MAX] -
      BoundaryLayerNum[Y_MAX] + 1;
   vBeta_PML_YHalf = _mm_load1_ps(&Beta_PML_YHalf[j]);
   vpHj_PML_Coeff_M_Lossless =
      _mm_load1_ps(&pHj_PML_Coeff_M_Lossless[j]);
```

```
vpusai_hxz_Y_MAX = (Vec4f *)pusai_hxz_Y_MAX[i][j-
    jshift];
vpusai_hzx_Y_MAX = (Vec4f *)pusai_hzx_Y_MAX[i][j-
    jshift];

vk = 0;
while (vk < vkmax)
{
 h_update_nonmagnetic_pml_sub(vBeta_PML_YHalf,
    vpusai_hxz_Y_MAX[vk], vpHj_PML_Coeff_M_Lossless,
    vez_max_hx[vk], vez[vk], vhx[vk], vDB, xmm0_Y_MAX);
 h_update_nonmagnetic_pml_add(vBeta_PML_YHalf,
    vpusai_hzx_Y_MAX[vk], vpHj_PML_Coeff_M_Lossless,
    vex_max_hz[vk], vex[vk], vhz[vk], vDB, xmm1_Y_MAX);

 vhx[vk] = xmm0_Y_MAX;
 vhz[vk] = xmm1_Y_MAX;

 vk ++;
}

h_update_nonmagnetic_pml_sub(vBeta_PML_YHalf,
    vpusai_hxz_Y_MAX[vk], vpHj_PML_Coeff_M_Lossless,
    vez_max_hx[vk], vez[vk], vhx[vk], vDB, xmm0_Y_MAX);

h_update_nonmagnetic_pml_add(vBeta_PML_YHalf,
    vpusai_hzx_Y_MAX[vk], vpHj_PML_Coeff_M_Lossless,
    vex_max_hz[vk], vex[vk], vhz[vk], vDB, xmm1_Y_MAX);

xmm0_Y_MAX = _mm_and_ps(xmm0_Y_MAX, *pMask2);
xmm1_Y_MAX = _mm_and_ps(xmm1_Y_MAX, *pMask2);

vhx[vk] = xmm0_Y_MAX;
vhz[vk] = xmm1_Y_MAX;
}

//pusai_X_MIN
if( i >= 2 && i <= 2 + BoundaryLayerNum[X_MIN] - 1 )
{
    if( id == 0 )
    {
        vBeta_PML_XHalf = _mm_load1_ps(&Beta_PML_XHalf[i]);
        vpHi_PML_Coeff_M_Lossless =
            _mm_load1_ps(&pHi_PML_Coeff_M_Lossless[i]);
        vpusai_hyz_X_MIN = (Vec4f *)pusai_hyz_X_MIN[i][j];
        vpusai_hzy_X_MIN = (Vec4f *)pusai_hzy_X_MIN[i][j];

        vk = 0;
        while (vk < vkmax)
        {
          h_update_nonmagnetic_pml_add(vBeta_PML_XHalf,
            vpusai_hyz_X_MIN[vk], vpHi_PML_Coeff_M_Lossless,
            vez_max_hy[vk], vez[vk], vhy[vk], vDB,
            xmm0_X_MIN);

          h_update_nonmagnetic_pml_sub(vBeta_PML_XHalf,
            vpusai_hzy_X_MIN[vk], vpHi_PML_Coeff_M_Lossless,
            vey_max_hz[vk], vey[vk], vhz[vk], vDB,
            xmm1_X_MIN);
```

```
            vhy[vk] = xmm0_X_MIN;
            vhz[vk] = xmm1_X_MIN;

            vk ++;
          }

        h_update_nonmagnetic_pml_add(vBeta_PML_XHalf,
            vpusai_hyz_X_MIN[vk], vpHi_PML_Coeff_M_Lossless,
            vez_max_hy[vk], vez[vk], vhy[vk], vDB,
            xmm0_X_MIN);

        h_update_nonmagnetic_pml_sub(vBeta_PML_XHalf,
            vpusai_hzy_X_MIN[vk], vpHi_PML_Coeff_M_Lossless,
            vey_max_hz[vk], vey[vk], vhz[vk], vDB,
            xmm1_X_MIN);

            xmm0_X_MIN = _mm_and_ps(xmm0_X_MIN, *pMask2);
            xmm1_X_MIN = _mm_and_ps(xmm1_X_MIN, *pMask2);
            vhy[vk] = xmm0_X_MIN;
            vhz[vk] = xmm1_X_MIN;

        }
  }

//pusai_X_MAX
if( i >= (memory_size - 4 - BoundaryLayerNum[X_MAX] + 1)
      && i <= memory_size - 4 )
{
  if( id == p - 1 )
  {
     ishift = memory_size-4-BoundaryLayerNum[X_MAX] + 1;
     vBeta_PML_XHalf = _mm_load1_ps(&Beta_PML_XHalf[i]);
     vpHi_PML_Coeff_M_Lossless =
        _mm_load1_ps(&pHi_PML_Coeff_M_Lossless[i]);
     vpusai_hyz_X_MAX = (Vec4f *)pusai_hyz_X_MAX[i-
        ishift][j];
     vpusai_hzy_X_MAX = (Vec4f *)pusai_hzy_X_MAX[i-
        ishift][j];
     vk = 0;
     while (vk < vkmax)
     {

        h_update_nonmagnetic_pml_add(vBeta_PML_XHalf,
           vpusai_hyz_X_MAX[vk], vpHi_PML_Coeff_M_Lossless,
           vez_max_hy[vk], vez[vk], vhy[vk], vDB,
           xmm0_X_MAX);

        h_update_nonmagnetic_pml_sub(vBeta_PML_XHalf,
           vpusai_hzy_X_MAX[vk], vpHi_PML_Coeff_M_Lossless,
           vey_max_hz[vk], vey[vk], vhz[vk], vDB,
           xmm1_X_MAX);

        vhy[vk] = xmm0_X_MAX;
        vhz[vk] = xmm1_X_MAX;

        vk ++;

     }
```

```
        h_update_nonmagnetic_pml_add(vBeta_PML_XHalf,
            vpusai_hyz_X_MAX[vk], vpHi_PML_Coeff_M_Lossless,
            vez_max_hy[vk], vez[vk], vhy[vk], vDB,
            xmm0_X_MAX);

        h_update_nonmagnetic_pml_sub(vBeta_PML_XHalf,
            vpusai_hzy_X_MAX[vk], vpHi_PML_Coeff_M_Lossless,
            vey_max_hz[vk], vey[vk], vhz[vk], vDB,
            xmm1_X_MAX);

        xmm0_X_MAX = _mm_and_ps(xmm0_X_MAX, *pMask2);
        xmm1_X_MAX = _mm_and_ps(xmm1_X_MAX, *pMask2);
        vhy[vk] = xmm0_X_MAX;
        vhz[vk] = xmm1_X_MAX;
    }
}

//pusai_Z_MIN

vpusai_hxy_Z_MIN = (Vec4f *)pusai_hxy_Z_MIN[i][j];
        vpusai_hyx_Z_MIN = (Vec4f *)pusai_hyx_Z_MIN[i][j];

k = vk = 0;

vey_max = _mm_loadu_ps(&ey[i][j][k+1]);
vex_max = _mm_loadu_ps(&ex[i][j][k+1]);

while (vk < vkmax_Z_MIN)
{

h_update_nonmagnetic_pml_add(vBeta_PML_ZHalf[vk],
    vpusai_hxy_Z_MIN[vk], vpHk_PML_Coeff_M_Lossless[vk],
    vey_max, vey[vk], vhx[vk], vDB, xmm0_Z_MIN);

 h_update_nonmagnetic_pml_sub(vBeta_PML_ZHalf[vk],
     vpusai_hyx_Z_MIN[vk], vpHk_PML_Coeff_M_Lossless[vk],
     vex_max, vex[vk], vhy[vk], vDB, xmm1_Z_MIN);

 vhx[vk] = xmm0_Z_MIN;
 vhy[vk] = xmm1_Z_MIN;

 k += 4;
 vk ++;

 vey_max = _mm_loadu_ps(&ey[i][j][k+1]);
 vex_max = _mm_loadu_ps(&ex[i][j][k+1]);
}

h_update_nonmagnetic_pml_add(vBeta_PML_ZHalf[vk],
    vpusai_hxy_Z_MIN[vk], vpHk_PML_Coeff_M_Lossless[vk],
    vey_max, vey[vk], vhx[vk], vDB, xmm0_Z_MIN);

h_update_nonmagnetic_pml_sub(vBeta_PML_ZHalf[vk],
    vpusai_hyx_Z_MIN[vk], vpHk_PML_Coeff_M_Lossless[vk],
    vex_max, vex[vk], vhy[vk], vDB, xmm1_Z_MIN);

xmm0_Z_MIN = _mm_and_ps(xmm0_Z_MIN, *pMask2_Z_MIN);
xmm1_Z_MIN = _mm_and_ps(xmm1_Z_MIN, *pMask2_Z_MIN);
xmmo_0_Z_MIN = _mm_and_ps(vhx[vk], *pMask3_Z_MIN);
xmmo_1_Z_MIN = _mm_and_ps(vhy[vk], *pMask3_Z_MIN);
```

```
xmm0_Z_MIN = _mm_add_ps(xmm0_Z_MIN, xmmo_0_Z_MIN);
xmm1_Z_MIN = _mm_add_ps(xmm1_Z_MIN, xmmo_1_Z_MIN);
vhx[vk] = xmm0_Z_MIN;
vhy[vk] = xmm1_Z_MIN;

//pusai_Z_MAX
vpusai_hxy_Z_MAX = (Vec4f *)pusai_hxy_Z_MAX[i][j];
vpusai_hyx_Z_MAX = (Vec4f *)pusai_hyx_Z_MAX[i][j];
vhx = (Vec4f *)hx[i][j];
vhy = (Vec4f *)hy[i][j];
vex = (Vec4f *)ex[i][j];
vey = (Vec4f *)ey[i][j];

k = kmin_aligned;
vkshift = vk = k >> 2;

vey_max_Z_MAX = _mm_loadu_ps(&ey[i][j][k+1]);
vex_max_Z_MAX = _mm_loadu_ps(&ex[i][j][k+1]);

h_update_nonmagnetic_pml_add(vBeta_PML_ZHalf[vk],
    vpusai_hxy_Z_MAX[vk], vpHk_PML_Coeff_M_Lossless[vk],
    vey_max_Z_MAX, vey[vk], vhx[vk], vDB, xmm0_Z_MAX);

h_update_nonmagnetic_pml_sub(vBeta_PML_ZHalf[vk],
    vpusai_hyx_Z_MAX[vk], vpHk_PML_Coeff_M_Lossless[vk],
    vex_max_Z_MAX, vex[vk], vhy[vk], vDB, xmm1_Z_MAX);

xmm0_Z_MAX = _mm_and_ps(xmm0_Z_MAX, *pMask3_Z_MAX);
xmm1_Z_MAX = _mm_and_ps(xmm1_Z_MAX, *pMask3_Z_MAX);
xmmo_0_Z_MAX = _mm_and_ps(vhx[vk], *pMask4_Z_MAX);
xmmo_1_Z_MAX = _mm_and_ps(vhy[vk], *pMask4_Z_MAX);
xmm0_Z_MAX = _mm_add_ps(xmm0_Z_MAX, xmmo_0_Z_MAX);
xmm1_Z_MAX = _mm_add_ps(xmm1_Z_MAX, xmmo_1_Z_MAX);

while (vk < vkmax_Z_MAX)
{
  vhx[vk] = xmm0_Z_MAX;
  vhy[vk] = xmm1_Z_MAX;

  k += 4;
  vk ++;

  vey_max_Z_MAX = _mm_loadu_ps(&ey[i][j][k+1]);
  vex_max_Z_MAX = _mm_loadu_ps(&ex[i][j][k+1]);

  h_update_nonmagnetic_pml_add(vBeta_PML_ZHalf[vk],
      vpusai_hxy_Z_MAX[vk], vpHk_PML_Coeff_M_Lossless[vk],
      vey_max_Z_MAX, vey[vk], vhx[vk], vDB, xmm0_Z_MAX);

  h_update_nonmagnetic_pml_sub(vBeta_PML_ZHalf[vk],
      vpusai_hyx_Z_MAX[vk], vpHk_PML_Coeff_M_Lossless[vk],
      vex_max_Z_MAX, vex[vk], vhy[vk], vDB, xmm1_Z_MAX);
}

xmm0_Z_MAX = _mm_and_ps(xmm0_Z_MAX, *pMask1_Z_MAX);
xmm1_Z_MAX = _mm_and_ps(xmm1_Z_MAX, *pMask1_Z_MAX);
vhx[vk] = xmm0_Z_MAX;
vhy[vk] = xmm1_Z_MAX;
```

```
          }
       }
    }
}

void compute_E()
{
    int thread_num, num_threads;

    #pragma omp parallel private(num_threads, thread_num)
    {
        thread_num = omp_get_thread_num();
        num_threads = omp_get_num_threads();
        int i, j, k;
        imin = 1;
        imax = memory_size - 1;
        jmin = Index_E_Boundary[Y_MIN];
        jmax = Index_E_Boundary[Y_MAX];
        kmin = Index_E_Boundary[Z_MIN];
        kmax = Index_E_Boundary[Z_MAX];

        float imaxf = (float)imax / (float)num_threads;
        for (i = imin + (int)((float)thread_num * imaxf); i <=
            (int)((float)(thread_num + 1) * imaxf); i ++)
        {
          for( j = jmin; j <= jmax; j++)
          {
             for( k = kmin; k <= kmax; k++)
             {
                ex[i][j][k] = CA * ex[i][j][k] + ( pEj_Coeff[j] *
                    ( hz[i][j][k] - hz[i][j-1][k] ) - pEk_Coeff[k] *
                    ( hy[i][j][k] - hy[i][j][k-1] ) );
                ey[i][j][k] = CA * ey[i][j][k] + ( pEk_Coeff[k] *
                    ( hx[i][j][k] - hx[i][j][k-1] ) -       pEi_Coeff[i] *
                    ( hz[i][j][k] - hz[i-1][j][k] ) );
                 ez[i][j][k] = CA * ez[i][j][k] + ( pEi_Coeff[i] *
                    ( hy[i][j][k] - hy[i-1][j][k] ) - pEj_Coeff[j] *
                    ( hx[i][j][k] - hx[i][j-1][k] ) );
             }
          }
       }
    }
}

void compute_E_PUSAI()
{
    int thread_num, num_threads;

    #pragma omp parallel private(num_threads, thread_num)
    {
        thread_num = omp_get_thread_num();

        num_threads = omp_get_num_threads();
        int i, j, k;
        imin = 1;
        imax = memory_size - 2;
```

```
jmin = Index_E_Boundary[Y_MIN];
jmax = Index_E_Boundary[Y_MAX];
kmin = Index_E_Boundary[Z_MIN];
kmax = Index_E_Boundary[Z_MAX];

float imaxf = (float)imax / (float)num_threads;
for (i = imin + (int)((float)thread_num * imaxf); i <=
    (int)((float)(thread_num + 1) * imaxf); i ++)
{
  for( j = jmin; j <= jmax; j++)
  {
    for( k = kmin; k <= kmax; k++)
    {
        ex[i][j][k] = CA * ex[i][j][k] + ( pEj_Coeff[j] *
           ( hz[i][j][k] - hz[i][j-1][k] ) -       pEk_Coeff[k]
           * ( hy[i][j][k] - hy[i][j][k-1] ) );
        ey[i][j][k] = CA * ey[i][j][k] + ( pEk_Coeff[k] *
           ( hx[i][j][k] - hx[i][j][k-1] ) -       pEi_Coeff[i]
           * ( hz[i][j][k] - hz[i-1][j][k] ) );
        ez[i][j][k] = CA * ez[i][j][k] + ( pEi_Coeff[i] *
           ( hy[i][j][k] - hy[i-1][j][k] ) -       pEj_Coeff[j]
           * ( hx[i][j][k] - hx[i][j-1][k] ) );

        //pusai_Z_MIN
        if( k >= Index_E_Boundary[Z_MIN] && k <=
           ( Index_E_Boundary[Z_MIN] + BoundaryLayerNum[Z_MIN]
           - 1 ) )
        {
           pusai_exy_Z_MIN[i][j][k] = Beta_PML_ZGrid[k] *
              pusai_exy_Z_MIN[i][j][k] +
           pEk_PML_Coeff[k] * ( hy[i][j][k] - hy[i][j][k-1] );
           ex[i][j][k] = ex[i][j][k] - CB *
              pusai_exy_Z_MIN[i][j][k];
           pusai_eyx_Z_MIN[i][j][k] = Beta_PML_ZGrid[k] *
              pusai_eyx_Z_MIN[i][j][k] +
           pEk_PML_Coeff[k] * ( hx[i][j][k] - hx[i][j][k-1] );
           ey[i][j][k] = ey[i][j][k] + CB *
              pusai_eyx_Z_MIN[i][j][k];
        }

        //pusai_Z_MAX
        if( k >= ( Index_E_Boundary[Z_MAX] -
           BoundaryLayerNum[Z_MAX] + 1 ) && k <=
           Index_E_Boundary[Z_MAX] )
        {
        kshift = Index_E_Boundary[Z_MAX] -
           BoundaryLayerNum[Z_MAX] + 1;
        pusai_exy_Z_MAX[i][j][k-kshift] = Beta_PML_ZGrid[k] *
           pusai_exy_Z_MAX[i][j][k-kshift] +
           pEk_PML_Coeff[k] * ( hy[i][j][k] - hy[i][j][k-1] );
        ex[i][j][k] = ex[i][j][k] - CB *
           pusai_exy_Z_MAX[i][j][k-kshift];
        pusai_eyx_Z_MAX[i][j][k-kshift] = Beta_PML_ZGrid[k] *
           pusai_eyx_Z_MAX[i][j][k-kshift] +
                             pEk_PML_Coeff[k] * ( hx[i][j][k]
           - hx[i][j][k-1] );
```

```
                    ey[i][j][k] = ey[i][j][k] + CB *
                        pusai_eyx_Z_MAX[i][j][k-kshift];
               }
            }

          //pusai_Y_MIN
          if( j >= Index_E_Boundary[Y_MIN] && j <=
                ( Index_E_Boundary[Y_MIN] + BoundaryLayerNum[Y_MIN] -
                1 ) )
          {
            for( k = kmin;k <= kmax; k++)
            {
                pusai_exz_Y_MIN[i][j][k] = Beta_PML_YGrid[j] *
                    pusai_exz_Y_MIN[i][j][k] +
                pEj_PML_Coeff[j] * ( hz[i][j][k] - hz[i][j-1][k] );
                ex[i][j][k] = ex[i][j][k] + CB *
                    pusai_exz_Y_MIN[i][j][k];
                pusai_ezx_Y_MIN[i][j][k] = Beta_PML_YGrid[j] *
                    pusai_ezx_Y_MIN[i][j][k] +
                pEj_PML_Coeff[j] * ( hx[i][j][k] - hx[i][j-1][k] );
                ez[i][j][k] = ez[i][j][k] - CB *
                    pusai_ezx_Y_MIN[i][j][k];
            }
          }

        //pusai_Y_MAX
        if( j >= ( Index_E_Boundary[Y_MAX] - BoundaryLayerNum[Y_MAX] +
            1 ) && j <= Index_E_Boundary[Y_MAX] )
        {
            jshift = Index_E_Boundary[Y_MAX] - BoundaryLayerNum[Y_MAX]
                    + 1;
            for( k = kmin; k <= kmax; k++)
            {
                pusai_exz_Y_MAX[i][j-jshift][k] = Beta_PML_YGrid[j] *
                    pusai_exz_Y_MAX[i][j-jshift][k] +
                pEj_PML_Coeff[j] * ( hz[i][j][k] - hz[i][j-1][k] );
                ex[i][j][k] = ex[i][j][k] + CB * pusai_exz_Y_MAX[i][j-
                    jshift][k];
                pusai_ezx_Y_MAX[i][j-jshift][k] = Beta_PML_YGrid[j] *
                    pusai_ezx_Y_MAX[i][j-jshift][k] +
                pEj_PML_Coeff[j] * ( hx[i][j][k] - hx[i][j-1][k] );
                    ez[i][j][k] = ez[i][j][k] - CB *
                    pusai_ezx_Y_MAX[i][j-jshift][k];
            }
        }
    }
}

//pusai_X_MIN
if( i >= 2 && i <= ( 2 + BoundaryLayerNum[X_MIN] - 1 ) )
{
    if( id == 0 )
    {
      for( j = jmin; j <= jmax; j++)
      {
        for( k = kmin; k <= kmax; k++)
        {
```

```
                pusai_eyz_X_MIN[i][j][k] = Beta_PML_XGrid[i] *
                    pusai_eyz_X_MIN[i][j][k] + pEi_PML_Coeff[i] *
                    ( hz[i][j][k] - hz[i-1][j][k] );

                ey[i][j][k] = ey[i][j][k] - CB * pusai_eyz_X_MIN[i][j][k];
                pusai_ezy_X_MIN[i][j][k] = Beta_PML_XGrid[i] *
                    pusai_ezy_X_MIN[i][j][k] + pEi_PML_Coeff[i] *
                    ( hy[i][j][k] - hy[i-1][j][k] );

                ez[i][j][k] = ez[i][j][k] + CB * pusai_ezy_X_MIN[i][j][k];
            }
        }
    }
}

//pusai_X_MAX
if( i >= ( memory_size - 3 - BoundaryLayerNum[X_MAX] + 1 ) && i <=
     memory_size - 3 )
{
    ishift = memory_size - 3 - BoundaryLayerNum[X_MAX] + 1;
    if( id == p - 1 )
    {
        for( j = jmin; j <= jmax; j++)
        {
            for( k = kmin; k <= kmax; k++)
            {
                pusai_eyz_X_MAX[i-ishift][j][k] = Beta_PML_XGrid[i]
                    * pusai_eyz_X_MAX[i-ishift][j][k] +
                pEi_PML_Coeff[i] * ( hz[i][j][k] - hz[i-1][j][k] );

                ey[i][j][k] = ey[i][j][k] - CB * pusai_eyz_X_MAX[i-
                    ishift][j][k];
                pusai_ezy_X_MAX[i-ishift][j][k] = Beta_PML_XGrid[i]
                    * pusai_ezy_X_MAX[i-ishift][j][k] +
                pEi_PML_Coeff[i] * ( hy[i][j][k] - hy[i-1][j][k] );
                ez[i][j][k] = ez[i][j][k] + CB * pusai_ezy_X_MAX[i-
                    ishift][j][k];
            }
        }
    }
}
}
}
}
}

void compute_E_SSE()
{
int thread_num, num_threads;

#pragma omp parallel private(num_threads, thread_num)
{

    thread_num = omp_get_thread_num();

    num_threads = omp_get_num_threads();
    int i, j, k,vk;
    imin = 1;
    imax = memory_size - 2;
```

```
jmin = Index_E_Boundary[Y_MIN];
jmax = Index_E_Boundary[Y_MAX];
kmin = Index_E_Boundary[Z_MIN];
kmax = Index_E_Boundary[Z_MAX];
int vkmax_H = kmax >> 2;

float imaxf = (float)imax / (float)num_threads;

Vec4f xmm0, xmm1, xmm2;

Vec4f *vex, *vey, *vez;
Vec4f *vhx, vhx_min_ey, *vhx_min_ez, *vhy, vhy_min_ex, *vhy_min_ez, *vhz,
    *vhz_min_ex, *vhz_min_ey;
Vec4f vpEi_Coeff, vpEj_Coeff, vpEk_Coeff;
    Vec4f vCA = _mm_load1_ps( &CA );

Vec4f *vpusai_exy_Z_MAX, *vpusai_eyx_Z_MAX;
Vec4f vhy_min_Z_MAX, vhx_min_Z_MAX;

for (i = imin + (int)((float)thread_num * imaxf); i <=
    (int)((float)(thread_num + 1) * imaxf); i ++)
{
    vpEi_Coeff = _mm_load1_ps(&pEi_Coeff[i]);
    for( j = jmin; j <= jmax; j++)
    {
        vpEj_Coeff = _mm_load1_ps(&pEj_Coeff[j]);
        vex = (Vec4f *)ex[i][j];
        vey = (Vec4f *)ey[i][j];
        vez = (Vec4f *)ez[i][j];

        vhx = (Vec4f *)hx[i][j];
        vhx_min_ez = (Vec4f *)hx[i][j-1];

        vhy = (Vec4f *)hy[i][j];
        vhy_min_ez = (Vec4f *)hy[i-1][j];

        vhz = (Vec4f *)hz[i][j];
        vhz_min_ex = (Vec4f *)hz[i][j-1];
        vhz_min_ey = (Vec4f *)hz[i-1][j];

        k = vk = 0;
        vhy_min_ex = _mm_setr_ps( 0.0f, hy[i][j][0], hy[i][j][1],
            hy[i][j][2]);
        vhx_min_ey = _mm_setr_ps( 0.0f, hx[i][j][0], hx[i][j][1],
            hx[i][j][2]);
        vpEk_Coeff = _mm_load_ps(&pEk_Coeff[k]);
        while( vk <= vkmax_H )
        {
            e_update_nonelectric(vCA, vex[vk], vpEj_Coeff, vhz[vk],
                vhz_min_ex[vk], vpEk_Coeff, vhy[vk], vhy_min_ex, xmm0);

            e_update_nonelectric(vCA, vey[vk], vpEk_Coeff, vhx[vk],
                vhx_min_ey, vpEi_Coeff, vhz[vk], vhz_min_ey[vk], xmm1);

            e_update_nonelectric(vCA, vez[vk], vpEi_Coeff, vhy[vk],
                vhy_min_ez[vk], vpEj_Coeff, vhx[vk], vhx_min_ez[vk],
                xmm2);
```

```
                vex[vk] = xmm0;
                vey[vk] = xmm1;
                vez[vk] = xmm2;

                k += 4;
                vk++;

                vhy_min_ex = _mm_loadu_ps(&hy[i][j][k-1]);
                vhx_min_ey = _mm_loadu_ps(&hx[i][j][k-1]);
                vpEk_Coeff = _mm_load_ps(&pEk_Coeff[k]);
            }
        }
    }
}

void compute_E_PUSAI_SSE()
{
int thread_num, num_threads;

#pragma omp parallel private(num_threads, thread_num)
{

    thread_num = omp_get_thread_num();

    num_threads = omp_get_num_threads();
    int i, j, k,vk;
    imin = 1;
    imax = memory_size - 2;
    jmin = Index_E_Boundary[Y_MIN];
    jmax = Index_E_Boundary[Y_MAX];
    kmin = Index_E_Boundary[Z_MIN];
    kmax = Index_E_Boundary[Z_MAX];
    int vkmax_H = kmax >> 2;

    float imaxf = (float)imax / (float)num_threads;

    Vec4f xmm0, xmm1, xmm2;

    Vec4f *vex, *vey, *vez;
    Vec4f *vhx, vhx_min_ey, *vhx_min_ez, *vhy, vhy_min_ex, *vhy_min_ez,
    *vhz, *vhz_min_ex, *vhz_min_ey;
    Vec4f vpEi_Coeff, vpEj_Coeff, vpEk_Coeff;
    Vec4f vCA = _mm_load1_ps( &CA );

    //pusai_Y_MIN
    Vec4f *vpusai_exz_Y_MIN, *vpusai_ezx_Y_MIN;
    Vec4f vBeta_PML_YGrid, vpEj_PML_Coeff;
    Vec4f vCB = _mm_load1_ps( &CB );
    Vec4f xmm0_Y_MIN, xmm1_Y_MIN;

    //pusai_Y_MAX
    Vec4f *vpusai_exz_Y_MAX, *vpusai_ezx_Y_MAX;
    Vec4f xmm0_Y_MAX, xmm1_Y_MAX;

    //pusai_X_MIN
    Vec4f *vpusai_eyz_X_MIN, *vpusai_ezy_X_MIN;
    Vec4f vBeta_PML_XGrid, vpEi_PML_Coeff;
    Vec4f xmm0_X_MIN, xmm1_X_MIN;
```

```
//pusai_X_MAX
Vec4f *vpusai_eyz_X_MAX, *vpusai_ezy_X_MAX;
Vec4f xmm0_X_MAX, xmm1_X_MAX;

//pusai_Z_MIN
Vec4f xmm0_Z_MIN, xmm1_Z_MIN, xmmo_0_Z_MIN, xmmo_1_Z_MIN;
    __declspec( align( 16 ) ) int mask2_Z_MIN[4] = {0x0, 0x0, 0x0,
    0x0}, mask3_Z_MIN[4] = {0xFFFFFFFF, 0xFFFFFFFF, 0xFFFFFFFF,
    0xFFFFFFFF};
Vec4f *pMask2_Z_MIN = (Vec4f *)&mask2_Z_MIN;
Vec4f *pMask3_Z_MIN = (Vec4f *)&mask3_Z_MIN;
int vkmax_Z_MIN = (Index_E_Boundary[Z_MIN] + BoundaryLayerNum[Z_MIN]
    - 1) >> 2;

// setup mask
int r_Z_MIN = (Index_E_Boundary[Z_MIN] + BoundaryLayerNum[Z_MIN] - 1
    + 1) % 4;
if ( r_Z_MIN == 0 ) r_Z_MIN = 4;
        for ( i = 0; i < r_Z_MIN - 1; i ++ )
{
    mask2_Z_MIN[i] = 0xFFFFFFFF;
    mask3_Z_MIN[i] = 0x0;
}

mask2_Z_MIN[i] = 0xFFFFFFFF;
mask3_Z_MIN[i] = 0x0;

Vec4f *vpusai_exy_Z_MIN, *vpusai_eyx_Z_MIN;
Vec4f *vBeta_PML_ZGrid = (Vec4f *)Beta_PML_ZGrid;
Vec4f *vpEk_PML_Coeff = (Vec4f *)pEk_PML_Coeff;
Vec4f vhy_min_Z_MIN, vhx_min_Z_MIN;

//pusai_Z_MAX
Vec4f xmm0_Z_MAX, xmm1_Z_MAX, xmmo_0_Z_MAX, xmmo_1_Z_MAX;
int kmin_aligned = (Index_E_Boundary[Z_MAX] - BoundaryLayerNum[Z_MAX]
  + 1) & (~3);
int vkmax_Z_MAX = Index_E_Boundary[Z_MAX] >> 2;
int vkshift_Z_MAX;

    __declspec( align( 16 ) ) int mask2[4] = {0x0, 0x0, 0x0, 0x0},
        mask3[4] = {0xFFFFFFFF, 0xFFFFFFFF, 0xFFFFFFFF, 0xFFFFFFFF},
        mask4[4] = {0x0, 0x0, 0x0, 0x0};
    Vec4f *pMask2 = (Vec4f *)&mask2;
    Vec4f *pMask3 = (Vec4f *)&mask3;
    Vec4f *pMask4 = (Vec4f *)&mask4;

    int vkmax = Index_E_Boundary[Z_MAX] >> 2;
    // setup mask
    int r = (kmax + 1 )% 4;
    if (r == 0) r = 4;
    for (i = 0; i < r - 1; i ++)
    {
        mask2[i] = 0xFFFFFFFF;
    }

    mask2[i] = 0xFFFFFFFF;
    for (i = 0; i < kmin - kmin_aligned; i ++)
    {
```

```
        mask3[i] = 0x0;
        mask4[i] = 0xFFFFFFFF;
}

Vec4f *vpusai_exy_Z_MAX, *vpusai_eyx_Z_MAX;
Vec4f vhy_min_Z_MAX, vhx_min_Z_MAX;

for (i = imin + (int)((float)thread_num * imaxf); i <=
    (int)((float)(thread_num + 1) * imaxf); i ++)
{

    vpEi_Coeff = _mm_load1_ps(&pEi_Coeff[i]);

    for( j = jmin; j <= jmax; j++)
    {
    vpEj_Coeff = _mm_load1_ps(&pEj_Coeff[j]);
    vex = (Vec4f *)ex[i][j];
    vey = (Vec4f *)ey[i][j];
    vez = (Vec4f *)ez[i][j];

    vhx = (Vec4f *)hx[i][j];
    vhx_min_ez = (Vec4f *)hx[i][j-1];

    vhy = (Vec4f *)hy[i][j];
    vhy_min_ez = (Vec4f *)hy[i-1][j];

    vhz = (Vec4f *)hz[i][j];
    vhz_min_ex = (Vec4f *)hz[i][j-1];
    vhz_min_ey = (Vec4f *)hz[i-1][j];

    k = vk = 0;
    vhy_min_ex = _mm_setr_ps( 0.0f, hy[i][j][0], hy[i][j][1],
        hy[i][j][2]);
    vhx_min_ey = _mm_setr_ps( 0.0f, hx[i][j][0], hx[i][j][1],
        hx[i][j][2]);
    vpEk_Coeff = _mm_load_ps(&pEk_Coeff[k]);

    while( vk <= vkmax_H )
    {

      e_update_nonelectric(vCA, vex[vk], vpEj_Coeff, vhz[vk],
        vhz_min_ex[vk], vpEk_Coeff, vhy[vk], vhy_min_ex, xmm0);
      e_update_nonelectric(vCA, vey[vk], vpEk_Coeff, vhx[vk],
        vhx_min_ey, vpEi_Coeff, vhz[vk], vhz_min_ey[vk], xmm1);
      e_update_nonelectric(vCA, vez[vk], vpEi_Coeff, vhy[vk],
        vhy_min_ez[vk], vpEj_Coeff, vhx[vk], vhx_min_ez[vk],
        xmm2);

      vex[vk] = xmm0;
      vey[vk] = xmm1;
      vez[vk] = xmm2;

      k += 4;
      vk++;

      vhy_min_ex = _mm_loadu_ps(&hy[i][j][k-1]);
      vhx_min_ey = _mm_loadu_ps(&hx[i][j][k-1]);
      vpEk_Coeff = _mm_load_ps(&pEk_Coeff[k]);
    }
```

```
//pusai_Y_MIN
if( j >= Index_E_Boundary[Y_MIN] && j <=
    (Index_E_Boundary[Y_MIN] + BoundaryLayerNum[Y_MIN] - 1) )
{
vBeta_PML_YGrid = _mm_load1_ps(&Beta_PML_YGrid[j]);
vpEj_PML_Coeff = _mm_load1_ps(&pEj_PML_Coeff[j]);
    vpusai_exz_Y_MIN = (Vec4f *)pusai_exz_Y_MIN[i][j];
 vpusai_ezx_Y_MIN = (Vec4f *)pusai_ezx_Y_MIN[i][j];
vk = 0;
while( vk <= vkmax_H )
{
   e_update_nonelectric_pml_add(vBeta_PML_YGrid,
       vpusai_exz_Y_MIN[vk], vpEj_PML_Coeff, vhz[vk],
       vhz_min_ex[vk], vex[vk], vCB, xmm0_Y_MIN);

   e_update_nonelectric_pml_sub(vBeta_PML_YGrid,
       vpusai_ezx_Y_MIN[vk], vpEj_PML_Coeff, vhx[vk],
       vhx_min_ez[vk], vez[vk], vCB, xmm1_Y_MIN);

   vex[vk] = xmm0_Y_MIN;
   vez[vk] = xmm1_Y_MIN;

   vk++;
  }
}

//pusai_Y_MAX
if( j >= (Index_E_Boundary[Y_MAX] - BoundaryLayerNum[Y_MAX] + 1)
    && j <= Index_E_Boundary[Y_MAX] )
{
    jshift = Index_E_Boundary[Y_MAX]-BoundaryLayerNum[Y_MAX]+1;
    vBeta_PML_YGrid = _mm_load1_ps(&Beta_PML_YGrid[j]);
    vpEj_PML_Coeff = _mm_load1_ps(&pEj_PML_Coeff[j]);
    vpusai_exz_Y_MAX = (Vec4f *)pusai_exz_Y_MAX[i][j-jshift];
    vpusai_ezx_Y_MAX = (Vec4f *)pusai_ezx_Y_MAX[i][j-jshift];
    vk = 0;

    while( vk <= vkmax_H )
    {
       e_update_nonelectric_pml_add(vBeta_PML_YGrid,
           vpusai_exz_Y_MAX[vk], vpEj_PML_Coeff, vhz[vk],
           vhz_min_ex[vk], vex[vk], vCB, xmm0_Y_MAX);

       e_update_nonelectric_pml_sub(vBeta_PML_YGrid,
           vpusai_ezx_Y_MAX[vk], vpEj_PML_Coeff, vhx[vk],
           vhx_min_ez[vk], vez[vk], vCB, xmm1_Y_MAX);

       vex[vk] = xmm0_Y_MAX;
       vez[vk] = xmm1_Y_MAX;

       vk++;
      }
   }

   //pusai_X_MIN
   if( i >= 2 && i <= (2 + BoundaryLayerNum[X_MIN] - 1) )
   {
```

```
    if( id == 0 )
    {
       vBeta_PML_XGrid = _mm_load1_ps(&Beta_PML_XGrid[i]);
       vpEi_PML_Coeff = _mm_load1_ps(&pEi_PML_Coeff[i]);
       vpusai_eyz_X_MIN = (Vec4f *)pusai_eyz_X_MIN[i][j];
       vpusai_ezy_X_MIN = (Vec4f *)pusai_ezy_X_MIN[i][j];

       vk = 0;
       while( vk <= vkmax_H )
       {
          e_update_nonelectric_pml_sub(vBeta_PML_XGrid,
             vpusai_eyz_X_MIN[vk], vpEi_PML_Coeff, vhz[vk],
             vhz_min_ey[vk], vey[vk], vCB, xmm0_X_MIN);

          e_update_nonelectric_pml_add(vBeta_PML_XGrid,
             vpusai_ezy_X_MIN[vk], vpEi_PML_Coeff, vhy[vk],
             vhy_min_ez[vk], vez[vk], vCB, xmm1_X_MIN);

          vey[vk] = xmm0_X_MIN;
          vez[vk] = xmm1_X_MIN;

          vk++;
       }
    }
}

//pusai_X_MAX
if( i >= (memory_size - 3 - BoundaryLayerNum[X_MAX] + 1) && i
   <= memory_size - 3 )
{
   if( id == p - 1 )
   {
      ishift = memory_size - 3 - BoundaryLayerNum[X_MAX] + 1;
      vBeta_PML_XGrid = _mm_load1_ps(&Beta_PML_XGrid[i]);
vpEi_PML_Coeff = _mm_load1_ps(&pEi_PML_Coeff[i]);
vpusai_eyz_X_MAX = (Vec4f *)pusai_eyz_X_MAX[i-ishift][j];
vpusai_ezy_X_MAX = (Vec4f *)pusai_ezy_X_MAX[i-ishift][j];
vk = 0;

while( vk <= vkmax_H )
{

  e_update_nonelectric_pml_sub(vBeta_PML_XGrid,
      vpusai_eyz_X_MAX[vk], vpEi_PML_Coeff, vhz[vk],
      vhz_min_ey[vk], vey[vk], vCB, xmm0_X_MAX);

  e_update_nonelectric_pml_add(vBeta_PML_XGrid,
      vpusai_ezy_X_MAX[vk], vpEi_PML_Coeff, vhy[vk],
      vhy_min_ez[vk], vez[vk], vCB, xmm1_X_MAX);

  vey[vk] = xmm0_X_MAX;
  vez[vk] = xmm1_X_MAX;

  vk++;

}
  }
}
```

```
//pusai_Z_MIN
vpusai_exy_Z_MIN = (Vec4f *)pusai_exy_Z_MIN[i][j];
    vpusai_eyx_Z_MIN = (Vec4f *)pusai_eyx_Z_MIN[i][j];

k = vk = 0;
vhy_min_Z_MIN = _mm_shuffle_ps(vhy[vk], vhy[vk], _MM_SHUFFLE(2, 1,
    0, 0));
vhx_min_Z_MIN = _mm_shuffle_ps(vhx[vk], vhx[vk], _MM_SHUFFLE(2, 1,
    0, 0));

while (vk < vkmax_Z_MIN)
{
  e_update_nonelectric_pml_sub(vBeta_PML_ZGrid[vk],
      vpusai_exy_Z_MIN[vk], vpEk_PML_Coeff[vk], vhy[vk],
      vhy_min_Z_MIN, vex[vk], vCB, xmm0_Z_MIN);

  e_update_nonelectric_pml_add(vBeta_PML_ZGrid[vk],
      vpusai_eyx_Z_MIN[vk], vpEk_PML_Coeff[vk], vhx[vk],
      vhx_min_Z_MIN, vey[vk], vCB, xmm1_Z_MIN);

  vex[vk] = xmm0_Z_MIN;
  vey[vk] = xmm1_Z_MIN;

  k += 4;
  vk ++;

  vhy_min_Z_MIN = _mm_loadu_ps(&hy[i][j][k-1]);
  vhx_min_Z_MIN = _mm_loadu_ps(&hx[i][j][k-1]);
}

e_update_nonelectric_pml_sub(vBeta_PML_ZGrid[vk],
    vpusai_exy_Z_MIN[vk], vpEk_PML_Coeff[vk], vhy[vk],
    vhy_min_Z_MIN, vex[vk], vCB, xmm0_Z_MIN);

e_update_nonelectric_pml_add(vBeta_PML_ZGrid[vk],
    vpusai_eyx_Z_MIN[vk], vpEk_PML_Coeff[vk], vhx[vk],
    vhx_min_Z_MIN, vey[vk], vCB, xmm1_Z_MIN);

xmm0_Z_MIN = _mm_and_ps(xmm0_Z_MIN, *pMask2_Z_MIN);
xmm1_Z_MIN = _mm_and_ps(xmm1_Z_MIN, *pMask2_Z_MIN);
xmmo_0_Z_MIN = _mm_and_ps(vex[vk], *pMask3_Z_MIN);
xmmo_1_Z_MIN = _mm_and_ps(vey[vk], *pMask3_Z_MIN);
xmm0_Z_MIN = _mm_add_ps(xmm0_Z_MIN, xmmo_0_Z_MIN);
xmm1_Z_MIN = _mm_add_ps(xmm1_Z_MIN, xmmo_1_Z_MIN);
vex[vk] = xmm0_Z_MIN;
vey[vk] = xmm1_Z_MIN;

//pusai_Z_MAX
vpusai_exy_Z_MAX = (Vec4f *)pusai_exy_Z_MAX[i][j];
vpusai_eyx_Z_MAX = (Vec4f *)pusai_eyx_Z_MAX[i][j];

k = kmin_aligned;
vkshift_Z_MAX = vk = k >> 2;
vhy_min_Z_MAX = _mm_loadu_ps(&hy[i][j][k-1]);
vhx_min_Z_MAX = _mm_loadu_ps(&hx[i][j][k-1]);

  e_update_nonelectric_pml_sub(vBeta_PML_ZGrid[vk],
      vpusai_exy_Z_MAX[vk], vpEk_PML_Coeff[vk], vhy[vk],
      vhy_min_Z_MAX, vex[vk], vCB, xmm0_Z_MAX);
```

```
        e_update_nonelectric_pml_add(vBeta_PML_ZGrid[vk],
            vpusai_eyx_Z_MAX[vk], vpEk_PML_Coeff[vk], vhx[vk],
            vhx_min_Z_MAX, vey[vk], vCB, xmm1_Z_MAX);

        xmm0_Z_MAX = _mm_and_ps(xmm0_Z_MAX, *pMask3);
        xmm1_Z_MAX = _mm_and_ps(xmm1_Z_MAX, *pMask3);
        xmmo_0_Z_MAX = _mm_and_ps(vex[vk], *pMask4);
        xmmo_1_Z_MAX = _mm_and_ps(vey[vk], *pMask4);
        xmm0_Z_MAX = _mm_add_ps(xmm0_Z_MAX, xmmo_0_Z_MAX);
        xmm1_Z_MAX = _mm_add_ps(xmm1_Z_MAX, xmmo_1_Z_MAX);

        while (vk < vkmax_Z_MAX)
        {
            vex[vk] = xmm0_Z_MAX;
            vey[vk] = xmm1_Z_MAX;

            k += 4;
            vk ++;

            vhy_min_Z_MAX = _mm_loadu_ps(&hy[i][j][k-1]);
            vhx_min_Z_MAX = _mm_loadu_ps(&hx[i][j][k-1]);

            e_update_nonelectric_pml_sub(vBeta_PML_ZGrid[vk],
                vpusai_exy_Z_MAX[vk], vpEk_PML_Coeff[vk], vhy[vk],
                vhy_min_Z_MAX, vex[vk], vCB, xmm0_Z_MAX);

            e_update_nonelectric_pml_add(vBeta_PML_ZGrid[vk],
                vpusai_eyx_Z_MAX[vk], vpEk_PML_Coeff[vk], vhx[vk],
                vhx_min_Z_MAX, vey[vk], vCB, xmm1_Z_MAX);

        }

        xmm0_Z_MAX = _mm_and_ps(xmm0_Z_MAX, *pMask2);
        xmm1_Z_MAX = _mm_and_ps(xmm1_Z_MAX, *pMask2);
        vex[vk] = xmm0_Z_MAX;
        vey[vk] = xmm1_Z_MAX;

        }
    }
  }
}

void transfer_H()
{
    if( id != p - 1 )
    {
      MPI_Isend( hy[memory_size - 2][0], 1, new_dtype, id + 1, 0,
          MPI_COMM_WORLD, &req[0]);
      MPI_Isend( hz[memory_size - 2][0], 1, new_dtype, id + 1, 1,
          MPI_COMM_WORLD, &req[1]);
    }

    if( id != 0 )
    {
        MPI_Irecv( hy[0][0], 1, new_dtype, id - 1, 0, MPI_COMM_WORLD,
            &req[0]);
        MPI_Irecv( hz[0][0], 1, new_dtype, id - 1, 1, MPI_COMM_WORLD,
            &req[1]);
```

```
    }

    MPI_Waitall( 2, req, status );
}

void transfer_E()
{
    if( id != 0 )
    {
        MPI_Isend( ey[1][0], 1, new_dtype, id - 1, 0, MPI_COMM_WORLD,
            &req[0] );
        MPI_Isend( ez[1][0], 1, new_dtype, id - 1, 1, MPI_COMM_WORLD,
            &req[1] );
    }

    if( id != p - 1 )
    {
        MPI_Irecv( ey[memory_size - 1][0], 1, new_dtype, id + 1, 0,
            MPI_COMM_WORLD, &req[0]);
        MPI_Irecv( ez[memory_size - 1][0], 1, new_dtype, id + 1, 1,
            MPI_COMM_WORLD, &req[1]);
    }

    MPI_Waitall( 2, req, status );
}

void add_source( int source_x, int source_y, int source_z )
{
    ez[ source_x ][ source_y ][ source_z ] = exp( -0.5 * pow( ( 20.0 -
        n ) / 6.0, 2) );
}

void source()
{
    if( id == source_owner )
    {
        add_source( source_position_x_local, source_position_y,
            source_position_z );
    }
        if( source_left_owner != source_owner )
        {
            if( id == source_left_owner )
            {
                add_source( memory_size - 1, source_position_y,
                    source_position_z );
            }
        }

        if( source_right_owner != source_owner )
        {
            if( id == source_right_owner )
            {
                add_source( 0, source_position_y, source_position_z );
            }
        }
}
```

```
void data_collect()
{
   MPI_Gather( ez[1][0], size, new_dtype, Ez_save[0][0], size,
       new_dtype, 0, MPI_COMM_WORLD );
}

void output_Ez()
{
   char step[10];
   char fileBaseName[]= "output\\Ez_Field_";
   sprintf(step, "%d", n);
   strcat(fileBaseName, step);
   strcat(fileBaseName, ".txt");

   fp = fopen(fileBaseName,"w");

   for( i = 0 ; i < nx + 1 ; i++)
   {
       for( j = 0 ; j < ny + 1 ; j++)
       {
           fprintf(fp, "%f\t", Ez_save[i][j][ source_position_z ]);

           sqrt(pow(ex[i][j][source_position_z],
               2)+pow(ey[i][j][source_position_z], 2) +
               pow( ez[i][j][source_position_z], 2)));
       }
       fprintf(fp, "\n");
   }
   fclose(fp);
}
```

References

[1] http://www.mcs.anl.gov/research/projects/mpich2/documentation/files/mpich2-1.4.1-userguide.pdf

[2] J. Liberty, *C++*, SAMS Publisher, Inddiapolis, IN, 1999.

[3] W. Yu, X. Yang, Y. Liu, et al., *Parallel Finite Difference Time Domain Method*, Artech House, Norwood, MA, 2006.

Index